PARADOXES OF UTOPIA

Anarchist Culture and Politics in Buenos Aires, 1890–1910

Juan Suriano

Translated by Chuck Morse

AK Press

Paradoxes of Utopia: Anarchist Culture and Politics in Buenos Aires, 1890–1910
by Juan Suriano

Translated by Chuck Morse

ISBN 978 1 849350 06 8
Library of Congress Number: 2009933026

© 2010 Juan Suriano

Translation © 2010 Chuck Morse

This edition © 2010 AK Press

Originally published, as *Anarquistas. Cultura politica libertaria en Buenos Aires, 1890–1910* (Buenos Aires: Manantial, 2001)

Cover Design: Chris Wright (seldomwright.com)
Interior Design: Margaret Killjoy (birdsbeforethestorm.net)

AK Press
674-A 23rd Street
Oakland, CA 94612
www.akpress.org
akpress@akpress.org
510.208.1700

AK Press U.K.
PO Box 12766
Edinburgh EH8 9YE
www.akuk.com
ak@akedin.demon.co.uk
0131.555.5165

This book was made possible in part by a generous donation from the Anarchist Archives Project.

Printed in Canada on 100% recycled, acid-free paper by union labor.

Contents

CHAPTER VIII
Anarchist Rites and Symbols 201

TRANSLATOR'S ACKNOWLEDGMENTS

My greatest debt is to Pablo Abufom, a Chilean friend and comrade, who cheerfully and patiently helped me work through nearly every obstacle that I encountered while translating this book, whether it was an obscure idiomatic expression or something that I should have been able to resolve on my own. I am deeply grateful for his help, good humor, and revolutionary commitments. AK Press's Charles Weigl, who is a friend, co-conspirator, and now a neighbor, offered countless editorial suggestions that improved the text immeasurably. He and all of the AK Press collective are an inspiration to me. I am indebted to the following individuals, who read over and commented upon a chapter or more of the translation: Jesse Cohn, Michelle Matisons, Joshua Stephens, Adam Welch, Louis Colombo, Michael Caplan, Eric Laursen, Mary Dearborn, and Yvonne Liu. A. Walker gave me access to the online databases at his university, which were invaluable to me. I also owe a debt of gratitude to subscribers to the Radical Translators and Notas Rojas email lists, as well as Paul Sharkey, Lesley Ray, and Salvatore Engel-DiMauro, who helped me with the Italian passages. Finally, I am thankful for the encouragement of my longtime friend and comrade, Peter Larsen, and, as always, for the love and support of my partner, Yvonne Liu.

NOTE ON CONVENTIONS

As Suriano makes clear in the text that follows, anarchists named their groups and publications very conscientiously: the choice of a particular term or reference was not incidental for them, but reflective of their broader cultural and political strategies. Given this, I decided to translate all the names of anarchist projects into English, with the sole exception of the newspaper *La Protesta Humana* / *La Protesta*, which is typically not translated in English-language literature on the movement. Those who wish to do further research can find the original Spanish names in the appendix.

Also, the Argentine socialist movement included but was not limited to the activities of the Socialist Party. I capitalize the word *socialist* only when it refers specifically to members of or activities of the Socialist Party.

To the memory of my father, and for Mirta, Lisandro, and my mother

AUTHOR'S ACKNOWLEDGMENTS

While this work bears multiple intellectual debts, most of which can be easily identified in the text, I must highlight the contributions made by certain individuals. In the first place, Luis Alberto Romero, who directed the dissertation from which this book emerged, carefully and patiently read each of its drafts. His comments and rich insights into Argentine history improved the text substantially. I owe many of the ideas articulated here to Leandro Gutiérrez, who was unfortunately unable to read the entirety of the work. Diego Armus offered affection and companionship as well as critical and challenging suggestions that led me to pursue unanticipated lines of inquiry.

Numerous colleagues and friends also provided comments that benefited me greatly, including Ricardo Falcón, Daniel James, Enrique Mases, Ofelia Pianetto, Dora Barrancos, José Emilio Burucúa (who read the last chapter), Mirta Lobato, Ricardo González, Fernando Rocchi, and Agustina Prieto, who frequently supplied me with important documents that were unknown to me. Juan Carlos Torre and Oscar Terán offered many insightful observations.

I am grateful to participants in the seminars offered by the Argentine Social and Economic History Program in the Department of Philosophy and Letters at the University of Buenos Aires and the Working Group on the Labor Movement and Popular Sectors, from whom I received helpful advice. I am indebted to my colleagues at *Entrepasados* magazine and the Argentine Social History Program at the University of Mar del Plata. Equally stimulating were discussions with students in seminars that I led in the Department of Philosophy and Letters at the University of Buenos Aires (in 1992 and 1995) as well as in the Humanities Department of the University of Mar del Plata in 1994.

I must underscore my gratitude to Diego Bússola, Florencia Levin, and Lisandro Suriano, who consistently and enthusiastically helped me gather data; to Ana Lía Rey, who made the entire collection of the magazine *Ideas and Figures* available to me; to personnel from the following libraries: Arus (Barcelona), Nacional (Buenos Aires), Nacional (Madrid), and especially Amsterdam's International Institute of Social History, without whose archives it would have been impossible to complete this book.

Writing this work required many years of exertion in the context of multiple teaching obligations. The salary I drew from my full-time position in the History

Department at the Department of Philosophy and Letters financed almost the entirety of the project. Grants awarded to me in 1991 and 1994 by the Secretary of Science and Technology of the University of Buenos Aires (UBACYT) helped fund part of the research. Being a visiting scholar at the Council on Latin American Studies at Duke University between October 10, 1997, and March 20, 1998 enabled me to complete the final revision of the text in its dissertation form. There, thanks to the hospitality of Daniel James and Lynn Di Pietro, I enjoyed the peace of mind necessary to finish the last stage of this work. The University of Buenos Aires generously supported my stay by affording me a paid leave during the time.

And, finally, even though it is conventional for authors to acknowledge their families, this is by no means a simple matter of custom for me. I am grateful to my son Lisandro, whose big heart and good character helped anchor me while writing this book, and to Mirta, whose tenderness, intellectual stimulation, and incisive commentary made the work possible. She has my deepest gratitude.

In the past historians could be accused of wanting to know only about "the great deeds of kings," but today this is certainly no longer true. More and more they are turning toward what their predecessors passed over in silence, discarded, or simply ignored. "Who built Thebes of the seven gates?" Bertolt Brecht's "literate worker" was already asking. The sources tell us nothing about these anonymous masons, but the question retains all its significance.

—Carlo Ginzburg, *The Cheese and the Worms*

INTRODUCTION

IN 1902, SENATOR Miguel Cané made the following statement to his colleagues in government: "Circumstances are serious. The Senators know what's happening in the capital right now and what might occur throughout the Republic. The strikes, doubtlessly the work of agitators who exploit the good faith of workers' associations, are starting to take on alarming dimensions and could put the commercial, industrial, and economic life of the country in jeopardy."[1]

Cané made this distressed, dramatic proclamation in response to the strike wave that swept through Buenos Aires between 1901 and 1902, culminating in the general strike of November 1902. The government replied by imposing martial law and passing the Residency Law, which Cané himself had drafted three years earlier. These events had provoked the Senator's concern and were a worry throughout the capital, even though conflicts between groups and factions had become routine. In fact, there had been much greater violence a dozen years earlier during the 1890 revolution in Buenos Aires, which claimed hundreds of lives. Neither the political violence nor the political repression and martial law with which the government responded were fundamentally new.

A different issue motivated Senator Cané. There had been a change in the nature of the conflict. It had become social and was led by workers and the emerging labor movement, which had recently organized itself into two federations. And it was not so much the strikes per se as their ideological overtones that troubled him, specifically the presence of anarchists, who played a central role in the turmoil and whose ideas had taken root among workers. Cané himself acknowledged in the same speech that the source of the problem lay not in workers' "legitimate" demands, but in "agitators who take advantage of healthy and useful strata; who, living for this agitation, are really impresarios of strikes."[2] This was an unambiguous reference to anarchists who, along with strikes and workers' organizations generally, had become increasingly important during the last two decades of the nineteenth century and influential in labor relations. Indeed, the anarchist movement had matured and became an important actor in the major social struggles unfolding in fin-de-siècle Buenos Aires. Long gone were the days of 1885, when Errico Malatesta had to stop publishing his libertarian magazine due to the indifference of local Italians. Establishing itself among the workers, the anarchist movement came of age between the turn of the century and the 1910 Centenary celebrations: it controlled the Argentine Workers' Federation and key unions within it; created a substantial number of centers and cultural circles where its militants delivered lectures, performed theatrical works, and held parties; published periodicals, pamphlets, books, flyers, magazines, and even a daily newspaper; spurred the creation of rational, free schools; and were crucial to the organization of tenement dwellers.

In this work, I analyze the anarchist movement as a cultural, political, ideological, and social movement. I do not focus on the anarchist movement's relationship to the labor movement, which other scholars have treated extensively,[3] but rather examine institutions directly linked to the anarchist movement, such as its circles, press, and schools, within which anarchists defined their political and cultural strategies. I focus my investigation on the city of Buenos Aires during the two decades between 1890 and 1910, although I privilege the latter of the two, because that is when the anarchist movement was most interesting and developed.

Why restrict the study to Buenos Aires? First, because the anarchist movement's national reach was very limited. Though it is true that there were groups and activists throughout the country, anarchists were mostly irrelevant in areas where more traditional social relations prevailed. It was in the large, economically dynamic cities along the coast that they had a meaningful presence: there, they had an influence on foreign-born and native workers who were swept up in the modernization process and provided them with a network of labor, political, and cultural institutions. Anarchists' much greater impact in the cities than in rural areas makes the movement of the period an eminently urban phenomenon. And although anarchists had an effect on numerous towns and cities in the Pampa region, there is no doubt that movement reached its greatest magnitude in Buenos Aires, which was and is the country's political center, its most important port city, and the site of much of its wealth, industry, services, and commerce. Deliberately or not, anarchists essentially selected this metropolis as the arena in which to mobilize and disseminate their ideas, and it was there that they evolved with the greatest vitality, which is not to deny their enormous influence in Rosario.[4]

The temporal limit is also deliberate. The study begins around 1890, when the social effects of the modernization process began to make themselves felt and libertarian propaganda began to produce tangible results. It was at this time that anarchists started forming groups, publishing periodicals, and defining the strategies that the mature anarchist movement would pursue a decade later. I do not mean, by concluding the investigation in 1910, to suggest that the anarchist movement disappeared then, only that this was when its decline began. Indeed, while the broader public continued to imagine it as a dynamic social actor, its practical relevance—in political, social, and cultural terms—started to shrink inexorably by the end of the first decade of the century.

Primary sources from the period—not only those produced by the libertarian movement but also those of other tendencies—indicate anarchists' influence and deep roots among workers.[5] There was anarchist control of the Argentine Workers' Federation (which became the Argentina Regional Workers' Federation in 1904 [FORA in its Spanish acronym]; their immense May Day mobilizations; the momentum and leadership that they provided to numerous labor conflicts, including some general strikes; anarchists' strong ties to the dispossessed populations such as tenants; and of course the government's worries. All of these things underscore the libertarian movement's vitality and significance.[6] And while government reforms undermined the movement's attractiveness for workers, it must be seen as an early trigger of the state's concern with labor and an inadvertent source of reformist perspectives in government.

Urban society at the beginning of the twentieth century was a rapidly changing, chaotic product of the modernization process that had begun in the 1870s. This process led to the formation of a workers' sphere constituted by an incipient working class employed in small factories, workshops, assorted businesses, and the service sector (the port and transportation, principally). A social order of this sort had features strongly favoring the establishment of vigorous oppositional tendencies: the most significant was likely the constant mobility, both horizontal and vertical (ascendant and descendant), within the social body, which permitted some workers to become well-off while consigning a large portion to destitution. Complicating this was the state's inability to address workers' most pressing problems. An Italian observer noted bluntly that the workers' plight was truly catastrophic thanks to "the state's disinterest in—if not aversion to—workers' demands." He saw no mechanism for mediating the differences between capital and labor, either legislative or otherwise. "The government of this country of immigrants," he said, "lacks the very idea of addressing issues that the working class finds important, just as it lacks a sense of decency with regard to foreigners. It responds to economic and social conflicts without realizing that sometimes it is just a matter of equity and justice."[7]

Circumstances such as these created an auspicious environment for anarchism and ensured the centrality of crisis and confrontation in local social relations. The battle between Buenos Aires's emerging working class and business owners and the state became violent on numerous occasions, heightening the ambience of discord. Indeed, the Centenary celebrations were the climax of a symbolic clash between the dominant groups and the most radicalized sectors of the population. The Italian commentator quoted above also noted that the Socialist Party was unable to enlist the workers, among whom, nurtured by anarchism, "instincts of violence and rebellion" prevailed.[8] Anarchism, whose defining feature was not reflection but action, became an integral part of the culture of conflict and flourished in arenas disregarded by the state and other governing institutions. These factors, combined with problems like inadequate housing, job insecurity, unemployment, low salaries, poor working conditions, and political exclusion made the libertarian project a compelling, credible, and appealing alternative for workers.[9]

To understand this, we must bear in mind the alienation, exploitation, and marginalization of a sizable percentage of workers. The vast majority of them were new to the city, being either immigrants or migrants, and thus lived among strangers in an unfamiliar setting. Most had come to Buenos Aires with dreams of ascending the social ladder, only to find that their aspirations were much harder to realize than anticipated. With their direct links to their homelands, families, and traditions severed, they were immersed in a hostile society in which neither the church nor the state nor other national institutions played a cohering role, with the partial exception of mutualist associations.[10] For the most part, workers could rely on little more than their capacity to work, their hopes, and their will to survive.

The need for an arena for addressing social conflicts became clearest when aspirations for upward social mobility were frustrated. Unions attempted to act on the most pressing economic demands, and the centers and circles were spaces in which to meet and socialize, places of belonging and participation where individualism was diluted and collective endeavors formulated. It was in these places, especially during moments of turmoil, that anarchists and workers encountered one another, and in which the discourse of the former seemed plausible to the latter, even if convincing workers to embrace the anarchist project was another matter. It was hard for anarchists to include workers organically in the framework of an alternative culture, primarily because of obstacles inherent in the construction of an efficient system of symbolic exchanges between anarchists and workers. Although anarchists intended to educate them and make them aware of the need for a vaguely defined universal emancipation, what they found was thousands of workers more inclined to fight for social and economic improvements than emancipation as such.

Anarchists' impact upon workers grew, especially in the eyes of outside observers, as social conflicts intensified and the harsher effects of the modernization process became most visible. And indeed, it was not merely a matter of perception: there was a large number of anarchist militants. Disregarding data furnished by anarchists, who doubtlessly exaggerated their own numbers, police estimated that there were 6,000 anarchists in the country in 1902. Two years later, the Interior Minister calculated that there were "more than 4,000" anarchist activists in the Federal Capital alone.[11] Anarchists' use of the streets and central public plazas to express themselves and mobilize their supporters probably made them seem more numerous than they actually were. Nonetheless, it was at this time that elites were most worried and the movement's dimensions (and potential) were at their greatest.

Elite concerns were not simply a question of incendiary rhetoric; the threatening social character that anarchists could imprint upon the workers' movement and protest generally also alarmed them. Every May Day and during large strikes, they watched as thousands marched through city streets with their red flags, banners, and vocal dedication to social change. This was the most radical expression of the social conflict and a logical consequence of the process of economic growth and social transformation, even if not all the actors saw it that way.

These political-ideological developments among labor did not disturb the typically circumspect newspaper *La Nación*, which defended workers' right to display their symbols.[12] But in 1905, halfway between the approval of the Residency Law and the Social Defense Law, the government banned the exhibition of the red flag, which it saw as "a symbol of war and disassociation" between foreign-born parents and their Argentine children. "On what grounds," asked Interior Minister Rafael Castillo, "can we embrace this collision of colors, in which some assert that the red flag represents their demands and rights, while their children need simply to recognize the flag of the Fatherland?"[13] Anarchists' rigid opposition to the state and any type of political integration found its counterpart in Argentine ruling groups equally resolute dedication to excluding them.

Nonetheless, the creation of an integrative strategy in the form of tentative state reforms, the expansion of suffrage in 1912, and the emergence of syndicalism, which seemed more resonant with workers' demands, caused a rupture between workers' expectations and libertarian premises.

This work treats the period in which libertarians had the strongest ties to Argentine workers up to the dissolution of their mass influence. I argue that the very attributes that enabled the anarchist movement to grow in fin-de-siècle Buenos Aires later became obstacles that, along with various structural factors, led to anarchists' marginalization. It was Argentine anarchism's dual, contradictory identity—which expressed as much individualism and collectivism (or communism) as its European counterpart—that allowed it to expand. And although I use the term *movement* when referring to local anarchists, it should be clear that I am speaking of a conglomeration of tendencies (groups and individuals) and a veritable chaos of doctrines (individualism, collectivism, vitalism, etc.). Indeed, multiple forms of anarchism converged into a movement whose only common feature was a shared commitment to negating state authority. This was also the case in the Spanish anarchist movement.[14]

Spanish and Italian anarchist immigrants created the first groups in the capital. While anarchist individualists leaned toward terrorism in countries like Spain and France, bombing and assassinations were rare in Argentina. Pro-organizational and collectivist anarchists prevailed over individualists, even though the latter were always a presence and participated in varied dimensions of the anarchist movement, including labor agitation. These tendencies, which appear so radically divergent, repelled and attracted one another in a way that endowed libertarians with a binary identity that allowed them to speak to issues of essential individual concern (such as immigration and social ascent) while also mobilizing to satisfy collective, social needs in the circles, centers, and unions. With a degree of discord, individualism and collectivism merged into a discourse that challenged Argentine capitalism on moral grounds and whose central characteristic was its transclass position. In other words, anarchists appealed to the entirety of the poor and dispossessed—the oppressed generally—without making class distinctions between them. While the collectivists helped spur the organization of resistance societies and circles, individualists gave the libertarian project its insurrectional disposition and revolutionary urgency, reflected in the constant agitation and mass mobilizations, in which direct action served as a means and an end.[15] This is the logic of Argentine anarchists' combative, aggressive rhetoric and symbolic arsenal (their celebrations and flags, etc.), whose purpose was to reinforce the construction of a cultural, political, and ideological alternative (circles, schools, the press, etc.) that would challenge the state and parliamentarianism.

These characteristics led the local anarchist movement to vigorously defend the individual rights of all the oppressed, rights that they conceived, fundamentally, in relation to workers' efforts to address basic deficiencies. Libertarian action was perfectly suited to the expression of some of these needs in a society undergoing construction and transformation. Anarchists flourished under such circumstances, especially in areas of society neglected and disregarded by the state and governing groups. But changes in the dominant politics began to occur around 1910 (e.g., the expansion of suffrage and the beginning of social reforms), in addition to modifications in the social structure (from urban transformations and changes in communication practices to alterations in the forms of workers' organization) that displaced the anarchist movement, which was unable to adapt its strategy and vision to the new circumstances. Society evolved quickly, but anarchists did not and, instead, remained imprisoned by their attachment to action and their disinterest in analyzing the particularities of the society in which they lived.

What prompts us to study the political, ideological, and social movements of the past? We typically think of history in terms of the present, which is logical and correct, although it tends to obscure issues and encourage inaccuracies, especially in the case of popular social movements. If we glance at the historical literature produced in the last twenty-five years in Argentina, we would obviously note a pervasive interest in Peronism, which of course makes perfect sense, given the extremely important role that it played in Argentine history in the latter half of the twentieth century. It is natural that historians would look for solutions to contemporary questions by delving into phenomena that, far less politicized today, seem to offer an inexhaustible resource for researchers. In this way, much of Argentine social history is now tied to Peronism, which has become a point of departure (and arrival) for many historians and social scientists.

But historians have paid little attention to social and political movements that existed prior to 1945. This is true even in the case of the Radical Party, despite its obvious present-day relevance. Categorized as a movement of the "middle sectors," it held little interest for researchers. It was only in the 1970s that a curiosity about the topic emerged, due first and foremost to the links between Yrigoyenian and Peronist populism. Certainly, the Radical Party's populist dimensions are a good place to look for the tradition that would later take shape as Peronism.

Historians have been even less interested in left-wing movements—due to their supposedly limited impact—which is why there are so few studies of Argentine socialists and communists.[16] However, paradoxically, anarchism is inordinately prominent in the literature that does exist on the left in the first half of the century, despite its early disappearance as a movement.

Interest in anarchism's impact on Argentina has a long history. Anarchist militants furnished the first and classical accounts, eager to provide their movement with a heritage and identity.[17] Their chronicles were self-congratulatory, replete with heroic deeds, and unflattering toward opponents. Their narratives were the sole accounts of the early-twentieth-century left available until the 1960s, when academic historians began to take an interest in the working class. Activist chronicles assumed a different status at this time: they became primary sources from which to extract data for the reconstruction of left-wing history. However, as has occurred with popular accounts of Argentine history from Bartolomé Mitre onward, presuppositions found in militant texts have endured and become part of historical common sense, despite the lack of supporting evidence. For example, there is the simplistic assertion, generally made by Marxists, that anarchism is theoretically impoverished, archaic, unreflective, and only capable of influence in backward, economically undeveloped societies, in contrast to socialism, which would impact industrialized societies.

Although they do not usually state it so bluntly, renowned intellectuals such as English historian Eric Hobsbawm have made this argument. Hobsbawm, whose views are based on Marx and Engels's criticisms of Proudhon and Bakunin, denies that anarchist thinkers made a contribution to revolutionary theory. Although he recognizes that anarchists offered some useful elements to the socialist camp (particularly, the critique of the dictatorship of the proletariat and the tendency toward state centralization and authoritarianism), he concludes that anarchism's defining trait and primary appeal was its strong, almost irrational, anti-intellectual, and emotional content. This, he claims, is why anarchists exalted idealism and the spirit of sacrifice and were absolutely dedicated to subverting capitalism. Hobsbawm finds these traits admirable, but inadequate to the task of creating a new society.[18]

In Argentina, such assertions have played a part in polemics between socialists and anarchists from the outset. For instance, José Ingenieros wrote numerous articles describing socialists' prevalence in industrialized countries in contrast to anarchists' influence in backward ones. Ave Lallemant, a German socialist leader living in Argentina, went further, reducing the analysis to near caricature: "It's extremely difficult to enlist Italian and Spanish workers … in the socialist cause," because most, he claimed, were totally ignorant and thus easily drawn in by anarchists. "If not for the German comrades," he said, "all the workers would have fallen into the hands of the anarchists … whose movement remains quite strong."[19]

This formulation became established in studies of the left and also in more general works on these formative years in the history of modern Argentina. For instance, one well-known author argued that "prominent [anarchist] activists were overwhelmingly semi-illiterate artisans who crisscrossed the Atlantic."[20] This view contends that anarchists were able to lay roots in Latin American countries such as Argentina, Uruguay, and Brazil because of capitalism's delayed, irregular development in such nations and that anarchists came from the thousands of European immigrants who retained ties to peasant, artisanal lifeways and had not yet become industrial proletarians concentrated in giant factories. While anarchism influenced the most backward sectors (artisans and peasants), Marxism carried the most advanced (the industrial working class).[21]

This interpretation schematizes and simplifies the link between ideology and social class. Anarchism's strength in Buenos Aires, Montevideo, and Sao Paulo—or Andalusia and Barcelona for that matter—reflects more complicated phenomena than the existence of "desperately poor, hungry peasants." In Buenos Aires, socialists and anarchists' relative strength in the emerging world of labor does not confirm the argument: both fought for influence among the same groups of workers and impacted the "advanced" and "backward" alike. No one can claim that workers active in the socialists' centers were fundamentally different from those in libertarian circles: Spaniards, Italians, or Argentines [*criollos*] with an artisanal, peasant, or industrial proletarian identity all occupied the common oppositional space that anarchists and socialists had constituted jointly, despite their differences. The programs advanced by either group were more important in determining workers' support for one tendency or another. This is how I explain anarchism's popularity in this work.

While most studies of anarchism written since the 1960s presuppose anarchism's "backwardness," other factors have come into play as well, particularly authors' identification with various political traditions. For instance, anarchism has been cast as an historical anomaly rectified only with the arrival of Peronism, which reunited the "national and popular."[22] Other works establish a continuity between the Montoneros (oppressed Argentines [*criollos oprimidos*]) and anarchist workers (oppressed foreigners),[23] some use anarchism to explain the working class's supposedly insurrectionalist tendencies,[24] and others see it as a movement that engendered heroic deeds and the turn to revolutionary justice, which was necessary given the futility of attempts to change society legally.[25]

However, most academic works treat anarchism not as a political, ideological, and cultural phenomenon in its own right, but in relation to the workers' movement. Indeed, in many studies it is difficult to distinguish the anarchist movement from other forms of labor radicalism.[26] To an extent, many of these works advance ideas found in the militant accounts. For instance, in his exhaustive reconstruction of FORA congresses, Edgardo Bilsky argues that the workers' and anarchist movements had completely merged by the time of the FORA's Fifth Congress in 1905. "The labor movement not only became the anarchist movement's political and organizational focus," Bilsky writes, "but also completely absorbed the latter, or at least its most dynamic elements, reducing its other activities to simple complements of that central commitment or relegating them to a secondary status, dependent on support from FORAist militants."[27]

The boundaries between the anarchist movement and the emerging workers' movement *were* ambiguous at the beginning of the century. Indeed, the libertarian movement itself was amorphous. Anarchists, unlike the Socialist Party, did not have clearly identifiable leadership or a well-demarcated strategy, although it is incorrect to contend that the workers' movement absorbed them, just as one cannot argue that communism and socialism were mere variants of labor radicalism. The anarchist movement's core identity, and the center from which its ideas radiated, lay in the cultural circles and press, whose discourse was directed to the workers, emitted not by workers themselves but by a vanguard that intended to guide and transform them. Paraphrasing Hobsbawm, one could say that the press and circles were the spark that drove anarchists toward the workers or at least what propelled anarchists' penetration of the workers' movement.

In this work, I show that a pole of political, ideological, and cultural power—anchored by newspapers like *La Protesta*, the cultural circles, and some unions—emerged from the multiple tendencies constituting the anarchist movement in the first decade of the century. I call this sector "doctrinally purist" to differentiate it from advocates of syndicalist or anarcho-syndicalist positions. It attempted to raise popular (not class) consciousness by educating workers about anarchist principles, calling for individual freedom and absolute opposition to authority as epitomized by the state. Anarchism's conceptual breadth allowed anarchists to take advantage of the disorder of an emerging social structure and an embryonic workers' movement, although this later became a hindrance. Increased industrialization, which led to changes in the organization of the labor movement; the state's initial attempts to engage the unions; the appearance and growth of syndicalism, which had a more straightforward and effective class appeal; and the universalization of male suffrage in 1912 helped undermine anarchism's appeal for workers. Anarchism was more suited to a society defined primarily by conflict and confrontation than the one that emerged during the interwar period.[28]

Anarchists, socialists, and syndicalists inaugurated practices and ideas that later became integral to the Argentine left: the notion of an alternative world, ideas of insurrection and social rebellion, the employment of certain rites and symbols (the red flag and May Day, etc.), street demonstrations, the dissemination of the workers' and oppositional press, forms of militant commitment, mobilizations for the liberation of political prisoners, and varied types of confrontation and even negotiation with ruling groups. They also embraced a combination of rationalism, moralism, and puritanism that permeated the entire Argentine left, from the Communist Party to the Montoneros.[29]

In the context of the formation of that left culture, it is important to consider another pervasive idea in the historical literature on anarchism. I refer to the tendency to frame libertarian discourse as autonomous and countercultural, emphasizing its uniqueness and difference.[30] This perspective implies that anarchist discourse represented an absolutely unique project that was uncontaminated by other discourses circulating at the time. It also reflects the tendency to perceive systems of ideas as functions of their content and immanent logic, isolating discourse from the social conditions of its production. Although there was a cultural, political, and ideological arena in Buenos Aires that was relatively independent of the state, ideological messages must be analyzed in their context, linked to the subjects that expressed them, the social and cultural environment in which they circulated, and their forms of production, emission, and reception.[31]

Such an approach presumes not only that libertarian messages *are* adulterated, but that they also share external influences, ideological crossroads, and practices with other ideological and political actors. The libertarian cultural message encompassed important paradoxes and contradictions. It was constituted by fragments and accents with diverse meanings.[32] It is thus better understood as alternative rather than autonomous or countercultural. This alternative contained discourses on education, art (theater, painting, and literature), the body and sickness, women, marriage, and religion that were not unique to anarchism but at least partially shared with socialists, liberals, hygienists, and even social Catholics. Importantly, these actors all had different goals, but anarchists did not possess an uncontaminated cultural capital but rather one blended with multiple influences. In fact, it was far less closed and independent than typically supposed: from rationalism to emotionalism (opposites that co-existed uneasily within ideals of the anarchist man); from the family to the role of women; from the influences of romanticism, realism, and naturalism to the strong moral dimension of its worldview; and, finally, from the concept of leisure time to anarchists' disdain for popular culture. Anarchist analyses of and convictions about these topics were not essentially original but reflected disparate influences and intersections with other philosophical and cultural currents.[33]

Nonetheless, to understand anarchism it is necessary to do more than simply highlight commonalities with other permutations of local thought or to make it into a countercultural tabla rasa, as Diego Armus recently seemed to suggest.[34] The issues should be carefully nuanced in a way that frames anarchism as a complex mosaic that incorporated myriad discursive and conceptual contradictions and oppositions. While some subsume anarchism's cultural content to its political and ideological components—its view of the state and politics and consequent practical strategies—this obscures anarchism's connections with other viewpoints, as well as its disconnections from them.[35] How many shared the libertarian view of the state and politics? Few held similar positions during the period discussed in this book. Neither socialists, liberals, nor free thinkers, much less social Catholics, endorsed libertarians' confrontational posture.[36] Is not this elemental resistance to the political system one of anarchism's distinctive features—the one that prompted ruling groups to declare it an out-and-out enemy?

Where is the real anarchism? Is it to be found where its cultural commitments intertwine and converge with other discourses, or is it something that is more confrontational and resistant to reconciliation? Possibly both. The problem resides in deciding which discourse to select, but it is not only a question of identifying a discourse and pinpointing the essence of its words. One must also understand how others received that discourse, even if it is true, as Stedman

Jones argued, that to analyze an ideology we must begin by looking at what a political movement says and writes.[37] A political, ideological, and cultural movement must be understood in terms of its multiple discourses and practices. In this sense, anarchism, while it was not countercultural per se, insofar as elements from other doctrines entered into its message, it was more subversive of the dominant order. In any case, the concept of *alternative* is capable of capturing and explaining the breadth of the libertarian project, provided that its cultural aspects are not separated from its ideological and political elements. It was the interaction of all of these levels that enabled anarchists to become an important radical social actor in fin-de-siècle Buenos Aires.

We have taken a good path. As we see it, the formation of social
study circles and the establishment of libertarian schools are
solid, protective bulwarks in our race toward emancipation. They
are the groundwork of the great revolution.
—*La Protesta Humana*, January 7, 1900

CHAPTER I

The Organization of the Libertarian Movement
and the Dissemination of its Ideas

B Y THE TURN of the twentieth century, Argentina had become a geo-
graphically circumscribed nation with a consolidated state that exercised
control over the national territory. Economic transformations in the
coastal region and the Pampas, above all, had radically transformed the country's
productive landscape and generated a dramatic expansion of the city of Buenos
Aires. In a short time, railroads, streetcars, ports, factories, electricity, government buildings, and green spaces became features of the new physical structure
of the city. Someone who had lived in Buenos Aires in the late 1860s would
have beheld a very different, nearly unrecognizable city just thirty years later.
However, the most important change had been in the social structure, due to the
hundreds of thousands of immigrants that had come to the country to take advantage of the apparently abundant jobs. Indeed, while our imaginary observer
would have counted fewer than 200,000 inhabitants in the city in 1869, the
population was well over one million by the Centenary in 1910: the population
of Buenos Aires had grown more than fivefold. The city had also undergone a
significant cultural and social evolution. It had become a multi-ethnic, multi-
cultural metropolis where native-born Argentines [*criollos*], Italians, Spaniards,
and tens of thousands from other parts of the planet crossed paths.[1] As José Luis
Romero noted years ago, there was "deep agitation in many levels of the social

structure."[2] One of those levels was linked to the formation and development of a working class, which would increasingly make its presence felt as the nineteenth century drew to a close. By the twentieth century, this new social actor had created forms of mobilization and political, labor, and cultural institutions defined by the new ideological tendencies of socialism and anarchism. The latter are the focus of this book.

1. ANARCHISM IN BUENOS AIRES: A BRIEF HISTORICAL OUTLINE

There were many libertarians among the waves of European immigrants that arrived in the late 1870s and early 1880s, especially among Spaniards and Italians and, to a lesser extent, the French. They typically came to Argentina to escape the police or simply in search of better living conditions in a country that seemed to offer both work and freedom. Many had participated in pivotal events in the European workers' movement such as the Paris Commune and the First International, and, like many other immigrants, often did not remain in the country permanently.

In the 1880s, local anarchist efforts were very modest and carried out by small groups usually united by ethnic and ideological affinities mirroring those found among anarchists in Europe. For the most part, they studied and discussed the most prominent libertarian theorists, without worrying much about practical initiatives or long-term social transformation. This changed with the arrival of two Italian libertarians, who helped the anarchist movement take shape in Buenos Aires. One was Héctor Mattei, who founded the Anarchic Communist Circle and, three years later, the Bakers' Union, the first union inspired by anarchism and one that would play an important role in the years ahead. The other was Errico Malatesta, who immigrated to Argentina in 1885. He had the greatest intellectual capacity of all the libertarian propagandists that passed through the country and, during the four years that he lived here, he did much to lay the basis for the growth of the anarchist movement through his organizing activities and theoretical contributions. He created the Social Studies Circle and the newspaper *The Social Question* and, surrounding himself with a group of mostly Italian militants, tried to construct a libertarian oppositional pole while minimizing the harsh and wearisome arguments in which anarchists liked to immerse themselves.[3]

This loose network dissolved after Malatesta departed in 1889 and for several years thereafter libertarian groups acted in isolation and limited themselves to publishing efforts. Most local anarchists identified with the individualist, anti-organizational newspaper *The Persecuted* (1890–1897), which had little influence beyond those isolated groups. Toward the mid-1890s, as labor conflicts intensified, some militants became active in resistance societies, perhaps inspired by similar experiences they had had in Spain or Italy, and a faction soon emerged that championed anarchist participation in the labor movement and the organization of unions. The arrival of Antonio Pellicer Paraire, Inglán Lafarga, and José Prat, Spanish anarchists who had participated in labor activism through the Spanish Workers' Federation, gave a significant impetus to pro-organizationalists, who were also encouraged by the 1897 appearance of the newspaper *La Protesta Humana* and the presence of Italian lawyer Pietro Gori, who lived in Buenos Aires between 1889 and 1902. All of these militants dedicated themselves to organizing newspapers, cultural circles, and resistance societies.[4]

The battle between individualists and pro-organizationalists gradually tilted in favor of the latter, which cleared the way for libertarian political action among local workers. A sizeable contingent of intellectuals, journalists, and activist workers constituted the solid core that made the expansion and diffusion of the libertarian doctrine possible. The anarchist movement abandoned the isolation and self-referentiality characteristic of its early period, during which it mechanically reproduced European ideas. It inserted itself into Argentine society through the creation of institutions for workers' self-defense, without losing its internationalism or disinclination to analyze local conditions. The anarchist movement took off, articulating and combining the most heterogeneous social forces in its resistance societies, countless centers and cultural circles, schools, libraries, and newspapers. Anarchists became the most significant oppositional force in Buenos Aires in the first decade of the twentieth century, which is not to deny the presence of socialists.

Anarchists and socialists created the Argentine Workers' Federation [FOA in its Spanish acronym] in 1901, although disagreements between them led the socialists to depart shortly thereafter and to form a separate federation Workers' Union, which gave anarchists uncontested control of the FOA for a number of years. Although it appears that there were relatively few dues-paying members in the FOA, it controlled key unions like the National Federation of Port Workers and the unions for the streetcar drivers, sailors, and stokers, and for the stall workers of the Central Fruit Market.[5] Anarchists also had a strong presence among the bakers, metal workers, construction workers, and ship workers (builders, boilermakers, and caulkers). This placed them in a position to put pressure on the mainstays of the agricultural export economy, since shutting down even a portion of ground transportation or port activity could disrupt vital elements of the Argentine economy, such as the export of meats and grains. In May 1902, these unions were involved in a series of disputes, culminating in the first general strike in Argentine history that November. Overwhelmed by the magnitude of the events, the government unleashed a heavy crackdown that was particularly hard on anarchists, who were the visible leaders of the turmoil.

The government imposed martial law and passed the Residency Law, which enabled it to silence the oppositional press and to imprison and expel foreigners suspected of subversion.[6]

Conflicts occurred constantly throughout the decade. There were seven anarchist-led general strikes,[7] the renters' strike of 1907, some partial but important strikes (the streetcar workers struck in 1902; the port workers, machinists, and ship stokers in 1904 and 1905; and the cart drivers in 1903 and 1906); the May Day mobilizations, which were particularly contentious in 1904, 1905, and 1909; and demonstrations on behalf of political prisoners in 1910. Demands for salary increases, improvements in labor conditions (the working environment, the eight-hour day, weekly days off, etc.), union rights (recognition of the right to organize, the rehiring of employees, etc.), and the solidarity inherent in the world of labor drove the dissent.

Anarchists mobilized a large percentage of Buenos Aires workers—port workers, cart drivers, coachmen, sailors, stokers, mechanics, painters, bricklayers, plasterers, bakers, and laborers—but their message went beyond mere economic demands to point toward the qualitative transformation of society. Workplace battles were merely a first step; their real goal was to rouse "workers' sleeping consciences" and build a different society. It was to that project that they devoted their best efforts.

2. PROPAGANDA, AN IMPORTANT TOOL: GROUPS, CIRCLES, AND STUDY CENTERS

Anarchists regarded the dissemination of anarchist ideas as a powerful weapon. They spread them in various ways and through disparate institutional mechanisms, such as groups and cultural centers, newspapers and magazines, and rationalist schools. Through their schools, anarchists waged a long-term battle to create a different type of person—freed from the "shackles" and "prejudices" of religious and patriotic education—whereas their publications, circles, and groups provided the organizational structure for the more immediate propagation of ideas.[8]

Political and ideological propaganda had become a force in Argentine society at the beginning of the century, particularly in urban areas that were linked directly to the agro-export economy. A series of novel circumstances made this possible. These included rapid urbanization; the dramatic development of communication technologies, particularly the press, which became a medium not only for elites but also for middle sectors; and the emergence and growth of left-wing associations, parties, and groups—including anarchists among others—who sought to recruit and influence popular strata through the transmission and diffusion of discrete ideological messages.

Anarchists were heirs of a radical political tradition, with roots in the French Revolution, that uses ideology to justify its action, although their opposition to party centralization put them at odds with their socialist and Marxist peers.[9] Anarchists attempted to organize in a manner consistent with their commitment to spontaneity and individual freedom and to reconcile two apparently contradictory imperatives: on the one hand, the need for politically effective organization and, on the other, the need of individual members of the organization for freedom. Anarchism had elements of the "artisanal character" that Lenin attributed to the Russian Social Democrats of the 1880s and 1890s. By "artisanal character," Lenin was speaking of theoretical and organizational incoherence and programmatic disunity. Lenin scorned such disorder and, in contrast, advanced an organizational model that various strains of Marxism would adopt in one form or another; it saw propaganda as the coordinated, organized, and unified action of a political party, led from the top down. This party had to have a regularly appearing newspaper at its disposal—the voice of the party—so as "to give each militant a reason to march *in rank and file*."[10] Anarchists categorically rejected this strategy, seeing it as authoritarian and antagonistic to individual freedom. They fought for their ideas in an utterly different manner, publishing newspapers and organizing groups, unions, and individuals on the basis of strongly individualist ideas and following a path that essentially ensured that efforts would be duplicated at times and that tactical and even doctrinal stances would diverge.

The anarchist movement as a whole was committed to transforming society and individuals through propaganda, to infiltrating systems of belief and worldviews that were deeply rooted in common sense. Libertarian propaganda was comprehensive and attempted to convince not only exploited male workers but also their wives and children. Because of this, local anarchists, like their Italian and Spanish counterparts, deemed the Catholic Church an archenemy. And even though tendencies toward superficiality and voluntarism led some libertarians to underestimate religion's power, others understood its intense persuasive capacities: "The Catholic Church," said Julio Molina y Vedia, "has excelled in selecting and deploying the means of influencing and molding man ... the priestly caste has a craftiness of the first order."[11]

Anarchists understood the difficulty of overcoming hindrances imposed by religion. They were especially concerned about religion's influence on the families of libertarian militants, since:

> The most blatant, inconceivable contradictions exist within it. While the father and son hang portraits of cherished social thinkers from their headboards ... the mother and daughter have effigies of the Virgin and the saints and don't read anything but

> the stupid prayer book ... the men go to study centers, the women
> go to church ... and when children are born, the father, this man
> of advanced ideas, this revolutionary and anarchist, enemy of all
> religious farces, tolerates all of these charades and acts oblivious in
> the most disgraceful way.[12]

Clearly it was difficult for anarchists to communicate their message to all workers. And while they generally focused their energies on active workers and preferred to propagandize in areas where they concentrated, the libertarian message was fundamentally universalist, directed to the individual as such, without distinctions of class or gender, and designed to draw everyone—men and women, manual and intellectual workers—onto the revolutionary path.

In the initial chapters of this book, I analyze the relationship between anarchist organization and the ideological, political, and cultural project of the groups, cultural circles, and social study centers, from which practically all libertarian activity radiated. There is no doubt that these institutions, in their totality, were what most resembled the Marxist revolutionary party while also being most compatible with anarchists' commitment to spontaneity.[13]

Circles, groups, and centers were an arena for the comprehensive education and indoctrination of the worker and his family, the latter being inaccessible to resistance societies, whose demands were directed to workers and limited to the working environment. To an extent, and in an informal way, the direction of the unions was subject to guidance from the publications and centers, groups, and circles. They were spaces for the development of activists—responsible for the education and indoctrination of popular sectors—and, linked to the workers' associative public sphere, they set the preconditions for the formation of resistance societies and unions. When labor institutions appeared and made economic demands, unattached to particular political tendencies, the groups, circles and centers endeavored to maintain an ambiguous doctrinal purity within them. Indeed, they tried with various degrees of success to influence the unions up to 1905, when anarchists enjoyed a fleeting political and ideological predominance in the FORA. These institutions continued to grow until the Centenary, although in many cases resistance societies fulfilled similar roles.

Circles, groups, and centers were formal, delimited environments for association. They helped participants satisfy social needs while remaining aloof from influences considered pernicious on the left—such as the café and bar, although libertarian activists frequently used these as places to meet and disseminate their ideas during the movement's formative years in the 1890s. In essence, the circle or center was to provide all the elements necessary for workers' well-being, from recreational pastimes to basic educational resources such as classes, libraries, and lectures. There was a utopian element, too, insofar as anarchists attempted to construct an almost ideal environment in the circle, center, and group, isolated from the perversions of the real world. It was an escape to the future. "In the anarchist commune," said Pierre Quiroule, "man will flee the darkness, shunning unwholesome settings."[14]

These anarchist institutions were a place for the construction of political and cultural bonds, whose origins go back to the popular clubs and fraternal societies of the French Revolution, which Masons also utilized. Initially, these spaces of sociability were formal bodies for the bourgeoisie, but were later used by workers as environments for political fraternization. Creating these sorts of institutions was a practical realization of workers' demand for the right to free association.[15] In Argentina, workers' organizations date back to the 1860s, when they first appeared under the guise of mutualist and ethnic groupings.[16] Shortly thereafter, parallel to early attempts to create resistance societies, libertarians formed their first groups and circles, which linked intellectuals and workers around the explicit ideological and political goal of liberating the former from the "oppression" of bourgeois society. These groups evolved politically, ideologically, and culturally: their history constitutes a little-known aspect of the class struggle, one rarely addressed by scholars of the working class, who are typically overly preoccupied with the labor movement's organizational and institutional dimensions.

The anarchist circles began as small nuclei with well-defined ideological aims, publishing pamphlets and newspapers. Although they were initially closed and barely communicated among themselves, in the mid-1890s they began to move toward political struggle, incorporating lectures into their activities in hopes of expanding their ranks. When they realized the limits of offering talks in one or two locations in the capital, they set out on propaganda tours throughout the country with the goal of creating anarchist institutions in the cities and towns of the interior. By the turn of the century, anarchist groups, circles, and centers had evolved into the cultural and political fabric of a comprehensive project that ran from publishing pamphlets and newspapers, sponsoring lectures, doctrinal courses, and creating study groups to more recreational activities like literary readings, theatrical performances, revolutionary song, folk dances and music, rural celebrations, and libertarian dances and parties.[17] Libertarian efforts touched on nearly every aspect of life, and ventured to present a cultural alternative that, in addition to having political and ideological components, put forward unique forms of theater, recreation, family life, health, everyday habits, and so on; to put it more succinctly, they tried to innovate new forms and norms of sociability. Thus, the libertarian circle was an environment in which a workers' culture emerged—through the exchange of individual experiences, workers became collective and began to assume a shared identity.

The topic examined and analyzed in this and the two following chapters is very important to comprehending anarchist practices and the meaning that libertarian militants attributed to them. I will begin by identifying the circles and describing their emergence and activity.

3. THE IMPORTANCE OF HAVING A NAME

Although there is not enough data to fully reconstruct the history of the network of anarchist groups, centers, and circles, existing data does reveal ideological tendencies, cultural and political patterns, anarchists' means of transmitting and elaborating their messages, and the tactics that they used to create centers of resistance and alternative models of political and cultural association.

It is also possible to conduct a sustained examination of the libertarian symbolic universe implicit in the groups and circles' names. Their names were their calling cards, and by no means irrelevant. They were a founding gesture designed to reinforce the anarchist symbolic framework and provide Buenos Aires workers with an identity that would enable them to resist the disciplining and moralizing activities of the state and civil institutions.

The names of the circles and groups expressed their worldview and cast elements of the libertarian symbolic universe into relief. In them, one can see their certitudes and beliefs, as well as their hopes for radical social change. The names were an important symbol, perhaps as important as the flags and banners that they carried in street demonstrations, and gave their institutions a distinct identity—a necessity in a tangled, complex, and cosmopolitan society, in which anarchists confronted and competed with a multitude of messages from the prevailing state, religious, ethnic, and nativist institutions that were also attempting to mold workers' identity.[18]

Some libertarian circles had names that expressed their identification with and commitment to the proletariat: Worker's Shout; The Proletariat; Slaves of the Counter, and Friends of the Worker. In other cases, class identity was diluted in favor of a generic reference to the exploited: Sons of the People; The Dispossessed; The Hobos; The Hungry; The Height of Misery; The Vagabonds; and Universal Pain. These names underscore anarchism's populist impulses, deemphasizing class differences in order to speak to the oppressed in universal terms. It is no accident that the anarchist institution par excellence was La Casa del Pueblo [The House of the People].

In many instances, the names used by groups, circles, and centers referred to their doctrine—for example, The Anarchos or The Libertarians—or combined that with mention of a specific neighborhood: The Los Corrales Libertarians, The Barracas Anarchists, and The Almagro Libertarians. In other cases, there was just the geographic term, such as The Mazzini Plaza Group and the Floresta Education Center. The need to oppose capitalism and subvert its values occupied a privileged place in the symbolic imagination of local anarchists. There were also appeals to violent, more-or-less individualist tactics: there were centers named The Struggle, Expropriation, Social Volcano, Agitator, Expropriation is necessary, The Rebel, La Protesta, The Conquest of Bread, The Conquest of the Ideal, The New Rebels, Determination, and Rebellion. Names of this sort were perhaps the most common, evoking combat and resistance to capitalism. Others pointed unambiguously to support for violence: Revenge, Vengeance, Pallás's Bomb, The Honorable Delinquents, The Dynamiters, Bresci, and Emulators of Ravachol.

Names often used imagery linked to light, fire, and the sun, which represented freedom and were to guide humanity to the revolution and a happy future: The Sun, The Dawn, Gleam, Children of the Sun, Dawn of the Future, and The May Sun. These names were also publication titles and reflected central themes in libertarian iconography, as they connoted the revelatory truth proclaimed by anarchists. As heirs of positivism, their truth rested on a firm belief in science and the progress derived from it. Science and reason were not only symbols but also weapons in the struggle against religious dogmatism. They had illuminating, revelatory powers that would guide humanity from ignorance to enlightenment, from authority to anarchy, from reaction to revolution and freedom. Many centers had names pointing to science's centrality in the construction of the new society: Labor and Science, Light and Progress, Initiative, Forward, New Directions, Creation, Aspirants to the Ideal, New Era, and Evolution.

Faith in science was not unique to anarchists but part of the dominant paradigm at the time. Indeed, anarchists shared signifiers with an extremely broad range of tendencies: even statesmen, whom anarchists scorned so passionately, were vocally committed to science and progress, and it was in their name that they led the modernizing process. People on opposite ends of the local political spectrum revered Auguste Comte and Herbert Spencer,[19] which shows how widely certain ideas were shared among partisans of all variants of the turn-of-the-century ideological framework. Libertarians' scientism was extreme at times. They were fully convinced that humanity would organize itself around scientific, positivistic, and exact laws—an assertion that would be untenable today, given power's uses of science in the twentieth century. However, like many others a century ago, anarchists thought science fundamentally liberatory and believed that the science of sociology would counteract the negative effects of capitalism. Their convictions led them to envision a new society based on analytic inductions derived from positivism and logic. Reflecting their commitment to sociology, anarchists had a longstanding tradition of organizing innumerable social studies centers, international social studies circles, libertarian social study centers, anarchist libraries, popular centers, educational centers, and modern schools. These efforts indicated their deep faith in education and study as instruments for social transformation, which they shared with many in turn-of-the-century

Buenos Aires. Education, science, and progress were quasi-universal concepts and formed part of the prevailing paradigm, although of course anarchists rejected state education.

In the spirit of rationalism, names frequently referred to nature or, specifically, to the belief in society's natural equilibrium and humanity's inherent goodness. Some evoked the harmony, peace, and happiness that would reign in the future utopian society, as well as the healthy, natural habits represented by vegetarianism: Freedom and Love, Love, Young Lovers, Health and Strength, Nature, Nature Center, and Free Love. Others suggested a future in which humans would live unburdened by subjugation or moral, religious, political, or social restraints: Neither God Nor Master, Human Emancipation, and Without God or Country. And armies would also disappear: some groups—The Deserters, The Soldier's Enlightenment, The Conscript, and The Barracks—focused on fighting patriotism and militarism.

Names also commonly pointed to the equality, fraternity, and justice that would reign after the anarchist revolution, which would liquidate the old society and erect a new order upon totally different values: Equality and Fraternity, Solidarity, Justice, The Free, Freedom, and Universal Family. Reiterating an image that anarchists used repeatedly, this new humanity would emerge on the ruins of capitalism: To Destroy is to Create and To Destroy and Build. This was a salient motto in libertarian discourse and iconography: anarchists assumed that the future society would have to be constructed on the rubble of capitalism, which is why they frequently depicted the revolutionary worker standing atop the debris of bourgeois society. Universal values that libertarians saw as absolute truths would structure this perfect, new society: The Truth or Did You Notice? Of course, it was the libertarians who would teach this truth and prepare the workers for a better world: The Gentlemen of the Ideal and The Defenders of New Ideals.[20] Some assembled under the banner of the martyrs of the long revolutionary struggle (The Chicago Martyrs and Heroines of the Future), others with the guidance of the great masters (Carlo Caffiero, Zola's Disciples, Élisée Reclus, Ibsen, Alberto Ghiraldo, Florencio Sánchez, Emilio Zola, and Francisco Ferrer). These names also bespeak the sundry ideological and philosophical sources from which they drew.

More than a few groups and circles focused on theater, especially during the second half of the first decade: Modern Art, Art for Life, Young Lovers of Art, Ibsen, Florencio Sánchez, Alberto Ghiraldo Philodramatic Group, Art and Solidarity, Modern Theater, Modern Dramatic Association, Art and Labor, and Glory to Art. The number of theater groups attests to anarchist enthusiasm for drama as a means of propaganda.

Thus, the names of the libertarian centers, circles, and groups endowed the anarchist movement with a distinct identity, articulated a symbolic framework, and, above all, emphasized modern secular values like equality, liberty, and solidarity.

4. THE EMERGENCE, PEAK, AND DECLINE OF THE GROUPS AND CIRCLES

It appears that the first group was the Bakuninist Center for Workers' Propaganda, which was active in the second half of the 1870s and linked to one of the Argentine sections of the First International. Its purpose was to polemicize against Marxists, although there is little information about its efforts or structure or the activity of other groups during the time.[21] We do know that the Italians Héctor Mattei and Errico Malatesta participated in founding some of the first circles and centers while they resided in Buenos Aires—the Anarchic Communist Circle in 1884 and the Social Studies Center in 1886—which disseminated libertarian ideas, educated militants, and polemicized against Italian republicans and socialists.[22] Malatesta also fostered a pro-organizational sentiment among anarchists and gave some coherence to the scattered libertarian community, which was predominantly Italian. Nevertheless, though his ideas lived on among local activists long after his departure from the country, his organizational influence was far less enduring: dispersion and fragmentation once again characterized libertarian activity in the years after he left Argentina.

Groups and circles popped up sporadically during those years, the most important being The Dispossessed, which was composed of Spanish immigrants. It sponsored regular lectures and, in 1890, became the driving force behind the important anti-organizational periodical, *The Persecuted*.[23] It was not until the mid-1890s that centers, groups, and circles began to appear regularly, which accompanied the consolidation of the organizationalist, anti-individualist current within the anarchist movement. Pro-organizational anarchists became a dynamic force insofar as they had devised a strategy of collective action whose purpose was to strengthen workers' oppositional capacity. Although they basically lacked coordination among themselves, all of the groups, whether made up by individualists or organizers, were committed to mobilizing against their perceived common enemies: the state, state-run schools, religion, and, on a different level of enmity, socialists.

There is evidence that six groups were active in the city of Buenos Aires in 1897. One, The Anarchos, was based in the Barracas workers' district and was extremely energetic, focusing its efforts on publishing revolutionary pamphlets and creating an anarchist propaganda library.[24] It also defined the circles' role in remarkably coherent terms in a pamphlet published in the year it was founded: the circles' primary task was to educate the workers so that they could overcome "misery and ignorance, smashing to pieces the systems and beliefs that suffocate our existence."[25] Responding to the linguistic diversity among local workers, they published the text in Spanish and Italian. They understood the circle as a key instrument for the transformation of workers into "revolutionary individuals," whose conduct would be exemplary in every respect: "In the workshops, producing more damage than value; in the street, on the avenue, in the café, and in all social relations, they will show that they are conscious, having no respect for the pillars of the present order." They would also disrupt "patriotic processions, ceremonies, and holidays" and would be beyond reproach in the private sphere too, "not coupling through religious or civil means, but through the free attraction of the sexes," and giving their children a secular education.[26]

Here one sees the emergence of the ideal of the complete militant, always ready for action and committed in all aspects of life, and who put the revolutionary cause before private concerns. In a city where new social forces appeared rapidly, anarchists constructed an image of a different individual, a "revolutionary individual," who was exemplary and dedicated to combat, sacrifice, and suffering. This image runs throughout the entire history of the Argentine left; according to Gutiérrez and Lobato, it "was embodied in fighting for the cause of the dispossessed, in the strength needed to challenge police persecution, in ideological clarity, and in the probity necessary to resist bourgeois enticements."[27]

Although the circles' action was still comparatively limited, anarchist propaganda became progressively more spirited as groups like The Anarchos grew more engaged in spreading a message of proletarian redemption and less involved in fruitless polemics within Buenos Aires's anarchist movement (although these never disappeared entirely). Local anarchism was beginning to look like a political movement.[28] The advent of *La Protesta Humana* in 1897 was very important in this context: it became a link between groups, provided a degree of coherence to their efforts, promoted the creation and growth of other groups, and documented their activities in endless articles and reports. With a certain triumphalism, an editorial in the third issue declared:

> It is with great pleasure that we, from the pages of *La Protesta Humana*, see the new complexion that propaganda has assumed. We intend to encourage it by using this section of the paper to publicize initiatives and projects carried out by groups in the capital and the interior of the country.[29]

By becoming a link for the still dispersed anarchist movement, the periodical implicitly presupposed the movement's capacity to become an agent for social change, a conviction that it would question many times but never abandon. *Social Science*, a theoretical-doctrinal publication that appeared the same year as *La Protesta*, also attempted to bolster the groups and circles' effort to create an organizational alternative for the general public. It called for an end not only to internal squabbles but also "dogmas," "conservatisms," and "sectarian passions." A dense fabric of institutions, publications, and activists began to emerge in Buenos Aires organized around providing workers with social, political, and cultural alternatives. The Sociological Bookstore opened at 2041 Corrientes at this time, owned by the Italian Fortunato Serantoni. For five years, it was the linchpin of the local anarchist movement and a center for the diffusion of libertarian ideas; it was the main provider of locally published and European anarchist literature, helped print and distribute an enormous quantity of publications, spread news about the circles and groups' activities, and was a point of reference for much of the Argentine libertarian movement. It also lent its space to nascent or new groups that did not yet have a meeting place, as well as to established groups that found themselves lacking a venue for one reason or another.[30]

There was an impressive growth in the number of groups and circles and also a peak in their activities between 1898 and the end of 1902, when the government passed the Residency Law and imposed martial law. "We have seen feverish efforts in field of propaganda for some time," observed a libertarian journalist.[31] Twenty-two circles existed in Buenos Aires in 1902 (table 1). During these years, the number of anarchist activists grew and an impressive number of well-known figures from other tendencies joined their ranks, like Pascual Guaglianone and Eduardo Gilimón, who had been active socialists, and Arturo Montesano, Félix Basterra, and Alberto Ghiraldo, who had been engaged members of the Radical Party. All were distinguished organizers, lecturers, and editors. Clearly, the anarchist movement's challenge was to win the workers to their cause and dispense with the inward-looking attitude typical of its earlier years. The goals of the International Social Studies Circles capture the aims of the centers during those years: 1) to prepare the proletariat for emancipation, cultivate its moral and intellectual cohesion, and ready it for the social struggle; 2) to spread the principles of modern economic science among the proletariat; 3) to support the foundation of a library, a lecture hall, and a libertarian school for children, facilitating the education of the workers and their offspring; 4) to offer itself to workers' societies for all types of sociological and social propaganda; 5) to hold propaganda meetings and debates in order to study the roots of underlying social problems.[32]

The growth in groups and circles reflected an increase in the size of the working class as well as the frequency of their meetings and the range of their activities. These included publication of pamphlets, books, and magazines; the organization of discussions, rallies, and lectures (these multiplied dramatically); the creation of libraries and educational programs; and, above all, the *veladas*, which would occupy a central place in libertarian activities during the first decade of the century. *Veladas* were multifaceted cultural events held in a large hall or theater that typically revolved around theatrical performances, poetry readings, lectures, the singing of revolutionary hymns, musical performances, or family dances.

The most ambitious project of this period was the attempt to construct a sustainable Casa del Pueblo, which would be the site of all anarchist activities. Anarchists had been working toward this end in one form or another from 1899 to 1902, although it appears that its full operation was only sporadic during the time. The Casa del Pueblo was part of anarchists' bid to provide a comprehensive alternative that would address workers' diverse needs. Located in a large rented hall at 353 Callao Street, it had two big halls with a capacity of 400 people. "In the first, a duly staffed cafeteria, illuminated by electric light, will operate, as well as a stage that will regularly showcase the best works of revolutionary theater, alternating artistic events with readings, a room for medical-legal research, and the editorial offices of our periodicals."[33] The second hall would contain a library, a libertarian school, and meeting spaces.

All workers, regardless of their ideological convictions, could participate in Casa activities. Organizers sold memberships for one peso per month, entitling a worker and his family to partake in all Casa activities, whereas non-members had to pay fifty centavos for each event.[34] The Casa opened in 1899 and regularly held meetings, lectures, theatrical performances, and parties for five months: "The *veladas* ... take place every week; in their amazing activity, all lovers of emancipatory ideas contribute their artistic, moral, and intellectual energies, enabling the city's workers to have a permanent source of ideas and pleasing recreation."[35] However, this optimism was short-lived: at the turn of the century, it was announced that financial problems were suffocating the Casa, and days later, the Administrative Commission reported that the institution would close.[36]

Table 1: Libertarian Centers in the City of Buenos Aires, 1897–1910

YEAR	NUMBER OF CIRCLES
1897	6
1898	18
1899	7
1900	7
1901	12
1902	22
1903	7
1904	51
1905	25
1906	37
1907	40
1908	38
1909	37
1910	22

Data from *La Protesta Humana, La Protesta, The Rebel,* and *The Future.*

Undeterred, a group of activists moved the Casa's belongings to a small site at 1557 Calle Cuyo (Calle Sarmiento today) and tried to continue its activities there under the name Libertarian Social Studies Circle.[37] It opened in mid-April, and reports indicate that it had some public support. Nevertheless, the ongoing financial problems—the great Sword of Damocles that always hung over anarchist activities—prompted one writer to issue a warning to the anarchist movement: "The circle must receive help or it will collapse again due to a lack of resources." Pointing a critical finger at his comrades, he said: "Collectively or individually, we're far less concerned about this than about how to propagate abstract ideas."[38] His recrimination points to one of the anarchist movement's great problems: the inability to sustain organizations and activities due to the strong individualist streak in the movement. Indeed, when organizers maintained a level of regularity, success crowned their efforts. Perhaps the best example is Rosario's Casa del Pueblo, a collaborative effort between ten different groups. The list of activities carried out in 1900 speaks for itself: they had their own building, where they set up a jobs exchange through which 446 people found employment; they had a library holding 380 books on science, art, sociology, and literature (250 in Spanish, 90 in Italian, and 30 in French); they also had a permanent orchestra and a theater group (named Ibsen) that staged thirty plays (nine of them translated in the Casa); there were twenty-eight *veladas* of various types, sixty-four lectures, and fifty-two libertarian compositions were sung and recited; they lent the hall to workers' associations twenty-two times; distributed 2,310 free pamphlets and 5,510 periodicals through voluntary subscription; and sold 2,670 books and pamphlets at cost. Lastly, they lodged fifty-six needy "comrades" in the Casa and raised $605 for diverse causes.[39]

Buenos Aires anarchists finally found a suitable location for their Casa del Pueblo in April 1902. It was the old Skating Ring at 1009–1049 Charcas Street, a big hall owned by an engineer named Peduzzi, who apparently had anarchist sympathies.[40] Like its previous incarnation, the Casa offered various services to workers: meeting spaces, rooms to shelter needy militants, a hairdressing salon, a medical office, a job listing service, and a planned popular university. They raised money and equipped the old storehouse, and it immediately became the site of intense activity. However, the anarchist movement soon divided over the experiment and the most significant sectors (*The Rebel, La Protesta Humana,* and the Federación Obrera) withdrew their support. They accused Peduzzi of embezzling funds and published a statement saying that it was "totally impossible for the Casa del Pueblo to operate in the Skating Ring," and urged their comrades to "refrain from giving money for that end."[41] The venture ended in failure.

In addition to the Casa del Pueblo, anarchist circles had become a familiar presence in Buenos Aires at the dawn of the century.[42] There were at least twenty-two in operation in 1902. They were scattered throughout disparate neighborhoods, typically those that had a high concentration of workers as well as union and socialist centers. The majority were in El Centro, Barracas, La Boca, and San Telmo, although there were also some in Almagro, Once, San Cristóbal, Parque Patricios, and Villa Crespo. Many threw themselves into intense activity and then vanished: this appears to have been the case with Land and Liberty, The Chicago Martyrs, The Light, and Libertarian Dawn. Others, such as The Torch and The Sun, managed to sustain operations for two, three, or four months, but then disappeared without leaving much trace, as their militants formed new groups or joined others in existence. The majority of circles survived for longer and, as a whole, their propagandistic offerings were remarkably broad: they sponsored lectures, meetings, *veladas*, parties, and innumerable fundraisers for magazines, schools, and libraries. Among those that stood out are the Boca Popular Center for Education, which put on two lectures every week between 1902 and 1903, The Seed, and especially The Gentlemen of the Ideal and The Defenders of New Ideals, whose efforts were extraordinarily consistent and sustained. The Defenders were active between 1901 and 1906 and The Caballeros from 1901 to 1907.[43]

Parallel to increased urbanization, which brought with it the growth of industry and the expansion of some service unions, the number of libertarian centers and circles grew in large cities such as Buenos Aires and Rosario, as well as in smaller, less significant ones. For instance, anarchists had a presence in Santa Fe, which had more than six centers in 1902 and disseminated propaganda to Rafaela, Cañada de Gómez, San Justo, Paraná, Colastiné, and Esperanza, all cities in which there is a record of anarchist groups. La Plata was also important, as well as the neighboring localities of Berisso, Ensenada, and Tolosa. After Buenos Aires, however, Rosario was the city with the most active libertarian movement. There were circles there as early as the 1890s, including the mythic Science and Progress, in which Dr. Emilio Arana played a distinguished role. For ten years, that circle regularly sponsored lectures and published pamphlets and periodicals such as *The New Humanity*.[44] There were sometimes as many as ten groups operating in Rosario in a given year during the first decade of the century.

There were also circles in port cities such as Ingeniero White and Bahía Blanca; in municipalities linked to Pampas agriculture like Bolívar, Chascomús, Juárez, Colón, Chacabuco, Pergamino, Chivilcoy, 9 de Julio, Junín, Tandil, Salto, and Coronel Vidal; and in the Paraná river corridor: Campana, San Nicolás, Zárate, Baradero, and San Pedro. Groups also began to appear in the new settlements in Greater Buenos Aires such as San Martín, Victoria, San Fernando, Quilmes, Lanús, Adrogué, Avellaneda, Banfield, and Lomas de Zamora.[45]

General Julio Roca's government unleashed a heavy crackdown in 1902 in response to the large strikes in which anarchists had played a central role. This brought the movement's growth to an abrupt halt. Martial law, the deportation of prominent libertarian activists under the Residency Law, arrests, the shutting down of periodicals, and simple police pressure all contributed to a momentary suspension of anarchist activity. The centers were particularly vulnerable in moments of turmoil, since martial law not only disrupted their programs but also severed the network through which they financed themselves. This is why most disappeared and those that managed to survive were essentially underground, reappearing a few months later, usually in different locations and with fewer militants.

The effects of the repression lasted for a number of months, but political and labor activity returned to previous levels of intensity in the middle of 1903. Despite having been battered, when anarchists reemerged they were stronger than they had been before, and they had also earned a degree of prestige among the workers due to their combativeness and resolve during the strikes. Anarchist activists, who were more numerous due to recruitment efforts in the labor movement, regrouped easily and organized more than fifty circles in the city of Buenos Aires in 1904, a rate that they would never again be able to repeat. Their maturation led to an extension of their geographic influence: in addition to the already noted expansion in greater Buenos Aires, anarchists were very active in and opened circles in Palermo, Villa Urquiza, and even in the then-remote neighborhood of Belgrano.

The libertarian movement was reaching its apogee and the circles were unusually dynamic at this time. Light and Life, which was headquartered on Montevideo Street between Charcas and Santa Fe, sponsored lectures, published pamphlets, and worked diligently to raise money to start a school in the seamen and stokers' union headquarters in La Boca. New Light, from Villa Crespo, put on more than a dozen successful lectures in four months. Almost all of the groups raised money for their own periodicals; many organized frequent propaganda tours in cities in the province of Buenos Aires, along the seacoast, and on river shores. Another group, Blue, published a weekly anarchist paper named *The Wake* for a time, to which Basterra, Guaglianone, and other distinguished anarchist writers contributed.[46] The Gentlemen of the Ideal were particularly effective: they organized dozens of events designed to help finance *La Protesta* and also raised funds for the victims of repression during May Day, the weavers of Valentín Alsina, the port workers, and the anti-militarist committee. The groups' multifaceted, comprehensive activity was complemented by workers' hair salons, schools, libertarian libraries and bookstores, two anti-alcohol and naturalist centers (Nature and The Natural), and the vegetarian restaurant Pomona.

The circles' rising levels of activity, which paralleled that of the anarchist movement as a whole, suffered a new blow during the Radical Party's failed uprising in February 1905. The government did not limit its repression to participants in the revolt, but rather extended it to the entire workers' movement and its political articulations—to socialists and especially to the anarchists. A new wave of detentions, deportations, and arrests, as well as the closing of political centers and periodicals had a significant impact on the circles. The imposition of martial law staunched political and union activities until the end of May, after which the circles renewed their activity.[47] Of the fifty-one centers in existence in 1904, a mere twelve were still operating after the repression following the Radical Party's rebellion, but thirteen new ones appeared during the year, yielding a total of twenty-five for 1905. The number increased to forty in 1907, just under that number in 1908 and 1909, and then dropped in 1910, a year distinguished by the application of martial law in the month of April and the debacle following the Centenary (see Table 1).[48]

The circles, groups, and centers, and the anarchist movement generally, reached a summit between 1904 and 1910. This was the result of anarchist influence in the labor movement through the FORA, which was an effective means of recruitment of libertarian activists. Along with a relatively favorable socio-economic context, it was also a consequence of the groups' decisive support for unionizing and mobilizing workers, as well as the propaganda carried out by libertarian periodicals, which attained circulation rates they would never again reach.[49] Other clear indicators of anarchism's importance during the period are the mass May Day demonstrations, libertarians' consistent involvement in all types of street actions and social struggles, and of course ruling elites' unconcealed anxieties about anarchist influence, which to them seemed poised to transform worker discontent from an inconvenience into a serious threat to public order. The government thought that it could address workers' discontent with labor laws and the anarchist threat with repressive laws. This was the logic behind the Residency and Social Defense laws (approved in 1902 and 1910, respectively). "It is not a matter of passing a law against strikes," said Senator Pérez during a discussion of Cané's legislation in 1902, "it is a question of stopping abuses, of preventing criminal deeds from taking place under the guise of strikes, of saving society from anarchist explosions." The law would "eliminate the agitators who exploit the unions' good faith."[50]

Though a declared enemy of the state, the anarchist movement did not pay much attention to the state's activities. Nevertheless, even though anarchist communism was not class-based per se, there is no doubt that anarchists encouraged the struggle between capital and labor in practice. Elites began to see anarchism as a menace to the degree that it received worker support.

The circles and centers' activity unfolded in an environment of conflict and crisis for the incipient-but-visible Buenos Aires working class, which immediately regrouped after the government lifted martial law in late May 1905. Circles such as Modern Youth, Social Studies Center, Love, Art and Freedom, the veteran Gentlemen of the Ideal and Art and Life, The Soldier's Enlightenment (a specifically anti-militarist group), the Social Studies Centers de Villa Crespo, Social Studies Centers de Belgrano, and the May Day center—to cite the most outstanding—feverishly organized meetings, *veladas*, lectures, libraries, and schools. They also sponsored innumerable fundraising events for the families of fallen comrades; the victims of the 1906 floods in Santa Fe; the deportees and incarcerated; *La Protesta* (to help it purchase a new rotary press among other things); the victims of the repression during the 1905 and 1909 May Day mobilizations; the Modern School; striking tenants in 1907; and Spain's *Land and Liberty*, to name the most important causes. Some centers had a very definite orientation, like the Anarchist Women's Center (1907–1908, which played an important role during the tenants' strike), or Love of Work (1906), Burevestnik (1908), and Friend of the Worker (1907–1909), which represented Russian anarchists living in Argentina.[51] A distinguishing characteristic of those years was the diverse offerings provided by the circles' choral societies and drama groups, which had multiplied and contributed their services to the many *veladas* organized by anarchists' groups and workers' associations.[52]

Despite being at the height of their influence, the most lucid anarchists understood that organizational problems limited the movement's growth and encouraged dispersion. Groups and publications proliferated, but the vast majority were short-lived, did not accomplish their goals, and did not coordinate their efforts with others. In 1907, a group of leading activists released a statement that called for harmonizing the groups' action though a large anarchist center in the Almagro neighborhood. The idea was to compose a list of pamphlets being published, educational centers and libraries, groups and theatrical organizations, in order to avoid the duplication of efforts.[53] The initiative progressed slowly, but when an attempt was made to create a committee to organize the work in an orderly fashion, most of the signers of the initial call spoke out against the project and it miscarried.[54] Anarchists could work together in unity during periods of repression, but dissolution and disorganization prevailed when crises passed.[55] And this inability to pull off unified actions frequently caused strife when activities were duplicated and when, as sometimes happened, activists obstructed events organized by their comrades simply because of doctrinal differences. Some anarchists saw this as a serious dilemma: "A heated atmosphere, poisoned by the absurd propaganda of a few, is the cause of these scenes. Due to this absurd propaganda, the discussion of ideas has come to resemble preaching … We have to clear the air."[56]

An environment of euphoria and optimism prevailed in the period leading up to the Centenary, between the "red week" of May 1909 and April 1910, when the government launched a bitter assault on the anarchist movement, dissipating anarchist exuberance and almost completely preventing libertarian groups and circles from functioning.

The assassination of Police Chief Colonel Ramón Falcón prompted the government to adopt a more repressive posture. It correctly believed that a crackdown would enable it to pull off the pageantry of the approaching Centenary, with all its symbolic weight. And the repression was exceedingly effective. The new Social Defense Law and the imposition of martial law provided the legal framework for closing public offices, muzzling the press, imprisoning dozens of activists, and deporting others (such as Adrián Zamboni and the mythic Eduardo Gilimón). But what made the repression around the Centenary so unique was its unprecedented duration and the draconian violations of individual and press freedoms that it entailed, which set a precedent for the repeated human rights' violations that would take place later.

To summarize, libertarian centers were typically located in parts of Buenos Aires with a high concentration of workers: Barracas, Constitución, La Boca, Parque Patricios, Once, San Telmo, Villa Crespo, and El Centro. There was also activity in Palermo, Flores, Belgrano, and Villa Urquiza. The anarchist circles reached their greatest diffusion and influence during the first decade of the century, parallel to the growth of the FORA, which anarchists also led. The increase in the number of anarchist circles coincided with the intensification of broader social antagonisms, and their diminution correlates to periods of heightened repression after peaks of contention (1903, 1905, and 1910, respectively).

Workers seemed to have found the anarchist vision more appealing when they felt the need to join forces and organize for their interests. When economic frustrations were linked to dissatisfactions about social, political, and cultural segregation, the centers, circles, and groups offered an alternative—or at least a compelling attempt at an alternative—that contained cultural, political, and ideological elements. It impacted all the arenas in which workers gathered: the factory, workshop, tenement, neighborhood, and places for recreation and political protest. The attempt to link all of these spheres to the unique space of the circle and group was what made the anarchist project embodied by these institutions so rich, even though scores of obstacles impeded its practical realization.

5. THE DIFFICULTIES OF ORGANIZING PROPAGANDA

How did anarchists establish the strategies and tactics that they would use to spread their ideas and enlighten the workers? Organizing propaganda was a complex undertaking for a political-ideological tendency with strong individualist impulses and a propensity toward disorganization and fragmentation that spread its energies outward like a fan, one that lived in a constant state of agitation and internal tension. In an earlier book, I explored the negative consequences that the deportation of large numbers of activists and spokespeople had on the anarchist movement, rupturing its coherence, internal continuity, and links to the workers.[57] I will not focus on that here; instead, I will examine how conflicts within the movement—perhaps even more than government repression— frustrated anarchist attempts to elaborate and articulate a cohesive message.

Anarchism's potent individualist, anti-organizational inclinations presented a problem for the systematic dissemination of the doctrine, especially in the early period, though pro-organizationalists mounted an effective challenge to this. The majority of the anti-organizationalists were associated with the periodical *The Rebel* (1898–1903). The pro-organizational ideas reflected the stance of the Workers' Federation of the Spanish Region, which was founded in 1881; this position was popularized in Buenos Aires by Spanish libertarians, particularly the Catalan Antonio Pellicer Paraire, who began extolling the virtues of organization as soon as he arrived in 1891. Organization, in his view, would rest upon "free accord," and through it, workers would fight to improve their lives and working conditions without authoritarian ties; unions would federate by profession and region.[58]

Pietro Gori supported this position enthusiastically, as did other important local propagandists like Félix Basterra, Alberto Ghiraldo, and Pascual Guaglianone. Under the organizational stamp, the anarchist movement as a whole would embark on an upward trajectory until the end of the first decade of the twentieth century. Pro-organizationalists were able to sink roots among local workers, who responded to economic necessities by organizing themselves into resistance societies, while the anti-organizational, individualist approach was less attractive to those eager to address problems like low salaries, poor working conditions, and unemployment.

Individualists released a statement calling for "the complete rejection of organization and the acceptance of anarchist propaganda as we see it—that is to say, leaving the individual free to work as he pleases, without burdening him with obligations of any sort."[59] This perspective implied the rejection of organizational programs, inter-group alliances, and, most of all, of individual leadership. For individualists, all the ills of organization were epitomized by the traumatic experience of the First International and the tragedy of the Paris Commune, both of which had imbued anarchism with a keen skepticism toward organization and encouraged its propensity toward individualism.

The gulf between the individualist and pro-organizational positions was difficult to bridge. Pro-organizationalists supported organizing the workers to change society and, in this sense, fit in more easily into the broader socialist tradition. Their individualist opponents did not have an equally substantive alternative and renounced efforts to unite men and women around institutions dedicated to improving their lives.[60] The anti-organizers shared socialists' commitment to creating a future without injustice or inequality, but their tactics for creating that utopia were different insofar as they privileged the role of the autonomous individual who was unaccountable to collective entities. They naively thought that individuals *qua* anarchists had an innate predisposition toward rebellion and would respond collectively "to every violation of their liberty, ego, altruism, and sense of justice, a response usually proportionate to the violation."[61] They also envisioned anarchists as all-around militants, capable of propagating the revolutionary "gospel" wherever they happened to be and always attempting to win over their interlocutors. Their vision of political activity was purely spontaneous and individualized, and propaganda understood in this way required neither organization nor parties.

For the anti-organizers, the lack of cohesion among anarchist groups that troubled their rivals was not a serious problem. In their view, "it is natural that one should begin struggling on his own";[62] unity would emerge spontaneously from the affinity among like-minded militants. Unlike those who hoped to organize new adepts into revolutionary institutions, the anti-organizers supported the slower, but in their opinion more effective, spread of anarchist ideas. *The Rebel* claimed:

> Although the number of individuals who are conscious of the full breadth of the anarchist idea and who embrace it in all its consequences grows slowly, today there is not one single thinking person who does not accept at least some of our demands.[63]

It added that, even if this was not the ideal path, the demolition of capitalism was nonetheless underway, thanks to the innumerable cracks in the system opened up by anarchists. It attributed this progress to the free initiative, autonomy, and decentralization among libertarian groups. In short, they were interested in the advance of the idea and intellectual cohesion among anarchists, not doctrinal unity or the creation of institutions.

In fact, the constant disagreements among anarchists, which would have alarmed most political activists, did not trouble them, because they believed that anarchists shared only a general commitment to securing "the individual's complete well-being [and] absolute freedom of action."[64] But of course there were different—and conflicting—ways to achieve this, and such differences clearly divided the movement. Although individualists prevailed during the early years and later lost influence, they never disappeared, since their views are inherent in anarchist thought. Even the Kropotkinian communism that predominated among local libertarians continually stimulated tendencies toward extreme autonomy, despite its avowed pro-organizationalism. In addition to the individualist streak in Kropotkin's ideas, the Spaniard Ricardo Mella promoted individualist ideas in the mature anarchist movement in Buenos Aires through his prolific writings, as did some of his followers, such as Julio Camba, a Nietzschean who worked with

La Protesta between 1904 and 1906 and gave courses on rationalist education until he was deported.

Nevertheless, at the turn of the century, a commitment to organization, doctrinal unity, and the federation of groups became a premise of anarchists' engagement in the labor movement as well as their political and cultural efforts, and would coexist with the centrifugal tendencies produced by individualism and the movement's innate drive toward autonomy. The contradictory and uncomfortable coexistence of these two tendencies was a cornerstone of the libertarian identity and constitutive of anarchist practice. The tension between them expanded anarchists' appeal and helped them win the sympathies and adhesion of large numbers of workers, although ultimately it led to a fatal dispersion and fragmentation.

However, opposition to organization did not prevent individuals from organizing themselves on the basis of ideological and political affinities. Dozens of groups and libertarian circles structured themselves in such a way, despite their fervent anti-organizational convictions. What these groups struggled to do was find a way to forge links among themselves for the purposes of carrying out joint actions, a task greatly complicated by their distrust of formal relationships between groups. The newspaper *The Rebel* championed the formation of groups, but categorically rejected federations or any sort of inter-group alliance that would require political and doctrinal uniformity. Appealing to the authority of the French libertarian Jean Grave, it argued that such alliances between groups necessarily led to the delegation of political will, the concentration of power, and the usurpation and limitation of individual freedom and initiative: "We join forces," said Grave, "and coordinate our efforts, but in a new way that presupposes a new concept of relationships, from individual to individual."[65] This implied that associations between groups would be limited to mutual acquaintanceship and the exchange of ideas. The challenge for them was to create harmony without homogeneity. Mirroring their idealistic view of the equilibrium of the natural world, groups would derive a sense of direction from the harmony between them: it would not resemble the centralized and authoritarian "line" of a Marxist party, but would be an orientation, a synchronization of groups premised on the libertarian doctrine's elemental commitments.

The anti-organizational, individualist perspective began to lose its preponderance in the latter half of the 1890s and the anarchist movement underwent an informal and irregular process of unification and doctrinal homogenization due to the ascendency of pro-organizationalists.[66] Of course, there was never anything resembling the sort of central committee one found among political parties like the Socialist Party, that outlined policies and established doctrinal boundaries. Anarchists did not need to organize or advance programs with elections in mind.

Toward the end of the nineteenth century, the need to create an institutional sphere in which workers could organize, but which was distinct from groups and circles, pushed the anarchist movement to accept broader organizational forms, such as resistance societies. This led to the challenge of balancing demands for universal human solidarity and individual autonomy and freedom.[67] At this time, hundreds of Argentine anarchist militants spontaneously began to organize themselves in a new way, with a strong commitment to individual autonomy and vague federalist notions concerning the role of certain unifying figures or institutions, even though these figures and bodies played this unifying role inconsistently due to the tendency toward dispersion.

This role was played by charismatic figures, like the Italian lawyer and propagandist Pietro Gori; some newspapers (mainly *La Protesta Humana*); study centers and cultural circles; as well as certain anarchist-led unions, such as the car drivers' union, whose building in Barracas was a central meeting space for libertarians for many years. Anarchists developed the lines of political unity in these arenas, which were naturally more cohesive during moments of greater conflict, when the anarchist movement was attracting workers to its ranks and enhancing its internal solidarity, joining together around its members' basic, shared goals.

Despite the objections to organization, at the turn of the century much of the libertarian movement recognized the need to not only form groups but also to federate them. For pro-organizationalists, it was a historically demonstrated truth that humanity is social and that it has to build forms of association that will enable it to meet physical and intellectual needs while enjoying complete freedom of action. The formula seemed transparent: "Through the exercise of individual autonomy, the group emerges. Through the exercise of collective autonomy, the association of groups arises in turn."[68] This was an important recognition, given anarchism's individualist impulses, even though the most extreme tendencies—terrorists, Stirnerites, and Nietzscheans—never had a significant following in Argentina.

The pro-organizationalists argued that while people in society might be happy or unhappy, free or enslaved, as individuals, they are always immersed in society and social by nature: "The individual is not independent of society, but a product of it. Without society, he would not have emerged from the sphere of brute animality or truly become a man. Without society, there would be no choice but to return more or less immediately to primitive barbarity."[69]

Instead of seeking a chimerical, total autonomy, people ought to try to create the conditions of their freedom and happiness in agreement with others, "modifying, in accord with others, social institutions that do not work for them."[70] Kropotkin's influence is evident in this statement: as Álvarez Junco points out, the Russian thinker had "an Aristotelian confidence in the human species's natural sociability, to the extreme of discounting the possibility of an individual, isolated life."[71] For Kropotkin, mutual aid was the mechanism through which men acted on their impulses toward human solidarity and the reality of their interdependence. Pushed to an extreme, such organizational ideas could suggest the idea of forming an anarchist party—not in the sense understood by socialists, but premised on association and a unity built upon the recognition that people must "agree among themselves, join forces, share out the tasks and take all those steps which they think will lead to the achievement of those objectives."[72] Advocates of these views thought that their ultra-individualist comrades condemned themselves to impotence by isolating themselves, wasted the movement's energies, and damaged the libertarian image in the eyes of the workers, who were confused by the contradictory perspectives. With some justification, they argued that anti-organizers were headed fatally toward inaction, dragging unsuspecting workers along with them.

Some went further and argued that anarchism, like socialism, was not a science but a project or proposition that the militants intended to put into practice, and the only way to do that was by formulating programs that could attract workers and link the circles, periodicals, resistance societies, and activists themselves in a common undertaking. "Organization," *La Protesta* said, "far from creating authority, is the only cure for it and the only means whereby each one of us will get used to taking an active and conscious part in collective work."[73] It seemed obvious that unity and organization were necessary for the defense of workers' interests. In point of fact, there were—unsuccessful—attempts to federate anarchist groups. The first, the Libertarian Federation of Socialist Anarchist Groups of Buenos Aires was formed in late 1898 by Pietro Gori and the following groups: Agitator, The Deserters, Polinice Mattei, The Scattered, Neither God Nor Master, and Light and Progress.[74] The venture began on a weak note, since it did not have the support of most local libertarian groups or the principal newspapers. Indeed, at least fifteen groups rejected the proposal and newspapers such as *La Protesta Humana, The Future,* and *Social Science* took an arm's length approach, as did, of course, the individualist newspaper, *The Rebel.* The Federation's Alliance Pact was the source of the skepticism; its attempt to coordinate the groups' activity aroused the suspicions of most activists. Although it stressed "the complete autonomy of individuals and federated groups in all initiatives in which collective action might be damaging, not useful, or counter-productive," it established operational requisites that limited individual and group autonomy.[75] For instance, in questions of general interest, agreements would be made by a simple majority vote of group representatives, which angered the individualists, who rejected the dual concessions to representation (the members of a group to their own delegate and the delegate, in turn, needing to submit to a collective of delegates). And although supporters explained that the majority's decisions did not bind the minority, the anarchist movement rejected the federation nonetheless. Other aspects of the Alliance Pact, such as the creation of administrative (administration and correspondence) and political (propaganda) positions, or the quasi-obligatory payment of monthly dues to sustain the body, also reinforced negative sentiments. After six or seven months, during which only a few meetings were held to discuss the project, the effort vanished from the local political scene.

There was also an attempt to federate libertarian circles in Buenos Aires in 1901. It was convened by the L'Avvenire group, which was linked to the newspaper of the same name and, along with *La Protesta Humana*, firmly defended the pro-organizational position. Hoping to boost propaganda, approximately one hundred militants met in Buenos Aires. Avoiding calls for uniform principles or an alliance pact, they tried to specify a framework for moderate coordination and some accord on methods of agitation. When the attempt to hold a large libertarian congress miscarried, they decided to create a "Flying Propaganda Group," which would periodically send representatives from groups, newspapers, and worker societies to distant neighborhoods like Caballito, Flores, Villa Urquiza, and Palermo, where the libertarian gospel arrived with greater difficulty, and to support propaganda efforts and create new groups in them. There was also an attempt to link all the centers and launch a coordinated propaganda campaign in the form of proselytizing tours and lectures. The goal was to win over the thousands of workers who were disillusioned and largely up for grabs, given the lack of organizations representing them. *La Protesta Humana* urged militants to:

> Talk to the comrades in their homes, in the cafés, wherever you can arrange a meeting; get to know them, gather them in groups, form small educational and propaganda centers, and the idea will march forward victoriously. There are comrades in every neighborhood and town who are powerless on their own, but who can do great things with others. Organize yourselves into groups and centers, in accord with your knowledge and strengths, and organize acts of propaganda.[76]

This call was made at a time when the pro-organizationalists were beginning to become unambiguously hegemonic in the anarchist movement. They did not conceal their intent to control it and were unsparing in their criticisms of their rivals. With the hyperbole typical of anarchist discourse, they accused individualists of wrecking libertarian propaganda and distancing themselves from the workers. Pro-organizationalist Pascual Guaglianone declared:

> The charlatans achieve all of this by introducing a very special sociology into the country. It is a product of unbalanced minds, a

sociology preached from lecterns in the back rooms of warehouses and from the columns of newspapers dedicated to amorphism, individualism, Ravacholism, and every other imaginable extravagance; cathedrals in which disciples of Nietzsche who had never even seen the covers of his books put forward new interpretations of anarchy and began telling us about the Superman ... these devotees of the Superman who don't even know how to read, but nevertheless talk to us all day about philosophical individualism, about degenerative factors, and countless other problems that they alone knew how to solve.[77]

He maintained that their approach to anarchism was totally ineffective, since the people neither liked nor understood it, and condemned individualists, somewhat puritanically, for using vulgar vocabulary: "Anarchism should express itself in a manner that is fitting for it, in a language of decency."[78]

Guaglianone's criticism reflected his recent socialist past as well as pro-organizational anarchism's attempt to discover and define an exemplary, educated, rational, and moral militant. This militant was an organizational intellectual who defended and extolled the superlative virtues of organization and the exclusion of those who did not toe the doctrinal line. In a sense, his standpoint was the reverse of ultra-individualism. This is why the editors of *La Protesta Humana*, fearing the reaction of those less identified with the pro-organizationalists, ran a piece immediately after his article that apologized for some of his exaggerations and also, though they themselves were undeniably partisans of organization, called upon all anarchists to join together in performing the shared tasks of propaganda.[79]

The task for pro-organizationalists was finding structures that were consistent with the anarchist doctrine and that did not compromise individual freedom or autonomy. The most widespread organizational model consisted of forming and multiplying specifically libertarian groups and circles, which would pursue political-doctrinal objectives, and resistance societies organized by trade, whose purposes were fundamentally economic. Libertarian organizations presupposed the free association of their members and federalist principles; that is, they operated without leadership or a predetermined orientation.

However, anarchists never managed to coordinate their efforts over the long-term: groups operated on their own or associated briefly on the basis of doctrinal affinity.[80] But the local anarchist movement did unite around two, clearly differentiated cores between 1897 and 1902: on the one hand, pro-organizationalist groups took the newspapers *La Protesta Humana* and *The Future* as their points of reference; and, on the other hand, the anti-organizers looked to *The Rebel,* although of course this is not to deny that many circles, groups, newspapers, and magazines were sympathetic to both camps. On occasion, doctrinal polemics between the two tendencies became personal, and accusations and recriminations flew. In early 1901, the already tense relations erupted due to the unequal distribution of proceeds from an event whose profits were supposed to be divided equally among the three periodicals. A strange arithmetic awarded *The Rebel* less money than the others and, as a result, the affair blew up into a scandal. Both sides accused one another of having bourgeois leanings, misappropriating funds, and using the cause for personal gain, making offensive comments about the intellects and personal lives of those involved. They aired these matters publicly without reserve.[81]

These internal disputes were set aside momentarily during the unusually intense social conflicts at the end of that year. They culminated in a strike wave—in which anarchists played a leading role—that brought most of the country's productive apparatus to a halt. The strife led to the formation of a solid workers' federation (the FORA), the government's passage of highly repressive laws, and the beginning of labor reforms.[82]

The anarchist movement acquired a new level of maturity and a new importance in Argentina's social and political scene after this conflict, which strongly benefited the pro-organizational tendency, given that the emergence of workers' protests made organizing the workers indispensable. Furthermore, the disappearance of the anti-organizational newspaper *The Rebel* in 1903 was symbolically important, as was the ostensible predominance from then on of the pro-organizational newspaper *La Protesta,* which become a daily shortly thereafter and served almost exclusively as the anarchist movement's voice until the 1920s. From then on, internal conflicts and battles for power within the movement would primarily express themselves in its pages and, to a lesser degree, those of other, ephemeral publications.

Thus, in the midst of internal conflicts and problems arising from strategic and doctrinal differences, anarchists reconciled—somewhat turbulently—two apparently irreconcilable imperatives in the circles, groups, and centers: they became politically effective, organizational instruments that also allowed for the total freedom of their adherents. In one form or another, libertarian groups and circles played an influential role in Argentine society. This began in the 1890s and intensified during the following decade, when a broad network of centers and groups spread throughout Buenos Aires and cities and towns in the interior of the country, generating the political ideological and cultural alternative that is the focus of this book.

These bodies were the nuclei in which Argentine anarchists defined their propagandistic strategies: "The center," stated *The Rebel*, "is indispensible to good propaganda."[83] And it fulfilled two fundamental tasks. First, by preventing dispersion and curtailing the tendency toward disorder, it permitted libertarians, in each town, neighborhood, or locality where they were present, to concentrate their propaganda (communications, correspondence, pamphlets, books, and newspapers, etc.) in one place. Second, it was a sphere of social, cultural, and political association whose primary goal was to educate the workers (and their families) and transform them into revolutionaries.

The International Social Studies Center released a declaration of principles that expressed these aspirations clearly when it stated it intended "to prepare the proletariat for emancipation, cultivate its moral and intellectual cohesion, and ready it for the social struggle."[84] This declaration pointed to the model followed by the vast majority of libertarian groups; to "prepare the proletariat" meant educating it in the anarchist doctrine and immersing it in an alternative worldview that would affect all aspects of the social and cultural life of the proletariat as a whole (men, women, and children).

We believe it necessary to abolish hierarchy among men.
—*The Rebel*, May 20, 1900

CHAPTER II

The Anarchist Appeal[1]

WHAT DID THE proletariat mean in anarchist discourse? And to whom did anarchists direct their message? To the working class or to the exploited generally? If the latter, did they direct it to all of the exploited or only its "conscious and intelligent" part? In order to analyze the complex views of social actors in the doctrinal mosaic of anarchism, it is valuable to consider the nature of the anarchist alternative and its social repercussions in greater detail. The tidy historical perspective that assumes an unambiguous link between the anarchist movement and the workers' movement obscures complexities in the former, which was far more than a species of labor radicalism. Without denying that anarchist discourse appealed primarily to workers, who were the most oppressed sector of society, or that anarchists encouraged class struggle in practice, libertarians thought of their message as universal and not class-specific. Anarchists believed that a class-based perspective subordinated the individual to an external class identity and that such a subsumption was unjust and authoritarian. However, although the doctrine was not classist, the movement did direct its political and social practices to workers, and this led to complications in its conception of social class and ambiguities and contradictions in its discourse. Anarchists' peculiar way of perceiving classes and class struggle gave rise to thorny internal debates and frustrated their attempt to lead the workers' movement.

1. THE ANARCHIST APPEAL: THE WORKING CLASS OR THE PEOPLE?

Social conflicts grew more acute at the turn of the century—particularly in 1902—and anarchist union and political activity intensified. This yielded a transformation within the anarchist movement: the bitter polemic between supporters and detractors of organization resolved itself in the favor of the former, who secured near-absolute dominance in the movement, even though the disputes never completely disappeared. "Anarchists shifted the center of gravity of their activity," Oved notes, "to the battle against an external enemy: the government, the employers, the church, and the army."[2] Relative unanimity on these basic questions strengthened anarchists and allowed them to focus their energies on a common opponent. This enabled anarchists to emerge from their isolation and become a significant social actor, although Oved's comment suggests a degree of homogeneity in the movement that did not exist. His perspective echoes remarks made by non-anarchist observers in decisive moments of social turmoil: the non-worker press, state institutions, dominant groups, and the socialists all saw anarchism as a coherent form of labor radicalism, even if, for some, it was a pathology to be extirpated from society and for others, a voice of extremism.

However, when studying periods of calm, it is easy to see that there was in fact a tangled fabric of contradictory ideas and tendencies and constant, vigorous debates between those that I denominate "doctrinal purists" and "heterodox intellectuals."[3] Doctrinal purists were anarchist activists, typically intellectuals and writers, who defended doctrinal orthodoxy and operated almost like party intellectuals, defining and delimiting the correct and incorrect lines. Made up of a small group of leaders, this group functioned as an intellectual elite that tried to persuade the militant base to accept their views and often used highly sectarian methods in their efforts to make this happen. By contrast, heterodox intellectuals—such as Alberto Ghiraldo, José de Maturana, Alejandro Sux, and Florencio Sánchez—were much more doctrinally open, often had roots in literature, and typically had attitudes that the purists considered reprehensible. For instance, purists reproached Alberto Ghiraldo when he, at the helm of *La Protesta* between 1904 and 1906, attempted to link the anarchist and socialist workers' federations. They also never forgave him for having been active in the Radical Party, seduced by its founder, Leandro Alem. Even worse, there were uncorroborated claims that he had tried to involve anarchists in the 1905 Radical Party rebellion.[4] The quarrel would never end, since even after Ghiraldo left the anarchist camp in 1914, there were others, like Julio Barcos or González Pacheco, who held similar ideas.

Whereas dispersion among anarchists caused by individualism limited the movement's growth during the earlier period, the prevailing current in the new stage tended to exacerbate its more rigid, sectarian aspects. I refer specifically to an inflexible attitude toward political activity and a focus on building unity around ideological affinity, which precluded alliances with other oppositional forces.

The purists, who feared deviations from core anarchist principles, were an important presence throughout the history of the movement and significantly constrained its political and labor activity. They seemed to be a natural corollary to the innate diversity of the libertarian movement, which was highly ecumenical—indeed, a veritable doctrinal chaos in which individualists, collectivists, communitarians, organizers, anti-organizers, and supporters and opponents of violence, among others, attracted and repelled one another. Its doctrinal breadth and laxity, its ability to represent a wide array of needs and positions, expanded anarchism's appeal and helped it lay roots among the workers and others discontented with the reigning social and economic arrangements. Unencumbered by the restrictions of a political party, it was able to speak to and for large portions of the oppositional spectrum.

This breadth had a direct connection to anarchists' ambiguous position on class. Unlike Marxists, they did not feel compelled to advance a conscientious definition of classes or class struggle: they were vaguely anti-capitalist and rejected the Marxist idea of class consciousness. They saw political participation as an individual choice, not as a necessary consequence of underlying economic contradictions. They were populists who hoped to free all of the oppressed from exploitation, even though their social practices unfolded in a context in which class conflict took practical and discursive precedence.[5] Anarchists constantly encouraged workers' battles against employers and the state without having a fundamentally class-based perspective. Their attitude toward the capitalist economy and the class structure arising from it differentiated them in important ways from Marxism.

Libertarians defined social actors not through their relationship to the means of production but in relation to forms of oppression. They were moralistic and universalistic, and their anti-capitalism, unlike that of Marxists, transcended a class-based outlook, resting instead on liberal political and philosophical presuppositions of natural rights, equality, liberty, and harmony. It leaned heavily on a notion of liberty, whose object was to make the individual happy, since it was humanity's natural right to be undisturbed by extraneous influences: "our liberalism," *The Rebel* argued, "is such that, while rejecting private property, we accept that if someone wants to stop others from using what is in his possession, then he should do so. But we also believe, without necessarily arguing that it will happen, that the needy should make use of resources with as much cruelty as they find necessary, and that this will produce an interminable struggle."[6]

Many Argentine anarchists relied on Kropotkin's work, widely distributed in local networks, to bolster their non-classist analysis. Readings of Kropotkin made by Spaniards José Prat and Anselmo Lorenzo were particularly important (Prat was among the co-founders of *La Protesta Humana*, indubitably the movement's most important newspaper). Indeed, there was pervasive support for Kropotkin's anarcho-communism among local anarchists. His writings were already widely circulated in Río de la Plata region in the 1880s: his pamphlets and articles were first published in Buenos Aires in 1887, two years later in Montevideo, and shortly afterwards they were reprinted in periodicals such as *The Persecuted*, *La Protesta Humana*, *The Rebel*,[7] and especially in *La Liberté*, a French paper put out by Pierre Quiroule that reprinted *La Révolte*, which Kropotkin had established in France. The groups also published a number of Kropotkin's pamphlets and books in the 1890s, but the peak of his influence occurred after 1905, when his predominance among doctrinal purists became unambiguous, anarchist communism was written into the FORA's statutes, and *La Protesta* serialized his *Memoirs of a Revolutionist* over one hundred issues.[8]

This non-classist approach prioritized the moral condemnation of social injustice over the critical analysis of the capitalist economy and advanced a more flexible, generic interpretive schema than that put forward by Marxists. It found the roots of social divisions not only in economic relationships but also in the enormous cultural distances between social sectors, which emerged because one social actor possessed knowledge that the other did not. This transcended the contradiction between the proletariat and the bourgeoisie to produce, in Kropotkin's terms, a broader divide between poor and rich, exploited and exploiters, dispossessed and privileged, and people and bourgeoisie. As Alvarez Junco notes, "the introduction of the ethical-critical element into the factors of oppression and dispossession changed the classical socialist focus in at least two ways: on the one hand, it expanded the group of the dispossessed ... and on the other hand, instead of defining history through progressive class polarization, it pointed to the possibility of overcoming the tension through the enlightenment of the oppressed."[9] Although anarchists continually spoke of the class struggle, they diminished its importance discursively and contextualized it within broader conflicts, leading to an attack on authority per se.

Anarchists aspired to represent the exploited as a whole and criticized alienation in very broad terms. For them, ethical and cultural elements had priority over specifically socio-economic determinations; they did not differentiate men and women by their position in the social structure, but rather by the ideals they professed. In this sense, social classes existed more in thought than reality. Man was above all an individual, a fact that was more important than whether or not he belonged to a specific social class. And when he embraced the libertarian ideal, he embraced anarchist universalism, not the particular interests of the proletariat. Although anarchists did not deny the class struggle, they regarded it as secondary and did not believe class interests were inherently revolutionary.

The libertarian doctrine offered an alternative to alienated workers, displaced intellectuals, marginalized elites, and those whose hopes to enter the middle class had been frustrated. As with English Chartism, though on a lesser scale, anarchists gave voice to popular misery and discontent, and provided a meaningful response to the malaise and dissatisfaction circulating in fin-de-siècle Buenos Aires.[10] Anarchists recognized that immigrants' thwarted dreams of material improvement furnished adherents to their cause. This idea is illustrated well in a dialogue that Gilimón imagined between two deportees. It takes place on the deck of the ship traveling from Spain to Argentina: "'See them?' asked one of the pair, pointing to immigrants heading to Buenos Aires. 'They are future anarchists. When disappointment comes, when their hopes fade, when brutal reality wounds them, their republicanism and americanism will go up in smoke. They've been deceived and their disenchantment will lead to fury.' 'Yes,' the other responded.... 'It's painful for these poor people, but perhaps it's for the better. Progress, like the gods, needs its victims.'"[11]

Anarchists tirelessly attempted to enlist these victims, exploiting the discontent, disappointment, and resentment of workers who had been unable to fulfill the dreams of prosperity that had prompted them to leave their homelands. Libertarians tried to turn any grievance into a full-scale rebellion. This is why they supported and led the 1907 renters' strike (while the Socialist Party busied itself debating whether or not a consumers' rebellion was a true strike); agitated on behalf of political prisoners; supported the cigar workers' quasi-Luddite battle against the introduction of modern machinery;[12] ran huge headlines in their newspapers denouncing the mistreatment of army conscripts, and even tried to organize them;[13] harshly criticized the persecution of prostitutes; and unsuccessfully urged the police to join the ranks of the rebellion. Their trans-class position, reinforced by their nearly theatrical rhetoric, was key to their ability to lay roots among popular sectors in moments of dissension, which is not to deny that socialist and anarchist messages were very similar, perhaps even identical, in specific labor conflicts. But the way that libertarian discourse was disseminated was very important; it was dramatic, eloquent, full of exaggerated gestures, and always accentuated social binaries. Socialist leaders Jacinto Oddone and Enrique Dickmann acknowledged that this rhetoric—which they saw as irrational—helped make anarchism attractive to workers, even if they did not join anarchist ranks in massive numbers.

2. REVOLUTIONARY URGENCY

The movement's ideological heterogeneity, the dynamic of its practical action, and its "categorical directness" made it a perfect fit for a chaotic, excessively cosmopolitan society with a heterogeneous world of labor, in a constant process of transformation.[14] Through their resistance societies, cultural circles, alternative schools, and broad network of publications, anarchists offered responses to workers' daily crises and hopes for a better life. And speaking to workers' aspirations did not require grand theoretical disquisitions or extreme ideological coherence. It was merely necessary to present where the needs arose. By doing so, anarchists were able to engage immediate, popular expectations and offer a framework for contention in a society where few were available.

A sentiment of revolutionary urgency permeated anarchist practices during the first decade of the century. On the one hand, this was a response to abrupt socioeconomic changes, marked by the disorderly character of urban Argentina, with its high degree of horizontal and vertical mobility that complicated attempts to form a coherent proletarian identity. This social, economic, and cultural dynamism may have also limited the libertarian movement's theoretical development, which was sacrificed to the need for rapid and forceful responses to pressing crises. Paradoxically, anarchist urgency about changing society did not lend itself to reflection about future alternatives, with the important exception of Pierre Quiroule's work.[15]

Revolutionary urgency was also inherent in the libertarian perspective itself. It subordinated thought to action and, to a degree, the long-term planning of the revolutionary process for immediatism although, as some have pointed out, there were really two stances toward the future society among anarchists: one, a by-product of individualism, celebrated spontaneity and rejected planning as inherently authoritarian and a violation of the natural impulses of the masses; the second, a constructive approach that originated with the organizationalists, tried very hard to design templates for life after the revolution.[16]

The urgency, immediatism, and attempt to accelerate political time that pervaded the local anarchist movement gave content to libertarians' alternative to socialist gradualism: they advocated the complete destruction of the state without intermediate stages or the intervention of a proletarian dictatorship. They believed that the preconditions necessary for spreading the anarchist ideal would emerge spontaneously. They also privileged action for its own sake, focusing less on the fulfillment of specific goals than the precipitous realization of an abstract end. This drove them to constantly champion spontaneous actions and throw themselves against the foundations of the capitalist state.[17] They took the maximalist position in every action in which they participated, always attempting to push the limits. The idea of all or nothing, of reaching goals immediately, was a factor in much of their activism: "Free men ought to go directly to the conquest of bread and not hang around picking up crumbs," said *The Rebel*.[18]

This militant urgency prioritized action and propaganda and reduced theory to the systematic, reiterative description of social problems. The vast majority of articles published in local anarchist publications denounced the ills of capitalist society from an exceedingly abstract, moralistic perspective: the state's perversion, the church's hypocrisy and lechery, the bourgeoisie's greedy and exploitative nature, and the proletariat's suffering—these were among the most common motifs. Libertarians frequently and consistently cast these issues in an ahistorical frame that obscured the specificities of the society in which they lived.

Indeed, the predisposition to simplification in anarchist discourse impacted their response to conditions in Argentina. Anarchists' habit of analyzing society on the basis of very general, imprecise postulates compromised their efforts to formulate compelling interpretations of local circumstances. While they tended to be very flexible in practice, anarchists were often unable to offer insightful analyses due to their tendency to relentlessly and mechanically repeat their formulas, and to their inclination to define social actors in terms that were so general that they would be of equal relevance anywhere else on the planet. Local propagandists were seldom subtle when it came to explicating the diverse social groups in motion, and their criticisms were fundamentally moral. Thus, the bourgeoisie, workers, priests, soldiers, and statist functionaries were stripped of national or local nuances and bore the same attributes in Argentina as they did in Italy or elsewhere. In part, the dearth of national particularities reflected anarchist internationalism and the geographic mobility of those who wrote for local newspapers and magazines, who typically stayed in Argentina only briefly. Indeed, in many cases, they began publishing articles shortly after their arrival and their pieces were often loaded with influences from their countries of origin. A mechanical transposition of previous experiences onto local society tinted their interpretations.

On the other hand, and despite the influence of positivism, anarchists had little interest in observing and quantifying social and economic data. Moralistic denunciations were the norm and solid structural critiques absent in most newspapers, books, and pamphlets that they released. Not long after the period discussed in this work, Abad de Santillán acknowledged the consequences of the libertarian movement's disinclination toward analysis: "Other than an occasional prisoner support campaign, we are too far on the margin of the economic, political, and spiritual life of the times; we are too withdrawn, too disinterested in everything that isn't immediately and visibly relevant to action. This condemns us to irrelevance."[19]

Félix Basterra was one of the few libertarians to analyze Argentine society, and the results were not impressive. In his book, *El crepúsculo de los gauchos* [*The Twilight of the Gauchos*], which was published in 1903, he used a positivist framework to explore the economic, political, social, and judicial realities of Argentina, but his empirical data and conceptual arsenal were impoverished.[20] Drawing on liberalism, he appealed to [former Argentine president] Domingo Faustino Sarmiento, and especially [Argentine political theorist and diplomat]

Juan Bautista Alberdi, to endow his diagnoses with legitimacy and to liken the situation of fin-de-siècle Argentina to that existing under Juan Manuel de Rosas's regime,[21] establishing a schematic continuity between the politics of the Rosas's confederation and those of Julio A. Roca.[22] Basterra argued that the country had not advanced at all during that half-century interval.

His conclusions were stained with a biological moralism that stressed the triumph of the rural (the bad) over the urban (the good) and of gaucho barbarism, caudilloism, and clientistic politics over immigrants and the idea of progress. His conclusion was drastic: he declared Argentina a "wasteful country, unequipped to innovate economically; amoral in its social exchange; dissolute in its morbid inheritance."[23]

We find ourselves dealing with very different approaches if we analyze the contributions of the two most important and active figures in Argentine anarchism at the beginning of the century, Alberto Ghiraldo and Eduardo Gilimón, who were doubtlessly the most prolific anarchist writers of the time and prominent throughout the entire period studied in this book.[24]

Ghiraldo, who had been active in the Radical Party, was spontaneous and emotional by nature. What makes the social critique in his work unique is his incorporation of the figure of the gaucho, which he celebrated in two ways. On the one hand, he exalted the gaucho's noble spirit: the gaucho, Ghiraldo wrote, is "a symbol of courage, abnegation, manliness, and civic pride … who never runs from danger, disappoints a friend, or breaks his word to someone who trusts him."[25] On the other hand, he extolled the gaucho's rebelliousness in an effort to incorporate native Argentines into social struggles and endow them with a tradition of resistance. Ghiraldo was attempting to counteract the pervasive idea that only foreigners were active in social protests and to demonstrate that Argentine-born workers were also engaged and had their own legacy of rebellion.

This was why he choose the emblematic name *Martín Fierro* for *La Protesta*'s weekly supplement, which was published from 1904 to 1905. According to Ghiraldo, the poem "Martín Fierro" was "a shout of the struggling class against the upper layers of society that oppress it, a protest against injustice."[26] He was not attempting to re-signify José Hernández's persecuted gaucho, but to advance a unique appropriation of the gaucho that extracted the Argentine-born man [*el criollo*] marginalized by progress from Hernández's image. The advance of modernity gave rise to a latent tension in Ghiraldo's views. David Viñas sees this in Ghiraldo's reclamation of Martín Fierro's rebelliousness: it was infused with populist elements, "conditioning factors that rendered the anti-industrialism of anarchist literature fatalistic and that mournfully exalted the artisanal, the gaucho, and the seamstress," while, on the other hand, "due to the effects of the strong liberal tradition," Ghiraldo joined Basterra in denouncing "barbarism, shadows, and caudilloism, appealing to enlightened reason."[27] The gaucho's struggle was a battle against the army, clientelistic and corrupt politicians, venal government, and the advance of private property: "They've knit over the Pampa with fences. The boss owns the desert, and keeps it a desert until he can sell it off. There's nowhere to build a ranch, a little clump of straw that has no owner.... Everything's fenced off. All paths closed."[28] He resisted the despised symbols of power against which anarchists also fought. The publication of the poem and photo of its author, or verse by Hilario Ascasubi and Estanislao del Campo in *Martín Fierro*'s "Clásicos Criollos" ["Creole Classics"] section, illustrate similar tendencies. The native Argentine was stripped of xenophobia and idealistically incorporated into the struggle of the people as a whole. The appearance of allegorical drawings depicting the gaucho and the worker side-by-side, or the use of gaucho slang and speech patterns, were also symptomatic of the effort to postulate a symbiosis between the native-born Argentines and foreigners.

By introducing the figure of the gaucho and related themes, Ghiraldo added something new to local anarchist discourse that was especially resonant with groups active among Argentine-born soldiers and rural farm workers from the interior. The line of analysis was also directly connected to certain doctrinal principles. To celebrate the gaucho was to exalt a figure who, at least in literature, intended to live without restraints and loathed the boss, the law, the fatherland, and the army. In his highly anti-militaristic work, *Alma Gaucha* (*Gaucho Soul*), Ghiraldo presented Cruz, the emblematic gaucho character, as a conscious, dignified figure who was condemned to death for deserting the army.[29]

The gaucho was portrayed as pure, thanks to his constant contact with nature: "The gaucho learned to love freedom passionately in the heart of the natural world, which surrounded him and taught him masterfully with the condor's majestic flight across infinite spaces ... with the guanaco, who dodges and weaves through the clouds of dust; he learned to defend his free will instinctively."[30] His life was idyllic, unrestricted, and unencumbered by the stifling pressures of property: "When he crossed the plains, he laid his eyes on the immensity of the fields, which were also a lesson in liberty for the soul."[31] Ungovernable, and impossible to discipline, he rejected any hint of authority: "Sarmiento understood this to the core," said González Pacheco. "A nation can be made with nomads like this, but not a state. It was necessary to restrain him, to turn him into a peon or a boss. 'Property is authority over things; authority is property over men.' Pugnacious by nature, he sensed this and shouted from the rooftops: 'They're building fences! They're fencing!'"[32] And the fencing exterminated his freedom and turned the gaucho into a proletarian or his hangman, a policeman or soldier. It was in these terms that some anarchists mythologized the gaucho, whom they cast as a moral exemplar. It was a gaucho lacking in flesh and blood, a literary device that was symbolically important in their attempt to envision a tradition of popular struggle. For anarchists, the gaucho bore the flag of liberty in an earlier epoch, whereas proletarians would do so in the present: "That instinct for freedom ...

we inherited it, we who are his descendants."[33] A problem raised by Argentina's extreme internationalism found a resolution in the intersection of positivism, the oppositional tradition of the gaucho, and the doctrine of the founding fathers of anarchism. If the foreign-born proletariat could identify with the Paris Commune or uprisings in Milan, native workers would find their heritage in the gaucho's legacy. Native-born [*criollo*] and immigrant struggles thus fused, giving shape to a distinctly Argentine worker-subject, and revealing that some of Argentina's unique realities had penetrated anarchist discourse.

However, many militants were indifferent to or even hostile to this position. While writers who came out of bohemian, literary circles, like Ángel Falco, José de Maturana, and Rodolfo González Pacheco, tended to react favorably, many regarded the celebration of the gaucho as a dangerous betrayal of anarchist internationalism, especially as the gaucho increasingly evolved into a nationalist symbol just prior to the Centenary. There was also a view among anarchists, tainted with biologism, that opposed not only the gaucho but also anything linked with native-born Argentines [*criollos*]. For instance, Basterra saw the gaucho as the embodiment of many prevailing social vices: a gambler, idle, xenophobic, ignorant, and quarrelsome, "vain, grotesquely narcissistic, boasting as if he were the center of the universe." While the long-suffering immigrant did all the manual and intellectual work, "the native Argentine [*el criollo*]," said Basterra, "is in the gambling den."[34]

Despite the discursive tensions created by the celebration of the gaucho and native-born workers in Ghiraldo's writings and those who sympathized with them, anarchist analyses of local society remained impoverished. Social criticism was reiterative, un-nuanced, and, typical of the era to a degree, endlessly repeated the same arguments about popular misery and governmental repression. Characters in anarchist novels were archetypes who reiterated their authors' dichotomous worldviews, while lectures and doctrinal articles attempted to seduce the reader-listener with an emotional pitch that mirrored literary postures and was awash with ethical messages and self-pitying sentimentalism.[35]

Eduardo Gilimón's case is different. Born in Spain, he was active briefly among socialists before joining the anarchist movement in the mid-1890s. He published articles in various newspapers and magazines and his signature appears continuously in *La Protesta Humana* from 1897 until 1910. His role in the anarchist movement's most important publication was mostly discreet, overshadowed first by Basterra and later by Ghiraldo. In 1906, after a fierce internal battle, he became the paper's central figure until the Centenary, when he was deported. Although he returned to Argentina years later and remained faithful to the cause, his activism had a lower profile and he wrote much less frequently for *La Protesta*. Gilimón was a doctrinal purist and in many respects the polar opposite of Ghiraldo. His militancy paralleled that of Ghiraldo, against whom he polemicized in *La Protesta*, accusing him of perverting the doctrine. He was much more inclined toward political journalism than Ghiraldo, who was really a politicized writer. His discourse was distinct, too, insofar as he addressed readers in a different register, using an ostensibly more rational language and demonstrating a degree of erudition in matters outside the anarchist tradition (although he saw himself as an expert in anarchist theory). His sympathies lay primarily with Kropotkin's anarcho-communism and the purpose of all of his (exceptionally unoriginal) work was to promote and defend what he regarded as the pure anarchist doctrine.

In the context of a flexible and porous movement like the anarchist movement, Gilimón acted like a party intellectual. He did battle against supposedly heterodox enemies like Ghiraldo or Julio Barcos (who were more open to political alliances and broad coalitions); opposed the unity of the workers' movement; worried over the growth of revolutionary syndicalism; and steadfastly refused to acknowledge Argentine specificities.[36] "The workers' cause is the same here as elsewhere," Gilimón wrote, "and he who feels the need to proselytize and rebel with the strength of his intellect and a conviction forged by reason understands that it is the same to fight for the emancipation of the proletariat in Argentina as elsewhere."[37]

Fixated on maintaining doctrinal purity, the purpose of most of his copious journalistic output was to expound the premises of the anarchist doctrine. His writings typically revolved around the concept of anarchy, the defense of the individual against authority, the critique of parliamentarianism and the state, tactics discussions ranging from union organization to the general strike, the defense of spontaneism and some forms of collective violence, and opposition to the idea of class struggle. In other articles, he polemicized against socialists and syndicalists and in others still, he railed against patriotism and militarism. He focused on the classical topics of the libertarian doctrine, which he often treated in highly abstract terms, and his reflections on Argentina's socio-economic structure lacked nuance, displaying his totally uncritical adhesion to anarchism.[38]

This was quite common in the local anarchist movement. Indeed, even though it became an important force in Argentine society, when placed in a broader historical perspective, anarchist proposals seem repetitive and inflexible in the context of the rapid social changes underway, especially in the political sphere. For instance, libertarians' opposition to the nationalization of foreigners (which would allow them to participate in electoral politics) might have seemed compelling at the turn of the century, in the framework of a highly restrictive electoral system, but it was much less appropriate fifteen years later, after the approval of the Sáenz Peña Law.[39] Anarchists' doctrinal rigidity, lack of pragmatism, and reluctance to analyze the particularities of Argentine society distanced them from the masses and undermined their ability to comprehend and transform the rapidly changing world around them.

Nonetheless, the relationship between anarchists' limited analytical attention to local society and their presence among the workers during the movement's high point merits exploration. Although naturally a complex issue, there is no necessary relationship between the intensity of social conflict and the intensity of ideological production. Coherence and theoretical depth are not requirements for attracting the masses to a political movement, as the history of Radical Party and Peronism clearly demonstrates. In a study of these issues among Spanish anarchists, one author observed that "an ideology is not a finished whole; it responds to social needs, and when it fails to do so, it loses its capacity to mobilize. What is important is not its theoretical coherence ... but its credibility and organizing power."[40]

3. PURE ANARCHISTS AND ANARCHO-SYNDICALISTS

The doctrinal purists' trans-class position was ubiquitous within the movement between 1905 and 1910, and this led anarchists to concentrate on doctrinal goals and set aside questions like the unity of the workers' movement. It also provoked spirited debates about the role of the labor movement that compromised anarchists' organizational potency. Doctrinal purists flatly opposed unifying the workers' movement as such because they believed it impossible to reconcile the diverse ideological strands within it (socialism, syndicalism, Catholicism, and anarchism). Workers, they believed, ought to organize themselves around shared ideals, outlooks, and tactical commitments. The end pursued was what mattered most, and labor unions, though important, were primarily a means for recruiting workers to the anarchist cause. This was the doctrinal purists' position from the FORA's fifth Congress in 1905 until its ninth Congress in 1915, when libertarians lost control of the federation and syndicalism became the dominant tendency in the labor movement.[41]

Nevertheless, libertarian activists engaged in the daily work of the labor movement believed that promoting unionization and workers' unity was the most important goal. Typically identified as anarcho-syndicalists, they acknowledged that most workers did not identify with anarchism but did not see that as a cause for great concern, because they believed that all workers had the same interests and were destined to be the core of the revolutionary process. The doctrinal purists' posture irritated them and they replied to it by arguing that if libertarians "only preach to the converted and isolate themselves from non-anarchists, then they're giving up the main objective, which has always been to recruit more anarchists, and the movement will atrophy without new blood."[42] Those who prioritized labor organization interpreted anarchist theory differently; for them, doctrinal purity was secondary.

These polemics reflected a battle for the ideological identity of the anarchist movement. It had become an important actor toward the middle of the first decade, although, unlike a political party (i.e., the Socialist Party), it lacked clearly demarcated positions and policies. Nonetheless, those who found a home under the anarchist banner recognized one another and shared some general principles such as anti-clericalism, anti-statism, anti-parliamentarianism, and opposition to the idea of the nation or—more precisely—the fatherland and its military expression, the army. Unity around these basic questions enabled the anarchist movement to appear, in the eyes of outside observers, as a relatively coherent opposition to the conservative regime, although scratching the surface reveals a movement struggling to confront deep-seated contradictions, ambiguities, and weaknesses.

In 1906, the doctrinal purists had control of *La Protesta*—the main voice of the anarchist movement—and their opponents were scattered in various short-lived periodicals in which they savaged the purists, who, in their view, were "constructing a new anarchist doctrine built upon useless reformisms, whose paladin is the confused paper, *La Protesta*."[43] In 1908, the newspaper *Light and Life* published an angry critique of the purists for, they alleged, having behaved violently and irrationally at a meeting held to benefit *La Protesta*: "Nevertheless, we understand these reprehensible events, given that all this suspicion, awkwardness, and tension necessarily had to come to a head, despite the intentions of those involved. A heated atmosphere, poisoned by the absurd propaganda of a few, is the cause of these scenes."[44] This statement underscores the serious conflicts within the movement.

Heterodox intellectuals like Ghiraldo and Maturana were at odds not only with the doctrinal purists, but also with the anarcho-syndicalists. They rejected the anarcho-syndicalists for their extreme workerism and because they seemed to embrace a division of labor that suggested that workers would perform manual as well as intellectual labor in the future society, which, in their view, implied reducing intellectuals to a secondary role focused on educational and journalistic tasks. The clash between the workerists and the intellectuals came to the surface in a long debate between the "manuals" and the "intellectuals."[45] Comments made by Dr. Juan Carulla about a workers' meeting that he attended during his time as a militant libertarian are suggestive: "My reaction," he recalls, "was to feel superfluous; a sadness consumed me similar to what Don Quixote felt when he came to his senses and realized that everything he had done in his gallant adventures was somewhat mad and vain; me, who thought he was fighting for the salvation of the weak."[46] Prior to the Centenary, heterodox intellectuals occupied a secondary position within the libertarian movement, although it was certainly more comfortable and secure than the role that they might have played in broader, non-anarchist literary and sociological circles.[47]

4. WHO IS THE REVOLUTIONARY SUBJECT?

The discussion of class unfolded not only among supporters and detractors of the idea of class struggle within the anarchist movement, but also within the recently emerged revolutionary syndicalist movement, and the disputes became bitter. Anarchism's conceptual breadth was a significant problem for those who tried to use *La Protesta* to define the ideological boundaries of the anarchist movement. The difficulty for the doctrinal purists was that syndicalism's class-based posture was hard to distinguish from some anarchist positions, which became especially confusing in the unions, where class-based discourse had broad resonance.

Indeed, the syndicalist movement became a formidable obstacle for anarchists. Its ambiguous anti-statism gave it a libertarian patina, and it used a language deceptively similar to that of anarchists, although syndicalists were always predisposed to negotiation and supported unity in the workers' movement. This rendered syndicalism attractive to workers, but deeply troubling to the purists, who seemed perplexed by its ultimate aims: "The strategy of the syndicalist doctrine," said Abad de Santillán, "of assembling all the ideological currents of the workers' movement into one organization, is derived from Marxism, not from Marx himself but from his followers. If not for syndicalist metaphysics, no one would have imagined that a revolutionary organization could exist without an end, unaccompanied by an overriding purpose. Simply to organize workers is not, in itself, to fight for the revolution."[48]

In addition to questions about the definition of class, these debates raised important issues about the transformation of society: who was the revolutionary subject and what were the oppositional movement's goals? Anarchists had to explain how society could be transformed and what role their cultural and labor institutions and press would play in the process.

Eduardo Gilimón, the central figure among the purists, was one of the strongest defenders of the trans-class position. Although he did not have a direct influence on the organized workers' movement, he exercised a strong influence over the libertarian movement, which did control the labor movement for much of the first decade. As an organic intellectual who positioned himself as an interpreter of the anarchist doctrine, he systematically attacked the quasi-Marxist, class-based perspective upon which the labor movement rested and that socialists and syndicalists had assimilated. He rejected class struggle and promoted the idea of a revolutionary elite of intellectuals and thinkers that would educate and enlighten the workers. For him, the revolution would not occur through class struggle but through the battle of the people against their exploiters. "The people"—a more inclusive category—encompassed an immense range of workers, people in the liberal professions, shopkeepers, and even "capitalists of all types." For him, "the people" also included the disinherited generally (the old, sickly, destitute, children, prostitutes, etc.), which reflected the Bakuninist idea of the masses as a source of revolutionary potential and political momentum. All revolutionary energies would turn against the state, which represented exploitation, repression, and the subjugation of society as a whole (of "the people"), not a particular class. It was on this basis that he concluded that the class struggle is not an anarchist process:

> It is not anarchic because anarchists do not fight against a social class, or an economic system, and do not come exclusively from a specific social class but rather from all of them. They are against a principle, the principle of authority, against a form of social organization that is authoritarian in its every dimension, from the political to the moral spheres, from the intellectual to the economic, and against all the social classes that oppose liberty, that oppose anarchy.[49]

For Gilimón, the working class was the most important source from which anarchists would recruit and from which the movement would derive its fundamental force, but nothing more than that. The dominant sectors, he believed, could also find allies among workers, since some would side with their oppressors due to an inability to dispense with servile habits, which is exactly what the forces of repression exploited when they tried to enlist workers. Indeed, being a worker was not in itself a virtue: at the very most, workers might mobilize around economic necessities in the unions, whereas anarchy was not "a system of improvements," wrote Gilimón, "but the abolition of the principle of authority as such ... men who belong to other social classes can embrace it—anyone with an elevated concept of individuality, dignity, and liberty.[50] In essence, the future of humanity hung on the balance of a struggle not between capitalists and workers, but between authoritarians and libertarians.

In opposition to the idea of class struggle, and particularly the Marxist idea of class consciousness that had penetrated anarchist discourse from multiple sources, the purists fought for a moral consciousness based on the values of the individual, liberty, rebellion, and human dignity. Years after the period we are discussing, Abad de Santillán reaffirmed the anti-classist posture in response to the spread of Marxism among radical workers and the impact of the Russian Revolution. Being a proletarian, he said, is not enough to make one a revolutionary, even if "Marxist demagogues ascribe an ineluctable historic purpose to workers and go to great lengths to spread the idea of the proletariat as a class; in their view, any rupture in class unity is an attack on the revolution."[51]

Santillán had a very different perspective. He did not believe that the proletariat was a unified class but rather a disjointed collection of human beings that filled the ranks of revolutionary forces and also—here he agreed with Gilimón—those of the oppressors. "In the revolutionary worker," he wrote, "there is a man before there is a worker; in the idea of the proletariat, there is the idea of humanity. In the consciousness of the proletariat fighting for a better world, you will find, in the first place, a human dignity offended by tyranny and oppression and only secondarily a shoemaker, a builder, or a carpenter.[52]

5. THE ENLIGHTENED VANGUARD

Anarchists did not believe that people converted to anarchism because they developed class consciousness, but rather through the revelation of the libertarian idea in an emotionally charged climate in which the possibility of a new moral order based on science and progress was evoked. This notion of popularizing revolutionary commitment through revealed truth seems to have been pervasive in Spanish anarchism as well. Activists who bore revolutionary ideas were less organizers than educators and agitators dedicated to revealing the gospel of a new world built around science, progress, and enlightenment. They were the chosen ones of truth and justice.[53]

This emotional temperament had roots in the pre-capitalist world, fit well with Hispanic cultural practices, and was ubiquitous in urban social movements such as the Argentine anarchist movement, which was specifically urban and, despite its rationalist patina, highly emotional and possessed of an undeniably moral understanding of the masses' conversion to anarchism. Although some would have differed with it, the following statement by González Pacheco captures the emotionalism in libertarian thought: "We anarchists are the spirit of the land; we possess the divine art of self-renewal. Our ideas, more than deductions from books, are vibrations of the eternal flesh, impossible to subjugate, immortal; they are living words, words of life."[54]

Many approached anarchism as if it were a faith revealed by apostles. Ghiraldo was not a libertarian activist formed in the discussion circles that read and analyzed Bakunin, Kropotkin, and Reclus, among others.[55] For him, Pietro Gori was the exemplary hero and venerated apostle who occupied the post that was left vacant when Radical Party founder Leandro Alem committed suicide. Ghiraldo, who believed that the Radical Party had betrayed its old leader, embraced anarchism with the same passion he had once felt toward Radicalism, guided by the person and the word of Gori. In his autobiographical recollections, he states that Gori "possessed all the traits necessary to proselytize: arrogance, refined manners, brilliant logic, and unfailing dedication." He later confessed that he absorbed the Italian anarchist's words like "a revelation" of "the new path that humanity had to follow to continue its ascendant march."[56] Gori's nearly divine words disclosed the anarchist doctrine to him and its "glorious" mission of freeing humanity from capitalism, religion, and the state.

Ghiraldo was not content with mere knowledge of the revealed truth and attempted to occupy the same place as his betters. He was only eighteen at the time of Alem's death and looked on helplessly at the leadership vacuum that had emerged in his absence. However, by the time of Gori's departure from Argentina, he felt able and obliged to become the moral champion of the oppressed. He openly aspired to lead their cause and autobiographical statements that he left behind emphatically corroborate suspicions of his excessive self-esteem. With constant laudatory self-references to "that formidable combatant," he shamelessly convinced himself that he possessed the "qualities of a real apostle." He also saw his newspaper, *The Worker* (1896–1897), as a battering ram and bastion "that daily lit a torch to enlighten the modern and cosmopolitan city." Even the dominant groups, he believed, had noticed the imminent revolutionary danger that he represented: "The conservative classes, preparing to defend themselves against the enemy arising in their midst, use every resource to fight and destroy it."[57] Ghiraldo was the embodiment of the revolutionary process.

Those who joined the movement for highly emotional reasons were not typically highly reflexive intellectually and had a propensity to uncritically use emotional, admiring, and apocalyptic language. Juan Carulla is a perfect example. In an article titled "The Agitators," he argued that "nobody has more right to our curiosity and admiration than the agitators," due to their courage and decisive action. "Take a glance across the vast social stage," he wrote, "and you will see your brothers feverishly waging a resolute battle for the conquest of the ideal; see them fluttering with the goodness of redemption, annunciating the good tidings of human justice in their sweet, virile voices."[58] As we have seen, these emotional, highly moralistic perspectives were often linked to a naïve celebration of visionary individuals, from Kropotkin to Gori, whose words unveiled the path to revolution.

It is thus no wonder that Gilimón saw thinkers and intellectuals as the visionaries and vanguard of the revolutionary movement: "On the front lines of the rebel camp," he wrote, "there are men who are not manual workers and who are, it is no exaggeration to say, the impetus of the rebellion, those who give form to the struggle, who lead, who make the critique of society."[59] For him, intellectuals were the axis of the revolutionary vanguard, a claim he thought reinforced by the heterogeneous pantheon of revolutionary heroes: Stirner, Malato, Bakunin, Pelloutier, Kropotkin, Spencer, Ibsen, and Marx. Not one, Gilimón noted, was a worker. Naturally, the pantheon's breadth also mirrored the movement's broad perspective on class.

Kropotkin understood anarchism as a branch of the progressive intellectual tradition, and especially of modern thought, which fought to liberate man from ignorance and authoritarian bonds.[60] Militant activist and anarchist historian

Max Nettlau placed anarchism in an equally expansive lineage: "Our idea is not revealed only in an elaborate system," he said, before celebrating intellectuals who were not libertarians per se but who had links to the tradition in one form or another.[61] Whitman, he said, could be valued for his singular and extreme dedication to freedom, Ibsen for his aversion to the state, Spencer for his criticism of the state's centralizing and oppressive role, and Stuart Mill for his socialist impulses. This flexible view of anarchism in Argentina—which was perhaps the most commonly held perspective in the movement—may have been even broader than in anarchist movements elsewhere. As an example of its heterogeneity, toward the end of the nineteenth century, stamps called "red sparkles" circulated in Buenos Aires that bore revolutionary phrases, which activists placed in public places as means of propaganda. The authors of the phrases offer a good indication of the movement's ideological diversity: Kropotkin, Reclus, Stuart Mill, Herzen, Pi y Margall, Saint Paul, and Plato.[62]

Anarchists believed that the vanguard's role was to educate, illuminate, and make people conscious—to teach the masses that the state and religion were the cause of social ills. The social question was thus central to the ideological and propagandistic scheme that anarchists directed to the workers. They asserted that a moral confrontation with, and comprehension of, these problems was a precondition of the advance toward revolution. But not everyone needed to accept the vanguard's transformative power: "It is sufficient, more than sufficient, if there is a large minority that takes advantage of any occasion in which the always-latent discontent manifests itself."[63] These ideas about the enlightening, combative role of the revolutionary elite (or "conscious minority") appear in Gilimón's thought and that of other local anarchist leaders. This position's origins seem to lay in Blanqui's views, who, after the failure of the Paris Commune, increasingly emphasized the positive role of the enlightening vanguard in opposition to the ignorant masses.

The idea had two important consequences on the social movement. On the one hand, fin-de-siècle French revolutionary syndicalists saw the working class as a proletarian elite whose mission was to lead the masses—who were incapable of doing it themselves—and train them for revolutionary action—this view was accepted by many in Argentina. On the other, Blanqui's ideas influenced Malatesta, whose ideas were also embraced by Argentine anarchists. Malatesta argued that anarchists only needed to organize a small minority and that the majority is inherently apathetic and hostile to transformation. He wrote: "The fact of having the majority on one's side does not in any way prove that one must be right. Indeed, humanity has always advanced through the initiative and efforts of individuals and minorities, whereas the majority, by its very nature, is slow, conservative, submissive to superior force and to established privileges."[64]

This minority had to be educated and made aware, although deprivation alone would be enough to mobilize the masses—who are "lacking in aspirations or ideals"—for the revolution. If there is a lack of daily bread, then revolution is possible. "The hungry masses are the revolution's dough, the anarchists are its yeast," was Gilimón's unambiguous metaphor.[65] His idea reflected the unmistakably romantic, Bakuninist, insurrectionary outlook that presumes that individuals (the people) have a natural, irresistible instinct for justice that will lead them to spontaneously destroy authority during periods of social convulsion. This idea was fundamental to the doctrinal purists' view of revolution. This is why Argentine anarchists tried to inflame every conflict that occurred during the first twenty years of the century and, it was in such moments, that the ignorant, oppressed masses and the "visionary" vanguard encountered one another. The anarchists saw themselves as the spark that would ignite the revolutionary bonfire and did their best to turn each clash into a revolution. And it was only from this vanguardist perspective that they were interested in organizing the workers' movement, which would eventually lead to a general strike and then revolution. They believed that the unions' role was not so much to win material improvements for the proletariat but rather to set off larger eruptions.

The more workerist sectors of the anarchist movement strenuously resisted the doctrinal purists' minimization of the class struggle, but lost their main vehicle of expression when they were displaced from *La Protesta*. After this, they launched many, mostly short-lived papers to disseminate their views. One of these, *Light and Life*, defined the history of civilization as a permanent battle between light and darkness, truth and deception, and the oppressed and the oppressors that, from the French Revolution onward, increasingly took the form of class struggle: "After the *Rights of Man*, two classes appeared that seemed to be friends, but that were really enemies; nobility, transformed into the bourgeoisie by the new organization, perpetuated indentured servitude under the name of citizenship; given the antagonism sanctioned by the republican constitution, the division between the workers and the bourgeoisie arose, and, from that came the class struggle."[66]

This newspaper would also voice the sharpest criticisms of Gilimón. In early 1908, it published a lecture that libertarian leader Esteban Almada had just given in the offices of the Cart Drivers' Society. Under the provocative title "Economic Determinism in the Class Struggle," he began by accusing his *La Protesta* rivals of being "shabby intellectuals with limited scientific or pseudo-scientific knowledge who think that they possess the absolute truth." He then argued for the centrality of economic forces in human life, given the inescapable pressure of material necessities. In his view, those who deny the influence of economic and material forces, like the doctrinal purists, obscure social conditions and spread a confusion that simply leads them to "a morbid regression to humanism … vainly hoping to harmonize the antagonistic interests of capital and wage labor

... denying the role of classes in our environment." Almada disputed Gilimón's claim that the prominence of bourgeois intellectuals like Bakunin, Marx, Reclus, and Kropotkin in the movement turned it from a class war into a social struggle. Their participation was exceptional and indicated their great sense of justice, but "we can find an elegant refutation of that fashionable theory in the fact that adepts of ideas of renewal are typically recruited from the poor, committed as they are to improving their physical and intellectual lives." Concluding on a highly reductionist note, he asserted that this was the case because economic factors totally determine sentiments and ideas and, as such, members of the bourgeoisie have no motivation to participate.[67]

The fact that Gilimón and his *La Protesta* colleagues held such amorphous ideas, and the existence of groups like those congregated around *Light and Life*, caused more than a few problems, since libertarian unionism had achieved real results and seemed to have become a foundation of the Argentine anarchist movement. Some libertarian leaders linked to unionism were irritated by those who argued that anarchism did not seek the emancipation of the workers, but rather humanity as a whole. They replied that anarchism, as a doctrine of social transformation, had to focus on the workers because "they are the part of humanity that needs emancipation."[68] In their view, intellectuals and anarchist thinkers' task was to educate and prepare the workers, so that they understood their part in the revolutionary process, but it would be the workers themselves who would make the revolution. This is why it was so important for unions to win things such as salary increases and reduced working hours for their members—they improve their lives in a material sense, give them more time to educate themselves, and foster a spirit of solidarity and rebellion.[69]

Given that intellectuals were to enlighten and lead the workers, calls for workers' independence and leadership made by an anonymous writer in the *La Protesta* seemed contradictory and ambiguous. They also brought to the fore an issue that had emerged in debates about the working class: the role of worker societies. After the libertarian movement embraced pro-organizational ideas, there was a tension for many years between those who privileged union action and those who saw it as only one of the movement's many activities, and not even the most important. The appearance of syndicalism in 1906 heightened this tension, insofar as it advanced views that were sometimes difficult to distinguish from those held by members of the anarchist FORA.[70]

La Protesta became a platform for the criticism of union action, especially after the doctrinal purists seized control of the paper.[71] And although it devoted a great deal of space to union activity and supported labor struggles universally, authors of its editorial statements and doctrinal columns argued that resistance societies were limited to improving workers' lives in material terms and that was not central to the battle against capitalism per se. This was so, they alleged, because an increase in salaries always resulted in a corresponding increase in the price of consumer goods (which negated the value of the improved wages). "Union activists must fight to make each worker a militant and ready for the realization of the ideal; they must focus on instruction as well as action."[72] Framed as such, union efforts were reduced to a tactical resource within a strategy that privileged trans-class, universalist assumptions.

For this sector of the anarchist movement, the unity of the working class was not a virtue in and of itself and would not ensure the transformation of workers' consciousness. This is why they insisted on organizing the workers around ideas or, more specifically, the principles of anarchist communism. This implied not so much workers' unity as a commitment to a broad vision of freedom that would allow individuals—not a particular class—to organize themselves on the basis of a common approach to social life.

Union activity was a tactic for recruiting workers to a more elevated undertaking: their education and enlightenment. For that reason, union funds and resources had to be spent not only on specifically labor-related necessities but also for educational activities like lectures, libertarian schools, and the publication of newspapers, magazines, pamphlets, and books. The ultimate goal of the anarcho-communist perspective that I have labeled as doctrinal purist was to educate the people and train them in the libertarian ideal, which would enable them to overthrow their enemies: the church, the army, capital, and parliamentary politics, all of which constitute and underpin the machinery of the state and keep the popular sectors in ignorance. "Let us fight against ignorance," said an article in *La Protesta*, "and we will have fought all ills."[73]

The purpose of all of our efforts and hard work is to disseminate ideas that are not in the popular consciousness.
—*La Protesta Humana*, January 12, 1901

CHAPTER III

Pamphlets, Books, Lectures, Militants, and Disseminators

As previously explained, anarchist circles, groups, and centers were forums devoted to educating and developing activists and to preparing workers to struggle for a new society. They were places of workers' self-affirmation and part of a discursive arena that Nancy Fraser has described as a "subaltern counterpublic."[1] In these bodies, local anarchists formulated messages intended to educate and enlighten the workers and activated webs of solidarity, recruitment, and consciousness raising. Almost all of their initiatives emerged from these arenas: their publishing efforts: their lectures, talks, debates, and propaganda tours; the training of militants; their activism within unions; the organization of rallies and street events; and the greater part of the recreational and educational cultural project found in the *veladas*. I will analyze these topics in this and the following chapter.

1. THE POWER OF SOLIDARITY

Despite the extreme heterogeneity of the local anarchist movement, there was consensus on the idea that militants' primary purpose was to educate and teach the libertarian doctrine to others in order to win converts and expand the ranks of revolutionaries. In one way or another, all the circles, centers, and groups' activities (lectures; the publication of books, pamphlets, and newspapers; parties, schools, classes, and libraries, etc.) reflected this goal, while also facilitating the education of militants. Building this cultural framework in circumstances of social turmoil and conflict was an arduous task that ran against prevailing tastes and relied heavily on libertarian militants' dedication and commitment to the idea that a fraternal union of men and women could transform the world. Indeed, solidarity was the local libertarian movement's driving force. It made possible the publication and distribution of anarchist literature, the operation of the circles, groups, centers, schools, and also the construction of a support network for needy comrades, whether they were imprisoned, ill, or relatives of fallen activists. In fact, as internationalists, anarchists did not limit their support to causes within Argentina: they also organized on behalf of the prisoners in Barcelona's Montjuich castle, the Spanish educator Francisco Ferrer and the Italian Bresci during their respective trials, the victims of demonstrations in Milan, and Spain's *White Magazine,* to cite some of the most significant instances. In addition to their fundraising events, they also raised money for allies through subscriptions.

Anarchists felt duty bound to provide solidarity to the weak and destitute, an obligation that they derived directly from anarchist morality and the doctrine generally.[2] "Among the natural premises of a free society," wrote Pellicer Paraire, "we must include the principle of solidarity, which encompasses the idea of reciprocity—the most beautiful concept of justice and practical fraternity."[3] The commitment to solidarity infused all anarchist practice, although it was only possible in small pockets of the world of labor in the present society— its complete practice would require the creation of a free society without competition between individuals and one in which relationships had no goal other than the common good. Anarchists held capitalism responsible for the lack of solidarity, but believed that it would prevail once capitalist competition disappeared.

However, the peculiar characteristics of the world of labor in turn-of-the-century Buenos Aires complicated the practice of solidarity. For one thing, there were pervasive national and even regional differences and in some cases this meant that acts of solidarity were restricted to a particular national or ethnic group, and, furthermore, there was always the danger that these differences would generate conflicts and rivalries among workers. Although they were not terribly common during the first decade of the century, they did occur, especially during strikes on the port, when the state and employers' associations set the mostly foreign-born port workers against the mostly Argentine-born laborers sent to replace them.

The diversity of the working class, and the fact that many had only recently arrived from Europe or from the countryside, meant an absence of common traditions or, at best, the superimposition of customs. Also, the unstable, volatile world of labor led to a degree of transience, inducing many to quit the city or ascend the social hierarchy, leaving the working class and union protests behind. For libertarian militants, the challenge was finding a way to practice solidarity in a competitive, urban society with a large immigrant population that included many who were focused on "making it" in the Americas. All of these conditions seemed to frustrate the construction of networks built upon reciprocity and mutual aid.

Nevertheless, the anarchists were optimists. They thought that capitalism inadvertently fostered practices of solidarity by oppressing and marginalizing the working masses and believed that mutual aid was an essential part of human nature that could overcome whatever social obstacles might be put in its way. In this case, as in so many others, Kropotkin was the source of inspiration. He regarded mutual aid as an essential component of anarchist morality. He took the concept of sympathy from Adam Smith's early work, *The Theory of Moral Sentiments*, that explained how individuals developed a moral sense of sympathy for those who had been aggrieved. This sentiment was neither religious nor mystical, but a physical fact of human nature. Kropotkin went beyond this, and even further than the Romantics' passionate attraction, when he attributed respect for the rights of others to the concept of mutual aid. In his view, mutual aid was innate to human beings and essential to the development of the capacity for free initiative. It led to cooperation and fraternity, not the Darwinian struggle for survival, and in that sense made human life and culture possible: the law of mutual aid was the law of progress.[4] This concept also suggested the idea of equality and mutual relationships, which express, as Alvarez Junco observed, "the old ideals of liberal radicalism: liberty, equality, and fraternity."[5]

Solidarity, a fundamental element of anarchist communism, could be and had to be put into practice by those who understood its importance. It was "neither humiliating charity, nor vain philanthropy, which are degenerate forms of solidarity," explained Pellicer Paraire, but a relational stance premised upon strong moral, ethical, and perhaps even puritanical virtues like tolerance, loyalty, friendship, and sincerity.[6] Superficially, these virtues do not seem very different from those extolled by Christians, but anarchists and even socialists promoted them systematically and, in point of fact, believed that Christian charity implicitly justified exploitation. For them, the church was cloaked in a shroud of hypocrisy that was absent from the libertarian approach to solidarity.

These ideas were omnipresent among local anarchists, and the network of solidarity that they constructed was broad and multifaceted. Circles, groups, and centers sponsored and organized most of the support efforts, and the newspapers and magazines did their part by publicizing where and when events took place. There were two types of solidarity actions: fundraisers for libertarian institutions and fundraisers in support of humanitarian undertakings. In the first case, militants organized events and subscriptions to benefit the libertarian press, secular or rational schools, libraries (to found them and buy books), union societies, and even propaganda tours, due to the high costs of activists' trips into the interior.[7] Solidarity efforts of a humanitarian character encompassed a wide spectrum of activities, such as aiding comrades injured in police crackdowns, the families of militants killed during actions, sick militants, the unemployed, prisoners, and deportees. The anarchist movement demonstrated its capacity to provide substantive assistance when the government deported more than fifty of its principal activists between December 1902 and February 1903. It supported deportees and their families in diverse ways, including the provision of economic aid that enabled them to afford day-to-day necessities and pay for their legal defense, although in many cases socialist and even liberal lawyers offered their services pro bono in solidarity with those affected by the Residency Law. Similar events occurred after each wave of repression.

Anarchist prisoner solidarity merits special attention. The phenomenon became an important part of libertarian practice after the mobilizations in 1901 and 1902, when there was a sharp increase in the number of people arrested—mainly anarchists—for union activism. Indeed, incarceration came to be a common experience for anarchists and the National Penitentiary, the La Plata prison, and the police's headquarters emerged as hated symbols of oppression, as did the Tierra del Fuego penitentiary, which many anarchists compared to the Barcelona's Montjuich castle, and the "floating prisons" in navy ships, where dozens of anarchists were held after the 1905 Radical Party uprising.[8] "Freedom for political prisoners!" became a battle cry, inaugurating a tradition of prisoner support on the Argentine left that continued in vigor until the early 1980s.

Anarchists showed profound concern for their detained comrades. They campaigned for their freedom, collected and sent them food, cigarettes, books, money, and clothes, and even sent similar items to their detainees' families. Although they were initially galvanized by their comrades' fate, discovering the terrible conditions suffered by those imprisoned for common crimes led them to extend their support to inmates as a whole. Consistent with their abstract defense of humanity's inherent goodness, they believed that people turned to crime only because the system had corrupted them. Anarchists also welcomed the chance to recruit in prison and carried out propaganda with that end in mind. In the prisons, "revolutionary propagandists encountered a fertile field, one crowded with those victimized by heredity, the environment, and social inequality. Accustomed to being treated like animals, their hearts hardened by crime and vice, they received the dignified words of the young inmates as if they were their first caresses."[9] Going beyond the defense of politicized prisoners, they fought for the humanity of all detainees: "Our voice, our warmth, should extend itself to all who suffer the consequences of the present social regime. It doesn't matter what crime they committed. They suffer, and that alone is reason enough for us to lend them our support."[10]

The issue of prisoners grew in importance as the social conflict intensified, to the point that there was a large, anarchist-led demonstration in Buenos Aires in May 1910 demanding the release of political prisoners.[11] The protest occurred in response to news that some of the many arrested during the long general strike in May 1909 had been tortured in the National Penitentiary. Unprecedented numbers attended the rally and the publicity generated by the events prompted the government to replace implicated prison personnel. The protest also called for the abolition of special-powers legislation as well as freedom and amnesty for political prisoners, but these demands were not met. Government repression during the Centenary ultimately put an end to anti-prison agitation.

Although the anarchist press actively supported these campaigns, the circles, centers, and groups were the practical, organizational foundation of the fundraisers. In some instances, they raised money through lists of supporters, but the most common method was putting on multifaceted *veladas* or theatrical performances, which of course also attempted to educate and recruit.[12] Militants announced these events with a good deal of advance notice and tried not to hold two on the same night in order to ensure sufficient attendees, a fact that also points to the limits of popular support for the anarchist movement's cultural and ideological efforts.

The press (not only libertarian) advertised the affairs, which generally took place in large theaters in the city center or in proletarian neighborhoods, since the anarchist halls were not big enough to accommodate large audiences. It was only during the Casa del Pueblo's short life that the movement could avoid renting rooms for such occasions. Otherwise, the preferred halls were the Iris theater and the Verdi hall in La Boca, the Doria Theater (2328 Rivadavia), the Casa Suiza (Rodríguez Peña y Cangallo), the Libertad theater (575 Ecuador), and the Italian community centers: Stella d'Italia (349 Callao), Unione e Benevolenza (the 1300 block of Cangallo), Lago de Como y L'Arte (1481 Cuyo). They also frequently used the following sites: Vorwarts (1141 Rincón), Centro Ciclista (444 Suipacha), and Orfeón Español; and the theaters Marconi, Olimpo (853 Lavalle), Apolo (1384 Corrientes), Roma in Avellaneda, and Cavour (764 Sarmiento). They raised money primarily through the sale of admission tickets, and also through raffles and lotteries. The raffles were quite frequent; they took place in centers, groups, circles, union societies, and especially *veladas*, where it was easier to sell tickets due to the large audiences. Militants or sympathizers donated the prizes, which ran from objects with a link to the revolutionary cause, such as political writings by Michelet, Zola, Pérez Galdós, Kropotkin, and Reclus; portraits of Louise Michel, Angiolillo, Reclus, and the martyrs of Chicago; to more functional items like watches, "a pair of gold earrings," "a couple of shirts," "six sets of women's stockings," and "three bottles of Chianti wine." One might also find "a revolver with a load of bullets" among the prizes, which is not surprising given how common it was for people to bear arms at the time.[13]

For the most part, these efforts yielded a profit, even if it was meager at times.[14] As the decade unfolded, the solidarity network grew more and more dense as a result of the increase in the movement's activities as well as its maturation and deepening roots among workers. Around 1910, the number of deportees, prisoners, and victims of the successive waves of repression had risen dramatically; the circles, groups, and centers multiplied and *La Protesta* went from being a weekly newspaper to a daily with a print run of more than 10,000 copies. Obviously, given the escalation of the social conflict, solidarity efforts deployed in 1900 would be insufficient ten years later.

2. THE POWER OF THE WRITTEN WORD: BOOKS AND PAMPHLETS

One of the basic goals of the circles, centers, and groups was to spread anarchist ideas among workers who were interested in the movement. "This pamphlet," one newspaper said of a publication by Barracas's Neither God Nor Master group, "exemplifies the anarchist doctrine and should be read by all comrades."[15] Anarchists' emphasis on publishing reflects their deep faith in the diffusion of the written word and the practice of reading, a conviction that they shared with many other tendencies active in this period of Argentina's modernization. Libertarians attempted to turn the act of reading doctrinal material into a public event that was accessible to all activists and the largest possible number of workers. To do so, they published ideological, political, and educational literature not commonly released by publishing houses or sold on the shelves of commercial bookstores.[16]

From the very beginning, anarchists tirelessly published pamphlets and books on the libertarian movement's principal thinkers and writers, something made possible by the state's tolerant attitude toward ideological literature and the broad freedom of the press. They also released magazines dedicated to "sociology, art, and letters," like *Social Science* (1897–1903), *The Social Question* (1894–1896), and *Seed* (1906), to name just a few, which contained numerous doctrinal articles and, at times, printed essays that were later published as pamphlets. On a few occasions, anarchist magazines, like others of the era, serialized the material in broadsheet form. Of course, anarchist newspapers also ran a large quantity of doctrinal pieces.

Publishing pamphlets was one of the main activities of circles, groups, and centers in the 1890s and throughout the period covered by this book, although anarchists put the greatest emphasis on public lectures and cultural events when they began to self-consciously direct their message to workers. The vast majority of the published authors were luminaries of the European libertarian universe: Kropotkin, Errico Malatesta, Élisée Reclus, Ricardo Mella, Jean Grave, and Pietro Gori, among others. They also published local authors such as Dr. Emilio Arana, Félix Basterra, and Alberto Ghiraldo. Along with material printed in Argentina, local booksellers imported and distributed a wide array of texts from abroad, mainly from Spain, Italy, and Paterson, New Jersey, but the high costs of imported material led to a preference for material published domestically.[17] Eduardo Gilimón identified two reasons for the strength of anarchist literary production in Argentina. On the one hand, reading was one of Argentines' favorite pastimes: "there are few nations in which people read as much as they do here."[18] On the other hand, printing costs were lower in Argentina than in Europe: "For a European worker … buying a book for one franc costs him the equivalent of a fifth of his working day," whereas a local worker can buy that same book for what amounts to only one tenth of his work day. "All of this helps explain why reading has more proponents in Argentina than in Europe and why anarchist theories have been so rapidly and exhaustively disseminated here."[19]

Despite the low costs, anarchists had to make extraordinary efforts to publish, given that print and paper qualities, and the size of a print run, could easily make printing expenses prohibitive. First of all, to publish a pamphlet, they had to raise enough money to pay for printing, which they did through subscriptions.[20] They put out many publications through this method, but at times it was insufficient: sometimes disinterest, mislaid subscription lists, or an inability to acquire enough money or to get the money acquired to the relevant group, caused the effort to fail. There were constant complaints in the movement press about the lack of financial support: "We sincerely hope that all who have received pamphlets from our library will be cognizant of the large debt hanging over it and will send in their contributions as soon as possible."[21] It was essential to recoup costs incurred when putting out a book or pamphlet in order to continue publishing, and this was especially difficult because the lack of commercial priorities among anarchists meant that they often sold literature cheaply, at a sliding scale, and likely gave a lot away for free.[22] This is why activists often had to help finance the publications with their own resources. These problems rendered the centers, groups, and circles' publishing efforts inconsistent, perhaps with the exception of the Anarchos group, which put out twelve publications in four years. Nonetheless, despite the discontinuities and publication problems, anarchists did pull off very sizable print runs in many cases.[23]

On many occasions, an effort succeeded and a publication sold out quickly. This occurred when prominent militants thought highly of the published author, multiple groups participated in the undertaking, and newspapers and booksellers promoted the endeavor. It was also important to release works in a strategic, timely fashion, taking advantage of moments of social convulsion or propaganda tours by well-known activists. For instance, the Sociological Bookstore announced the publication of Carlo Cafiero's pamphlet *Anarchía e Comunismo*, "which had a large print run, considering the propaganda tour that comrade Gori and anarchist groups have initiated in the Republic."[24] Such tactics helped them ensure the successful publication and distribution of a work, although naturally there were failures too: on numerous occasions, copies piled up in libraries and workers' centers, whether because of public disinterest, bad decisions made during the editing process, inadequate distribution, a poorly chosen author, or simply because the group behind the effort disappeared.

The publishing groups typically selected the best-known authors of the libertarian milieu for publication. Although they released many Italian works and circulated them among Italian workers, the vast majority of texts were in Spanish; many were reprints and others were translated (not always very carefully).[25] They chose works for their ability to communicate the doctrine forcefully and didactically. This is why Kropotkin was one of the most frequently published writers. He clearly and systematically expounded the ideals of anarchist communism in *The Conquest of Bread,* explaining that nature's riches must be appropriated and distributed equitably among individuals; in *The Place of Anarchism in Socialistic Evolution*, he explained how evolution culminates in anarchy; in *Law and Authority*, he outlined the historical development of both institutions and defined anarchism's stance toward them; in the widely-circulated *The Spirit of Revolt*, he explained how the revolutionary individual should mold himself. Malatesta was another highly esteemed author, whose most oft-published works included a critique of the electoral system (*Against Parliamentarianism* and *Universal Suffrage*); a didactic explanation of the doctrine through an entertaining dialogue (*At the Café*); and harangues to the rural workers, complemented by Élisée Reclus's *To My Brother, the Peasant*.[26] There were also frequent publications attacking the church, which was an obsession for anarchists and one of their favorite targets: *Religion and the Social Question* by the Catalan Joan Montseny; *God's Crimes* by Sébastien Faure; and Most's *The God Pestilence* were some of the titles assailing the church and religion. Anti-militarism and anti-patriotism were similarly important topics: *On the Fatherland* by Augustin Hamon, *The Soldier's Manual* and *Militarism and Anarchists' Attitude Toward War* by the Dutch libertarian-pacifist Domela Nieuwenhuis were often discussed. Another series of more demagogic texts argued that a parasitic minority exploited the workers with impunity and that anarchists would "rouse the oppressed individual."[27] Likewise, they published a series of brief and widely circulated treatises that, addressing women specifically, anticipated contemporary feminism: Soledad Gustavo's *To Women Workers* and Anna Maria Mozzoni's *To the Daughters of the People* and *To Girls Who Study*. These pamphlets spoke of women's conditions—condemned to servitude from birth and a double exploitation as wives and workers—and concluded by inciting women to make themselves into revolutionaries and rebel.

A high degree of abstraction and universalistic didacticism was very common, even in the few texts published by Argentine authors, such as Basterra and Arana. Virtually no works addressed the particularities of Argentine society. Among the few exceptions, there is a pamphlet by Alberto Castro y García Balsas, *Críticas al proyecto González* [*Criticisms of the González Legislation*], which is a longwinded criticism of the 1904 labor law.

Anarchists had to overcome enormous economic and organizational obstacles to put out their publications. Political persecution was also a factor, not to mention the challenge of getting poorly educated workers to read typically arid, doctrinal literature, despite such favorable conditions as high literacy rates, the increase in the habit of reading, press freedoms, and relatively low costs. Anarchists approached the undertaking spontaneously and haphazardly—like everything they did—but managed to get massive amounts of ideological literature into the hands of the reading public. Given the available data, it is impossible to determine the size of print runs and sales with any precision, much less compose a detailed profile of readers (beyond the activists), although one can suppose that anarchists produced approximately 20,000 to 40,000 pieces of literature each year.[28] The rate does not say much when contrasted to the circulation rates of commercial literature during the time, but it is highly impressive when one considers the barriers that anarchists had to confront and the customary abstraction and density of their publications.[29]

3. THE POWER OF THE WORD: LECTURES

The publication of doctrinal literature did not always have the effect desired by anarchists: workers might receive a pamphlet, book, flyer, or newspaper, but not all knew how to read and of course there was no way to guarantee that those who did would actually do so. Other strategies were necessary: although anarchists had always understood the importance of the spoken word for propaganda, in the mid-1890s, public readings and lectures became an elemental part of their strategy.[30]

Both the middle sectors and the working class expanded in Buenos Aires as a result of economic changes in the last three decades of the nineteenth century. This, along with growing secularization and literacy, produced a noteworthy expansion and diversification of the reading public and the ideological currents in circulation, which culminated in what Halperín has called a "new climate of ideas."[31] The appearance of anarchists and socialists as a force was a novel event that took place in the context of this new climate, and both groups sought to receive and transmit messages for an audience of workers. Along with the press, they saw public readings and lectures (especially) as vital tools for educating and recruiting workers.[32] Anarchists appropriated and re-signified these new forms of communication, although they were not alone in extolling their virtues. Indeed, educators had been doing so for some time, and some saw public readings as the most effective means of popular education. Former Argentine president Domingo Faustino Sarmiento, for instance, defended the practice, which he regarded as a form of entertainment in which the reader or orator transmitted ideas in a rational but also emotional manner, thereby pleasing listeners while contributing to their education, complementing what they might receive in schools.[33]

Anarchists and socialists saw public reading in similar terms, but attributed different meanings to it: it was a way for workers to acquaint themselves with the oft-inaccessible, great works of philosophy and literature and also, reflecting the almost puritanical morality in the libertarian world, helped keep workers out of the café. One observer, delighted by a public reading, noted the following: "They were a long way from the café, billiards, cards, and the emotional incompatibilities that fatally disrupt the peaceful harmonies of workers' homes."[34] And it was, principally, a tool of apprenticeship and indoctrination for militants themselves, a means for recruiting new adherents through the organization's reading groups in workers' centers, circles' libraries, and even prisons. A somewhat idyllic prison scene painted by an anarchist author evokes some of the virtues attributed to reading: "A circle of prisoners spent the morning listening attentively to chapters from Kropotkin's celebrated book, *The Conquest of Bread*, periodically interrupting the reader with questions about points that were too obscure for their rudimentary minds."[35]

Despite the utility of public readings, lectures were more practical and the preferred tool for reaching workers. Public readings tied the reader to a text and, while retaining some of the intimacy of a reading in a bourgeois club or salon, they were inaccessible to the great masses of workers, given that they usually took place in cramped rooms in libraries or workers' centers. Lectures, on the other hand, still allowed a direct relationship between the speaker and the audience but were no longer essentially private and could engage much larger numbers. The growth of the working class definitively expanded the audience to which anarchists and socialists directed their lectures and through which they constituted an alternative propagandistic space.

There were two lecture circuits in turn-of-the-century Buenos Aires: one was literary, in which the speakers were writers who spoke to a smaller, more learned, and refined middle-class audience;[36] the other was popular, directed to workers, and comprised of anarchists and socialists. Both circuits shared topics and even audiences to an extent, which reduced the distances between them. Indeed, the most common themes (patriotism, militarism, women's rights, alcoholism, hygiene, education, divorce, sexuality, individual ethics, and religion) were not exclusive to either group, but reflective of concerns shared by anarchists, socialists, liberals, freethinkers, Masons, and even Methodist pastors and Catholic priests. Although they had very different views, their audiences intermingled to a degree,[37] even though there is no doubt that anarchist and socialists made a unique contribution by "inventing" a worker audience and creating a forum in which to discuss topics from the world of labor.[38]

Workers were apparently reluctant to attend lectures during early years and struggled to pay attention to the orators. "The undertaking was so difficult and thankless at first!" said Dickmann. "There was tremendous ignorance among the masses, which we had to overcome patiently and with tolerance."[39] He made this comment while speaking about a lecture on health given in the Cart Drivers' building in 1897, but noted that, ten years later, more than one thousand people gathered in perfect order to listen to speeches in the very same building. Although his assessment of popular ignorance is debatable, there was a positive change over the first ten years of the century due to the politicization and education of workers as a result of the growth of the circles, groups, and centers and unions. The increased number of lectures put on by anarchists and socialists reflects this.

Table 2: Anarchist Lectures (1898–1910)*

YEAR	QUANTITY
1898	10
1899	20
1900	39
1901	48
1902	130
1903	23 **
1904	193
1905	83 ***
1906	165
1907	242
1908	285
1909	293****
1910	102*****

* The data, which is approximate, comes from *La Protesta Humana* (1897–1903); *La Protesta* (1904–1910), and *La Prensa* (1902, 1905, and 1908).

** The imposition of martial law in November 1902 greatly limited libertarian activities.

*** Martial law between February and May.

**** Martial law between November and December.

*****Martial law from April onward.

Toward the second part of the first decade, lectures became a favored method for disseminating ideas, not only for anarchists and socialists but also for many other groups.[40] They were ubiquitous in Buenos Aires, and the enthusiasm for lectures even surprised Gilimón: "More people attend lectures [in Argentina] than in Europe," he observed.[41] There was a sort of blind faith in the goodness of the word that multiplied the lectures and led people to fill the most varied public theaters where they were held. The abundance of lectures startled a foreigner visiting Buenos Aires around the Centenary, who composed an ironic portrait of the lecturer, as a personality typical of the times: making lectures a way of life, he talked a lot while saying little, but was fully confident "in spreading the knowledge that he carries within him through the word; he intends to lead a portion of Latin America along the path of progress and to sow the seed that will ultimately flower in the field of humanity and liberate still-dormant peoples."[42] The author's irony is less important here than his perception of the climate of the period and indication of the pervasive faith in the word's transformative power, shared by all social sectors, and the public's eagerness to learn. Shortly before the Centenary, numerous foreign personalities came to Argentina and gave scores of lectures to packed rooms in large halls throughout Buenos Aires. Among those demonstrating their oratorical prowess were Rafael Altamira, Jean Jaurés, Enrico Ferri, Vicente Blasco Ibáñez, and Anatole France.[43]

Initially, the lectures were not attractive to workers. They were accustomed to assemblies and rallies but not to listening attentively to speeches that went on for two hours or more, and few militants could give coherent talks. During the 1880s, especially the latter half, meetings were held frequently that focused on topics relevant to workers, and there were also habitual debates between anarchists and socialists, but there were few lectures or available lecturers. One exception was Malatesta, who often gave informal, spontaneous lectures in cafés and bars as well as in the Vorwärts hall and in Italian centers. There was also Rafael Roca (1859–1893), an individualist, who came to give three or four lectures daily in neighborhoods throughout Buenos Aires.[44] In some cases, the lectures had no time limit and the audience grew impatient and trickled out; other times the topics were so abstract that they were nearly incomprehensible. "We cannot recall," complained a writer in *La Protesta Humana*, "having ever heard so many stupidities said so earnestly. It is painful to see comrades hurl themselves into oratorical labyrinths from which they themselves can't escape just because they hope to seem more knowledgeable than the others."[45] An additional problem was that anarchists still had not clearly defined their desired audience, and though some lectures focused on workers, those focused on ideological disputes, either with socialists or within the anarchist movement, were far more common and bore little relevance to the common worker; these were attended primarily by militants or sympathizers.

This situation changed radically after the turn to organizationalism. Pietro Gori, who arrived in Argentina in 1898, played an especially important role in this. He had vast experience as a lecturer not only in Italy but also in the United States. Consistent with his pro-organizational perspective, he helped change the meaning attributed to lectures: he saw them as an essential tool of anarchist propaganda, a view that the emerging libertarian movement would soon embrace.[46] Gori did not disapprove of internal polemics and actually encouraged them, but he was also dedicated to disseminating the anarchists' "gospel" among the workers. His first lectures in the country condemned the individualist, anti-organizational wing of the movement, a stance reinforced consistently by *La Protesta Humana* and *The Future*. He also tried to draw attention to the dynamism of the world of labor as a field in which to wage the battle against capital, and urged libertarians to break out of the self-referential universe in which they had found themselves. This is why he gave numerous lectures arguing that workers would be the protagonists of the coming social revolution and asserting that organization was a foundation of that revolution.[47]

La Protesta Humana, *The Future*, and other pro-organizationalist forces, eager for Gori to spread his ideas, put together an extensive speaking tour that would bring him to cities close to Buenos Aires as well as more isolated places like Salta among other sites around the country. They organized the tour together because they saw "an urgent need for the workers to become educated about the current situation and prepare themselves to defend their dignity and means of life."[48] Thus, in January 1899, he visited Luján, Mercedes, and Chivilcoy. Later, traveling along the southern railway line, he spoke in Ayacucho, Azul, Chascomús, Maipú, Tandil, Juárez, Necochea, Balcarce, Lobería, Bahía Blanca, and Mar del Plata. He decided to stay in this last location for two weeks, presumably attracted to its incipient world of labor as much as its qualities as a vacation town.

Gori lectured in buildings occupied by the circles and centers where they existed, in Italian associations, and in rented halls. The goal was to spur the creation of new anarchist groups. He talked to workers about the social question, their friends and enemies, the evils of politics and political parties, the church's malevolent influence, and—this was one of his favorite topics—workers' present and future. He asserted that they were the real protagonists of history: "The workers are the neglected heroes of the great deeds, to which they always contribute so profoundly."[49] Gori spoke about exploitation, and explained that all workers under capitalism have shared interests. With his straightforward, emotionally charged eloquence, he asked, "Who deserves credit for building the Brooklyn Bridge? Who gave dozens of lives to the river while completing the endeavor? Who does the heaviest work in the Argentine countryside and city?" He explained that workers, who make up 90 percent of humanity, receive low salaries, mistreatment, and insecurity in exchange for their sacrifices. In sum, their reward is misery. It was a moving, uncomplicated, and effective speech. Gori's tour of the country, and the dozens of lectures that he gave in Buenos Aires were successful, if one considers the massive audiences that came to listen to him and the overwhelming number of workers among them.

Gori was a criminal lawyer and journalist, not a worker, and while workers celebrated him, he was also popular in academic circles. Founder of the *Modern Criminology Magazine*, he divided his activities between the labor movement and the academic sphere, which was the source of frequent speaking engagements for him. For instance, he gave a speech about "The Duel and the Evolution of Moral Valor" in the Círculo de La Prensa [Press Circle] that was introduced by Samuel Gache.[50] One author noted that Gori possessed a dual identity shared by many libertarian intellectuals, "resulting from a double articulation with the vicissitudes of popular sectors and certain aristocratic values advanced by the small intellectual community in the Río de la Plata region."[51]

But it was his oratorical skills and capacity for public seduction that made the Italian anarchist such a successful lecturer. This was particularly the case for women, who attended Gori's lectures in large numbers. A journalist from Mar del Plata's *El Progreso* expressed his pleasant surprise at "the numerous women present at his lectures … who were soon overcome by Gori's passionate words; there were abundant applause and cheers at the end."[52] Lectures were one way for working women to access forms of sociability that were otherwise beyond reach, although middle-class women also attended his lectures frequently. Indeed, Gori was a very talented speaker, who put forth his arguments clearly and demonstrated them with ample proofs. Even his political rivals acknowledged his virtues in this respect; leading socialist Enrique Dickmann regarded him as "a great orator whose lectures scaled literary heights, simultaneously attracting and captivating."[53] He was also quite versatile, being able to communicate with diverse audiences. He was praised for his lectures in the Círculo de la Prensa and the staid Department of Law, but was equally capable of engaging workers with his straightforward, clear terms. These qualities were highly valued in fin-de-siècle Buenos Aires and allowed anarchists to enlist a significant number of workers and some intellectuals and writers, such as Alberto Ghiraldo, Félix Basterra, and Pascual Guaglianone (who became an accomplished lecturer in his own right).[54]

Anarchists believed that lectures were a powerful tool and that the word had great transformative power.[55] Lectures were important not only because of what was said but also because of the symbolic power of an event in which there was an orator in the center, seducing the audience while his comrades distributed literature among attendees or collected money for one of their many causes. At times, these events spilled out of the theater and into the street, particularly when the lecturer was famous. For instance, according to *La Protesta Humana*, when Gori left Mar del Plata, "a large demonstration accompanied him to the station, including the Garibaldi band, which played the International."[56]

Anarchists and socialists came to see lectures as a privileged tool for propaganda by 1900. Organized primarily by groups and circles, they held them in their own buildings or in theater halls rented for the purpose, in addition to organizing lecture tours throughout the country. Open-air lectures in plazas and public parks also became common around this time. Enrique Dickmann claims that he put together the first one in 1897 after seeing how the Salvation Army proselytized in plazas on Sunday afternoons:

> I listened attentively to the evangelical sermon, their reading of passages from the *Bible*, their religious chants, infused with a mystical and pacifist spirit. I admired the patience and composure of the men and women, straightforward and humble, who gathered around a banner and impassively endured the mockery, gibes, and even insults from the ill-mannered ruffians who amused themselves by taunting them. It then occurred to me that we socialists could do the same thing—raise our platform in the open air and preach socialism's gospel, the new evangel of proletarian emancipation and human redemption, in the city's streets and plazas.[57]

Lecture topics in the early period can be divided roughly into two categories: on the one hand, there were general, doctrinal speeches that were directed to a broad audience and designed to educate militants; while on the other, reflecting the pro-organizational turn and consequent recruitment efforts, there were speeches on topics of interest to workers. These became increasingly important to libertarians.

Lectures in the first category were often highly abstract: for example, they treated science and anarchy; the society of the future; the origins of the state and its social function; libertarian morality and its differences with bourgeois morality; the social role of art and religion, among other concerns. Anarchists were obsessed with the topic of religion and felt a strong need to argue for the non-existence of God on scientific grounds.[58] Other themes were more concrete, such as those dealing with alcoholism; medicine in anarchy; women and the family; free love and marriage, etc. Two common doctrinal subjects bore strong links to the vicissitudes of the moment: militarism, which the border conflict with Chile made timely; and parliamentarianism, which was pressing due to Socialists' imminent participation in Buenos Aires elections.

The second group of topics reflected the libertarian movement's almost unanimous decision to address its discourse to the workers. Lecturers tackled issues such as the workers' past, present, and future; their rights; labor conditions;

salaries; the need for union organization; general and partial strikes, etc. Being internationalists, they also organized lectures on the Italian workers' movement and commemorations of historic events like the Paris Commune and the Haymarket affair.

Anarchists held frequent debates with socialists and representatives of other tendencies. For example, in 1902 Torrens Ros faced off against Manuel Hervas, editor of Baradero's *El Republicano*, and Félix Basterra did the same with a priest in Mar del Plata. In 1906 and 1907, there were numerous debates with socialists; in 1908, the most common topic was the relevance of the class struggle. There were also disputations over issues that were more internal to the anarchist movement, such as comprehensive education, organization, and neo-Malthusianism, although debates between anarchists and socialists were far more common. In the early 1890s, anarcho-individualists often crashed socialists' orderly events in order to challenge them on points of doctrine. These interventions typically ended poorly. For instance, during a lecture by Adrián Patroni in 1895, the anarchists, whom the socialists neither invited nor welcomed, tried to mount the rostrum and a pitched battle ensued: "Someone turned off the lights, people began throwing tables and chairs, punching and clubbing one another as firearms were drawn."[59] These comments, made by Dickmann, are credible—he assiduously participated in debates and was roundly praised for his judiciousness. "Thanks to his valiant and friendly disposition," a libertarian writer said of Dickmann, "he quickly became the anchor of all the good will in that chaotic environment."[60] Socialists agreed to participate in the debates in 1895, which became a routine though not always peaceful. Reflecting the absence of a straightforward anarchist orientation toward workers, the debates during the early years were often abstract and turned inward toward the militant milieu. For instance, a debate between anarchists and socialists took place in 1896 in a bar in the basement of a grocer's warehouse on Tucumán and Pellegrini streets. There, in an ambience filled with "smoke and booze," they argued over topics such as property, religion, science, and the future of humanity for three days and nights in front of an audience composed primarily of anarcho-individualists.[61]

The ascendancy of the pro-organizational wing of the movement around the turn of the century changed the debates significantly—convincing the audience became the priority. Anarchists and socialists, who were competing for the same population, regarded debates as an ideal way to contrast their ideas and explain them to workers.[62] Thought of as oratorical tournaments, victors of a debate won returns in the form of the new recruits to their cause. This is why both anarchists and socialists sent their best speakers to the podium, such as Gori, Guaglianone, Basterra, Oreste Ristori, and Bertani for the anarchists and, for the socialist side, Dickmann, Patroni, Nicolás Repetto, and even Dino Rondani, an Italian deputy who took part in these meetings actively during his visit to the country in

1902. They also sent militants to act as blocks of support, who applauded their comrades or interrupted rivals at opportune moments. This gave the events the feeling of an assembly, which would typify of the practice on the left thereafter. During 1902, a pivotal year for the left as a whole, "public debates were the order of the day"[63] and occurred with exceptional frequency, filling myriad halls, including the large Doria (later Marconi) theater, which was among the most important.[64] There were also debates in cities in the interior of the country.

By 1900, there was a much greater supply of libertarian speakers than there had been ten years earlier: the student Julio Molina y Vedia, Santiago Locascio, Pascual Guaglianone, Manresa Herrero, Manuel Reguera, Doctor Arturo Montesano, Luis Solitro, Teodoro Ros, Altair, Félix Basterra, Rómulo Ovidi, Adrián Troitiño, Oreste Ristori, and Spartaco Zeo were among the most acclaimed names on a roster that was overwhelmingly male (with the exception of "*compañera* Reyes") and that set out, with the support of the rest of the movement, to win over the workers.

Judging from the increase in the number of lectures and the size of their audiences, this propagandistic activity was fairly successful. Nevertheless, anarchists themselves were not always satisfied; some called for a more careful selection of orators because, they complained, many of their comrades were inept lecturers who simply liked to hear themselves speak. *La Protesta Humana* pilloried the oratorical excesses: "Comrade Telarcio then closed the event with some good words, although at times he was less than reasonable and, inspired by the enthusiastic speech, he went so far that he lost himself altogether."[65] This was a difficult problem to resolve for a movement in which individual autonomy and dilettantism were common coin.

Despite these hurdles, the content and number of lectures grew notably after 1904. If the names of previous lecturers dropped from the list, whether because they had given up activism or had been deported, an even larger number of propagandists and writers appeared in their stead.[66] Notwithstanding the distrust of the workerist anarchists, there was also a robust expansion of the topics, especially due to the influence of literary types and educators. The first to add themselves to Ghiraldo's ranks were: Ángel Falco, José de Maturana, Alejandro Sux, Tito Foppa, and Rodolfo González Pacheco. They gave a strong push to lectures on revolutionary art, particularly theater.[67] Educators Julio Barcos, Mario Chiloteguy, and Lorenzo Mario, who were also suspect in workerist eyes, spoke frequently about free schools and rational education. Doctors Juan Carulla and Ucar often gave speeches—the former speaking about hygiene and health and the latter about naturalism and the natural curative system. And in contrast to the previous five years, there was now a strong battalion of female lecturers who excelled at oratory and pressed for the full incorporation of women into the struggle. Virginia Bolten, a prominent militant from Rosario, was at the head of this group.[68] Religious, doctrinal, and philosophical themes, as well as militarism and patriotism specifically, continued to be favored subjects, although militants placed the greatest emphasis on concerns related to the world of labor, which included topics linked to the social question, forms of social and union organization, and anarchist strategies for influencing unions.

They directed the vast majority of their emancipatory messages to the workers and it was workers who made up most of the audiences, although there were also some students and intellectuals. Spectators were largely male, and during the early years, organizers commonly lamented the absence of women: "A throng of people gathered to listen to the word ... but it was mostly men," said *The Future*.[69] The struggle to attract women achieved better results when the lecture was part of a *velada* organized by the circles; the festive and familial character seems to have provided a better context for them to respond to the libertarian call.

Most lectures took place indoors, especially in the Unione e Benebolenza, Casa Suiza, cart drivers' building, Verdi, Vorwarts, Cavour, and the Iris, but more and more were held outdoors as the first decade unfolded. Spectators had to seek out the lecturer when they occurred in theaters and halls, whereas organizers of open-air lectures were essentially seeking out the audience. They typically happened around nightfall on weekdays, so as to engage laborers who were on their way home from work, or on Sunday afternoons, in order to draw in those enjoying the city's parks and plazas in neighborhoods like Once, Flores, Villa Crespo, Parque Patricios, Avellaneda, Centro, Barracas, and, to a lesser degree, Floresta, Liniers, Belgrano, and San Fernando.

4. THE POWER OF THE WILL: MILITANTS AND DISSEMINATORS

The anarchist movement did not revolve around powerful theorists or charismatic organizers: figures like Pietro Gori, who galvanized dispersed militants and played a prominent leadership role, were exceptional.[70] Evidence suggests a division of activists into two categories. In the first group, there is the large population of propagandists who made up the movement's base; the hundreds of militants who organized in the factories, workshops, on the port, in the central market, among transport workers, tenements, and elsewhere. Most were poorly educated but highly committed to the doctrine and occasionally capable of great mobilizing feats. They put together most of the anarchist movement's public events and were the prominent militants in labor conflicts.

The immense majority of these activists were manual laborers: bakers, typographers, construction workers, mechanics, shoemakers, painters, cart drivers, and hairdressers, etc. There was also a large number of unskilled workers like laborers, day laborers, and longshoremen, and it was not unusual to find some office workers and storekeepers among them too. In 1903, police sent a circular to the interior provinces listing 524 individuals suspected of being anarchists (who had been expelled, were on the run, or were under surveillance) and identified their professions in 159 cases. They were: twenty-five bakers, eleven mechanics, two hairdressers, six shoemakers, seven painters, two butchers, six tailors, seven cart drivers, two coachmen, seven typographers, four carpenters, two adjusters, one foundry worker, one blacksmith, one tanner, one cigar maker, one brush maker, one lathe operator, one tinsmith, nineteen day laborers, four longshoremen, five office workers, four storekeepers, one traveling salesman, one photographer, and one musician. Only ten had a basic formal education and performed intellectual labor: there were four journalists, four educators (teachers and professors), one attorney, and one bookkeeper. Police issued another list a year later that contained a total of forty-one suspected anarchists: thirty-two were manual and skilled workers, seven unskilled, and only two were educated (a journalist and a writer).[71]

These largely self-taught, proletarian activists made up the overwhelming majority of anarchist militants. Their knowledge of the doctrine typically came from publications and lectures and many, after doing a quick study in anarchist rudiments, felt confident enough to become lecturers and publishers themselves, which they could do easily thanks to the absence of party structures. The varied levels of intellectual facility are evident in comments that a police informant added next to the names of anarchists in his dossier: a longshoreman had a "regular education in social matters"; a baker was "endowed with average intelligence"; a mechanic had a "clear mind and often gave lectures"; a typographer enjoyed "great prestige due to his cleverness and perseverance in propaganda," etc.[72] Clearly, the groups, circles, and centers were producing activists, as intended, despite their lack of coordination and impermanence. Doubtlessly, these characteristics were key to the movement's success during those years: the self-education of militants, the organizational disorder and heterogeneity, the doctrinal breadth, and the ease with which an activist could acquire prominence (and enjoy the prestige that it implied in the world of labor). Such traits were compelling in local, urban society at the turn of the century.

In addition to that mass of base activists, there was a much smaller core group that disseminated libertarian ideas through the press, lectures, educational projects, and *veladas*. Naturally, the boundary between disseminators and base militants was porous—the distinction primarily reflects degrees of political initiative and education.

There appears to have been a greater percentage of native-born activists among the disseminators than the base militants, especially in the second half of the first decade. Disseminators such as Alberto Ghiraldo, José de Maturana, Alejandro Sux, Juan Carulla, Julio Barcos, and Teodoro Antilli were Argentine;

Florencio Sánchez, Edmundo Bianchi, and Ángel Falco were Uruguayan. These disseminators worked as advertisers, journalists, teachers, and, much less frequently, self-educated manual workers, such as typographer Torrens Ros, bakers Joaquín Hucha and Francisco Berri, and Inglán Lafarga, who was a carpenter.[73] They were organic intellectuals, but of a peculiar sort because their ties were not to a party but to a circle, group, center, newspaper, union, or theater group. Many wrote—dramas, novels, essays, and doctrinal pieces—and lectured, but did not generally produce original theory or literature and mainly limited themselves to translating and expounding the ideas of the European thinkers.

One libertarian writer condemned the disseminators: "Get rid of Guaglianone, get rid of Ghiraldo, get rid of Altair, get rid of Basterra, get rid of those four or five who know what they think, where they're going, and how to express it! And tell me: what reduces the value ... of all the others who are unknown for some reason?"[74] Nonetheless, the nucleus of disseminators was much larger than this writer suggests and they played a vital role in making anarchism a major political and social actor during the era.

The group included distinguished pro-organizational anarchists like Pietro Gori and Antonio Pellicer Paraire. Gori, who was born in Messina, Italy, was a well-known lawyer who balanced his legal profession with intense political activism in several countries: Germany, the United States, and Italy, from which he fled in 1898 after participating in an uprising in Milan. In Argentina, he engaged tirelessly in partisan activity and traveled the country, giving dozens of lectures in support of union organization. His legal knowledge gave him access to academic circles, who often invited him to speak. Antonio Pellicer Paraire was a Spanish typographer born in Barcelona in 1851 who had participated actively in the Spanish section of the International and published vast quantities of articles in Spain's *Anarchy* and *The Producer* newspapers. After a militant pilgrimage through Cuba, Mexico, and the United States, he arrived in Argentina in 1891, where he remained for the rest of his life. Like Gori, he was central to the pro-organizational tendency's ascendency in the anarchist movement.[75] He died in Buenos Aires in 1916.

Of course, other activists, in addition to these two, were central to the emergence of the mature anarchist movement: Francisco Berri (a.k.a. René Osita) was a working-class Spanish baker who participated actively in the formative period. An administrator of *La Protesta* during its early years, he played an important role in the formation of the Argentine Workers' Federation, in which he occupied leadership positions. Torrens Ros, a Catalan typographer who arrived in Argentina in 1897, was vital to the organization of the Federación Obrera and the Casa del Pueblo. He was pivotal in organizing efforts among port workers and the 1902 general strike. Like Berri, he fled to Montevideo in early 1903 to escape state repression. Inglán Lafarga, also Catalan, first worked with

The Persecuted and later directed *La Protesta* from its appearance in 1897 until 1902. He was an industrious lecturer and union organizer, although gave up political activity after the repression in 1902. Juan Creaghe (1841–1920) was an Irish doctor who lived for many years in the city of Luján, where he published *The Oppressed* (1894–1897). He directed and administered *La Protesta* various times and helped sustain the paper economically. He went to Mexico after the Centenary, where he supported the Magonists. Héctor Mattei, a bookkeeper by profession, was born in Italy in 1851 and, after having been active in the First International, settled in Argentina in the early 1880s. He worked with Malatesta during his years in the country and was a member of the Anarchic Communist Circle in 1884. He founded the bakers' union and published *The Bread Worker* in 1894. In 1901, he began participating actively in the Federación Obrera.

Although there were no brilliant intellectuals among Argentine anarchists, those listed and a large number of speakers and writers actively disseminated anarchist ideas: Félix Basterra, Pascual Guaglianone, Virginia Bolten, Felipe Layda, Oreste Ristori, Spartaco Zeo, Elam Ravel, Arturo Montesano, Eduardo Gilimón, Mariano Cortes (Altair), Federico Gutiérrez (Fag Libert), Julio Camba, Pierre Quiroule, Orsini Bertani, Teodoro Antilli, Santiago Locascio, Roberto D'Angió, Julio Molina y Vedia, Lorenzo Mario, and Edmundo Calcagno.[76] Others such as Adrián Zamboni, Carlos Balsán, Francisco Corney, Esteban Almada, and Francisco Sarache alternated between union activism and propagating anarchist ideas. Fortunato Serantoni and Bautista Fueyo became major booksellers and publishers in the anarchist movement for many years. Doctors Emilio Arana and Juan Carulla also played distinguished roles, in addition to the well-known educator, Julio Barcos. Alongside the journalists and speakers, there was also the more literary figures: José de Maturana (1889–1917), editor of *La Protesta*, publisher of *The New Paths* (1906–1907), and a dramatist who composed *La flor de trigo* (*Wheat Flower*, 1909) and *Canción de primavera* (*Spring Song*, 1912). Alejandro Sux, who was born in Buenos Aires in 1888, worked with *La Protesta*, to which he contributed a column about local customs called "My Sundays." Author of *Bohemia Revolucionaria* (*Revolutionary Bohemia*, 1910), he became a correspondent for *La Prensa* during WWI. Rodolfo González Pacheco (1881–1949) founded *The Seed* with Teodoro Antilli (1885–1923), and, starting in 1908 and for many years thereafter, was a prominent editor of *La Protesta*, where he wrote his famous "Carteles" ["Posters"]. In 1910, he was the architect behind the appearance of the short-lived libertarian evening newspaper, *The Battle*. In 1907, he published his book of prose, *Rasgos* [*Features*], and his *Las víboras* [*Vipers*] brought him recognition as a dramatist in 1916. The theatrical work of Florencio Sánchez (1875–1910) is well known. He had links to the anarchist movement in 1897, before he was famous, and his play, *Puertas Adentro* [*Inside Doors*], premiered in an anarchist circle in Montevideo. Although he was openly sympathetic to libertarians, his relationship to the movement was informal and his commitment declined as his celebrity grew.

Finally, there is Alberto Ghiraldo, the most well known of the libertarian writers. Born in Mercedes (a province of Buenos Aires) in 1875, he died in voluntary exile in Santiago, Chile in 1946. His political and poetic activity (the latter of dubious quality) began very early; activism in support of Leandro Alem and the revolution of 1890 served as his political baptism and his first literary foray was a piece on [President] Juárez Celman, attacking him and calling for his death, which prompted a rebuke from Alem himself. Poets Almafuerte, Espronceda, and Becquer initially had the greatest influence upon him as a writer, although the poet Rubén Darío later captured his interest and became a friend. Between 1897 and 1903, he published *The Sun*, which began as a literary publication but ended up as a social criticism broadsheet. It was during *The Sun*'s final period that he embraced anarchism, drawn in by the allure of Pietro Gori's personality. He was continually active in libertarian ranks from then on, and partook in every type of literary activity linked to the movement: he authored nearly a dozen works of theater and many works of prose; he lectured prolifically; directed *La Protesta* between 1904 and 1906 and briefly in 1913; and he edited and led the literary magazines *Martín Fierro* (1904–1905) and *Ideas and Figures* (1909–1916). He was also active in the labor movement, where he represented various resistance societies in the Argentine Workers' Federation. His personal ambition, independence of views, and apparent belief that he was the only anarchist intellectual that mattered caused innumerable conflicts with his comrades. In 1915, isolated from the movement, he went to Spain and withdrew from activism. He settled in Chile twenty years after that.[77]

These activists, along with many others whose names are now lost, were the core disseminators and visible, identifiable spokespersons and intellectuals of the local anarchist movement. They were a heterogeneous group and their degree of commitment and time in libertarian ranks varied widely. Indeed, many had very weak links to the movement—particularly writers drawn to the movement through a modernist, anti-bourgeois aestheticism (Alberto Ghiraldo is the most well-known case).[78] Their relationship to the movement was generally short-lived, much like the French symbolists who briefly supported the French anarchist movement under Mallarmé's inspiration. In addition, due to a skepticism about intellectuals and their fleeting commitments, relatively few libertarians welcomed their presence: "There's not much behind their large hats, romantic long hair, and Lavalliére neckties," wrote *The Libertarian*. "Nothing more than superficialities and exhibitionism. They became anarchists because they couldn't become anything else, and because they have always assumed that being one would not require anything more than just saying so."[79]

Among the notable exceptions in Argentina were Rodolfo González Pacheco and especially Alberto Ghiraldo, who militated in anarchist ranks for almost two decades. Ghiraldo's many years in the movement were not bereft of tension due to his political and ideological heterodoxy, which frequently put him at odds with more dogmatic anarchist leaders in the workers' movement and with the doctrinal purists. The turbulent relationship typified the anarchist movement's difficulty in building lasting bonds with intellectuals due to its enduring hostility toward those with roots outside the world of labor. The relationship was plagued with mistrust and misunderstanding, which partially explains why intellectuals were so quick to depart. "Very few remained in the movement," wrote Abad de Santillán, "some went over to diametrically opposed camps, others simply forgot their youthful ideas and the excitement that their work had generated among the revolutionary masses; some lost all character and creative ability to the extent that they distanced themselves from anarchist ideas."[80]

Bohemian literary circles also led some intellectuals—Alejandro Sux, for instance—to the anarchist movement, although these recruits were the weakest and least enduring. They were infatuated with the romance of revolutionary action and, in the oppositional climate of the time, dazzled by the aura of heroism and courage that surrounded libertarians. Their short-lived participation in the movement was based almost exclusively on admiration for figures of desperation and the defense of nebulous principles of liberty and justice. These intellectuals generally did not enjoy the sympathy of the doctrinal anarchists or publish much in the partisan press, but they occasionally wrote for marginal literary and artistic publications as well as important ones like *Martín Fierro* and *Ideas and Figures*.

Some socially conscious, intellectually inclined youth also got involved with the anarchist movement and linked their intellectual interests to activism. They disseminated libertarian ideas, created magazines, translated and published pamphlets, and lectured, although most of them left the movement quickly.[81] Pascual Guaglianone and Félix Basterra's cases are illustrative. Both came to anarchism around the turn of the century, attracted by Pietro Gori's ideas and person. Guaglianone—who was born in Buenos Aires in 1882 and died there in 1938—joined the Socialists when he was very young, but broke with them shortly thereafter to join the anarchist movement, in which he was active between 1899 and 1907. He contributed frequently to *La Protesta Humana* and was an energetic and talented lecturer who was as articulate in Spanish as Italian. He became one of the principal and most lucid critics of the socialists, and his public debate with José Ingenieros caused a stir. He also organized and agitated in Montevideo. Like many intellectuals in the anarchist camp, he ultimately traded his activism for another activity: university teaching, in his case. According to Santillán, Guaglianone "was a highly educated man, a bit eclectic ... [who] distanced himself from the movement and, it appears, the ideas of his youth, concentrating on technical, pedagogical labors without great significance."[82]

Basterra began participating in the anarchist movement when he became an editor of the magazine *Social Science*. He later played an important role in *La Protesta Humana*, which he directed briefly in 1900. He demonstrated his intellectual independence in the publication when, challenging the other editors, he expressed support for the individualist *The Rebel*'s position toward the organization of the International Congress in Paris. Although this cost him the leadership of *La Protesta Humana*, he remained a regular contributor until 1906, when he joined the staff of the newspaper *La Nación*, a brusque ideological shift for which he was violently condemned by the anarchist movement.[83]

Though sketched only briefly here, these two men's paths are typical of the period. The leading figures of the movement, most of them immigrants, were "doubly foreigners in the Latin American periphery"—in the literal sense of the word and also because, as foreigners, they were excluded from the court circle of the local intellectual elite.[84] Anarchist propaganda, whether in the form of journalism or lectures, provided a means through which they—middle-class intellectuals lacking in "cultural capital"—could articulate their views and sometimes launch a career. This was the case with Basterra and Guaglianone: the former began as an anarchist orator and became a university professor; the latter began as a writer and then jumped to salaried journalism. In a few instances, anarchist activism served as a trampoline for a degree of fame, as occurred with Alberto Ghiraldo, who earned a certain acceptance among established dramatists. Professionalization often followed reknown: as Julio Ramos said, "journalism is the best way to make a living as a writer,"[85] especially for a foreigner.

Basterra's trajectory provides a good example of anarchist activism as a mechanism for intellectual and professional legitimation, and the wrath of the anarchist press toward him suggests a suspicion of such motives. *La Protesta* avowed that he had accepted the *La Nación* post because "being a foreigner prevented him from maintaining himself through public employment, especially in this country, to whose children he gave such a beating in his pamphlet, *El crepúsculo de los gauchos*."[86] In reality, more than a few intellectuals vacated the cultural margins as soon as they had the chance to do so.[87] Guaglianone left anarchism to join the more comfortable academic field, which gave him a salary, professional legitimation, and, despite the fact he did not hold a university degree, a post in Ancient and Religious History in the La Plata Humanities Department.[88] Parallel to this, he traversed all the steps of the Education Ministry that would take him to the post of inspector general of secondary education.

It is difficult to know how many anarchists followed this path, although probably many fewer than would have liked to. Nevertheless, regardless of their success or failure, it is clear that there was an extremely weak link between intellectuals and the anarchist movement. In 1917, a disenchanted old libertarian lamented the opportunism and lack of conviction of many of his old comrades.

As he saw, Basterra had resolved his economic problems, "with a government job after singing the praises of [President] Figueroa Alcorta. Guaglianone liquidated his accounts with demagogic oratory, trading it in for a job as a mediocre school inspector and elevating his *compañera* to the category of spouse. Montesano, after the odyssey of the Residency Law, become a respectable, well-mannered bourgeois."[89]

Very few of the core disseminators persevered in their anarchism, perhaps the exceptions being Eduardo Gilimón, Alberto Ghiraldo, and Rodolfo González, and not one of them seemed to have possessed the talent necessary to become a leader of the anarchist movement per se.

The comrades and their families savor a moment of pleasure;
they are transported as this sublime piece of revolutionary theater
excites and pleases them. It is an impassioned work
of propaganda.

La Protesta Humana, May 14, 1899

CHAPTER IV

Free Time, Parties, and Theater

1. HOW TO USE FREE TIME

THE COMMENT ABOVE captures the purpose of anarchists' *veladas*. They were attempts to respond to workers' social needs and engage their non-working hours with a cultural project that was fun and also instructed them in the libertarian ideal. To do this, they deployed refined artistic and educational practices—such as theater, musical performances, and lectures—as well as more traditional recreational pastimes like games and festivities.

Leisure time was not a minor concern at this juncture in the history of Buenos Aires, as it was at least partially during non-working hours that workers' habits and conduct were formed. Although most had not won the eight-hour day, nearly all participated in some type of leisure activity, whether or not political vanguards deemed it desirable. Occupational patterns among Buenos Aires workers were varied in the two decades between 1890 and the Centenary: some earned livable wages and had regular, stable employment; others received subsistence salaries; and others still worked only intermittently and suffered periodic bouts of unemployment. Whether an individual fell into one or the other of these categories typically determined if that person had enough money and free time to participate in public entertainment. As Stedman Jones put it, "work type and schedule conditions leisure."[1]

But, regardless of their levels of comfort or deprivation, all workers needed recreation and rest, and they satisfied these needs in manifold ways: they might pass the time in the street, whether in the city center or in the quieter neighborhoods; others preferred to socialize in tenement courtyards;[2] and from early in the city's history, many, especially families, amused themselves in Buenos Aires's numerous parks, plazas, and public fields, where they could enjoy some respite from the tenements and slums, which were typically dark, airless, and unhealthy.[3] The hundreds of cafés and taverns in the city were highly attractive too, though frequented almost exclusively by men.[4] There were also picnics, country retreats, circuses, theatrical performances, among the other diversions that proliferated in Buenos Aires at the turn of the century and grew increasingly appealing to and affordable for working people. According to the 1909 municipal census, the number of attendees at public spectacles (operas, operettas, zarzuela, comedies, plays, circuses, cinemagraphic productions, etc.) rose from 1,488,529 in 1900 to 8,424,220 in 1909.[5] This surge reflects rapid and deep-seated changes in the culture industry and the social fabric of Buenos Aires generally. While these figures do not specify which social sectors were involved, there is no doubt that workers were among those in attendance.

Free time changed along with a worker's employment status. A fully employed person had designated periods of rest: the Sunday day off, religious and national holidays, and sometimes a working day shortened by organized pressure. But free time was forced when workers were unemployed or employed irregularly. They often passed the time in the café or on the street, and many associated joblessness with the temptations of gambling, whether legal or illegal, offered by the scores of gambling dens, lottery agencies, fight houses, and horse races taking place in Buenos Aires's three hippodromes.[6] Given this, it is easy to understand why groups advancing a social project—alternative or otherwise—framed free time in normative terms. Indeed, from different perspectives and in different ways, liberal reformists, social Catholics, civil servants, medical hygienists, and socialists all tried to determine how free time should and should not be used. This was true of anarchists as well.

Veladas and parties were foremost among anarchists' strategies for engaging free time. They hoped that they would discourage workers from patronizing bars, brothels, cabarets, Carnival celebrations, and other sites that supposedly promoted debauchery and alcoholism: "Entertainment … has great value when framed by individuals with a spirit of initiative," said *La Protesta*, "and it is a very good thing, too, because it relieves people of boredom while getting them out of the cafés, bordellos, and bars."[7] Anarchists energetically campaigned against alcohol—joined by socialists, social Catholics, evangelists, liberal reformers, and even the Salvation Army—in an effort to dissuade people from consuming liquor.[8] Anarchists believed that poverty caused alcoholism, but also that social pressure, custom, and the simple pleasures of drink could lead to alcohol abuse and the resultant moral degradation. Militants were to be exemplary in such matters: to consistently demonstrate the proper, educated, and dignified use of time, money, and the intellect.

Libertarian asceticism echoed calls for temperance found in domesticity handbooks addressed to workers that were circulating in Buenos Aires at the time. Those guides envisioned workers reconciled to the capitalist system, whereas anarchists wanted to emancipate them from it, but both agreed on the need for a restrained, venerable conduct. In opposition to arenas of licentiousness, they sought to create an ideal space, removed from worldly perversions. This is one of the reasons why they constantly stressed that anarchist parties were family affairs and encouraged the participation of women and children.

2. WOMEN AND THE FAMILY

"Don't stop your husband, boyfriend, son, or daughter from taking part in strikes or rebellions—let them join in!" urged *La Protesta*.[9] Anarchists tried tirelessly to enroll women into activism. The circle was the privileged space for their reception and, just as there were many lectures addressed to women specifically, libertarians also hoped that *veladas* would be a way to enlist them. They organized frequent dances, poetry readings, and theatrical performances that were directed to both sexes and included female spectators and performers (although there were no women among the anarchist dramatists). Accounts of anarchist parties in the newspapers sometimes distinguished attendees by gender, indicating libertarian interest in the topic. Their accounts indicate that a significant number of women—one-third of attendees—were present at such gatherings.[10] We do not know if these women attended the *veladas* because of their interest in the libertarian cause or simply to accompany their husbands, parents, or brothers.

Why involve women? Should they fight on equal footing with anarchist men? The topic of the role of women—"that other half of the human race"— and their emancipation occupied a central place in libertarian discourse. And while that discourse unfolded in the broader framework of liberal thought, anarchists devoted greater attention to the subject than any other tendency and were indisputably the vanguard in putting, to paraphrase Dora Barrancos, a transgressive discourse about women, marriage, the family, free love, and—even more audaciously—sexuality into "locution." This is not to deny that anarchists' views rested on the scientific paradigm of the time, or the presence of eugenicist and neo-Malthusian ideas in their convictions about birthrate control and the happy reproduction of the species. "Reasoned and limited procreation," argued a writer in *Gleam,* "is clearly advantageous. Reducing the population helps us ensure that we don't end up with too many mouths to feed and makes it possible to give children a good education and superior physical development." It would also, they said, reduce hunger and misery among workers and stop so many from becoming servants of the forces of repression. Some even thought of it as a way to boycott capitalism: "limiting procreation will help put an end to exploitation."[11]

Anarchists held that women were doubly exploited, as workers and as women. And it was upon the latter point—man's oppression of women—that they focused their attention. They interpreted women's subordination anthropologically, culturally, and historically, often in somewhat paternalistic terms.[12] In their view, there was a historical continuum between the present and very distant eras of human life: primitive man controlled women through violence, whereas modern man did so with a combination of force and cunning in the home, an isolating environment that undermined women's intellectual development. Furthermore, they believed that the rise of the bourgeoisie intensified female submission through marriage and other legal contrivances that were "made by men, for men."

> With respect to domination, reading the law books immediately makes it clear that men authored the laws. The way legislators speak of wives' duties and rights, and the difference in how they judge a female adulterer as opposed to a male one; the manner in which they treat a young mother and an illegitimate child; all of this is truly ridiculous. Men are innately egoistic and cynical. One can justifiably say that the husband's legal power is unlimited, whereas the wife's is null and void.[13]

They also rejected the idea that women are naturally weak. Their fragility was not innate, libertarians argued, but a consequence of a division of labor that historically assigned childrearing to women and thwarted their intellectual development, an injustice shrouded by ideals of feminine frailty and delicacy. Indeed, in the present society, schools, churches, and other institutions trained females from infancy to occupy a subordinate position as a housewife. *The Gentleman of the Wilderness* called upon its comrades to "prevent the clergy from obstructing our influence on women."[14]

But what exactly did "our influence" mean? Did it mean the influence of anarchist doctrine or of anarchist men? Anarchist discourse is unclear and contradictory on the point, perhaps because men wrote the vast majority of treatments of the "woman question." While some called for women's total emancipation—economic, legal, social, and sexual—others took a much more ambiguous, protective, and paternalistic stance: "Woman should be free, completely free—to think, to work and to love, *but always sheltered and safeguarded by man*."[15] This posture seems to have been pervasive among Argentine-born anarchists [*anarquismo criollo*]. It reflected the notion that women are childlike, unable to access freedom on their own as a result of centuries of subordination and oppression and that they, unlike girls, had acquired venal habits like flirtation, vanity, and ostentation, which rendered them superficial, fragile, and malleable.[16] Despite anarchists' continual assertion of the intellectual equality between men and women—which was significant in the context of prevailing ideas—their statements sometimes had a patronizing tone and gave the impression that they were directed to persons of limited intelligence.

This attitude caused tension in the anarchist movement, although public debate on the issue was rare. The most important exception occurred in 1896, with the appearance of *The Woman's Voice,* a libertarian newspaper made exclusively by and for women.[17] Its publishers declared in its lead editorial that the paper was necessary due to the shortage of voices addressing women's "submission and slavery" and, while they primarily blamed capitalism for women's subjugation, they also criticized men as a whole, who also bore responsibility, they said, for women's economic and sexual domination.[18] The eruption of this radically feminist perspective enraged some of their male counterparts, who, their self-esteem wounded and surprised to be accused of "sexual exploitation," disavowed their critics as immoral and irrational. Redoubling the challenge in its second issue, *The Woman's Voice* called its masculine colleagues "false anarchists" who only wanted to have a "submissive *compañera*" at their side to raise their children, cook their food, and do their laundry. "To you," they said, "a woman is nothing more than a pretty piece of furniture," and they threatened to go to their homes and reveal that they were "all a bunch of chickens and crabs who talk about freedom but only want it for themselves."[19] The critique's harshness gave rise to a firestorm of reproaches and insults—to which libertarians were so prone—as well as the emergence of a group of male supporters. All of this underscores the complexity of the anarchist movement's response to the question of women's emancipation.

In reality, all agreed that there would be sexual equality, the abolition of marriage, free love, and the disappearance of the nuclear family in the post-revolutionary future,[20] but matters were complex when it came to anarchists' actual practice in the present. While the doctrine rejected the marriage contract as a transgression upon nature, prevailing customs led quite a few anarchists to moderate their views and even marry.[21] Something similar occurred with the family: the doctrine condemned it as a coercive institution based on property and authority that was represented by the father, who transmitted the dominant social values to the children while controlling his spouse as if she were a belonging, and yet, despite this radical critique, very different ideas—ones much closer to those criticized in *The Woman's Voice*—appear to have reigned among actual anarchist families.[22]

Anarchists also upheld an ideal of a self-sacrificing, valiant, compassionate, and hardworking mother that closely resembled dominant maternal archetypes: "If each home had a woman with the elevated moral qualities of my upstanding mother," said one libertarian writer, exulting in the sacrifices that his mother had made for her children's education and well being. With eugenicist overtones, he continued along lines that would have made some anarchists uncomfortable: "Mother, who ensures the continuity of the species ... the fate of the human race depends on her defeat and triumph," because, if she enjoys good physical, intellectual, and moral health, "the product of her entrails will necessarily bear the progressive virtues of a regenerated race."[23] Of course, the goal of this eugenicist view of the woman-mother was not to facilitate the reproduction of healthy workers, but rather robust and dynamic revolutionaries. The ideal woman-mother had to raise her children well and teach them about the vices of religion, the nation, and the state. While the qualities that anarchists attributed to women were unconventional, their perspective still privileged the woman-mother's function in the family-home, which was quite unlike the family and home that they envisioned for the future. For some, it was vital that the woman-mother play that reproductive role, because otherwise "the home and the family will never become the coveted paradise of love, the charm of our ideals."[24]

Anarchists' emphasis on women's emancipation was unique, and introducing the topic into discourse was transgressive, but, as we have seen, some questions were difficult to resolve. Libertarians accorded women a different purpose in the revolutionary home, but their sphere of action was still fundamentally domestic. And while anarchists implored them to participate in their parties and *veladas*, such affairs were essentially extensions of the libertarian home. Women's presence at these functions transformed them into family affairs—which libertarian journalists constantly emphasized—and thereby endowed them with a degree of respectability that they otherwise would not have had. Newspapers often issued statements describing "the overwhelming cordiality at this absolutely familial *velada*."[25] Children's involvement also reinforced the uprightness of the events: kids read poetry, played music, and took part in theatrical performances. There were even *veladas* dedicated exclusively to children, such as one put on by the Women's Labor Association in the Cavour Theater in 1904, which followed a program similar to those of the *veladas* for adults.[26]

3. THE SEARCH FOR HEALTHY AND RATIONAL ENTERTAINMENT

Anarchist recreation and entertainment encouraged solidarity and respect for all participants. The *velada*, one of their favored models, typically included a wide array of activities: poetry, lectures, choral singing, orchestral music, theatrical works, and dance. The *veladas'* programs followed a rational cultural template (also embraced by socialists) that mixed learned and popular culture in the order, type, and content of the proceedings. The mixture was a source of some tension within the movement. For instance, dance was difficult to integrate into the libertarian cultural framework. Anarchists initially incorporated it into the *veladas* because of its popularity among workers, not its inherent virtues, and it quickly became a strategy for attracting people turned off by the heady lectures. Dance was one of workers' preferred forms of entertainment, regardless of their nationalities. Musicians played songs and rhythms from their assorted countries and people danced spontaneously at parties in tenements and other places where large numbers of working people gathered. Any occasion could trigger a party— an anniversary, a victorious strike, or simply a day off—and this commonly led to dance. A journalist dedicated to chronicling tenement life attested to the importance of these pastimes among popular sectors:

> Everyone steps out in the afternoon and those who know how to play an instrument perform the pieces in their repertoire while others dance. Right after a joyous tarantella, one hears the simple, harmonious moans of a sad one, or one played in the Argentine style by skilled hands on the guitar; just as the last notes ring out, the sounds of a galopa are heard. The international diversity of tenement residents expresses itself in the music; each one takes pleasure in playing or listening to the melodies of his homeland.[27]

Several styles of popular dance were consolidated and developed at this time, such as the haberna, milonga, and especially the working-class dance par excellence: the tango.[28]

Anarchists did not discourage these practices, but they did not encourage them either, and were actually somewhat suspicious, particularly of the tango, which they, like their conservative counterparts, considered a lascivious, immoral music of the brothel. But they did incorporate family dances into the *veladas*, despite some resistance. A libertarian journalist writing as "Antropón" vented his indignation at the dance style that had come to workers' societies and criticized his comrades for using it to attract workers. With a puritanical attitude presumably shared by some of his comrades, he argued: "We should not lower anarchy to men's vices, but make them shed their vices and rise to anarchy. Workers' events should provide instruction and recreation, and I don't think dance is either recreational or instructive. Frankly, it's tiring and confusing." Reflecting a rigid attitude reiterated in libertarian discourse, he concluded his article by saying: "In my view, workers' societies must prioritize workers' material and moral well-being, without giving in to these stupid customs and brainless routines. They don't accomplish any real regenerative work and aren't useful at all."[29]

This was not the reigning view after dance became integral to the libertarians' *veladas* and popular parties.[30] But, notwithstanding their acceptance of dance, anarchists did seek to regulate entertainment, dignifying it by trying to ensure that reason prevailed over the senses, encouraging moderation, and eliminating wildness. This was the only way to build the anarchist man, who would be austere, measured, and rational. "Entertainment," said Gilimón, "like everything else, should reform in accord with psychic progress and the development of culture. Above all, we must be sure to prevent it from having—like the Carnival—a regressive influence on the individual spirit."[31]

4. WAR ON THE CARNIVAL

The Carnival was a potent source of anarchist frustration and their response to it illuminates their complicated relationship to popular entertainment as well as their attempt to curb its dangers by molding workers' leisure time. Anarchists' interpretation of the Carnival was symptomatic of their discomfort with popular tastes generally, which extended to activities like the circus, comedy, wrestling, and (later) soccer, among other local pastimes. Carnival celebrations were the most well-attended and playful festivities in fin-de-siècle Buenos Aires; thousands participated annually. Native Argentines and foreigners mixed, indistinguishable behind their disguises, which often betrayed the influence of rural, pro-gaucho motifs that novelists and playwrights were cultivating increasingly.[32] Anarchists objected to what they saw as the Carnival's deeper meaning; their model of entertainment presupposed a fervent, acritical enthusiasm for reason that necessarily rendered the Carnival an irreducible antipode. They saw it as absolutely irrational: "When the god Momus rules," said *La Protesta*, "the god Reason blushes and hides impotently among the spider webs soiling the library books."[33] They saw the Carnival as an occasion in which the senses were freed from reason and people's logical and moral capacities undermined. This view fused with the idea that the Carnival was a coarse amusement and a regression to times of unbridled decadence typified by Saturnal pagan celebrations during the Roman Empire.[34] Thus, in addition to being irrational, the Carnival was a product of tradition and "when tradition commands, common sense is lost."[35]

The Carnival's apparent irrationality was enough to elicit libertarian disdain.

They denounced it as an instance of depravity that fomented unreasonable conduct among the masses, who ceded to intemperance behind the anonymity of their masks and disguises. They were incensed that people participated in these celebrations, joyfully embracing pleasure and vice as they expended energies that should have been invested in the emancipatory cause. Like many naturalist writers and conservative moralists of the time, they saw the Carnival as a wellspring of degradation.

Anarchists also held it responsible for the "fall" of many young women into prostitution:

> We see scores of unhappy girls who, on the heels of resisting the temptation of some venomous reptile, finally attend these parties in revealing blouses, half naked, showing off their natural beauty, shamelessly imitating obscene postures and, after dancing and feeling the effects of liquor, become intoxicated by the sweet talk of some schemer and give in, throwing themselves into the shameful mires of stultification and harlotry.[36]

Their analysis was conclusive: the Carnival embodied myriad social blights (lechery, prostitution, triviality, alcoholism, and ignorance, among others), prevented the rationalization of behavior, and squandered revolutionary energies.

Anarchists saw themselves as an educated, rational, and enlightened vanguard. They spoke in the name of health, high-minded conduct, dignified entertainment, and authentic laughter, which they counter-posed, in the words of a poem by Ghiraldo, to the Carnival's "malignant and repugnant laughter"— they celebrated "the fraternal laugh, the good laugh / that which satisfies noble bodies / currents of virtue that reinvigorate / the generous laugh / that elevates the spirit."[37]

Their opposition to festivities like the Carnival points to a profound contempt for the "unthinking masses," who had failed to swell the audiences at the *veladas* and who were, in libertarians' view, predisposed to follow their senses. They spared no depreciative adjective when describing these masses; they considered them "perpetual slaves of the Laconians, coarse and uneducated, an ignorant and pliant multitude, habitually drunk … submissive and timid workers … consumptive little producers withered by the factory."[38] They employed aggressive rhetoric of this sort not only in the context of the Carnival and other derided forms of entertainment, but also whenever they felt that the masses were ignoring their alternatives. Anarchists believed that the cathartic, unbridled revelry of the Carnival made it easier for people to go back to work in the factories and workshops, where they were exploited with impunity. They even argued that business owners, the government, and the church encouraged these types of recreational activities: they were "the first to promote such bacchanalia, knowing very well that it only takes three words to put the people to sleep: hunger, parties, and gallows."[39]

Anarchists' perfunctory analysis prevented them from understanding that even though the Carnival reinforced the system, it subverted it too. Some authors have described it as a "rite of inversion," in which signs of identity are lost behind the masks and charades. Rubén Darío grasped this after witnessing the Carnival in Buenos Aires in 1896:

> There are Marquises, Italian dukes, Spanish students, and Turkish chiefs. They are the revenge of the humble classes, a spontaneous and involuntary negation of democracy. The most twisted and crippled Neapolitan grocer becomes Adonis, a soldier, or a nobleman. A worker holds forth on anarchy and socialism more vehemently than any of his of comrades while walking around in disguise. Colonna or Doria of Barracas. Brave and excellent workers! They saved all year just to pass a few hours as Carnival princes. The muscular, steely legs of porters sheathed in colored stockings are visible among them, stout faces of the slums.

A decade later Emilio Becher ascribed a highly subversive meaning to the Carnival.[40] He argued that the external transformation of a mask produced a radical internal change that allowed people, in an insurgent theatrical moment, to insult and condemn their enemies. However, notwithstanding the claims of anthropologists and historians, anarchists did not define the phenomenon in such terms.[41]

Just before and during the Carnival every year, anarchist publications ran articles decrying the festivities, expressing their indignation at popular involvement in a rite that they believed contravened the rational spirit of the times. The Carnival was even a major adversary for some: "We include the Carnival among the numerous false institutions upon which we have declared war, one of the many that we must demolish."[42] Anarchist condemnation was not only rhetorical; they also attempted—with limited success—to discourage popular attendance by organizing anti-Carnival events and called several times for it to be boycotted. Lectures, public gatherings, and events or counter-events were weapons of symbolic warfare with which they intended to displace the ritual. They even put together "choral groups" modeled on groups that sang revolutionary songs in public plazas: when a crowd gathered, they launched into fiery speeches on the demerits of capitalism and the merits of anarchism. Anarchists were brave enough on occasion to take up the fight within the Carnival celebrations themselves: "Some bourgeoisie put together a masquerade that attempted a veiled ridicule of our comrades, but this was answered on the Carnival's eighth day with an allegorical carriage, covered in fabrics brilliantly painted by comrade Nardi that depicted revolutionary allegories."[43]

5. THE LIBERTARIAN CULTURAL MODEL

Although it appears that their anti-Carnival agitation did not catch on among the workers, libertarian discourse on the topic helps illuminate anarchist models of festivity and entertainment. Their recreational pastimes were to be pleasurable while also consolidating awareness among militants and winning new adepts to the cause. Furthermore, they were to symbolically bind anarchist codes with values that workers supposedly embraced, and exhibit the libertarian worldview to them. Anarchists' cultural alternative contained a critique of elite as well as popular culture. As Boris Fausto observed, ethical boundaries framed their perspective entirely: on the one hand, there were libertarian approaches to festivity (well-mannered, enlightened, healthy, and teetotaling) and, on the other, the degraded and banal, epitomized by the Carnival, creole circus [*circo criollo*], popular theater, and (later) soccer.[44]

Anarchists thought of their *veladas* as an alternative to both elite and popular variants of festivity. Although their template intersected with both models, it was closer to the former than the latter, insofar as its championed learned, erudite culture, which it appropriated and re-signified with content consistent with the libertarian doctrine. Anarchists who organized *veladas* were generally not workers but rather déclassé disseminators and spokespeople with a sort of double identity (simultaneously worker and intellectual). While their convictions aligned them in the camp of the oppressed, their cultural roots lay with erudite culture. It was from this vantage point that they sought to impact popular culture or—more precisely—workers' conduct, trying to mold their behavior and persuade them of the virtues of the anarchist model. Anarchist culture existed in an uneasy field of tension between cultural messages transmitted by the church, state, and school system, which also endeavored to edify popular sectors, and popular culture itself. Anarchists tried to undermine the influence of the establishment forces and transform popular culture.[45] The libertarian parties or *veladas*, with their songs, lectures, theatrical works, poetry readings, and family dances were spheres for processing anarchist culture and models for the workers, who were supposed to distance themselves from aspects of popular culture that were deemed regressive.

As their programs make clear, the *veladas* were long and sometimes overloaded with lectures and dramatic performances, although anarchists shortened them toward the end of the first decade in an effort not to wear out the audience. The structure and goals were invariable: the purpose was to educate those present about the ills of capitalism (proletarian oppression and misery, ruling-class immorality, etc.) and the well-being and freedom they would obtain in an anarchist future. The *velada* was always planned beforehand and consistently began with the collective singing of revolutionary anthems, preferably "The Sons of the People" or "The International." This was an attempt to bind the audience, and it was important insofar as singing the hymns indicated that the function had started. Revolutionary songs were integral to the workers' movement generally and anarchist events in particular, whether they occurred indoors or out of doors. They were not merely decorative, but a constitutive element of the cultural-political ritual that was the libertarian *velada*.[46] The songs, which were a counterpoint to the speeches, communicated anarchist convictions while interjecting a highly emotional note. "Sons of the people, chains oppress you / And that injustice cannot continue / If your existence is a world of grief / It is better to die than remain a slave"[47] were the opening lines of "Sons of the People," anarchists' favored anthem. The crowd sang standing, fists raised, typically accompanied by a band and choir, heightening the solemnity of the experience. The most common anthems were "Sons of the People" and "The International," but a wide range of their own and others' songs circulated and were performed. There was "Il Canto dei Ribelli" ["The Rebels' Song"], "Inno dei Malfatori" ["The Evildoers Anthem"], "Il Canto dei Lavoratori" ["The Toilers' Song"], "La Marseillaise," and "Il Canto degli Affamatti" ["Song of the Famished"]. They also adapted famous anthems like "La Bataille" ["The Battle"] to the bars of the "La Marseillaise" or the "Acrático" [Anarchic] and "Anárquico" [Anarchic] anthems to the music of the national anthem, whose second verse was replaced by:

Listen, mortals, it's the sacred shout
of anarchy and solidarity,
listen to the sound of bombs exploding
in defense of freedom.[48]

The symbolism of the anthems is clear. In addition to being an alternative to patriotic songs, they voiced libertarians' desire for the emancipation of the proletariat, to whom they held out a happy future in which the following would reign:

Progress, art, and science,
Justice, peace, and freedom,
Love and harmony among men
and a dawn of light and truth.[49]

There was also the critique of the church:

The vile clergy spits in your face.[50]

War against the class enemy:

The worker who suffer proclaims
… the defeat of the bourgeoisie is near.[51]

And of course opposition to government:

The oppressing governments
with unrivaled stupidity
make law upon law
fighting the ideal.[52]

The critiques acquired greater descriptive detail and a more forceful denunciatory tone in adaptations of popular rhythms like milongas and tangos, which anarchists and people connected to their networks seemed to have enjoyed, as indicated by the sale of revolutionary songbooks containing anarchist songs in these styles by the Sociological Bookstore and Bautista Fueyo's bookshop. While the tango was a specifically urban style, the milonga combined urban as well as rural elements, and its simple musical structure made it more adaptable than the tango. Anarchists appropriated these popular musical forms and grafted their own messages onto them: in clear, simple language, the lyrics of the libertarian milongas and tangos testified to the woes of the present society and their solutions. Like the anthems, the lyrics were didactic: they informed rural and urban workers that everything that they produce in exchange for their miserable salaries enriches the property owners, who hide behind the government and fatherland. But, in contrast to the universalism of anthem lyrics, those in this genre often referred to specifically Argentine realities. One song linked workers' exploitation and misery to the corruption and avarice of the rulers, who:

sold railroads
sold the fatherland as well;
exhausted all banks
and pawned the nation.[53]

The songs normally concluded on an optimistic note. They spoke of ending infamy through anarchy, and the abolition of the state, exploitation, borders, and "impious religion." They promised that:

> the priests and rulers
> that cause of our pain
> will be swept away any day now
> by the social revolution.[54]

And, with anarchy, the "light of freedom" will arrive and the land and tools will be owned and used by all.

In addition to adopting popular rhythms like the tango and the milonga, anarchists embraced other styles that were fashionable in Europe at the time, from solemn anthems to choral songs, from grandiose operatic arias to variety songs. Several pieces of music were normally performed at the beginning and end of each *velada* and during the intermission between the lecture and theatrical performance, or between these and the readings. There were romances, décimas, and, preferably and typically, arias of operas by Verdi or Puccini. "The tenor Patrone," *La Protesta* announced, "will sing parts from the *Manón Lescaut, La Boheme*, and *Fedora* operas."[55] The taste for lyric was deeply rooted among Italians, anarchist or otherwise. An old libertarian militant, who recalled that Italians were huge opera fans, said that "It's hard to even imagine an Italian community without a lyrical ensemble."[56]

Choruses and the duets were also commonplace, as were instrumental fragments from operas and symphonies. Anarchists were proud of their choral groups, and their bands and choral societies; they livened up the *veladas* with anything from anthems to popular rhythms of family dances (waltzes, paso doble, and polkas, etc.). The Libertarian Choral Society was prominent among the many short-lived musical groups: it performed at the most important anarchist parties and events between 1904 and 1910. When anarchists were unable to use their own musical groups, they turned to those from neighborhood or national associations, such as the Banda Musical from Barracas or the Spanish Choral Society.

Like song and music, readings were integral to the *veladas* and evidently well received. Also linked to the expressive strategies of elite culture, these rhetorical exercises were generally performed by children ("the Bongiorno girl," "the Reyes child," "little *compañera* Fernández"), who participated in the events as junior revolutionaries. In stern, resolute voices, they recited poetry ("To Anarchy," "Triumphant," "The Ideals," "No Mercy," "The First of May") or oppositional prose, condemning the behavior of dominant groups and extolling the proletariat. "That's why the workers," a child declaimed, "who are just meat for exploitation, raise a flag of struggle as an emblem of their yearning and prepare to choke their plunderers' arrogant throats, to deliver the crushing blow that will free them." Concluding praise was reserved for the libertarian vanguard: "the red libertarian multitude, a completely rebel world, advances, leaving behind the fateful shadows of Chicago, Buenos Aires, Montjuich, Milan, and hundreds of other touchstones; it pushes forward powerfully, imperceptibly."[57]

6. LIBERTARIAN THEATER

Theater was central to the libertarian *velada*, especially in the latter part of the first decade. Like song and reading, it also served as written and oral propaganda. In fact, many anarchists thought that drama was a better means of propagandizing ideas than lectures and books because it embodied them physically and because the force emanating from the stage galvanized the audience. In their view, the fictive nature of the performance enhanced the message's didactic power, and the emotional climate that it generated brought spectators closer to the libertarian ideal while also entertaining them: "Last Sunday was a good day for propaganda," said *La Protesta Humana*. "Hundreds of comrades and their families gathered in the theater hall to enjoy some relaxing moments in an environment of friendship and shared aspirations."[58]

The growth of libertarian theater paralleled the emergence and maturation of Argentine national theater and, in fact, some libertarian dramatists (Ghiraldo, Sánchez, and González Pacheco) directed their work to the latter arena. The minor form, particularly the comedic sketch, became popular in the 1890s, while the major forms (rural, urban, social, and historical dramas) became part of national theater around the start of the century. Many dramatists and theatrical companies also surfaced at this time—by 1911, there were no less than fifteen theater halls operating in the Federal Capital.[59]

Anarchists integrated theater into their efforts between 1896 and 1897, as elements of *veladas* and as independent performances. Initially, they had only one theater company, the Ermete Zacconi Drama Academy, whose namesake was a famous Italian actor who visited the country in 1904.[60] It was performed only in Italian (since most of its members did not speak Spanish). During those years, anarchists staged works by well-known foreign authors like Hauptmann, Mirbeau, Sundermann, Urales, and Cavallotti. They began incorporating Argentine dramatists at the beginning of the century, generally propagandists, such as Felipe Layda, Talarico y Costa, C. D. González, Jorge San Clemente, Manual Anguera, A. M. Lanzoni, and Jaime Berseni. Libertarian theatrical offerings expanded notably after 1904. There was a rise in the number of dramatists and drama groups, which hovered around ten between 1906 and 1909. The quantity of performances also increased: The Gentlemen of the Ideal group alone put on thirteen performances between May 1905 and October 1906, raising $2,800 for *La Protesta* in the process.[61] The thought of "revolutionizing the people through art" gained numerous advocates, even if not all anarchists embraced it.[62]

The notion of the theater as propaganda reflected anarchists' conception of social art, an art committed to the cause of the oppressed as opposed to art-for-art's sake. Predicated on this definition and the binaries typical of anarchist discourse, they subsumed all art under one or two categories: commitment or evasion. They considered non-political art mere rhetoric or empty talk, and their critique implied a transformation of the meaning attributed to art, exchanging the concept of expressed beauty for the harsh self-assurance embodied in a slogan that was dear to anarchists: "The good is beautiful and the bad is ugly."[63] For anarchists, aesthetic values were meaningless if bereft of philosophical and social convictions, if the artist was not dedicated to the cause.[64] By adopting the idea of a social art, Argentine anarchists embraced a combative aesthetic in the service of revolution. "There must be an art for the people," said Alberto Ghiraldo "one that educates, instructs, and inspires noble sentiments."[65]

Libertarians' approach to theater implied a rupture with the professional drama circuit. "Bourgeois" theater depended on the economic structure generally and its salability in particular, whereas anarchist's principal concern with theater was not profit but the dissemination of ideas. Anarchists thus built an alternative to the commercial theater network, as we shall see, although the principal libertarian authors did not compose their plays for specifically anarchist audiences. Florencio Sánchez wrote his pieces for commercial theater, with the exception of his earliest works, *Ladrones* [*Thieves*] and *Puertas adentro* (1897), which he authored for performance in Uruguayan anarchist centers.[66] Alberto Ghiraldo, José de Maturana, and Rodolfo González Pacheco, the three major dramatists engaged in anarchist activism, premiered their dramas on Buenos Aires's main commercial stages. Indeed, they hoped to become nationally recognized playwrights, which required acceptance among the broader public and critics. Dramas that Ghiraldo and Maturana wrote during this time were performed in the mainstream theatrical circuit almost exclusively. Commercial theaters staged Ghiraldo's *Alas* (1904) and *Alma Gaucha* (1906); Pablo Podestá's company premiered the second and Guillermo Bataglia did so four years later. Even though drama critics disparaged his work, Ghiraldo was invited in 1910 to participate in the creation of the Sociedad Argentina de Autores Dramáticos (Argentine Society of Dramatic Authors, later Argentores), which he served as president from 1911 to 1913, indicating a degree of recognition among his peers. Something similar occurred with Maturana: Podestá's company premiered his *A las doce* [*At Twelve*] in the National Theater in 1906 and the rural drama, *La flor del trigo* [*Wheat Flower*], in the Apolo Theater on August 17, 1908. While González Pacheco's theatrical work belongs to a later period, he also wrote for the professional circuit. The Muiño-Alippi Company staged his first work, *Las víboras*, in the New Theater in 1916, although anarchists read and discussed his work and their papers often published it.[67] Nonetheless, their plays were not featured in the *veladas* nor were they members of the anarchist drama groups, even though

Maturana and Ghiraldo lectured regularly at anarchist events.

There were multiple reasons for this disconnection. For one, there was anarchists' well-known distrust of heterodox intellectuals, which, in Ghiraldo's case, was exasperated by his prominence in the movement and tendency to sing his own praises. Some fervently defended his *Alas*, but the majority objected to its unrestrained modernism and excessive symbolism.[68] Critics fixated on the contradiction between his passionate vindication of social art and the plot of *Alas*, a work that never captured the interest of libertarian drama groups. The problem was deeper with *Alma Gaucha* due to his incorporation of native Argentine discourse through Moreirist personages who served as archetypes of rebellion.[69] "There is an attempt to redeem Moreirist values," commented David Viñas, "through the mediation of an anarcho-populist rebellion that exalts the savagery represented by the gaucho character, Cruz."[70] As noted previously, many anarchists rejected the celebration of the gaucho and Ghiraldo's views about the importance of regional particularities for art were probably also a source of dissonance. Like González Pacheco and Maturana, Ghiraldo thought that each people (from every region) had its own unique art—this included Argentines, hence his exaltation of the gaucho. Given the libertarian's propensity toward generic archetypes (the bourgeoisie, the worker, the priest, the soldier, etc.), his beliefs about the particularities and peculiarities of each people jarred with—and, to some, contradicted—libertarian precepts.[71]

Anarchists' approach to theatrical performance raised truly vexing issues: specifically, the designation of dramatists, actors, and directors, and their respective roles. Ghiraldo rejected authorial improvisation, which was dear to anarchists. Seeing himself as an heir to Ibsen's theater of ideas, he envisioned himself as a nationally-celebrated dramatist, performed by the best companies, who supplied his redemptive art to the workers and opened their minds. By contrast, anarchist drama groups adhered to assumptions held widely in the anarchist movement and, in that sense, were doctrinally "purer": their approach, whose roots can be found in Amadeo Dejacque's *Humanisferio*, reflected the notion that theatrical performance is natural to all individuals, given humanity's innate need to express itself. This led them to suppose that anyone could be an artist (an actor or dramaturge) if only the potentiality to do so was awoken within them. They argued that anyone could put on a play so long as he or she was drawn to performance, had voluntarily decided to participate in a production, and was committed to building a non-professional, theatrical circuit. This seemed tenable in the context of the great variety of short pieces and linear content staged in the Buenos Aires's libertarian scene: sketches, farces, short social dramas, *juguetes cómicos*, *petit piezas*, dialogues, interludes, monologues, symbolic portraits, and comedic and social fantasies. They saw theater as a means of direct communication with the audience and an act of collective creation, which, in fact, it was if we consider its actual operation just prior to the Centenary. From this perspective, theater was *from*, *for*, and *by* the people, whereas Ghiraldo endorsed a theater *for* the people but *from* and *by* the playwright. Nonetheless, these differences were not manifest in the content of the works: with the exception of his regional perspective, Ghiraldo shared other anarchist dramatists' predilection for melodramatic tones and characters that were archetypical and binary.

Anarchists' commitment to a free theater was another matter. Amateur actors—libertarian militants and sympathizers, generally—volunteered to participate in the productions and made up the drama groups. Anarchists believed that the performances encouraged cooperation and the emergence of collective sensibilities, despite the fact that the vast majority of the actors were male (organizers' hopes notwithstanding). Some families apparently resisted women's participation in an activity considered extremely advanced. "Female comrades are enthusiastic, but cannot take part, except in rare circumstances," lamented *La Protesta,* "because their fathers, boyfriends, comrades, and brothers stop them from doing so."[72]

The group selected a work and read and discussed it. They were usually simple pieces, due to the use of rudimentary stages and the near impossibility of acquiring materials necessary for sufficient set design. Then they distributed the roles, from the director to the actors, and rehearsed briefly, during which the "actor-militants" tried to memorize their lines and master the appropriate delivery and declamation. Evidently the results were usually quite poor, judging from comments in the libertarian press. Some charged those involved with carelessness and theatrical ignorance and there were frequent complaints about the actors, who appear to have been almost universally deficient: "From an artistic point of view … the productions premiered in the matinee left a lot to be desired."[73] Though devoted and willful, the actors lacked experience, improvised excessively, forgot their lines, mimicked in an exaggerated manner, and read poorly.

Problems also arose with the playwrights. While aesthetic or content-related qualms might arise when staging acclaimed dramaturges like Ibsen, Mirbeau, Urales, or Hauptmann, things became more complex with amateur dramatists. Anarchists applied the idea of collective creation to the composition of plays and encouraged sympathizers and militants to write dramas that would educate and enlighten the workers: "Our mission," said a member of The Gentlemen of the Ideal drama group, "is to teach those ignorant people."[74] Numerous amateur playwrights emerged from activist circles, most of whom never saw their "works" performed due to poor writing and occasionally incoherent premises and plots: "Sometimes dramatists turn up with improbable, artificial, uninteresting plays that are supposed to be social because someone burns down a factory, torments a bourgeois, or knocks around a priest, all of this in three or four acts and countless scenes."[75] Some resistance to free theater and excessive dramatic spontaneity emerged among anarchists: responding to this issue, and the shortage of original scripts, the Seed drama group organized a "literary artistic" competition in order to improve the quality of plays composed in Argentina. They did not reject free theater, but called for a greater commitment to study and rehearsal and a distribution of roles that was more consistent with participants' abilities. The effective propagation of ideas, they argued, required a good script, competent acting, and an audience that is delighted and entertained.[76]

The thematic content of libertarian theater was invariable. It was internationalist, like nearly all of the movement's discursive production, and the country or region in which the proceedings took place was only rarely identified (Ghiraldo's *Alma Gaucha* being an exception). The temporal framework was also typically unclear, framed by capitalism, but with ambiguous socio-political processes, other than the customary references to popular rebellions and the repression that followed. The subject matter and forms did not change over the years.

Anarchists cared little about dramatic or aesthetic nuance. It was not the artistry of the scenes but the dialogue—the effective, forceful expression of the message—that mattered to them. This is one of the sources of their proclivity for histrionic, demonstrative language. Indeed, their plays relied on the word and they paid scant attention to visual accessories, although actors' performances were extremely important to them. Underscoring this, angry comments followed the poor performances during the premiere of Federico Urales's *Ley de Herencia* [*Law of Heredity*]: "In our view, *Ley de Herencia* depends on the tight movement of the characters and on the script being well-spoken."[77] Ideally, the actors, in an intertextual operation, should verbalize libertarian theories. Libertarian theater was a social theater that tried to transform spectators by identifying problems and showing that society would inevitably evolve toward a harmonious, anarchist future.[78]

The libertarian repertoire was unoriginal, repetitive, and uniform in its exposition of ideals of social redemption. Characters were Manichean and archetypal, and dialogues and monologues laden with ideology and allegories. For example, each character in Palmiro de Lidia's *El acabóse* [*The Worst*] embodied a specific social type and bore the corresponding accoutrements: the people in rebellion raising their work tools represented justice, virtue, freedom, and fraternity; the three individuals associated with institutions that oppress the working class represented the bad: the general (the army) with his sword, the bishop (the church) with his silver crucifix, and the judge (the law) with his ornately bound law books.

The dramas revealed a world divided between exploited and exploiters, typically lacking in nuance or originality in the depiction of oppressor-oppressed relationship. The duality was characteristic of anarchists' enunciation of "a system that structures all, that operates on all levels of the sentence," which became immutable due to the Manicheanism inherent in anarchist thought.[79] There were "characters who were absolutely good and pure; identified with the working class and the subjugated, counter-posed to the villains, capitalists, bosses, strikebreakers, and authorities."[80] These binaries framed a wide range of social relationships, always expressing domination. There was sexual oppression in male-female relations: in Joaquín Dicenta's *El crimen de ayer* [*Yesterday's Crime*], a man seduces a woman, fathers her children, and then leaves her. The forsaken mother kills her lover, not because of infidelity but because he abandoned their children and deprived them of his name.[81] Stories of men (the exploiters) who took advantage of women (the exploited) were common, though their endings varied. When the wrongdoer was remorseful, he usually escaped punishment and was redeemed, although in other plays he did not acknowledge any culpability at all. Antimilitarism manifest itself in the civilian-soldier opposition; in his drama *El héroe*, Santiago Rusiñol describes the iniquities and perversions of barrack life and their effects upon conscripts at the mercy of sadistic officers.[82] Pietro Gori's *Senza Patria* [*Without a Country*], which premiered in Argentina in 1899, built upon this idea—Gori portrayed the merits of a world without borders, contrasted to the failings of the army and the fatherland.[83] The bourgeoisie-proletariat conflict was also a topic in many works; among them Hauptmann's social drama *Los tejedores* [*The weavers*] was a favorite of libertarian audiences. It told the story of the 1844 rebellion of the weavers of Silesia, who had grown tired of their misery and oppression. The plot didactically celebrated the process through which the workers emerged as a collective force and their acquisition of the deep social awareness necessary for a confrontation with capitalism.[84] For libertarian playwrights, proletarian rebellion was a consequence of the bosses-bourgeoisie's excessive exploitation of innocent workers—they frequently emphasized the binary, good/bad character of the labor relation. In Llana y Rodríguez's *El pan del pobre* [*Bread of the Poor*], an employer wickedly exploits the workers, relentlessly pushing them to revolt.[85] Convinced of individuals' transformative capacity, anarchists believed that social redemption was not only collective but also an individual task. In *Redimida* [*Redeemed*], by the Argentine Felipe Layda, an orphan is compelled to become a prostitute, but redeems herself by using the money she earns to finance an education (i.e., for enlightenment), which allows her to access more dignified spheres of society and stop selling her body.[86]

Generally speaking, these were the topics treated in Argentine libertarian theater. Formally, it was unoriginal, constituted by melodramatic resources taken from late Romanticism, realism, and newspaper serials. The principal protagonists were usually workers, who were always desperately exploited and on the verge of rebellion, much like romantic heroes straining under the pressure of powerful enemies. While libertarian dramatists sometimes depicted defeat, their emphasis was usually on the moral victories of the oppressed: a people in revolt may be crushed, female proletarians might become prostitutes, the workers may take the wrong path, but victory inevitably awaits at the end of the road, when the victims finally become aware of their exploitation and vanquish their oppressors. This optimistic view of social transformation linked libertarian theater to the realist aesthetic and distanced it from naturalism to a degree, although both idioms intermingled at times. Anarchists loved and admired Emile Zola, but criticized naturalism for its defeatism, for its fatalistic characters, and for offering an anatomical or photographic image of society.[87] By contrast, they embraced realism because it went beyond mere description, subordinating artistic questions to an analysis of the causes of social problems and human behavior, which in turn were subordinated to the goal of social transformation. Local anarchists' admiration for realist writer Octave Mirbeau expressed this perspective: "In his work, everything is just as it is, whether or not it offends: if there is brutality, it is because it exists; if perversion and cruelty emerge and are repugnant, it is because they persist; if there is pus or blood, that is because it pours from the open, rotting wounds."[88] Social ills had to be shown in the crudest possible way to rouse the dormant consciences in the audience and enlist them in the anarchist cause.

Who made up the audience at the libertarian theater? Was it workers or only devotees and sympathizers? Anarchists believed that dramas—and the *veladas* generally—were crucial to encouraging association and shared ties among those inspired by anarchism. And it was precisely these people who comprised the audience: individuals with a basic knowledge of anarchist ideas, probably activists and sympathizers who occasionally brought along a co-worker. It was apparently the same people who attended the lectures and read the movement press. The growth in audience sizes reflected the increased participation of women and children: "a large number of women," commented one writer, "that half of humanity that our cause must conquer at all cost, put in an appearance, accompanied by their companions or fathers."[89] As with those attending the parties, anarchists expected a specific conduct from theatergoers, based on proper manners, respect, attentiveness, and silence and engagement at the appropriate moments. Apparently it was not easy to create these model spectators, judging from journalists' recurrent complaints about unseemly behavior: some "laugh and talk aloud," *La Protesta* grumbled, just when the "drama's sad scenes move the heart to weep,"[90] others, said *The Rebel*, "transgress the interests of propaganda, good will, and the audience generally," when they "make everyone victim of their juvenile insolence" and ruin the event.[91]

Needless to say, anarchist theater did not draw the massive audiences that could be found at the circus or one-act farces. It was probably also a different audience, one that did not attend public events indiscriminately, although some likely took in performances of the emerging national theater, watching plays by

Florencio Sánchez, José de Maturana, García Velloso, Nicolás Granada, and others. Anarchists' interests were qualitative: they were not attempting to compete with commercial theater or popular spectacles, but to attract an audience of militants and potential militants. Indeed, attending a libertarian theatrical performance was itself an act of commitment, given that tickets generally cost the same as they did at the commercial theater (as noted previously, activists hoped that these performances would raise money for anarchist undertakings). Likewise, when plays were part of a *velada*, this meant that the attendees not only witnessed a performance but also participated in a militant function in which songs were sung and lectures delivered. It was essentially an affair for initiates.

Considering this, it appears that the audience was substantial, even if it probably did not extend beyond anarchist networks. Excepting periods of martial law, there were approximately four performances in the city of Buenos Aires every month during the opening decade of the century, although sometimes as many as nine or as few as one or two. In part, these rates reflect the fact that performances only occurred on weekends—the audience and the majority of the actors were workers and thus mid-week shows were impractical—and also suggest that anarchists understood that there were not enough devotees to justify holding more than one performance at a time. There was an average of 500 spectators at each, though occasionally more than 1,000 or just around 100; there were roughly 2,000 attendees monthly or 24,000 annually. In keeping with the growth of libertarian influence, these figures rose slightly toward the end of the decade.[92] The modest increase in the size of the audience evidences workers' level of interest and also inadequate promotion, which was restricted to the anarchist press and, less frequently, posters. Commenting on the slender profits garnered by recent gatherings, one writer said: "There are various reasons for this, but the main issue is the lack of promotion. Most groups and societies publish the program in *La Protesta* and leave manifestos on whatever corner, which makes it extremely difficult to find the program." The author called for reaching beyond the newspaper's readership.[93]

Based on the concept of solidarity among the oppressed, anarchists constructed a small but significant alternative cultural space from which they transmitted their messages as an oppositional, enlightened, and rational vanguard. That space had to create and recreate activities that would occupy workers' free time, a free time viewed as productive time and not mere leisure. They also helped generate and model a workers' audience, one that attended the lectures and theatrical performances and supposedly stayed away from unsavory sites like the Carnival, café, and tavern. However, their alternative did not grow as the organizers had expected it to, fueled by social discontent: it appears that most workers who participated in the strikes and street protests did not embrace anarchists' cultural projects. They did not take the step from simply protesting to making the militant commitment to "*give up ignorance.*"

There are multiple reasons for this. In the first place, Buenos Aires was in the midst of massive changes, in which instability and fluctuation complicated the constitution of a coherent social subject. Ascendant and descendent social mobility tended to make the barriers between groups very porous which, in addition to the limited development of industry, hindered the articulation of a common workers' identity. Thus, urban society at the beginning of the century had a working class in formation and transformation, and this doubtlessly hampered anarchists' ability to popularize their cultural alternative.

The customs and fragmented traditions that Buenos Aires workers bore also played a part. They were a heterogeneous mix of internal migrants and—especially—immigrants from around the globe, and their prior experiences were as diverse as their national origins, although they shared habits linked to the tavern, drink, popular dance, the circus, Greco-Roman wrestling, festivities like the Carnival, as well as novel forms of recreation like soccer and cinema, which made themselves felt later. It is likely that most workers preferred lighter entertainment than that offered by the *veladas*, with their heavy ethical content, emotional density, and repeated calls for the destruction of a capitalist system that seemed to enjoy excellent health. This would help explain the relative success of anarchists' rural retreats and picnics. Surely the open space of the forests of Palermo, Maciel Island, or some suburban estate offered an attractive freedom of movement. While these outings replicated the song-lecture-drama format, they were interspersed with dance, hearty lunches, sack races, obstacle course games, "thread the needle for the girls," and soccer. Open-air gatherings had a slightly more balanced combination of productive free time and recreation.

Workers (and non-workers) interested in "serious" culture also had a wide range of institutions at their disposal (socialist, union, neighborhood, parochial, and educational), as well as a large quantity of amateur drama groups, whose offerings had a great deal in common with what anarchists provided. Obviously the libertarian's *velada* partook of this broader context and competed for (and sometimes shared) the audiences with other tendencies. The cultural model embodied in the *velada* was a presence in political and neighborhood centers up to the rise of Peronism.

It is also important to understand the limited popularity of anarchist recreational activities in the context of the explosive growth of the culture industry throughout the decade. It expanded dramatically, as other spectacles complemented the circus and wrestling, which were once forms of entertainment enjoyed exclusively by popular sectors. Soccer and cinema became prominent, drawing 2.5 million spectators in 1909. The national theater took off during those years and the number of theater halls almost doubled between 1906 and 1911. There were cinema and theater houses in El Centro, Boca, and Barracas and in remote neighborhoods like Once, Flores, Belgrano, and Villa Crespo; the same is true of soccer, whose neighborhood context was already undeniable. The growth of the culture industry bore a direct relation to a reduction in the price of circus spectacles, cinema, and theater, which allowed viewers to enter paradise for the price of a ticket. The City of Buenos Aires's 1910 census corroborates the trend: between 1900 and 1909, the number of attendees at diverse spectacles multiplied eightfold, exceeding eight million by the latter date.[94] Many of the attendees were presumably more privileged workers who, encouraged by having Sundays off, perhaps visited the spectacles monthly.

The construction of a libertarian cultural alternative did not occur in a vacuum but paralleled the creation of a culture industry that quickly attracted a popular audience. It was appealing because it focused on entertainment and amusement, during which the worker could momentarily forget his or her sundry problems (the risk of unemployment, a salary that did not cover living expenses, educating the children, the cost of a trip to one's native country or bringing over family members who had remained, etc.). The workers, or at least a significant portion, supported strikes and protest demonstrations when they looked likely to yield material benefits, but preferred to spend their leisure time on more superficial pastimes than the libertarian's "serious and rational" offering, where recreation and free time were seen as productive time and engaged with the libertarian doctrine.

No intelligent person could be unaware of the impact of the press.
—*La Protesta*, June 26, 1906

CHAPTER V

The Anarchist Press

IN THE PREVIOUS chapter, I explained the importance of lectures, theater, and the publication of books and pamphlets as means of anarchist propaganda. Disseminating the written word through newspapers was also central to their political and ideological strategies and their cultural apparatus as a whole. Indeed, one could argue that newspapers were their most powerful tool.

Pellicer Paraire expressed some of the reasons for this:

> The study circle gathers forward-thinking individuals, educates them, harmonizes them, and creates the elemental revolutionary force; the libertarian school molds the new army that will fight for our emancipatory ideals until victory; the pamphlet, broadsheet, and book instruct the people and familiarize them with new ideas and the need for their realization ... but the libertarian newspaper has all of these beautiful qualities and goes even further; just like the school, circle, and pamphlet, it instructs, illuminates, and harmonizes, but even more efficiently.[1]

Libertarians wrote countless articles on the utility of the press and its influence on public opinion.[2] They set out to create an alternative journalistic arena that was directed to workers primarily. It would challenge their supposed passive consumption of "bourgeois" papers and engage people who did not typically read the press. At the cost of tremendous effort, they published incalculable newspapers and magazines that became a conspicuous part of the landscape of fin-de-siècle Buenos Aires, although they did not manage to attract the bulk of workers and their readers came largely from within the anarchist movement.

1. THE CONTEXT

The publication of ideological and political texts has been crucial to political life since the French Revolution. *The Declaration of the Rights of Man* established the free expression of ideas as a fundamental prerogative of individuals as such: all men are entitled to speak, write, and publish their views. It was solely the bourgeoisie that exercised this privilege before the revolutions of 1848, when access to the press (and advertising) typically required education and property. But non-bourgeois strata, especially workers, entered politics and its institutions, including the press. As Habermas has shown, there was a dramatic growth in readers and a transformation of the basic meaning of the press.[3]

Modern political groups and parties used their papers to organize and coalesce supporters, disseminate and define their views, and to do battle against competitors. They simply could not have existed without them. In Argentina, the press also played a vital role by enlisting people in the processes of urbanization and industrialization underway in the latter half of the nineteenth century. As Mirta Lobato explained: "Journalism as an activity allowed speakers and writers to exercise a type of political leadership and social influence, and was also a means for constituting a body of representations about the new country and its citizens, including immigrants."[4]

There was an expansion of the public sphere after the Battle of Caseros in 1852, when the press took on a new vitality and centrality to politics. As an arena of debate and political contest, newspapers typically needed political sponsorship to survive, a fact that also facilitated the integration of journalists and national associations into political life.[5]

Modern newspapers appeared in the country between 1870 and 1880. Their point of departure was the publication of *La Capital* from Rosario (1867), *La Prensa* (1869), *La Nación* (1870), and *El Diario* (1881), as well as the first cable service to Europe, which Havas, a French firm, established in 1877. Coinciding with national unification and the concordant economic growth and social diversification, publications with graphics expanded rapidly, although not so much the size of print runs as the number released and their thematic diversity.[6] The press was remarkably advanced by the turn of the century, but papers tended to come and go quickly—notwithstanding the tireless efforts of their publishers—and the metamorphosis of large newspapers into capitalist businesses was the overriding trend. The papers modernized their appearance, incorporated the latest technologies, and utilized novel strategies like multiple editorial departments, foreign correspondents, telegraphic agencies, and more flexible approaches to information.[7]

Scores of periodicals burst upon the scene as the market expanded, immigrants arrived, and literacy spread. There were dailies, weeklies, biweeklies, monthlies, and magazines; the topics covered ranged from general reportage to trade-specific information, from ethnic and political publications to those focusing on religion, comedy, literature, current events, finances, economics, sports, etc.

A broad arena of popular engagement with reading had taken shape around 1900. Newspapers were decisive in the construction of the new public reader, but this was only possible because of the dramatic rise in literacy levels. Though impressive in the late nineteenth century, the increases were particularly striking in the beginning of the twentieth. For instance, as an indication of the general tendency, between 1905 and 1914 the number of elementary students surged from 122,144 to 203,756 in the province of Buenos Aires and from 118,151 to 190,317 in the capital.[8] The expanded reading audience provided a seemingly inexhaustible reservoir for the new political and ideological tendencies also emerging at the time.

Thousands of workers became readers, encouraged, in part, by the countless publications that spoke to them in some capacity—from the large newspapers to innumerable journals and magazines that specialized in current events, politics, literature, sports, science, religion, etc. *Martín Fierro*, and the gaucho-themed literature derived from it, also made a notable contribution by incorporating the common man into reading, as Adolfo Prieto has shown. While it is difficult to know if anarchists and socialists grasped the depth of the transformations that were underway, they clearly recognized the fertility of the arena, since publications addressed exclusively to workers did not exist. Indeed, the growth of the socialist and anarchist movements was directly linked to the development of the workers' press.

2. ANARCHISM AND THE FREEDOM OF THE PRESS

In addition to expanded literacy, two additional circumstances greatly favored the extension of anarchist publishing: the relatively low cost of printing and distributing literature and the existence of a free press, without which it is extremely difficult to express opinions that the government and elites find "dangerous." Unlike the political press during the final decades of the nineteenth century, which helped topple government coalitions but did not challenge their institutional foundations, anarchist newspapers set out to overthrow "bourgeois" institutions themselves, even if their ambitions remained primarily on the discursive plane. In point of fact, their fiery rhetoric and aggressive attitude toward the state notwithstanding, the anarchist press was able to express itself largely unmolested in the movement's early years. This changed during the strikes of 1902 when anarchist discourse and worker discontent began to fuse, leading authorities to start censoring ideas and restricting oppositional publications.

Article Thirty-Two of Argentina's Constitution decreed the freedom of the press; it prohibited any interference from the parliament or the executive power. In the 1870s, when the anarchist press appeared, most newspapers were factious and partisan and criticized opponents harshly and freely, publishing what today would be considered slander. The press generally escaped government meddling, although crossing certain lines sometimes resulted in punishment. For instance, authorities shut down the *La Nación* newspaper in 1874, 1890, 1893, and 1901—in the latter year simply for objecting to the unification of the national debt.[9] Anarchist publications were perpetually on the margins of the permissible and, despite occasional calls to ban them, authorities were generally tolerant and did not persecute them.

Official attitudes changed as social conflict exploded in late 1901 and the government came to see anarchists as central actors in the turmoil and its newspapers as instigators of the rebellion. The imposition of martial law, reinforced by the approval and application of the Residency Law, gave the government legal tools with which to silence the oppositional press. It closed *La Protesta* five times between 1902 and 1910: between November 22, 1902 and January 31, 1903, when there was martial law during the strikes on the port and in the Central Fruit Market; from February 5 to May 14, 1905, during the Radical Party's uprising; from October 8 of that year to January 1, 1906, when martial law was decreed during the October 7 general strike; from November 14, 1909 to January 16, 1910, after a young Russian anarchist assassinated Police Chief Ramón L. Falcón; and, finally, from May 13, 1910 until late 1911, as a result of Centenary festivities and the wave of repression that followed them. Likewise, as occurred with the press generally, the government periodically seized copies of *La Protesta*, even when it had not decreed martial law, if it objected to an article's tone or content.

Debates about limiting press freedoms grew more spirited as the government saw it, increasingly, as a threat. Interior minister Joaquín V. González declared the press was a menace because of its effect on the "most numerous classes," and argued that authorities should step in when it fails to moderate itself. He issued a warning as soon as martial law was lifted in 1904: "We remind the press that it is duty-bound to effect the utmost composure, to draw inspiration from patriotic ideals, and, when popular sentiments turn against the concept of government, be sure to direct them toward the noble causes of liberty and national defense."[10]

As the conflict escalated and anarchists' prominence among workers blossomed, a consensus emerged in the government about the need to limit the press. In 1908, Buenos Aires Police Chief Colonel Ramón L. Falcón proposed a law curtailing oppositional groups' freedom of speech, a notion to which he had been committed for some time. He justified it with the following allegation: "Some socialist and anarchist newspapers have crossed the line, articulating their ideas in ardent articles that are seditious as well as senseless, openly advocating attacks on property, assassination, plunder, and arson." After declaring that such publications could not be tolerated, he claimed that they were responsible for common crime, and, as a result, banning them did not violate the Constitution's Article Thirty-Two.[11] His argument rested upon an edict issued by the attorney general granting police the right to impede the circulation of anarchist publications if they incite public disorder.

The anarchist movement responded by immediately forming a Freedom of the Press committee. Constituted by eleven libertarian groups (Life and Work, To Destroy is to Create, Iron, May First, On March, Freedom Lovers, Friends of the Worker, Evolution, Universal Family, *La Protesta* Russian Group, and International) and three resistance societies (Sandal Makers, Sign Makers, and Shoe Makers), the committee organized rallies and public meetings against police machinations.[12] However, it was the reaction of the broader public, which regarded the proposed law as an abhorrent violation of the freedom of expression, that was most decisive in defeating the initiative. The newspaper *La Razón* argued that the measure threatened the freedom of speech generally, since it gave police unlimited power, which was "repugnant to liberal sentiments and contrary to the progress of thought." The paper, which was not at all sympathetic to anarchists, also questioned the breath and ambiguity of the concept of "disorder" and attacked the notion that anarchist propaganda was subversive per se as a transgression of the freedom of thought. In the paper's view, only manifestations of anarchism that contravene the stated norms of the Constitution should be censored. In essence, *La Razón* saw the maneuver as a breach of the freedom of the press as a whole: "It intends to subject the pen to the sword," concluded the newspaper.[13] Its suspicions seemed to be confirmed after the "Red Week" of May 1909 when Colonel Falcón again called for limiting the oppositional press, while also charging many commercial papers (*El País*, *La Argentina*, *El Diario*, *El Nacional*, and *Última Hora*) with "preaching subversion" because they had taken issue with police actions during the bloody events—even though their criticisms had far more to do with opposition to Figueroa Alcorta's government than solidarity with the strikers. Authorities were also irritated by gestures like the one made by the newspaper *La Argentina*, which asked the Strike Committee for permission to publish and transport its paper normally, implicitly recognizing the Committee's authority.[14]

While that particular attempt to restrict the freedom of expression miscarried, the government was more successful with the Social Defense Law, which was approved in mid-1910 as a means to suppress the anarchist movement. Its Article Twelve stipulated sentences of one to three years for those who "publicly defend crime, either verbally, through writing, printing, or any other means or deed" and, basically resuscitating Falcón's stratagem, it granted police power to censor and castigate whomever and whenever they wanted.[15]

Availing itself of the climate of intolerance around the Centenary, the government managed to limit the freedom of expression without inciting the public's ire. By linking the restriction of ideas to the exigencies of public security, the men ruling Argentina thought that they had found a viable legal formula. The application of this law silenced the libertarian press for most of 1910 and part of the following year, and visibly curbed public freedoms.[16] It was also the first step in a series of actions in which the state, in the name of public security, became increasingly belligerent toward the freedom of expression. During the period of martial law in 1910, authorities looked on as armed gangs of civilians attacked anarchist and socialist centers, damaging these institutions and their presses, anticipating the anti-democratic practices that would grow even more severe after the tragic week of 1919.

3. THE LIBERTARIAN PUBLICATIONS

The government inflicted serious damage on libertarian periodicals every time it shut them down during periods of martial law. It not only disturbed their publication schedules but also frequently confiscated subscription lists and arrested and deported publishers, who were often difficult to replace. But, nonetheless, anarchists were able to publish and articulate themselves without restriction for most of the period examined in this book.

The first anarchist (and socialist) periodicals appeared during the explosion of publishing in the late 1870s and early 1880s. Between 1879, when *The Wretch*, the earliest-known libertarian periodical was released, and 1890, an assortment of short-lived broadsheets with limited print runs circulated. Many were published in foreign languages and reproduced the content of European broadsheets. For instance, there was *La Liberté*, a Kropotkinite weekly put out by Pierre Quiroule in 1893, which faithfully reprinted articles published in the French libertarian press. There was also *The Social Question*, which Errico Malatesta published in 1885, during his time in the country. It duplicated material from its namesake in Florence and largely consisted of doctrinal articles and diatribes against the republicans of *L'Amico del Popolo* [*The Friend of the People*]. Only ten issues appeared before Malatesta shut it down in the face of the apparent disinterest of the Italian community (to whom it was directed) and *L'Amico del Popolo*'s refusal to respond. It had lasted only three months.[17] However, beginning in 1890, publications began to acquire a certain presence and durability. Between that year and 1896, the Dispossessed group published 102 issues of *The Persecuted*, which became the principal, generally regular newspaper of the individualist, anti-organizational tendency. Its print run fluctuated between 2,000 to 4,000, making it the most influential libertarian publication of the time.[18] *The Oppressed*, whose purpose was to polemicize against the individualists of *The Persecuted*, also had a degree of continuity; Dr. Juan Creaghe published its thirty-five issues between 1894 and 1897, initially in Luján and later in Buenos Aires.

These periodicals upset a census taker in 1895: "All social interests are represented in the Argentine Republic," he said, "even socialism and anarchism, like a black mark on the sun of progress!"[19] Others, particularly those who understood that the libertarian press constituted only a small portion of publications released in Buenos Aires, found the phenomenon less worrisome.[20] The first feminist newspaper in the country, *The Woman's Voice*, appeared in 1896 and, as previously mentioned, was a combative broadsheet that came out for ten issues before folding under the pressure of financial difficulties and, possibly, the antipathy it evoked among many male activists. Between 1897 and 1903, there were three relatively regular publications, whose aggregate print runs were between 6,000 and 9,000 (to cite the lowest credible estimate), that became the backbone of the anarchist movement during those years.[21] First, there was *La Protesta Humana,* which lost the qualifier "Humana" in 1903.[22] Second, there was *The Rebel*, which came out from November 11, 1898 until May 28, 1903. It was the main adversary of *La Protesta Humana* and the pro-organizational tendency generally; it was weekly and biweekly alternately, with a print run vacillating between 2,000 and 3,000 copies. *The Future* was the third consequential publication; its position was similar to that held by *La Protesta Humana*, with whom it battled against the anti-organizationalists. It came out weekly from 1896 to 1904, when it stopped publishing in order not to duplicate *La Protesta*'s efforts. It published a total of 249 issues in Italian.

More than a few Italian-language newspapers and magazines circulated in the 1890s, as well as some that were bilingual. The quantity dropped substantially in the following decade due to the increase in the percentage of Spanish libertarians and the relative "Argentinization" of the anarchist movement—a process reflecting the presence of numerous Argentine-born activists as well as anarchism's growing roots among native workers. But, nonetheless, given that a large number of Italian workers did not read Spanish, *La Protesta* published a daily column in Italian in 1907 and 1908 until the columnist (Roberto D'Angio) was deported under the Residency Law. *La Protesta* discontinued the feature after being unable to find an Italian-speaker to replace him, a fact that underscores the "Argentinization" of the anarchist movement, especially among its disseminators.[23]

There were also magazines like *Social Science* or the annual *Illustrated Almanac* of *The Social Question*, both of which had particularly rich graphic and editorial content. The tireless Fortunato Serantoni directed *Social Science*, subtitled "a magazine of sociology, arts, and letters," which was the best theoretical publication produced by local anarchists during the four years of its existence. It included articles by the usual European thinkers—William Morris, Élisée Reclus, Sébastien Faure, Errico Malatesta, Jean Grave, and Carlos Malato, etc.—as well as domestic authors such as Altair, Julio Molina y Vedia, Félix Basterra, and Juan Creaghe. The publication featured a portrait and biography of an influential thinker for anarchists in every issue: Grave, Malato, Faure, Morris, and Hamón among others. It folded under economic pressures in 1901. The *Almanac Illustrated* was slightly more didactic but otherwise very similar; it included revolutionary songs and the characteristic calendar featuring events related to the workers' and libertarian movement instead of patriotic and religious anniversaries. Neither publication ran articles about local social issues.

The social conflict expanded during the remainder of the first decade and so did the anarchist press, although it was not so much the quantity of publications that was remarkable as their thematic variety, regularity, and print runs. Magazines on sociology, art, and letters multiplied (such as *Martín Fierro, The New Paths, Seed, Letras, The Lie,* and *Ideas and Figures*), which were energetically promoted by writers such as Alberto Ghiraldo, José de Maturana, Rodolfo González Pacheco, Juan Mas y Pi, Pierre Quiroule, Alejandro Sux, Julio Barcos, Santiago Locascio, and Fag Libert. Publications focused on education began to appear (*Modern School Bulletin, Francisco Ferrer,* and *The Popular School*) as well as anti-militarism (*The Barracks* and *The Soldier's Enlightenment*). There was even a short-lived cartoon magazine *(La Debacle)*.

The most important moment for the anarchist press during this time was *La Protesta*'s transformation into a daily, which occurred on April 1, 1904. With the exception of government closures during periods of martial law, *La Protesta* came out daily from that date until May 13, 1910, when it was shut down for more than eighteen months, only renewing regular publication in 1912.[24] Although it was host to innumerable internal quarrels and enormous financial challenges, it managed to survive because of a readership made up largely of devotees and sympathizers who remained faithful to the paper, despite its vicissitudes, presumably because of its doctrinal content and practice of social denunciation. It was more modern than other libertarian periodicals, which also helped it endure: it provided systematic reports on the workers' movement, with daily accounts of various conflicts; incorporated information received by telegraph; ran advertisements; was sold on the street, and published illustrated supplements like *Martín Fierro* (led by Ghiraldo between 1904 and 1906), and a monthly supplement for eleven months in 1908 (supplements became sporadic after this).

La Protesta was exceptionally long-running and consistent for an anarchist publication, although it operated at a much smaller scale than commercial papers like *La Prensa* and *La Nación*. Max Nettlau, the most distinguished chronicler of the global anarchist press noted that he knows of no other libertarian newspaper as long-lived as *La Protesta*, "a rare and notable phenomenon."[25] Its print run oscillated between 4,000 and 8,000 copies daily until 1909—figures that were far from stunning or satisfactory for its publishers—although the print run increased in early 1910 to roughly 16,000 copies. The greater demand, which was likely a consequence of the heightened turmoil and climate of discontent at the time, led the publishers to try to engage a portion of the evening market by releasing a second paper, *The Battle*, which came out in the late afternoon. According to Santillán, this is the only instance of a libertarian newspaper with a morning and an evening edition.[26] The paper, whose main editor was Rodolfo González Pacheco, was short-lived: it first came out on March 7, 1910, and could only publish twenty-six issues before it was closed along with *La Protesta*.

4. A WORKERS' OR ANARCHIST PRESS?

The anarchist press spoke to and drew sustenance from new readers. As noted, anarchists and socialists availed themselves of the expansion and diversification of the reading audience and raised issues from the world of labor for consideration, constructing an oppositional press that helped create a worker readership. However, the libertarian press was not specifically workerist, even though it was directed to workers, distributed at their meetings, lectures, workplaces, union congresses, and actions—and many subscribers were workers.

There was a series of union publications, which mostly leaned toward anarcho-syndicalist and kindred postures, focusing on specifically labor-related issues, whereas the anarchist press had a trans-class position. Libertarian newspapers generally concentrated on universal emancipation and privileged the diffusion of the basic principles of the libertarian doctrine. Although they provided information about the world of labor, they concentrated on topics such as individual freedom, the nature of the state, and especially science—the deus ex machina that would resolve all of humanity's problems. The lead editorial in *La Protesta Humana* is eloquent on this count. Addressed to all of the oppressed, it highlighted the redemptive role of science, which had helped identify society's challenges: "observation and study," it said, "have revealed the cause [authority] of the terrible ailments afflicting humanity" thereby illuminating reality and "making men conscious."[27] Anarchists viewed the newspaper itself as a scientific instrument in the service of emancipation and, despite the doctrinal discrepancies among them, all utilized a universalist, pseudoscientific discourse in which Darwinism, Spencerism, and neo-Malthusianism mixed. This was a mostly unoriginal perspective that they shared with the socialist press and even some "bourgeois" newspapers. At least some anarchists still read the latter, as indicated by complaints that appeared when Aníbal Latino took the mantle at *La Nación* in 1901. Militants bemoaned a drop in quality ("it has become excessively commercial") and a lack of tolerance ("it's a conservative mess"). "We've lost a decent bourgeois paper," they grumbled, and called upon workers to stop reading it.[28]

In 1900, editors of *La Protesta Humana* bewailed their own paper's neglect of "the workers and the labor movement,"[29] although the amount of space dedicated to labor increased over the ensuing decade as the social conflict intensified. *La Protesta Humana* and other newspapers (*The Future* and *The Rebel*, to a lesser extent) instigated and promoted union action. They reported on it and organized resistance societies and country-wide propaganda tours, like the one undertaken by Inglán Lafarga, editor-in-chief of *La Protesta Humana*, who spoke as a representative of the Argentine Workers' Federation in 1901. Nonetheless, they did not become labor newspapers, and the doctrinal content of the libertarian press did not change, even in papers like *The Future* and *La Protesta Humana*, which actively supported anarchist participation in the labor movement. There are good reasons to be skeptical of Abad de Santillán's claim that *La Protesta Humana*'s editors and contributors "were generally workers, who lived from the product of their labor and were in continuous contact with the working class."[30]

Although Inglán Lafarga, its first editor-in-chief, was a cabinet-maker and scores of workers—manual laborers, primarily—contributed, most of its writers in the first decade were literary types and intellectuals, whether purist or heterodox. Among the former: Santiago Locascio, Antonio Pellicer Paraire, Emilio Arana, Mariano Cortes (Altair), Alfredo López (Jean Valjean), Félix Basterra, Pascual Guaglianone, Carlos Balsán, Máximo Aracemi, Roberto D'Angio, Pierre Quiroule, Lorenzo Mario, and Eduardo Gilimón, who personally wrote more than six hundred articles for *La Protesta* between 1898 and 1910. The following individuals were among the heterodox: Julio Molina y Vedia, Federico Gutiérrez (Fag Libert), Alejandro Escobar y Carballo, Juan Carulla, Julio Barcos, Rodolfo González Pacheco, José de Maturana, Juan Mas y Pi, Alejandro Sux, and Alberto Ghiraldo.[31] These were the people who produced the newspaper, although readers played a dynamic role and occasionally had a very direct impact. Readers participated in different ways: from serving as judges in literary competitions to pressing editors by threatening to suspend their subscriptions when they disagreed with some viewpoint expressed.[32] Among the many responses to the readers, editors Mariano Forcat, Lorenzo Mario, and Eduardo Gilimón published an interesting piece in 1907 complaining about the "intemperance" of readers who cancel their subscriptions when opinions appear in the paper that contradict their own.[33] Clearly readers were actively involved in the anarchist press, although we do not have enough information to determine which ones were workers. Editors defined the overall doctrinal line and incidental pieces by readers-workers had a limited bearing on the overall identity of a specific periodical.

Spearheaded by Eduardo Gilimón, doctrinal purists responded aggressively when Alberto Ghiraldo became the editor-in-chief in 1904 and tried to put *La Protesta* at the service of the Argentine Workers' Federation. They wanted it to be independent, claiming that "the federation has anarchic overtones, but is fundamentally a labor organization, in which there are workers without sociological ideals and also socialists. *La Protesta* … runs the risk of ceasing to be an anarchist publication."[34] Frustration with Ghiraldo also grew when he attempted to negotiate an alliance between the FORA and the Socialist Workers' Union. Pressure from purists ultimately led Ghiraldo to depart two years later; they retook control of the newspaper and eliminated the editor-in-chief's position in order to bolster the power of the editorial department and allied circles.

Conflicts over the leadership of the paper were ongoing. With the exception of Gregorio Inglán Lafarga's long tenure—apart from a short leave, he directed it from its 1897 appearance until he was deported in 1902—the editor-in-chief's position changed hands frequently. The following men occupied the post between 1902 and 1906: Félix Basterra, Juan Creaghe (three times), Alcides Valenzuela, Elam Ravel, Eduardo Bianchi, and Alberto Ghiraldo. Other than the 1902 change, the replacements were the result of personal and ideological disputes. This was also the case with the composition of the editorial staff from 1906 onward, which constantly changed in response to battles within the movement. The anarchist movement's doctrinal breadth, lack of clear leadership structures, and freedom of initiative encouraged interpersonal skirmishes; in many cases, the desire for power and simple jealousy were as important as ideological disagreements. But *La Protesta* was the movement's most prestigious newspaper and its only daily, and those facts alone were enough to ensure that competing tendencies would fight to control it and make it a battleground for clashes between opposing lines.

Militants linked to the FORA and other union societies launched a new assault in 1908, in hopes of securing control over the paper. In a strategic move, they convened a large meeting to discuss *La Protesta*'s fate, at which they submitted a motion for a new Administrative Committee. More than 1,000 people endorsed their proposal, which meant, in essence, subordinating the publication to militants in the FORA's orbit. The editors (doctrinal purists) balked at the gesture and made it known that they would not relinquish editorial power under any circumstance. Raising the flag of ideological fidelity, they provocatively asked: "Should *La Protesta* continue cornered in the closed circle of unionism? Do these groups embrace the anarchic ideal or are they actually dissidents launching a veiled attack on our revolutionary tactics?"[35]

The doctrinal purists regained their supremacy and their opponents had no choice but to retreat and release their own publications, which were typically short-lived. As an example, in June 1908, under the leadership of Esteban Almada, a group of anarchists linked to the FORA began putting out *Light and Life*, which reported on the labor movement and supported the class struggle. It tried to do battle with *La Protesta*, but could only publish six issues before dissolving.

As a whole, the anarchist press—*The Rebel, The Future, Social Science, New Route*, and particularly *La Protesta*—were not workers' newspapers even if they were addressed to workers and read by some of them.

What content did the papers contain and who read them?

5. A DOCTRINAIRE AND IDEOLOGICAL PRESS

The anarchist press was fundamentally ideological and its goal was to transform the workers through an aesthetic-doctrinal message that was different from that articulated by the commercial, informational press. It sought to do this through a language privileging "discursive strategies of the sensible," that is, "a dialogue of sensations and sensibilities between the enunciator and the interlocutor."[36] The article titles themselves appealed to emotion—emphasizing, exclaiming, utilizing dramatic, sharp, and categorical phrases that were adjectival assessments, ideological definitions, and value judgments. "The Victims of the Horror"; "The Bloody Wake"; "Montjuich!"; "National Disaster"; "Redeemed"; "Bark, Dogs!"; "Those Catholic Circles!"; "Those Who Live from What Is Not Theirs," etc. There were also imperatives pressing readers to define themselves: "Be Men," "To Those Who Are Indifferent," "We Learn to Struggle," etc. In addition to having an emotional function, anarchist language played a "conative" role in which the "enunciator exerts pressure upon the interlocutor."[37]

Anarchist discourse tried to shake readers' inner fibers with histrionic, emotionally charged declarations: "Oh, bourgeois vampires! You, on one side, and Jesuitism on the other: you have robbed the people, condemning them to eternal suffering."[38] Their penchant for inflamed discourse often led them to employ extravagant terminology and affected expressions that sometimes bordered on the incomprehensible. For instance: "An endless number of characteristic types mill around in the distended belly of the great cosmopolis"; or, "A shapeless protoplasm that only the Carlylian heroes or the pseudo-Nietzschean supermen could ferment or mold."[39] Litvak has noted a similar tendency among Spanish anarchists—they tried to dignify their discourse with rarified jargon, even if at times they did not know what the words they were using meant.[40]

Some anarchists understood that their verbal excesses were counterproductive. In 1902, *The Rebel* printed a lucid, three-column article on its first page titled "What Our Press Should Be." It listed a series of blunders in anarchist discourse, from the use of "coarse language" and gratuitous aggression toward non-anarchists to the habitual use of arcane vocabulary. "To call a hypocrite a tartuffe," it said, "is to write in a way that ensures that absolutely no one will understand you."[41] The author concluded by urging his comrades to do their best to communicate in a more colloquial manner, in a way that would be intelligible to the masses. But few heeded this rare call for discursive flexibility, and libertarian writing remained unchanged.

As was the case with their drama, anarchist journalism pointed to a polarized world of social contrasts that seemed to contain two absolutely different forms of life that did not interact with one another or even inhabit the same universe. The bourgeoisie—a vague, generic term in libertarian discourse that typically included employers, priests, and soldiers—were always heavily loaded with negative attributes. Indeed, anarchists were far more interested in reviling them than executing a reasoned analysis of their activities or specifying local nuances. The bourgeoisie "supports itself without producing anything," said *The Rebel*, "living at the expense of the unfortunate worker, annihilating and exploiting the people, condemning them to the most horrendous misery."[42] Their opposite, the workers, were conflated with the oppressed in general and were the victims of suffering, misery, hunger, and overwork, and immersed in a quotidian exploitation that stultified them and prevented them from reacting. "The just, good, hard-working man is a victim of the capitalist, the authority, the priest, and the soldier. And it couldn't be otherwise, given today's social arrangements. One is either a victim or victimizer, exploiter or exploited."[43]

Articles were frequently illustrated with allegorical drawings reinforcing the discursive binaries: the bourgeois were depicted as robust and well fed, wearing luxurious garments, and with faces betraying a lascivious, lecherous attitude. The workers, on the other hand, were malnourished, pained, and ragged. The vast majority of these articles concluded with fiery rhetoric enjoining the workers to dedicate themselves to the revolutionary cause: "Come with us, workers of the world, come swell the ranks of the anarchic ideal, in her you will learn to be men, to know yourselves and understand who the real wrongdoers are."[44] Or they harshly warned the "exploiters" about the fate awaiting them at the end of the road: "Continue, continue your criminal deeds, so that the people in its sublime rages will hurry to crush you under its gigantic steps, murderers that you are! Don't try to escape the people's work. You're doomed!"[45]

The libertarian press did not attempt to inform in same way as "bourgeois" papers. It did not contain sections on domestic politics, international affairs, sports, crime, or entertainment. When articles on those topics appeared, it was to illustrate doctrinal points: if there were reports of military conflicts, it was to criticize war and patriotism; if there was an account of street crime, it gave rise to angry declarations about social inequality; comments on the dealings of the legislative chamber set the stage for condemnations of parliamentary politics, etc. The anarchist press was an alternative press and, even though publications from other tendencies shared some of its discourse (on science and art, for instance), it was different in fundamental ways, from the papers' names to the type of material that they contained.

As with the circles, the publications' names expressed anarchist convictions and goals. There was the spirit of resistance and combat: *The Workers' Struggle, Emancipation, Social Demand, The Revolutionary, La Protesta, The Social Revolution, The Rebel, Revolt, Justice,* and *Awake.* Others pointed to the centrality of the workers and the exploited in the revolutionary process: *The Worker, The Persecuted, Misery, The Oppressed, Labor, The Voice of the Slave,* and *We Work.* Some voiced the commitment to social change: *The Seed, The New Times, The Social Question, The Dawn of the Twentieth Century, The New Paths, The New Era, The New Civilization, Gleam, New Route, Light and Life, The Torch,* and *Social Dawn.* Other titles communicated anti-militarist convictions: *The Barracks* and *Soldier's Enlightenment.* And the minority that supported terrorism had *Caserio* and *Ravachol's Voice,* which, between both, did not publish more than three issues.[46] The sole feminist mouthpiece was *The Woman's Voice.* There were also special publications marking anniversaries: *November 11* and *September 20.* The names were unoriginal and, with the exception of *Martín Fierro,* all bore a universalist stamp and could be found in other latitudes. For instance: *La Protesta Humana* had equivalents in Valladolid, Madrid, Sabadell, Cadiz, Chicago, San Francisco, Túnez, and Boston; *The Social Question* had them in Trieste, Valencia, Paterson, and New York; *The Seed* in Chicago, London, Melbourne, Cadiz, La Coruña, Reus, Tarrasa, Sao Paulo, and Trieste; *El Libertario* in Madrid; *Light and Life* in Oviedo; *Tiempos Nuevos* in Gijón; and there was *Social Science* which, according to Lily Litvak, a group of Spanish anarchists created in Buenos Aires in the image of its Barcelona analog.[47] The newspapers' names were typically accompanied by the ideological declaration "Anarchist Newspaper" and subtitles underscoring their oppositional identity: "Why are you talking about liberty? The poor are slaves" was the motto of *The Social Question* in 1895; or, "To the degree that workers, who are the multitude, are conscious, the victory of the Social Revolution will be easier" was the Élisée Reclus quotation that *The Anarchist Ideal* ran in 1899.[48] *The Rebel* used Proudhon's emblematic "Property is theft."

When technically possible, the libertarian publishers used different fonts for emphasis and to help readers locate regular sections. They also utilized varied font sizes and bold letters within columns to signal contrasts. For example, the previously cited article criticizing *La Nación* concluded by urging workers not to read that paper but, instead, *El Trabajo* and, immediately after, a notice for the preferred newspaper appeared in large, bold letters: "*El Trabajo,*

Diario del Pueblo. Published in Montevideo. Subscription cost for Argentina: 1.70. Send requests to *La Protesta Humana*."[49] Capital letters were also used for urgent items like calls for subscription payments and meeting notices: "IMPORTANT MEETING: TAKING PLACE ON TUESDAY" or "IMPORTANT ANNOUNCEMENT."

Despite the differences between them, most anarchist publications had the same regular features, which made it easier for readers to find desired information. The first page, the most highly valued space in the paper, was dedicated to editorials and doctrinal articles (on the revolution, property, the state, law, the individual, liberty, women and the family, the nation and militarism, religion and the church, and science, etc.), which often ran into the second and third pages as well. These pieces were sometimes unsigned or signed pseudonymously, though often they bore the signatures of local speakers and writers or were reprints of pieces by the luminaries of anarchism such as Kropotkin, Malatesta, Reclus, Tolstoy, Hamon, and Malato, who also authored the majority of the books and pamphlets. Publishers clearly saw the doctrinal articles as the heart of the periodical. "We want intelligent readers to share in our ideals," *La Protesta Humana* said in its first editorial.[50] Convinced of words' transformative power, anarchist publicists thought that these articles revealed a different, alternative world (and future) that would rouse the sleeping consciousnesses of the readersworkers—"revolutionary criticisms enlightening readers and inciting the masses to concern themselves with the *res publica*."[51] Above all, to enlighten meant publishing a copious amount of doctrinal essays: "Authority and Justice" explained the evils of the state and law; "Don't Vote," the futility of parliamentary politics; "Fanaticism," the irrationality of religion; "Anarchist morality," libertarianism's superiority over capitalism; "The barbarities of militarism," the cruelty of the army; "For the Woman" and "The Need to Make Women Combatants," sexual equality and women's importance to the social struggle.[52]

Their approach did not change substantially over time, although *La Protesta*'s engagement with the social question, local politics, and topics directly related to Argentine conditions grew less abstract after it became a daily and especially after Ghiraldo took the helm. It also incorporated more topical information: pieces about the police, social life, the presidential palace, parliamentary politics, scientific issues, and the workers' movement, etc. The newspaper adopted a structure that closely resembled commercial papers, although the purpose of its news sections was not to inform but to provide a platform for illustrating doctrinal points.

To buttress their ideological messages, anarchist newspapers and magazines frequently inserted short phrases throughout their pages. These had different titles depending on the publication: they were "Brief Thoughts" in *The Rebel*, "Evangelisms" in *Seed*, and "Rebel Aphorisms" in *La Protesta*. These epigrams might appear at the end of an important article or grouped together, either anonymously or signed, printed in bold letters and framed to make them more visible. Containing no news, they were dictums that summarized anarchist goals and attempted to "penetrate readers' minds." For instance, *The Rebel* published a long piece about work and personal savings, explaining to the worker-interlocutor that he is real owner of his labor power and the product of his exertions. It ended with a call to rebellion and, immediately afterward, there was a "Brief Thought" commenting on the benefits of revolution: "Evolution will inevitably bring revolution and social harmony will follow."[53] The messages' brevity and their prescriptive, admonitory character were totally consistent with libertarian modes of expression. They always stressed doctrinal fundaments: on religion, "If there is no creator and that which is born dies, religions are a lie";[54] on government, "Government is organized and legitimized injustice, but the subjugated have the force of reason and must make it the reason of force to abolish government";[55] and on militarism, "Parents who let their sons become soldiers are vile!"[56]

Social denunciation was another common feature of the libertarian press, and one that occupied large amounts of space. Here authors abandoned the typically abstract tone of anarchist discourse. The denunciations were not only generic (capitalism, law, the army, and the police, etc.) but also related to specific individuals and situations: clashes in factories and workshops; police actions; and difficulties in workers' daily lives like unemployment, low salaries, alienation, illness, and housing problems. It was in these pieces that readers could most easily identify with those who produced the periodicals. One of the best examples is *La Protesta*'s coverage of the 1907 tenant strike, during which it provided day-by-day, neighborhood-by-neighborhood reports on the vicissitudes of the conflict.[57] Moral condemnation infused these pieces, which at times shaded into forms of folklore, featuring a constant emphasis on social contrasts.[58] Of course, the binaries of anarchist discourse were expressed fully here. While the bosses and police were favored targets due to their "constant abuse" of workers, the priests (the "monastic ogres"), tenement owners, moneylenders, soldiers, prisons, and judges were also a daily concern for anarchists who, beyond the repetitive and monotonous quality of their denunciations, anticipated campaigns for social rights insofar as they asserted that each person is entitled to just and fair treatment.[59]

Although the anarchist press was not a workers' press, it dedicated an increasing number of pages to the world of labor as the social conflict intensified and anarchism's standing in resistance societies grew (and as libertarians saw their ideas becoming a presence in workers' struggles). The press reported on union activities, workers demands, strikes, social gatherings, and the vicissitudes of the international labor movement. Such items might appear anywhere in the paper, but they occupied the first page and central, interior pages when there were strikes and other conflicts. In such cases, anarchists did not relate the details of the dispute (or they did so only partially), because their priority was putting forward their binary oppositions: denouncing business owners, police, and government (who were undignified and brutal) and defending the workers (who were dignified and valiant). As the quantity of reports on the workers' movement grew, so too did the amount of space devoted to polemics with other tendencies on the left (socialists and syndicalists) and among anarchists. Most of the libertarian press was doctrinally purist and, accordingly, saw union action as secondary and it positioned itself—vaguely at times—against the battle between classes. In this sense, alongside information about labor, one can perceive the frictions internal to the libertarian movement.

Anarchist reportage on the workers' movement—strikes, disputes, demonstrations, and repression—put the social question into discourse and facilitated the construction of anarchist traditions. Pieces on the "individual sacrifices" made by terrorists like Angiolillo and Ravachol also did so, although these were much more common in the individualist publications of the late 1890s such as *The Rebel, The Social Question, Ravachol's Voice, Caserio,* and *The New Civilization* than the mature anarchist movement's press. There were many articles recounting the great deeds and travails of the masses that nurtured these traditions: there were essays on the French Revolution, the Paris Commune, the executions in Chicago that led to May Day, executions in Barcelona, repression in Milan, and countless confrontations in Argentina. Anarchist newspapers also included notices of anniversaries of major events in the history of the proletariat, which further bolstered the new traditions.

Topics explored often pointed to a mix of anarchism and tendencies with roots in liberalism and positivism. The anarchist press allocated significant space to the practice of alternative lifestyles: from relationships and free love to vegetarianism (not accepted by all militants), naturalism, the crusade against alcohol, etc. Likewise, as champions of family planning, they published numerous articles defending neo-Malthusianism as well as pieces counterposing secular, rational, and free schools to state education. Libertarian papers also committed progressively more pages to art in general and literature and theater in particular, in addition to releasing specialized publications on these topics, such as *Martín Fierro, Letras,* and *Ideas and Figures.* This was particularly true after heterodox intellectuals like Alberto Ghiraldo, José de Maturana, and Rodolfo González Pacheco became active. Although already a regular practice for *La Protesta, La Batalla* dedicated almost a complete page to commentary on the offerings of Buenos Aires theater, which doubtlessly reflected the theatrical interests of its editor, González Pacheco, anarchists' concern with workers' free time, and the rapidly growing importance of mass entertainment.[60]

The amount of literature published also increased. Short stories appeared frequently, which were typically unoriginal, as Diego Armus aptly noted while commenting on the sentimental, melodramatic character of anarchist fiction, which had more in common with commercial novels than countercultural works.[61] Taking an old tradition from the commercial press, *La Protesta* and *The Battle* had a section for daily installments of serials, generally in the lower part of the last page. Between 1904 and 1910, *La Protesta* serialized the following works among others: *La novela roja* by Catulle Méndez; *Del cautiverio* and *El libro de la crueldad* by Giges Aparicio; *En los bajos fondos* by Maxim Gorky; *Sangre y oro* by Alberto Ghiraldo; *Notas del tiempo* by José de Maturana; *Espumas y plomo* by Joaquín Dicenta; *Un sueño de amor* by Leda Rafanelli; and *La isla de los pingüinos* by Anatole France. This was apparently an effective strategy for capturing readers' interest, although doctrinal texts often displaced literary pieces. The following items among others were serialized: *Organización, agitación y revolución* by Ricardo Mella; *Memorias de un revolucionario* by Kropotkin; *En la ciudad de la utopía* by William Morris; *El trabajo envilecido y maldito* by Anselmo Lorenzo; *Nuestro orden y vuestro desorden* by Pietro Gori; *El comunismo* by Augustin Hamon; and *Teoría del préstamo usurario* by August Blanqui.

Another recurrent feature of the libertarian press reflected anarchists' emphasis on solidarity: typically, several sections on the last page focused on the periodical's internal life and the anarchist movement as a whole. These commonly included a list of books, pamphlets, newspapers, and magazines received; ads for libertarian books or announcements of forthcoming titles; notice of correspondence with individuals and groups in Argentina and abroad; information (and commentary at times) about *veladas*, lectures, and meetings; various subscriber lists; and reports on the publications' finances. The latter was a particularly compelling topic given that the newspapers were seen as the property of all readers.

Anarchists hoped to construct an alternative communication network with their press, one that would at least partially neutralize readers' passive consumption of media and the commercial and governmental press's effect on the public, particularly workers. This is why all anarchist publications had a section announcing forthcoming works and acknowledging the receipt of publications from Argentina and worldwide. In it, they reviewed, commented upon, and encouraged readers to consume these materials and sometimes described the content of the works, which could be acquired at the Librería Sociológica or the papers' offices. The material received was diverse: there were numerous publications from Argentina (from Rosario, Bahía Blanca, San Pedro, Zárate, Ingeniero White, Córdoba, and myriad towns in the province of Buenos Aires); and, reflecting anarchist internationalism and the constant travels of many activists, there were periodicals from around the world. For example, during the opening years of the century, the following newspapers and magazines arrived regularly: from the United States there was *Free Society, La Questione Sociale, El Despertar* (Tampa), and *L'Alba Sociale* (Tampa); from Spain there was *Idea Libre*, the prestigious *Revista Blanca, El Productor*, and *Fraternidad* among others; *O Despertar* from Brazil; *El Librepensamiento* from Peru; from France *L'Anticlerical, L'Humanité Nouvelle, Le Libertaire, L'Auve Meridional* (Montpelier), and the paradigmatic *Les Temps Nouveaux; El Derecho a la Vida* and *The Dawn* from Uruguay; and Rudolf Rocker's *Arbeter Fraint* from England.[62] Libertarians hoped that this network would unify the libertarian cause and give it a universalist character.

Although there is not enough evidence to establish a detailed profile of readers, the papers were clearly addressed to workers, which was also the case with most of their advertising. For example: "Workers … Pirol bitters Regenerates – Strengthens – Improves Appetite – Aids digestion. Try it once and you'll never want another aperitif."[63] Anarchist publications were sold and distributed in factories and workshops, at pickets, tenements, assemblies, parties, and lectures. However, the size of the print runs make it clear that only a minority of workers bought them. Publishers naively voiced their surprise that workers "happily read" the very papers that "justify" their exploitation, the high cost of living, and speculation. "And to think that the workers who buy these enemy newspapers, increase their circulation!"[64] *La Protesta* even ran an article alleging that most of its readers came from the middle sectors—it claimed that 70 percent of the 8,000 copies published daily in 1908 were "consumed by the middle class, bourgeoisie, and professionals." However, this assertion should be taken with a grain of salt, given that it was made in the context of the polemic with the FORA and was intended to minimize the FORA's merits.[65]

6. IRRESOLVABLE PROBLEMS OF THE ANARCHIST PRESS

In addition to the fact that the publications' ideological dimensions limited their readership, there was another, no less weighty difficulty: the simultaneous production of various publications dispersed energies and weakened the totality of the anarchist press by fostering competition for readers. Some militants criticized this dispersion and the consequent loss of quality. For instance, in 1906, a newspaper attacked publications from the Gentleman of the Wilderness group for their "elemental vulgarity and naïveté, suggesting that they should devote some of their free time to study, which would surely enrich their anarchism."[66] But the profusion of publications was inevitable due to the decentralized, heterogeneous nature of the movement. The libertarian press also included myriad genres (sociology, letters, arts, philosophy, and politics) and doctrinal positions (individualist, vitalist, Nietzschean, naturist, collectivist, anarcho-communist, and anarcho-socialist). In light of the individual/collective, organization/anti-organization, class/people binaries, it is easy to see why each tendency would release its own publications: *The Rebel* "came into being ... to fight a dangerous trend among the anarchist groups,"[67] facing off against *La Protesta Humana*, *The New Civilization*, and *The Future; Gleam*, according to Abad de Santillán, was created to challenge Ghiraldo's leadership of *La Protesta*;[68] *New Route* and *Light and Life* were published in 1906 and 1908, respectively, also to do battle with *La Protesta*. This is just a handful of the publications focused on ideological debates within the movement.

The multiplicity of publications also reflected the strong individualist impulses among anarchists—a group or individuals could put out a broadsheet without feeling obliged to consider the needs of the movement as a whole. Prominent media often encouraged this: "If you don't like the papers that exist, then create your own! What could be better?" said *The Rebel*. "The more, the better! It shows that the anarchic idea is spreading."[69] Many anarchist groups tried to raise money to help *La Protesta* after it became a daily and surely it would have collapsed without their aid; but even so, publications continued to multiply, given that not all welcomed *La Protesta*'s centrality. In 1908, Gilimón harshly criticized the individualism evident in the proliferation of anarchist periodicals, which drew readers from *La Protesta*. He wrote:

> Every propagandist seems to want to be a pontiff, an editor-in-chief, the only one who knows how to make the anarchic idea touch the people. They argue bitterly among themselves and compete constantly and yet no one prevails, since they all defeat one another, tearing each other down and, with it, propaganda itself.[70]

These conflicts also limited the distribution of *La Protesta*: a group displaced or marginalized by the publishers would withdraw their support, take subscriber lists with them, and in some cases put out another publication. It is likely that *La Protesta*'s drop in sales during Ghiraldo's leadership was due to the antipathy that he aroused among militants. Similarly, the 2,500 copies that *Gleam* published during its few months of existence probably took readers from *La Protesta*.

Distribution problems were equally vexing. It was difficult for anarchists to circulate their papers in the capital and adjacent areas and even more so in remote parts of the country, which required onerous mail and train shipments that were routinely delayed. Distribution in the interior improved over the years thanks to the creation of a network of sales agents. In 1904, *La Protesta* had agents in Rosario, Mendoza, Santa Fe, San Pedro, La Plata, Mar del Plata, Junín, Los Toldos, Paraná, Tucumán, and Zárate. They apparently played a crucial role:

"*La Protesta*'s success and influence in a particular town depends more on the agent more than any other factor," wrote Diego Abad de Santillán.[71]

The best-known publications were sold in the Librería Sociológica (Corrientes 2041), the Librería Francesa (Esmeralda 574), at Rivadavia 2339; and at kiosks in the following plazas: Independencia, Lavalle, Rodríguez Peña, Monserrat, Constitución, 11 de Setiembre, Victoria, and Lorea. In addition to professional booksellers and distributors, there was a network of neighborhood agents made up by activists and sympathizers from the groups. In 1904, *La Protesta* reported on its new agents: the hat makers' leader Juan Dussio for Coghland and Villa Urquiza; the port leader Constante Carballo for La Boca; and the Initiative group for the Belgrano neighborhood.[72] It was difficult to enlist individual street venders, who were reluctant to carry newspapers with smaller sales. *La Protesta* only managed to do so sporadically, and nearly all of the scarce mentions of sales via this route concern street vendors' refusal to carry the paper due to supposed police harassment.[73] Furthermore, during periods of martial law, authorities not only shut down the publications but also confiscated their shipments in the mail, thereby preventing readers in the interior from getting their copies. This occurred in normal periods too.

The irregularity and transience of the publications was another issue that hampered anarchists' ability to reach a mass audience, although such problems were by no means exclusive to the anarchist press: a high percentage of publications from Buenos Aires, commercial or otherwise, disappeared quickly. In the 1880s and 1890s, partisan broadsheets were often unable to support themselves through sales, which was also the case with many commercial publishing ventures. Naturally, such quandaries were more extreme for anarchist papers and magazines.[74]

The quantity of anarchist publications reflected the relative ease with which one could publish in fin-de-siècle Buenos Aires: groups simply had to raise some money from activists and supporters and put together a two-or-three-person editorial team in order to make this happen. Sustaining regular publication was the challenge: the lion's share of publications did not put out more than a dozen issues; quite a few, including many that we only know by name, published once or twice and then vanished. Although not a main cause, persecution—shutting down the papers and imprisoning their managers and editors—also contributed to libertarian periodicals' short life spans. It is fair to assume that most persecuted publications were the most widely distributed.

As for the most long-lived undertakings, such as *The Rebel, The Future, La Protesta,* and *Ideas and Figures,* anarchists worked indefatigably to put them out and, despite countless obstacles, made every attempt to do so regularly. Some militants argued defensively that "the punctuality with which a publication comes out is not the primary indicator … of its value."[75] This comment, made by a writer in *The Rebel*, minimized the importance of regularity in order to defend voluntary subscriptions as a means of financial sustenance, which had become a matter of debate. *La Protesta Humana*, the only survivor from the era, took a more pragmatic—and one might say professional—approach when it set a fixed cover price after it went from a biweekly to a weekly publishing schedule in 1900. Its editors ran a long letter explaining that they had to do so because many voluntary subscribers did not send contributions. "Thus, we hope that each reader conscious of the paper's value will pay his due, ending the abuse represented by the useless shipment of newspapers."[76] They understood that the paper had to come out regularly if it was to persevere. *The Rebel* was biweekly, *The Future* biweekly and then weekly. *La Protesta Humana* was biweekly for the first ten issues; from issue thirty to ninety-eight; weekly from issue eleven to thirty, and from November 1900 to April 1, 1904, when it became a daily. Without regular publication, readers as well as the advertisers withdrew. For instance, unions that announced their functions in the anarchist press could not communicate with supporters in a timely fashion when the paper did not come out on schedule and, when this happened, they responded by ceasing to purchase ads or make contributions.

This points to a dilemma that was almost impossible to resolve for papers such as *La Protesta*, which operated at an enormous technological and financial disadvantage compared to their commercial counterparts. Although it is true that the anarchists did not hope to compete with them, technological and financial limitations were a significant barrier to their evolution. As Manuel Tuñón de Lara remarked, "technology is a question of investment, and investment depends on the judicious distribution of profits."[77] At a time when many papers were instituting technological enhancements (new rotary presses, news agency subscriptions, distribution improvements, the purchase of a building, etc.), the libertarian press, which struggled to meet printing costs, was unable to keep up. This rendered it less competitive and less attractive to readers, particularly because of the limited use of graphics. Readers complained about poor printing (ink-stained or barely legible pages), distribution problems, and delayed schedules. The publishers generally laid the blame on poor production conditions: "The machine that we use to print *La Protesta* is inadequate to the demands of the print run. Printing cannot begin before 2:00 in the morning, when the last union reports come in. Our present print run is 8,000 copies and the machine can't print more than 800 an hour, which means that we're unable to deliver our papers until just after 12:00." The article concluded by urging readers to be patient and not to compare it to "bourgeois newspapers."[78] Nevertheless, they tried very hard to overcome the technological limitations, which they partially achieved in 1907 when they bought a new rotary press that could print 10,000 copies per hour and accommodate larger paper sizes, which enabled them to print six columns per page. They also added a Tipograph typesetting machine three years later.

While commercial newspapers were commodities produced for profit, the anarchist press pursued ideological, not financial, ends (except of course when it was attempting to raise money for movement necessities). Even so, it was extremely difficult for *La Protesta* to remain solvent, especially after it became a daily: there were printing expenses, paper costs, distribution fees, and salaries for graphic personnel and full-time editors, etc. The salaries were a source of discord among anarchists, since many viewed publishing as a form of activism and thus necessarily unpaid. *La Protesta Humana* broke with that standpoint in 1901 when it created a professional position with a salary that was the "equivalent to that of a bricklayer's mate."[79] The publishing group justified this by citing the impossibility of putting out the paper every week in their free time: editing, management, printing, and shipment greatly exceeded volunteers' labor capacity, which is why "the group responsible for this paper has decided, with full awareness of its meaning, to provide a salary for the work required for publication (which cannot be done in off hours)."[80] *La Protesta* stuck to this strategy and also ended up compensating multiple editors simultaneously as well as typesetting and administrative staff.[81] Some argued that these paid positions were merely launching pads for careers in journalism and, in fact, they were the first step in that direction for more than a few writers: Félix Basterra became a journalist for *La Nación*, Edmundo Calcagno for *Última Hora*, Alejandro Sux for *La Prensa*, Ghiraldo wrote for *La Razón,* and Julio Barcos, Florencio Sánchez, and Juan Carulla contributed to various "bourgeois" papers. Some anarchist publishers never accepted the idea of paying editors. In an undisguised jab at *La Protesta*, a rival libertarian publication gloated, "We are delighted to make it known that *Gleam* does not provide any type of remuneration to anyone."[82]

Publishing a newspaper that would be read by the working masses required at least some income and the question was how to acquire it. Pellicer Paraire commented on the issue: "Unlike bourgeois parties, we don't have capitalists who, with utilitarian ends, contribute part of their wealth to their mercenary papers. We have to supply the capital through the masses and through organization, assuring the press's existence on the basis of the labors of nuclei throughout the republic."[83]

Groups played an essential role in distributing the press. They disseminated papers free of charge and organized parties and raffles and applied the takings to the press's debts. *La Protesta Humana* had support groups as early as 1900. In response to financial difficulties that the paper faced in late 1904, various groups and activists started collecting donations to pay off its deficits.[84] Four years later, a number of groups formed the Committee to Expand *La Protesta*, which had the (unrealized) goal of buying a building for the paper so that it could avoid expending 2,600 pesos annually on rent.[85] The groups were also industrious propagandists: they distributed the newspaper to passersby, at meetings, lectures, public rallies, worker restaurants, grocery stores, and generally anywhere that popular sectors gathered. Help from some individuals was vital too. For instance, Dr. Juan Creaghe was a veritable patron of *La Protesta*. The Irishman—who was economically comfortable and possessed of deep libertarian convictions—gave a significant portion of his resources to the paper and, in fact, his support made it possible for it to become a daily and buy its first rotary press in 1904. "The underwriter [Juan Creaghe] has signed the contract with the equipment vender and paid 2,400 of the 4,200 pesos due, which includes all the necessary materials and installation."[86] The paper would not have survived without his assistance. Creaghe lived in Argentina for many years and between 1894 and 1897 published and sustained the *Oppressed* newspaper (initially in Luján, where he lived, and afterward in Buenos Aries), which he ultimately shut down in order to avoid competing with *La Protesta Humana*. He opened and financed libertarian schools and came to the aid of *La Protesta* various times for more than a decade, serving on several occasions as its editor without charging a salary. In response to continued requests for money, he was obliged to make a declaration: "Many think that I have enormous sums at my disposal, but that's not the case. The truth is that I won't be able to give any more for another twelve months, approximately."[87]

Subscriptions were the anarchist press's main source of income until 1901 or 1902. When payments were voluntary, newspapers did not survive: from 1897 until 1900, when *La Protesta Humana* set a fixed subscription price, publishers complained about economic shortfalls in every issue, bemoaning subscribers' lack of payments. This was a pervasive issue for libertarian publications, although they were fairly stable once they set a fixed price, so long as they did not attempt huge print runs. The subscription system was onerous: each paper created subscriber lists (containing between ten and twenty subscribers) in the name of a group or individual who took responsibility for collecting the money and delivering it to the newspapers' publishers. As straightforward as this would seem, numerous problems arose. For instance, subscribers were often difficult to find, especially because the vast majority used pseudonyms.[88] And newspapers had to mobilize large numbers of collectors to gather money from lists in the province of Buenos Aires and other areas around the country. Sometimes groups or individuals responsible for the lists disappeared because of ideological disputes, emigration, or for no apparent reason at all, often taking their lists and the money that they had collected with them. Subscriptions could serve as a base for a publication, but could not sustain it over the long haul.

Financial burdens multiplied when *La Protesta* became a daily, and this required anarchists to enlist more subscribers. They asked for help from the libertarian movement as a whole, calling for subscriptions as if they were a duty: "We're not asking for charity or pleading. We are insisting that each one of you fulfill his obligations. Every good comrade has a responsibility to help sustain the common cause."[89] Echoing this, while pointing toward those in better economic positions, Creaghe pressed for greater contributions from comrades who were not workers, reminding them of Kropotkin's maxim, "from each according to his ability, to each according to his needs."[90]

Street sales were increasingly crucial during the initial decade of the century: they expanded the reading audience and also alleviated some financial pressures. *La Protesta* used them, whereas newspapers like *The Rebel* remained faithful to distribution by voluntary subscription (although it was ultimately sold in kiosks) and never accepted ads. *The Rebel* alternated between periods of deficit and surplus and almost collapsed on several occasions. In June 1900, it reported that it was "on the verge of dissolution," but endured into 1903, when a drop in sales produced an insuperable financial crisis. While *La Protesta Humana–La Protesta* evolved in some respects, primarily in its coverage of the workers movement, the content of *The Rebel* did not change substantially between 1897 and 1903. It claimed that it was "written by the workers and for the workers," but retained its highly ideological-doctrinal approach as well as its original objective of challenging the pro-organizationalists. However, Argentina and the anarchist movement had not been inert between 1897 and 1903. *The Rebel*, which had, disappeared.

However, even with street sales, penury was ubiquitous for the anarchist press. The quarterly and monthly financial reports published by *La Protesta Humana– La Protesta* between 1897 and 1910 indicate that it was usually insolvent, which sometimes stopped it from coming out or, as occurred in 1902, compelled it to cut back to two pages. Debts were paid when there was a surplus and anything left over was saved. The paper used money set aside in 1907 to buy a new rotary press but, even though there were surpluses throughout 1908, there was not enough to pay off the machine. One can see *La Protesta's* sources of income in one of the few detailed monthly accountings it published: documenting November 1904, it registered a total of 3,748.73 pesos in income, which it earned through the following methods: 44 percent from subscribers; 34 percent from street sales; 3.5 percent from sales at the Librería Sociológica; 7 percent from gatherings organized by the groups; 3 percent from raffles; 5 percent from donations; and less than 1 percent from advertising.[91] These portions changed slightly in the years immediately preceding the Centenary, due to a rise in revenue from street sales and ads.[92]

It was necessity more than conviction that prompted the new approach to advertising. Initially, when most anarchists saw the press as a service, the advertisements published were barely profitable, purchased mostly by activists and sympathizers, with the exception of a few clearly commercial ads such as those for Quilmes and Bieckert beers. The need to support a newspaper and expand its readership challenged this practice and led anarchist publications to begin actively selling space in their pages. *La Protesta Humana* fully incorporated advertising in its first issue as a daily on April 1, 1904. It advertised: Carpintería de Benito Puente, Sastrería de Ernesto Bettini; the *Martín Fierro* magazine; Librería y Cigarrería de Bautista Fueyo; Cigarrillos Fígaro y Federación Obrera; Antonio Loredo's Peluquería Germinal; Fotograbados de Luis Giustti; and Taller de Sastrería de Camilo Marotta. All these advertisers had links to the anarchist movement in one way or another.[93] In 1906, two pages were devoted to ads for large firms like Bols and Pilsen (Bieckert) among others. In 1909, the paper eliminated the free classifieds and job opening listings it had introduced in 1904. Integrating advertising was not without conflicts: although publishers saw the need for it, reader-activists were intensely critical and accused them of connivance with exploiters. Likewise, advertisers like Bieckert, Quilmes, and Bols, who were eager to attract workers and more than willing to pay for ads, demanded guarantees that the newspapers would not call for a boycott of their products if a conflict with their employees were to occur. Though tensions and contradictions remained, by 1910 newspapers like *The Battle* and magazines like *Ideas and Figures* had modestly increased their use of advertising as well as the revenue earned through it, without, however, resolving underlying financial difficulties.[94]

The anarchist press had a significant presence among readers linked to the world of labor, and at the same time, a complex, hazardous existence marked by uncertainty and the ever-present risk of dissolution. In the context of favorable conditions like growing literacy, active popular reading, press freedoms, and the relative ease with which one could publish, anarchists managed to create a sustained, prolonged core of publications constituted by newspapers like *The Rebel, The Future, The Persecuted, The Battle,* and—especially—*La Protesta Humana–La Protesta,* in addition to magazines like *Social Science, Martín Fierro,* and *Ideas and Figures.* The totality of these publications, along with the centers and circles, were the foundation that helped consolidate the anarchist movement in Buenos Aires and endow it with a voice, despite the absence of a centralized party. The libertarian press also made an indispensable contribution to the formation of left wing, oppositional public opinion, whose principal readers were supposed to be workers.

However, beginning in the years following the Centenary, the press began a slow, inexorable decline and progressively came to see itself as the voice of a small minority. Why was this its fate? In addition to the structural changes that caused the broader disintegration of the anarchist movement, and a commercial press that was more attractive to the reading masses (including workers), the libertarian press did not know how to overcome its limitations in order to fully access a proletarian audience. These limits resided principally in the doctrinal, closed character of its journalistic discourse, which yielded a series of interrelated problems. It prevented libertarians from expanding their readership, which caused financial shortfalls that prevented them financing technological improvements necessary to compete in an increasingly sophisticated market, which jeopardized the financial viability of the publications as such. Anarchists did not know how to break out of this vicious circle, and perhaps did not want to.

In the incessant, titanic struggle to overthrow social prejudices and conventions, the dense web that increasingly shrouds the mind of contemporary man, undermining and confusing the development of his intellect, in that unflagging, generous battle that we libertarians wage against the present social organization, the question of libertarian education, inspired by modern scientific discoveries and based on the natural reason of things ... has to mean molding the character and intellect of the men of tomorrow upon the healthy, philosophical principles of anarchism.
—*The Rebel*, July 14, 1901

CHAPTER VI

The Educational Practices of Argentine Anarchism

I N THIS CHAPTER, I analyze libertarians' fragmentary and mostly unsuccessful attempts to create an educational alternative in Buenos Aires at the turn of the twentieth century. Though very modest in its achievements, it helps us to understand the anarchist movement and the popular sectors to which it addressed itself, revealing points of encounter and disconnection, of contact and rupture, between the workers and those hoping to represent them politically and ideologically. Educating the workers was an integral part of the anarchists' ideological framework and examining their inability to successfully generate an educational alternative illustrates some of the broader discursive and practical difficulties that restricted their ability to mobilize the populace around the anarchist cause.

I do not focus on strictly pedagogical concepts. Instead, I argue that Argentine anarchists' educational efforts were an ideological attempt to cultivate a proletarian identity organized around opposition to patriotism, militarism, and religion and based upon the exaltation of rationalism and the combination of manual and intellectual work in instruction.

1. EDUCATION AS A TOOL FOR TRANSFORMING THE INDIVIDUAL

Within the broader socialist camp, anarchists were the most vigorous defenders of Enlightenment educational ideals and the progressive tradition born of the French Revolution. They firmly believed in reason's capacity to transform society and eliminate ignorance, and saw the latter as a principal cause of popular misery and oppression. Like many of their peers, they thought education pivotal to liberation and embraced many of the pedagogical ideas that began circulating in the second half of the nineteenth century but whose roots lay in the Enlightenment. From Rousseau to English pedagogue Reddie, from Paul Robin to Catalan educator Francisco Ferrer, these reformers all asserted that education was central to individual liberation.

Anarchists were convinced that education would enable humanity to become conscious of potentialities rendered dormant by economic exploitation and religious obscurantism. They regarded the growth of such self-awareness as a process of paramount importance for the improvement of humanity in the present and the future, as it would prepare men and women for individual as well as social redemption. Given education's liberating power, they fought to make it available to everyone as a means of moving toward a society without privilege or hierarchy.

Libertarians' faith in rationalist ideas was unwavering. They held that science would free humans from toil and allow them to produce abundantly and live comfortably and happily. They believed that science undermined the prejudices of religious dogmas and bourgeois "philistinism." And furthermore, in their decidedly schematic variant of positivism, they thought that the same laws governed the natural and the social worlds and that, as a result, the natural and social sciences shared the same logical structure. Humans, they maintained, would find equilibrium in an anarchist society built upon natural processes. They thought these processes inconsistent with capitalism, which thwarted nature while producing social disequilibrium, immiserating the portion of humanity that works (the majority) and enriching those dedicated to leisure (a small minority). For them, capitalism disorganized and divided humans, who were naturally equal.

Anarchists were not alone in their rationalist and scientific fervor. In fact, their views paralleled those voiced by Sarmiento in 1881: "We educate children in exactly the same way that the North American Mann, the German Froebel, and the Italian Pestalozzi have shown us that they should be educated: following rational precepts, we teach them everything taught today in schools around the globe."[1] And educators as a whole shared their belief in education's capacity to overcome backwardness and ignorance. However, anarchists amplified this faith exponentially when they asserted that organizing society around scientific precepts would dislodge political and religious authorities and yield a utopian, "rational" order without social ills.

Anarchists' confidence in science's revolutionary power had direct links to their belief in the malleability of the individual, which was the premise of their notion that education could make humans aware of oppression. They were convinced that study, instruction, and doctrinal propaganda were fundamental both for acquiring a liberated consciousness and counteracting the cultural monopoly of dominant institutions. This is why the creation of an alternative culture seemed so crucial for the resolution of social problems. Disseminating and popularizing their "new culture" laid the preconditions for the masses' assimilation of the new insights. Their uncritical zeal for rationality notwithstanding, anarchists were more committed to the ideals of scientific progress than militants from any other ideological tendency, including socialists.

Anarchists challenged the state's monopoly on education on at least two grounds. First, they believed that it reproduced social inequalities and protected dominant groups, and, second, that it disseminated nationalist falsehoods that obscured life's realities, fostered xenophobia, and legitimized political hierarchies. This is why they held that government schools could not address workers' needs. As noted, while anarchists appealed to the people generally, they privileged workers in their discursive scheme and defended the value of manual labor. Accordingly, they advanced a comprehensive, educational vision that called for a combination of manual and intellectual instruction that would promote social leveling while endowing workers with a sense of responsibility, confidence, and technical proficiency.

With respect to the treatment of students, anarchists rejected the disciplinary practices and rewards and punishments typical of the authoritarian educational system and, in contrast, passionately defended children's creativity and critical spirit. They also called for coeducation and healthy, open-air living.[2] Although these ideals were not exclusive to anarchists, they were a way to advance the revolutionary cause. Libertarian militants embraced the principle of education for liberation.

2. ANARCHISM AND PUBLIC EDUCATION

Anarchists regarded conventional education as a means of dominating and alienating the working masses. The process began in the family and with the subjugations inherent in paternal authority itself. Libertarians saw that authority as among the most tyrannical because it was exercised without limit or fear of rebellion. The child had no ability to resist his or her oppression—paternal authority was total and weighed upon the child from birth until he or she individuated. The father, by imposing his views during the many years in which the child's mind was malleable and personality weak, accustomed the child to obedience, respect for the law, authority, and bourgeois institutions generally. He also prepared the boy or girl for the class-based, nationalist, and religious instruction that he or she would receive in school.[3] "To the degree that he has a truly creative mind, he will have to destroy everything that he has learned and reconstruct his intellectual world," declared *The Battle*.[4]

At this stage, said anarchists, the child was supposed to move on to be dominated by the public school. "Pedagogy, as presently understood, offers nothing but mediocre teachers and stultified students," argued *La Protesta*. "It corrupts and thwarts growing minds."[5] Libertarians hoped that their alternative would prevent this by counteracting the state's monopoly on education, its capacity to integrate the oppressed into the system, and its ability to dull the individual's critical spirit. This is why anarchists thought it essential to create an educational alternative, even though they were never able to do so on a wide scale.

Libertarian interest in education in the first ten years of the century must be placed in a context of intensifying government control over education and heightened efforts to fortify an Argentine national identity. War-like hostilities with Chile as well as diplomatic quarrels with Brazil—with which Argentina had an age-old enmity—also caused patriotic sentiments to swell.[6] And, of course, there was the virulence of the social conflict, which further accentuated nationalist pressures. Elites, worried they might lose their grip on social power, linked social turmoil to foreigners generally and anarchism specifically. This led to the approval of a series of repressive laws; the Residency Law was only the most conspicuous.[7]

All of these developments had a palpable impact on the school system. In 1909, on the eve of the Centenary celebrations and in an ambience of social violence, the National Education Council resurrected an 1884 legal clause to mandate that all uncertified private-school teachers register with the Council and take an authorizing exam. The Council also prohibited foreigners from teaching geography, history, and civics and decreed that only native-Spanish speakers could provide instruction in the language. Similarly, it standardized curricula and declared its right to review curricula used in private classes before the beginning of the school year.

The council also obliged teachers to mark the May 25 and July 9 national holidays and devote classes to their meaning.[8] Additionally, it compelled students to swear to the flag. All students were ordered to do so daily during the patriotic euphoria around the Centenary, although the practice had already been mandated in some school districts where foreigners were a majority, such as in Consejo Escolar IV, which had jurisdiction over fifteen schools in La Boca neighborhood. The indifference shown by some students—primarily foreigners—to national symbols troubled educational authorities. They were worried not only by students' foreignness but also by the presence of "exotic ideals that are incongruent with the Argentine temperament" and violate "the elevated sentiments of love of country and respect due our institutions." The Council implemented two measures reflecting these concerns. In 1904, it resolved that the Argentine flag must be raised during class hours and, two years later, ordered the salute to the flag.[9] Patriotic fever spread to all levels of the school system. At the Council's request, the famed writer Leopoldo Lugones wrote an article on "aesthetics and patriotism" and Martín Malharro, a well-known Post-impressionist painter named inspector general of drawing and manual work, published an essay called "Free Drawing and Patriotic Education."[10]

The strengthening of nationalist attitudes drew from diverse ideological sources, from the Sarmientinian admiration for the North American educational system to Ricardo Rojas's nostalgia for Hispanic forebears. The most significant application of the nationalist framework, inspired by positivism and sponsored by the state, was realized under the leadership of Ramos Mejía. Halperín's account needs no commentary:

> He [Ramos Mejía] imposes civic, ceremonial rituals of an almost Japanese intensity on primary school students: children learn to daily decipher and repeat formulas in tormented verse and stilted prose that commit them to defending the flag to their last drop of blood. They shout these pledges in front of an altar of the Fatherland, which all teachers are obliged to keep adorned with fresh flowers.[11]

The effort to rally children around the nation—one supposedly or actually threatened by foreign countries and doctrines—was not an attempt to exclude immigrants but rather to integrate them into the national community through their offspring. And the school was indispensable to this as a means of fostering a sense of national identity among the country's new residents. It required modifying some linguistic and cultural practices, but also provided an excellent mechanism for social assimilation.[12]

Libertarians were very sensitive to the nationalist content in education. "Educating for the Fatherland," wrote a commentator in *La Protesta*, "is to educate against the well-being of one's fellow man, to defy the love of humanity, life, reason, and justice."[13] Viewing the state as a monolithic, homogeneous entity, they believed that its educational programs were a malevolent, disciplinary tool. "The science of education," they argued, "has always been in the hands of the government and the church, which is why the former has been able to survive for so long as institution and the latter continues to regulate conduct, imposing a morality of its liking."[14] It is for this reason that they set out to construct an educational alternative that would neutralize the state's monopoly on education.

Anarchists' model of alternative education also sought to act on the workers, making them into thinking individuals while fighting the "deformations" instilled by government schools and popular commonsense. They saw education, furthermore, as a tool for molding the revolutionary vanguard and producing exemplary militants: the cultured, educated activist who was able to communicate effectively and rationally and enlist the workers in the revolutionary cause.

But anarchists confronted two major obstacles. The first was the relative success of state-sponsored education, which worked efficiently on popular identities and became ubiquitous in Argentine society. Indeed, even though the educational system was by no means fully formed at the time, it facilitated a dramatic expansion of literacy and enjoyed high levels of public acceptance.[15] For a population with a large immigrant component, education offered a means of upward mobility and, by disseminating patriotic symbols, assimilation. Local anarchists, though grasping the meaning of government-led educational programs, naïvely urged popular sectors to renounce them: "It's time for the submissive and deceived parents to realize the horrible meaning of patriotic education," implored *La Protesta*.[16] Anarchists did not understand that the appeal of the nation and its insignia was more complicated than deception and submission, and that public schools offered more than mere literacy. A will to assimilate was a decisive factor. For anarchists, the great challenge was to ensure that their educational alternative offered something that was both new and desirable to ordinary men and women.

3. EDUCATION: BEFORE OR AFTER THE REVOLUTION?

Differences within the anarchist movement were the second obstacle to the construction of a libertarian educational alternative, which of course complicated other attempts to advance projects that needed the support of the entire libertarian community. Although anarchists were united under the umbrella of anti-statism, anti-clericalism, and their oversized faith in rationalism, the range of positions within the movement produced a destructive dynamic that caused initiatives propelled by one camp to be ignored or even boycotted by the others. Educational efforts are a good example of this, and a case in which the movement's internal contradictions clearly contributed to their prompt failure. While no one questioned the importance of education, the "educationalists" strove to create libertarian schools in the here and now while others thought that popular education had to wait until after the revolution. These divergent views among Argentine anarchists paralleled differences among their European counterparts. Those who relegated education to the "day after the revolution" were indebted to Bakunin, who thought it impossible to provide an alternative education in a capitalist society because men's actions and conduct were "products of natural and social life, of the physical and social conditions of the environment in which each individual is born and continues to develop." Educating an individual differently required different conditions—the existence of conditions of equality. "To make men moral," he said, "it is necessary to make their social environment moral." They must first be emancipated politically and then can be educated.[17]

The "educationalists" had a different position. They were heirs to Barcelona's Modern School, which Francisco Ferrer i Guardia (1859–1909) directed from 1901 until the year of his tragic death. Its pedagogy was unique because of its atheism, commitment to coeducation, mixture of economic classes, emphasis on scientific principles, and the broad latitude that it gave to students (which included eliminating the system of rewards and punishments). Ferrer drew inspiration from French educator Paul Robin, but, unlike Robin, his efforts were fully integrated into the community, its supporters embraced anarchism explicitly, and the libertarian movement as a whole backed his work. This earned Ferrer constant police persecution and, ultimately, execution by the Spanish government, which baselessly held him responsible for bombings and assaults. This tragic dénouement elevated a simple teacher with alternative commitments into one of the preeminent martyrs of the international anarchist movement. Although his modern schools ceased functioning not just because of persecution but also because of numerous practical problems, they still became the model that anarchist educators in Argentina—where Ferrer's work had an enormous impact—would attempt to follow.

The "educationalists" believed that a revolution could occur only if there was first a radical transformation of the individual through education. Ferrer drew upon the Rousseauian idea of natural goodness—that children are good by nature—and, against Bakunin, asserted that revolutionary education could change the individual in contemporary society. For this to happen, he or she would have to be educated freely, without coercion, and shielded from the effects of state education. This led Ferrer to call for the creation of a network of rational schools that would inculcate a commitment to science, freedom, and solidarity among students, avoiding the authoritarianism and parochialism of bourgeois schools which he thought yielded acquiescent and undiscerning adults. Ferrer and his Argentine followers intended to use the school for the purposes of workers' moral and intellectual emancipation. While that liberation would be collective and the oppressed would have to build institutions to free themselves from bourgeois rule, the revolution would rest on a personal, individual choice to become enlightened and cast off the influence of the church and state. Rational schools would accomplish the essential task of helping children grasp the origins of economic inequality and the fallacies of bourgeois society (religion, the fatherland, politics, etc.).[18]

Consciously or not, most local anarchists embraced the Bakuninist view, which had an innate affinity to the revolutionary urgency and insurrectionalism so pervasive in the movement. The "educationalist" minority, by contrast, was gradualist. It envisioned the revolution as a long-term process that first required the transformation of the individual. These two currents contained numerous sub-currents, yielding additional disputes. Once again, the problem of the anarchist movement's mixed, heterogeneous, and occasionally contradictory messages revealed itself. And although anarchists and the rest of the socialist camp believed that the mental transformation of the working masses was a central step on the revolutionary path, unlike Marxists and socialists, they did not think it necessary to create a party to organize and lead the workers. This also set them apart from the Leninists, who accorded a central role to the enlightened vanguard of the proletariat, which would define the proletariat's course and the "correct" ideological and political line for the development of class consciousness. It is not that anarchists rejected vanguards per se—in fact they were a vanguard and thought of themselves as such—but they were characteristically disorganized and decentralized as a result of their emphasis on individual freedom. Their extreme individualism was often destructive of their collective endeavors.

However, all anarchists believed that leveling the aristocracy of intelligence was fundamental to the struggle against authority. Qualitative differences in educational offerings produced and deepened existing social inequalities. Therefore, anarchists deemed it vital to construct an alternative that would counteract the values inculcated by government schools, generate new ones that would enlighten the workers, and strengthen individuals' natural impulses toward freedom. They intended to contest the state's monopoly on education, which is why they tried to create an educational alternative.

4. "GET OUR CHILDREN OUT OF OFFICIAL SCHOOLS"

"Anyone who understands will be with us; except for the ill-willed, only imbeciles oppose us."[19] It was in these simple terms that some anarchists saw their educational efforts, which they thought would have a devastating impact on bourgeois society.

Their ventures, however, were fragmentary and not well thought out. Many of their projects, which at times shared educational premises with socialists, Masons, and freethinkers, unfolded chaotically and were beset with polarizing tensions. There were the stresses of their David-and-Goliath battle against the public school system and also the debilitating divergences within the anarchist movement, which is what is of interest here. Although anarchists instinctively conceded education's importance, sometimes their enthusiasm was merely rhetorical. In reality, beyond a general consensus on the issues, they held conflicting views on education's role in the revolutionary process that reflected, as noted, differences between Spanish rationalism and Bakuninism. These differences acquired a particular slant in Argentina and, along with popular disinterest, helped terminate practically all anarchists' educational initiatives and, in the wake of the Centenary, led rationalists to constitute a tendency of their own, distinct from anarchism and with aspirations of complete political and ideological independence.

During the opening decade of the century, tensions between those who believed that workers' education could occur in the present society and those who thought it had to wait until after the revolution had a decisive impact on the contours of anarchist educational practice, although explicit polemics on the issue were rare. Indeed, no one frontally attacked educational efforts and all acknowledged that they were an elemental part of the long-term revolutionary project. Education, like direct action, was a moment in a dialectical relation between the present and the future. However, Argentine anarchists, like anarchists internationally, had at least three positions on the role of education, even if they are only latent in the incomplete record of the partisan press from the time.

In a fiery call for the creation of schools that would "improve the spirits and expand the minds" of the people, Esteban Almada urged his comrades to use good sense and avoid the extremes of "exaggerated optimism or crushing pessimism. Those are the fates ... of those who put their faith in labor organizing exclusively or those who, like individualists, reject it with Olympian disdain. Both sides share a common point of departure: ignorance of the topic that they either extol or disparage."[20] The thrust of his critical comments was directed at the editorial department of *La Protesta*, then headed by Eduardo Gilimón, a doctrinal purist. Some criticized the paper for not supporting or writing about the Modern School in Buenos Aires, although in reality it published myriad pieces about it, including financial reports, announcements for parties, meetings, lectures, and even essays by Julio Barcos—director of the Modern School—outlining its aims and criticizing anarchists who appeared indifferent to it. Educational concerns were clearly a priority for *La Protesta*, but there were disagreements, which I will analyze below.

It is important to clarify the doctrinal purists' position on rational education. At no time did they deny its importance, as *La Protesta*'s support indicates, but they did not accord it the same priority as the rationalists. "Education is education for us, nothing more," said Gilimón. "We do not seek any utilitarian end in it at all. We're not trying to make anarchists."[21] This statement points to a central issue: the notion that education, training, and culture are liberating in themselves, because they allow individuals to expand their horizons and comprehend social ills. Displaying an uncommonly open-minded attitude, Gilimón even commented on the merits of Argentina's secular education as contrasted to the extreme clericalism of Spain's educational system: Argentines' approach shielded children from the religious influences prevailing in most homes and encouraged them—partially of course—to think with a certain freedom in religious matters. Without saying so openly, he was acknowledging that secular, government-sanctioned education had snatched an important flag from libertarian educational efforts.

Of course, Gilimón was not defending government education and, like all local anarchists, he lamented the damage that authoritarian, nationalist public schools supposedly did to children. It was precisely because of that damage that anarchists deemed it crucial to create schools that allowed absolute freedom of expression and thought: "Education cannot have any goal, end, or aim other than education itself. Introducing anything else is destructive and only ensures that some men deceive others in the name of a distraction."[22] This is why Gilimón called for structuring education around a body of positive knowledge that would help develop children's capacities for comprehension, discernment, and reason.

He voiced a clear commitment to free education, but also concerns about restrictions that alternative schools might impose on the freedom of thought. His worries were prevalent in the more individualist wing of Argentine anarchism that, echoing Spanish anarchist writer Ricardo Mella, questioned practices in rational schools that seemed to replace religious, nationalist dogmas with secular, political ones, a critique as applicable to anarchists as socialists. They believed that schools simply ought to be a nurturing environment where young people develop and grow and in which ideas and doctrines are described not imposed. Mella argued for explaining but not teaching political doctrines: including anarchism, which, ultimately, was only one doctrine among others. Taking the idea of individual freedom to the extreme, he said that children should be allowed to embrace it freely when they become adults and not coaxed or pressed into doing so by educators. Education should not be propaganda, but rather neutral and based on science, which did not have one truth, given that each individual, a free thinker by nature, had the ability to reason. That implied that there was no single, universal reason.[23]

The individualist perspective engendered an ambiguous attitude that neither rejected nor celebrated educational projects. This cohered with individualists' vision of the intellectual vanguard's role in the revolutionary process. It was the vanguard that revealed and explained social ills, marking out the path that must be followed by the masses, who were generally and involuntarily uneducated because they did not have the time to educate themselves under the prevailing social arrangements.

With respect to educational alternatives, Gilimón and most of the libertarian movement embraced a form of revolutionary urgency that put them in synch with the Bakuninist notion of educating the masses after the revolution. They paid little attention to educational initiatives, even if they consistently voiced their enthusiasm for them, including some that were not truly alternative. The doctrinal purists focused on forming militants by educating and recruiting a minority of workers that would populate the ranks of the revolutionary vanguard. Rational or comprehensive education for all the exploited was unattainable under capitalism.

Likewise, anarchists oriented toward the labor movement did not devote significant energy to the creation of an educational alternative. Most believed that the environment of solidarity in the resistance societies was an excellent instructor and educator of workers. Congress resolutions of the Argentine Workers' Federation affirm this. In its first congress (1901), the issue of education was not on the agenda and confusion about the editing of the final declaration suggests that it held only marginal interest at the time.[24] The organization later expressed tepid support for free schools. It was only at its third congress (1903) that it declared it urgent to found schools. It articulated its vision:

> Spurning all denominational education, the child is exposed to the greatest sum of knowledge, thus avoiding cerebral deformations and fostering broad capacities for discernment, which will enable him to discuss and compare all types of doctrines. The schools' motif will be freedom in education, and artistic training and manual apprenticeship will unite with scientific instruction, always having the comprehensive development of all of the child's faculties as its goal.[25]

This resolution implicitly differentiates between rational and revolutionary education. Concerned with workers' education, the congress also called for initiating nighttime programs for adults in the free schools. Drafted by Alberto Ghiraldo, the proclamation has roots in rationalist pedagogy and favors the creation of an educational alternative. Later congresses affirmed this, urging labor societies to start libraries, publish pamphlets, and apply some of the money normally spent on social events to these undertakings. At the sixth congress, there was a proposal to establish an educational council that, under FORA leadership, would organize educational initiatives.[26]

These good intentions grew more pronounced in later congresses. But even as anarchists secured their predominance in the federation, the labor movement failed to become a primary source of educational endeavors. While doctrinal purists and anarcho-syndicalists considered education vital but, in practice, left it for the future, a third tendency within the revolutionary movement thought education as significant as labor organizing and the press. Advocates of this position did not clearly emerge as a tendency until the middle of the first decade when, inspired by Ferrer, Julio Barcos irrupted into the anarchist movement and began to endow the current with a unique pedagogical profile. This was especially the case after the 1906 founding of the Lanús Secular School, one of the most interesting efforts in the period under investigation.

5. THE FIRST STEPS OF LIBERTARIAN EDUCATION

Before Barcos appeared on the scene, dispersion, voluntarism, and an almost total ignorance of pedagogy in general and rationalism in particular characterized anarchist educational initiatives. The initial steps were stammering and, except in one instance, attempts to create schools did not get beyond the planning stage. For example, in 1898 a student named Julio Molina y Vedia, with the backing of the Los Acratas group, presented a detailed plan for a libertarian school that would operate on vaguely eugenic precepts. "The two supreme principles of the educational method employed," his proposal declared, "will be the preservation and regeneration of the human species and student happiness."[27] Shortly afterward, Molina y Vedia reported that the undertaking had to be suspended due to an absolute lack of interest. The failure likely reflects an absence of faith in the proposal's author as much as the disinterest of the broader anarchist movement. Imbued with individualist strains at the time, the idea of creating alternative schools was untenable as an immediate goal, notwithstanding the fact that Molina y Vedia was active in the individualist camp.[28]

It was individualists who one year later launched the first libertarian school, which operated for approximately three years. Los Corrales Libertarian Propaganda Group, which had a clearly anti-organizational orientation, sponsored the venture. It had broad support among Buenos Aires anarchists: the anti-organizational *The Rebel* and the pro-organizational *La Protesta* both promoted the school, which was located in Parque Patricios.

The convening group thought it imperative for anarchists to create a rationalist and scientific educational alternative whose teachings would be "diametrically opposed to the dogmatic education that Argentine children receive in so-called places of learning"[29] and that would counteract the damage done by state schools' religious and patriotic instruction. Indeed, religious education occurred not only in parochial schools, but also in the relatively more secular state schools, where belief in God remained a premise. Anarchists saw religion as a principal cause of children's future submission to the system: "It is clear that the chimerical notion of God, the creator of all things, binds thought with iron ties and undermines the will with endless old wives' tales that, after being hammered into children's minds, cause moral death as soon as the youngster begins to smile."[30] The second major reason to build alternative schools was nationalism's growing presence in the official educational programs which, as indicated, was by no means an anarchist fantasy but a palpable reality.

The Los Corrales libertarian school struggled with multiple obstacles. Despite having a large number of students—seventy-nine in 1900 and seventy in 1901—it was not economically self-sufficient, probably because students paid their fees irregularly and because funds provided by the libertarian movement were inadequate. The convening group worked diligently to support the school: it organized *veladas*, lectures, and excursions to the countryside to promote it and raise money. But, even so, crippling financial problems endured, given that these activities only rarely brought in a sizable profit. The group released a desperate call in early 1901, stating that it can "barely attend to the school's needs, which grow daily."[31]

There was also pressure from the local school board. Apparently, its concern was not the content of the instruction but the school's physical infrastructure. Militants from Los Corrales issued another call for help to the libertarian community. If they did not receive aid, they said, "the school will definitely disappear; the clerical-bourgeoisie exploiters will shut it down without even a peep of protest on the pretext that we do not have enough space for the large number of children who come here and, as a result, are unhygienic."[32] The primary causes of the school's ultimate collapse were economic, the relative indifference of residents, and a lack of initiative from the anarchist movement.

Nonetheless, the experiment was an important step in the maturation of anarchists' educational initiatives and set the stage for consistent and serious discussions of the role of education in the revolutionary process. Indeed, a number of pieces appeared in influential libertarian newspapers calling for alternative education. For instance, in mid-1901, while the Los Corrales school was still operating, *La Protesta Humana* published a letter from a sympathizer that proposed expanding the ventures;[33] *The Rebel* argued that education would help the oppressed become conscious of exploitation and dissuade them from the temptation to make mere economic demands. At the same time, a profile of an ideal activist emerged who, thanks to education, would be reflective and not beholden to the excessive, unhealthy voluntarism prevailing among anarchist militants. A columnist in *The Rebel* wrote:

> An educated comrade does so much more for propaganda than an uneducated one; the ideas and opinions expressed by someone who is informed have greater moral force, produce a more powerful impression upon the spirit and in the mind of someone who is unaware, than the awkward, cumbersome speech of someone who struggles to put his thoughts into words and often says the exact opposite of what he means.[34]

The author even argued that education had the same strategic importance as the press, although their purposes were different. The press's objective was to "agitate, move, and propagate" anarchism among popular sectors, whereas education helped individuals reason and reflect more deeply, providing the "serenity necessary to study and comprehend problems."[35]

Veteran Catalan activist Antonio Pellicer Paraire, perhaps the most prominent anarchist leader in the country at the time, made a crucial contribution to the discussion. In a long, front-page article in *La Protesta Humana*, he effusively and enthusiastically celebrated the formation of the Los Corrales school. He argued that the era of ultra-individualist, verbose digressions was coming to an end and the creation of collective revolutionary interests had begun. An advocate of organized action, he used the founding of the school—largely propelled by individualists—as an opportunity to extol the virtues of collective efforts, thereby scoring a point in the ongoing debate between pro- and anti-organizationalists. He was one of the few libertarians to explicitly call for a comprehensive strategy for social change. Unions, cultural centers, and alternative schools could not succeed in isolation, he thought; instead, libertarians should fight together for a common goal. Enthusiastically, he declared:

> Reason has prevailed at last, yielding the rapprochement of all those tired of slaving away without being able to count the number of people who are convinced and dedicated to emancipatory work, without being able to realize any idea in practice, without being able to enjoy the pleasure of seeing an army marching toward the conquest of social freedom.[36]

In his view, the anarchist movement had taken the right path. Libertarian schools would provide solid, protective strongholds for advances secured on other fronts.

However, the Catalan militant's optimism was unjustified and enthusiasm within the anarchist movement for opening an educational front was not consolidated, despite the example of the Los Corrales school. Indeed, a good deal of the momentum built during the opening two years of the century disappeared with that school. Anarchists overwhelmingly dedicated their energy to founding and strengthening workers' societies and regional federations after witnessing the impact of the labor movement.

Anarchists did not advance a coherent educational project until the middle of the first decade and none of the few attempts that they made to start schools between 1902 and 1905 came to fruition. In 1902, a group composed primarily of longshoremen launched the Friends of Free Teaching association; its goal was to create a libertarian school that would provide a rationalist education to workers' children. Also that year, a small notice in a newspaper appeared announcing the establishment of a night school that would give classes in arithmetic and grammar. The only hint of activity in 1903 was an offer to donate money for the creation of a rational school. The following year, with the support of the local sailors and stokers' society, militants formed the United Comrades Center for Popular Teaching of La Boca. Its purpose was to found a secular school. Around the same time, the Art for Life center ambitiously but unsuccessfully tried to establish a modern school with branches in different neighborhoods.[37] Although the Residency Law weighed heavily upon the anarchist movement after late 1902, it appears that it did not directly affect anarchists' educational endeavors. As far as we know, practically no libertarian educational initiatives were operating in late 1902. It is difficult to determine if "militants with teaching responsibilities" were deported since lists of those expelled from the country do not contain clear data on the topic. Julio Camba, who tried to open a night school several months before the government ejected him, is the only deportee that we know to have been associated with educational projects.[38]

Libertarians were unable to launch a sustainable educational alternative for two, principal reasons. First, not enough workers wanted such an alternative. Many working-class families were not terribly interested in educating their children in a regular, systematic way and, instead, preferred to have them learn a trade and go to work in order to help out the family. Many withdrew their kids from school after just a year or two of study.

The second reason was anarchists' tepid commitment to establishing their own schools. Midway through 1903, *La Protesta Humana* sought to change this by serializing a chapter from Kropotkin's *Fields, Factories, and Workshops* entitled "Manual and Intellectual Work," which it hoped would help anarchist militants get acquainted with the precepts and relevance of rational pedagogy. Many were unfamiliar with anarchist educational ideas and some were even hostile. Once, for instance, a number of activists protested an anonymous comrade's decision to donate a large sum of money to create a school. This prompted educationalists harshly criticize the resistance societies that refused to contribute funds to educational initiatives while being, in their view, more than willing to waste them on long strikes that they generally lost.[39] Indeed, popular indifference and internal movement conflicts, not repression, were the greatest obstacles to the establishment of an educational alternative; the government was far more preoccupied by the labor movement and quite confident in its own educational programs.

In 1905, a large group of anarchists made another attempt to institute an alternative, this time with unique resolve. They organized a Free Schools Committee whose primary goal was to "get our children out of official schools, which atrophy minds and quench lofty sentiments."[40] In contrast to previous efforts, this project had the backing of a substantial number of libertarian cultural groups (The Conquest of Bread, Art for life, Gentlemen of the Ideal, The Seed, Modern Youth, Tailors, Light and Progress, The Modern School, Dawn Group, and New Dawn). Also expressing its enthusiasm was *La Protesta*, which, under the leadership of Alberto Ghiraldo would consistently back undertakings of the sort. The Committee held regular meetings and created a school board charged with formulating curricula and coordinating written and spoken propaganda on behalf of the project.

Its members had an ambitious vision. The plan was to set up neighborhood subcommittees throughout the city that would carry out local propaganda, relieving the Committee of that task, and work toward founding schools. The subcommittees would locate suitable sites for the schools, sponsor informational lectures, and try to cultivate enthusiasm among residents. Clearly, the Ministry of Education at least partially inspired this organizational model. But those involved greatly overestimated their capacities. They managed to put together two subcommittees—one in Palermo and the other in the area encompassed by Entre Ríos, Caseros, Paseo Colón, and Rivadavia streets—but the project disintegrated before they managed to launch a single school.

Once again, the failure reflected a lack of demand and inadequate support from the anarchist movement. While it is true that the state launched a bitter crackdown in February of that year on libertarian militants, who had little or no relation to the defeated Radical Party uprising, this did not have a decisive impact on the Free Schools Committee. The absence of union enthusiasm was also significant, considering that resistance societies were supposed to provide part of the funds, buildings, and some of the students, and that one of the project's primary goals was to get workers to enroll their children in free schools. The debacle also points to the Committee's limitations. It was barely alive twelve months later, without having accomplished any of its principal tasks. There is even evidence that it did not provide aid to the only anarchist-led free school, which was located in Barracas and extremely penurious. The libertarian press complained bitterly about the "inadequate materials and elemental deficiencies with which [the school] operates. It is painful to know that beautiful and altruistic initiatives like these do not flourish but, instead, are totally unstable due to the lack of assistance from all those comrades dedicated to finding and fomenting better means of libertarian propaganda." The article concluded by urging the Committee to help the school.[41]

6. IN SEARCH OF A RATIONAL SCHOOL

Although that project came to naught, a wing of the anarchist movement began to materialize that was specifically dedicated to building an educational alternative. The group, still embryonic and without recognized leadership at the time, raised two very important questions about the libertarian pedagogical experience. On the one hand, there was a shortage of teachers trained in the principles of rational education. "Do we have even one instructor," asked the Free Schools Committee's secretary, "that has properly understood these innovations?"[42] He answered his own question with a categorical no and proposed that the Committee attempt to train teachers, as their French and Spanish counterparts had done. On the other hand, this brought up the thorny topic of educational freedom. Rational education implied that no doctrine—including anarchism—should be imposed. A free school signified total freedom of expression and thought: "There will be no external pressure of any sort, either on the school, the teacher, or the children ... we will not teach any ideology of any kind, only science. We don't want to turn children into sectarians; they will choose their own paths with a healthy capacity for judgment and"—concluding with typical rationalist optimism—"we assure you that they will choose a good one."[43]

More interesting educational endeavors emerged in the libertarian camp during the second half of the first decade, as the social conflict reached unprecedented levels of intensity. I refer specifically to the Lanús Secular School, the Modern School of Buenos Aires, and, to a lesser degree, the modern schools of Villa Crespo and Luján. A discernible rationalist tendency had surfaced under the leadership of Julio Barcos, doubtlessly the most distinguished local representative of rationalism between 1905 and 1920. Born in 1883 in Coronda (Santa Fe), Barcos dedicated himself to teaching at an early age. He taught at and directed the Lanús Secular School and the Modern School of Buenos Aires; he was the principal force behind the League for Rationalist Education, in whose administrative council he held various positions; he edited the League's newspaper—*The Popular School*—between 1912 and 1913, and authored numerous articles on issues related to rationalist pedagogy. In 1901, he played a central role in the creation of the first teachers' union, the National Teachers' League, and, a decade later, helped to found the Teachers' International of the Americas.[44]

It was not libertarians but the socialist-led Secular Education Society who founded the Lanús Secular School. This institution enjoyed the support of a broad spectrum of activists, including followers of [Socialist Party leader] Juan B. Justo, anarchists, freethinkers, liberals, and Masons: all united around the goal of "building a school for training and educating children of both sexes with the most modern teaching methods and on the basis of the most progressive educational precepts that are, therefore, bereft of all political and ideological predilections."[45] Initially, the school's ideological framework was socialist, as indicated by the use of the term *secular* (socialists' favored term for their educational projects); the typical speakers (Ángel Giménez, Pascuala Cueto, and Enrique Dickmann); and the structure of the parties (they sang the "Hymn of the Workers," not the "Sons of the People").[46]

The school began offering courses in late August 1906 under the direction of Ramona Ferreira, a teacher who described herself as a journalist and freethinker and who had the socialists' backing. Anarchists found her objectives and methods untenable. She argued that the school ought to try to win children's hearts "through scientific notions and moral maxims, while inculcating in them respect for the legally constituted institutions and hierarchies, the only foundation upon which we can build the citizens of tomorrow."[47] Of course, this was intolerable for libertarians, who hoped to use education to accomplish the opposite: to undermine the "legally constituted institutions and hierarchies." Not surprisingly, a conflict erupted almost immediately after the school opened and Ferreira quit shortly thereafter. She circulated a public letter claiming that the school's directive council supported "sectarian and libertarian ideas," subverted disciplinary norms, disturbed the pedagogical system "in defiance of order and morality," prompted the teaching personnel's insubordination toward school authorities, and did not recognize the principle of authority in any capacity. She justified her resignation by appealing explicitly to the principle of authority. "Without discipline," she wrote, "there can be no morality and without morality, there is corruption."[48] Demonstrating their inability to work with other progressive tendencies, the anarchists on the directive council that had harassed Ferreira celebrated her departure, accusing her of being authoritarian, opposing coeducation, and violating the principle of free thought. The organization of school members, now under anarchist control, named Julio Barcos as director. With the teacher Corona López, he began giving courses to students in the first through fourth grades. Notwithstanding the sectarianism of those who had installed him in the leadership, Barcos operated with marked flexibility and encouraged the involvement of his socialist and freethinker colleagues.

The Lanús Secular School operated until the end of 1909 when, already in decline, it received the coup de grace during the repression that followed the assassination of police chief Ramón L. Falcón. Doubtlessly the most successful anarchist educational experiment, it functioned without interruption for three years with an average of more than 100 students annually. In 1908, 125 students attended the day classes and 30 partook in evening classes.[49] There is evidence that students in the first through the fourth grades received classes and that basic night classes, propagandistic lectures, artistic events, and Esperanto courses were given to adults. Julio Barcos directed the school until 1907, when he left to take over the Modern School of Buenos Aires. Mario Chiloteguy oversaw the school until October 1908, when he was replaced by Pedro Bruny for a few months and then, finally, by Emilio Osorio, who led the school until it closed.

In addition to its classes, its library and regular public events made Lanús Secular School a neighborhood hub for socializing, culture, and recreation. The school's public functions almost always occurred on Saturdays, Sundays, and weekday evenings, so that students' parents, to whom a large part of the activity was directed, could attend. Lectures focused on disseminating the principles of rational education, but were generally more didactic than ideological, running from a course on public hygiene taught by Doctor Alicia Moreau to historical talks by José de Maturana. There were also many recreational events, including cinematic and theatrical functions, excursions to the countryside, dances, and school parties with a distinctly communitarian flavor. The purpose of all of this was to make the school's programs attractive to those living nearby.

Activists hoped that the school would challenge the Catholic Church's strong presence in the neighborhood. Some saw it as a principal rival. "Jesuitism rules openly here," said an anarchist sympathizer. "They have multiple schools and hand out money and clothes to get students, and cause trouble and spread slander in an attempt to chase our school out of the area."[50] Activists complained that Catholic schools reinforced the church's already pervasive impact on working class families, especially on mothers. Male militants repeatedly lamented the religious influences in their homes, which—placing the blame on others—they often attributed to the fact that their spouses took charge of their children's education.

This is why Julio Barcos thought that they should expand educational and cultural endeavors, which would raise the consciousness of "popular elements" and enlighten "the spirit of parents who send their children to the school," neutralizing state and religious interference:

> I think it advisable to put on all types of lectures and family gatherings for residents, and take advantage of any opportunity to engage the parents—in straightforward, sensible terms—in a discussion of the problems that constantly arise at school and at home. Up until now, the school and the home have marched along different paths, one undoing the work of the other but without counteracting the pernicious forces in either.[51]

Barcos was a realist. In 1907, the school had only one teacher to attend to fifty-eight students with various levels of education. The school's building was totally inadequate and its books and other educational materials worse than insufficient.[52] But, even so, he saw the Lanús Secular School as the embryo of a "beautiful project" and attributed its problems to a lack of support from the anarchist movement.

Anarchist hesitations about educational projects were especially pronounced in the case of Lanús Secular School, despite its successes. Some found its name troubling. It used the term *secular,* whereas *modern* or *comprehensive* were the preferred adjectives for anarchist schools. The word *secular* reflected the fact that socialists had originally named it, and Julio Barcos, perhaps because he had a broader perspective than his comrades, prudently decided not to change it. The Boilermakers' Society of Buenos Aires, underscoring union activists' distrust of intellectuals, explicitly criticized the school's name and accused it of lacking a revolutionary character. The school's Administrative Commission responded harshly, expressing its irritation with those troubled by trivial issues like the school's name while having nothing to say about its educational work. The Commission pointed out that state-sponsored schools described themselves as "modern" and "comprehensive" and yet anarchists' use of those terms never met with objection. All of these words were indeterminate, "equally empty and ambiguous with respect to the moral and intellectual content that revolutionary thought must imprint upon the child's spirit."[53] Underscoring the cultural distance between educators and union activists, the Commission said that it would do its best to provide a simple overview of the school's approach, but that it is "very difficult to explain it in two words to those who don't have even a rudimentary grasp of the topic."[54]

A year later, the Commission reproached the libertarian movement broadly for its lack of support. Its indifference may have been the result of the doctrinal amplitude with which Barcos and, later, Mario Chiloteguy led the school. Both were libertarian militants and firm defenders of rational education, but cognizant of state and religious education's appeal. Being more judicious than their comrades, they tried to avoid alienating locals with sectarian content and encouraged the rest of the progressive spectrum to participate. This is demonstrated by the fact that Alicia Moreau and Enrique del Valle Iberlucea were invited to lecture at the school. An article defending the school in *La Protesta* argued that anarchists' skepticism toward it was absolutely unjustified and denigrating to those who sustained the project. Those who attack it, said the piece, "show by their words that they are completely ignorant of this school's educational system." They should "visit when classes are in session so that they can see for themselves the good things that occur at the Lanús Secular School."[55]

This conflict became bitter around the Modern School of Buenos Aires. Modeled on Ferrer's Modern School of Barcelona, the plan for the school, advanced in 1907, was more elaborate than that of previous anarchist educational projects. With prior failures in mind, coordinators prioritized raising enough money to support the infrastructure necessary for an educational experience that would be serious and appealing to parents and students alike. To compete with state education and attract students, the coordinators insisted on a comfortable, spacious building that was ventilated in the summer and heated in the winter, books and other basic implements, and teachers who were well-educated not only formally but also in rationalist pedagogy. Organizers pleaded with the entire anarchist movement for support and the response was auspicious. Representatives from around twenty resistance societies linked to the FORA, as well as various groups and publications, attended the founding meeting of the Administrative Commission, which was charged with moving the endeavor forward. The nomination of Julio Barcos as director was also promising, as was the hiring of the teacher José Sagristá, who had taught in Barcelona's Galileo School.

Nonetheless, it was difficult to get the project off the ground and progress was very slow. Almost twelve months after its formation, the Administrative Commission released a worried statement: "Few anarchists have participated thus far."[56] It was only with great effort that they managed to organize some night courses a year after the school opened in a building provided by a resistance society in Barracas. There were other problems too, as made evident by laconic announcements appearing in *La Protesta*. There was a shortage of instructors, the Pro-Modern School Group had collapsed because of insufficient members, and the morning session had to be suspended in the winter of 1909 because students could not bear the freezing temperatures in the classroom.[57] Initial optimism notwithstanding, the school operated precariously for approximately one year with an average of one hundred students until it closed for the same reasons as the Lanús Secular School.

Led by Julio Barcos, the group sponsoring the school blamed anarchists generally for the failure, accusing them of "shamelessly boycotting" the experience. They were especially angry with the editors of *La Protesta*. Gilimón responded to their criticisms by asserting that the Modern School had enjoyed unprecedented support from Buenos Aires anarchists and that it was the group responsible for the project that bore responsibility for the meager results. He criticized Barcos for attempting to open a large, prestigious, well-equipped rationalist school instead of launching small schools simultaneously in diverse neighborhoods, as the territorial strategy advanced in 1905 had recommended.

The differences were deep. Barcos and his group envisioned a long-term project focused on alternative education, whereas Gilimón, the doctrinal purists, and the anarcho-syndicalists were frustrated by the lack of immediate results and concerned primarily with the present. With the typical revolutionary urgency, Gilimón declared, "We're not enamored of plans: it's the facts that matter. The school should be a reality already—it has been a plan for long enough."[58] Reflecting the factions' basic strategic disagreements, Gilimón's comments suggested that educational initiatives should be reduced to a secondary role, made into complements of political and labor activity. However, as previously mentioned, no one disputed the importance of education, which was an elemental part of libertarian tactics. Proof of this is available in the dozens of articles and hundreds of announcements published in the libertarian press between 1905 and 1910; the discussions of modern, comprehensive, and rational education; and the overstated, abstract, and nearly ritualistic eulogies to Ferrer's efforts in Barcelona.

This is why the frankness and realism of two pieces that appeared in the *La Protesta* are surprising. After analyzing the fate of the school, both proposed postponing such projects if they could not be carried out more effectively. They cited various reasons for their failure. The first was the total incompetence of the teachers who, except in rare cases, did not have adequate training in or knowledge of the postulates of rationalist education. Most were simply militants who assumed teachers' duties in an ad hoc manner. This was a problem "because an individual can be endlessly knowledgeable about various topics but still a terrible teacher."[59] The second reason was teachers' transience. They often changed in the middle of a course and their replacements rarely had the same ideas about teaching or methods. The pervasive ignorance of rationalist pedagogy helped perpetuate this problem. And, finally, there was not enough money for the basic school infrastructure. In August 1909, the City of Buenos Aires closed the Modern School in Villa Crespo after verifying that seventy students were receiving classes crowded into one room in a dilapidated building. "How is it possible," asked an author of one of the *La Protesta* articles, "to compete with state education?" Answering his own question in unusually pragmatic terms, wrote, "It's impossible. And I don't think that we should reopen the schools that were closed if we can't do so with better resources and teachers than the government's."[60]

However, the rationalist group saw things differently. They acknowledged that the Modern School had been shaky and almost inert for the last year, but they rejected their rivals' claims that it was because of their incompetence. Instead, alleged that unaddressed differences, skepticism, and egoism among anarchists were the roots of the problem. And they raised an issue that signaled the approaching schism between rationalists and the doctrinal purists: "Are we extraneous or do some envy our combat posts? They can have them. But don't forget that revolutionary men have one primary trait and that's a willingness to adapt their practices to their ideas."[61]

The repression in late 1909 and around the Centenary was disastrous for the anarchist movement in general and especially its weak educational flank. The nearly year-long interruption of classes during martial law caused the few schools then operating to virtually disappear. The three libertarian schools functioning in Buenos Aires and the surrounding areas (the Modern Schools in the capital and in Luján and the recently reopened one in Villa Crespo), which had a total of approximately 250 students, were closed under various pretexts, but it was obvious to all that the real issue was their links to the anarchist movement. Administrators and activists involved with the schools were detained and prosecuted. Rationalists protested educational authorities' collusion with police: "It has been demonstrated that the National Board of Education acted under orders from the Police command, whose pedagogical authority is evidently unimpeachable."[62] The persecution even extended to oppositional teachers employed in state schools. For example, Pedro Maino, who had more than twenty years experience as an educator, was removed from his director's post in a San Pedro school "for being a known anarchist" and arrested.[63]

7. THE RATIONALIST EDUCATION LEAGUE

These events, the spread of public schools, popular indifference, and anarchists' growing weakness undermined enthusiasm for creating a libertarian educational alternative. Although there were still isolated attempts, only the rationalist core remained firmly committed to organizing an educational project that would be superior to the official one.[64] I use the word "superior" advisedly, because the idea of building an "alternative" had practically disappeared from rationalists' lexicon. Even though they still had anarchist support, and *La Protesta* continued publishing their announcements and articles, the rationalists had—without proclaiming it—broken with anarchists and evolved into a group of intellectuals with an educational program that was available to progressives generally. Of course this included anarchists, whom they preferred, but their link to them was no longer inherent. And while they did not express it outwardly, some were drawn to the idea of reforming state education from within. Hints of this are visible in the first article of the Rationalist Education League's statement of purpose: "To make the efforts of those who understand the need to reform contemporary education converge, for the development of an approach to education and curricula that realizes the scientific, humanitarian ideals of modern pedagogy."[65]

Founded in mid-1912, the Rationalist Education League's purpose was to fight religious and nationalist influences on education, reopen the Modern School, and build a broad educational alternative that all Argentines would want to access.[66] It created its own media to promote its activities and disseminate ideas. The *Francisco Ferrer* magazine was its voice in 1911; *The Popular School,* which came out until 1914, succeeded that paper after the creation of the League.

Julio Barcos led the League, with the support of participants in previous projects and other educators that backed its cause. Although it had some internal conflicts, the League's stance on the postulates of rational education was largely homogenous and stable.[67] The group no longer saw rationalism as an anarchist tactic or an instrument of any ideology, but as an independent structure of ideas that would one day have a status similar to that of other recognized ideologies: "Socialist, anarchist, and rationalist theory, like the Hegelian, positivist, and Darwinian, are all philosophical systems with political and social applications that are either true or false in the context of the present reality, but not illicit before the law."[68] They believed that rationalism would redeem humanity insofar as it lends itself to human regeneration, happiness, and freedom.

Overthrowing the bourgeoisie through proletarian revolution was no longer the pivotal step in the creation of a new society. Instead, the rational education of human beings would, in the words of *The Popular School*, lead the forces of good to victory by "molding individuals who will be able to live in the society of the future on the basis of scientific knowledge and positive philosophy; forming mind-sets bereft of dogmatic ideologies, tolerant, but not indifferent to the opinions of others; cultivating unbiased spirits that tackle problems by following the path of positive philosophy and the truths of the experimental sciences; fostering healthy and robust individuals, [and] capable of enjoying the moral and material pleasures of life."[69] Going even further, *The Popular School* asserted that the scientific and philosophical content of rational education elevated it above ideological dogmas, which generate anti-rationalist prejudices among believers who fear that "it won't lead their children to join the political party of their preference."[70]

Even though *La Protesta* continued to publish abundant information on the Rationalist Education League and articles by Julio Barcos, the rationalists had split with the harder variants of doctrinal anarchism. Underscoring this, the League's secretary expressed his irritation when the socialist paper *La Vanguardia* described Barcos as a "known anarchist." Such statements, he complained, helped police confuse rationalism's aims and ensure that the people will never realize "that we rationalists are not dangerous."[71] Tellingly, he did not dispute the paper's pejorative use of the term "anarchist." Relations with the anarchist movement became openly hostile shortly thereafter. An unsigned article in *La Protesta* described League leaders as "failed caudillo types," to which the League's Administrative Commission responded with an angry statement protesting the "malicious caricatures of an anonymous feature writer."[72]

The rupture is even more transparent if we consider rationalists' acceptance of the idea of transforming the official educational system from within. Illustrating this, the League joined the Teachers' Confederation, which had two main goals: improving teachers' economic circumstances and "substantially transforming the means and ends of the present educational system within state schools."[73] Julio Barcos himself conceptually endorsed this tactic in a work entitled *La Crisis Educacional y el Magisterio Argentino* (*The Educational Crisis and Argentine Teachers*), which contained a harsh criticism of state education, but one emerging from a different perspective than that traditionally employed by anarchists.[74] He framed education as a matter of concern for all progressives, whether oppositional groups or even reformists functioning within the educational apparatus like inspectors Raúl Díaz and Carlos Vergara. Self-critically, he accepted part of the blame for the disastrous condition of public education: "We are all responsible, because we were all indifferent when our shared educational challenges were discussed." In his view, the state's educational system had totally failed to educate the youth and needed to be completely reformed, from its assumptions to its goals. The failure had occurred primarily because education had been organized around political not educational principles. Somewhat naively, he asked why military men and not the teachers' union had been able to set the terms of the system. But he had broken with a pillar of libertarian doctrine by asserting that the state, though responsible for many educational problems, was not a monster to destroy. The state also lost the abstract quality that it typically had in anarchist discourse. Rationalists recognized it as an interlocutor and set out to change it.

While retaining clear libertarian inspiration, the League and the Teachers' Confederation fought to prevent politicians from securing leadership posts in state educational institutions. It called for "reforming the present system of government schools, creating a republic of teaching in which teachers have the ability to elect their own superiors." It sought to generate an autonomous educational system in which real educators would be responsible for issues related to education. To achieve this, the teachers, subjects of the revolutionary process, would have to transform themselves intellectually and morally. For this, the League and the rationalists, educators of the educators and creators of the transformative project, were there to help.

Barcos and the rationalists were pragmatists. By distancing themselves from the ideological certitudes enclosed in revolutionary rhetoric, their work had greater viability among educators. Rationalist discourse was reformist and progressive, in contrast to the revolutionary urgency of the doctrinal anarchists, with whom they always had an uneasy coexistence. It is no surprise that disagreements between the two groups came into the open after the Centenary. The rationalists had not stopped being libertarians in the broad sense, but they lost their impatience for social transformation. They accepted that social change would be a long process and that the "free, rational, healthy, and unprejudiced" education of the individual would have to lay the foundation for a better, future society.

These views were by no means exclusive to the rationalists; educators from diverse currents embraced at least some of their principles. Barcos himself recognized this: "Official educators, who are not necessarily shortsighted just because they are educators, have begun to understand that there is a need to transform schools on a rational, scientific, humanistic, and free basis."[75] Rationalist discourse was part of a broader discursive field than that occupied by the doctrinal purists, one that even included reformists within the state educational apparatus. The latter had no reason to object to rationalists' goal of creating a "school that is friendly to progress," built upon scientific and rational principles, and that stimulates children's capacity for thought, curiosity, investigation, and intuition. While these goals were perfectly consistent with libertarian revolutionism, they could also be extracted from—and even rendered incompatible with—anarchist doctrine. Indeed, Barcos's turn to the Radical Party shortly afterward is easy to understand. To reward him for the switch, he received a position in the National Education Council, where he would continue preaching his views in a more moderate though more effective form.

During Spain's "Tragic Week" in 1909, revolutionaries burned churches and religious schools in the name of rational education. In its exaggerated and implacable response, Maura's government executed Ferrer and shut down 130 rationalist schools. These facts help us place the Argentine experience in a comparative perspective: the repression in Argentina during the Centenary resulted in the closure of less than one dozen libertarian establishments, which had operated on a much more precarious footing than their Spanish counterparts. The number of schools closed indicates the magnitude of the respective undertakings. Rationalism's success in Spain was due to the backwardness of that country's educational system, which was torn between the prevailing religious, quasi-medieval pedagogy and the Spanish government's lukewarm efforts to fight pervasive illiteracy, a problem that was also aggravated by regional differences.

The Argentine public school system operated effectively on popular sectors, and the role of education took shape just as the modern state was being formed. It did not matter how many mistakes were made in the birth and development of the statist educational apparatus, what mattered was that it spread literacy successfully and disciplined residents under the leitmotif of universal, free, and obligatory education. This doubtlessly undermined the appeal of libertarians' educational initiatives. Government schools also had an infrastructure that was incomparably better than what anarchists could offer (not only good buildings and materials but also specialized teachers). In fact, libertarians' precarious, modest efforts were not even very attractive to libertarian activists themselves. Police calculated that there were 5,000 to 6,000 anarchist militants in Buenos Aires during the first ten years of the century and yet libertarian schools never had more than 200 or 300 students, indicating that very few anarchists enrolled their own children in these schools.

Due to a lack of conviction and internal differences, anarchists could never articulate a coherent alternative to the state's monolithic programs—and the state practically ignored libertarians' educational exploits.[76] Militants threw themselves en masse into cultural activities and, above all, the labor movement, where they hoped to harvest more immediate results. Anarchism's labor front paid little attention to educational endeavors and, like the doctrinal purists, its support for alternative education did not correspond with practical steps in that regard.[77] Perhaps they saw the solidity of the state apparatus as an insurmountable obstacle, or perhaps the idea of instituting a comprehensive, rational educational alternative that would combine manual and intellectual work seemed best postponed to the post-revolutionary future.

The weakness of anarchist educational efforts contributed to the failure of the libertarian revolutionary project as a whole, although many elements of rationalist pedagogy were assimilated into other progressive educational tendencies and, in that sense, not all of their contributions disappeared in the dead ends into which anarchists turned.

The individual will not be free or happy so long as the state survives.
—*La Protesta Humana*, May 1, 1902

The law was established to preserve and strengthen the dominant minority; thus, at a time when the minority's weapon is money, the law's principal goal is to keep the rich, rich and the poor, poor.
—Rafael Barrett, *Notas críticas*

The fatherland is a myth: the entire world is our home. We don't need to defend borders or a little plot of land.
—*Gleam*, March 25, 1906

The idiots, the slaves, the mentally castrated are the ones who vote, those satisfied with bread and circuses while they live a life of misery.
—*No Votamos*, pamphlet from the Anarchos group, Bahía Blanca, November 22, 1907

CHAPTER VII

The State, the Law, the Fatherland, and Argentine Anarchists' Political Practices

A NARCHISTS AND SOCIALISTS worked assiduously to construct a social arena in which workers could constitute and express a distinct identity. Of the two groups, it was anarchists who most vigorously opposed integration into the political system and who fought hardest to create a practical political alternative. Their opposition to the state led them to reject not only the institution as a whole, but also aspects of it such as the legal system, the idea of the fatherland, the army, and electoral politics.[1] They saw themselves as outside of the state's restrictive, fraudulent system—an institution, it so happens, that slowly and inexorably transformed the residents of Buenos Aires into citizens.

With their characteristic revolutionary urgency, anarchists rejected ideals of citizenship, representation, and political participation, and posited a more spontaneous approach to doing politics that included the general strike and, to a lesser degree, propaganda by deed. They believed that these strategies would enable them to eliminate the state, classes, and social inequality.

Historians of the Argentine anarchist movement often take for granted the affinity between anarchist apoliticism and workers' indifference to the political system. This simplifies the relation between political vanguards and workers insofar as it fails to scrutinize libertarians' reasons for challenging representative politics or the difficulties inherent in their perspective. This also obscures issues germane to understanding this formative stage of modern Argentine history.

This chapter, which focuses on the first fifteen years of the century, examines Argentine anarchists' view of and practical response to the state, legal system, fatherland, army, electoral politics, direct action (particularly the general strike), and tactical use of violence.

1. THE STATE

In 1904, Interior Minister Joaquín V. González had to withdraw his proposed National Labor Law. As a response to the social conflict, its purpose was to regulate labor relationships and deter anarchist intervention. Its demise reflected the parliament's limited interest and also decisive opposition from industrial sectors in the Argentine Industrial Union as well as workers in the anarchist-led Argentine Workers' Federation.[2] In other words, the most pertinent actors rejected government intervention in a matter that they considered the prerogative of bosses and workers. Anarchists celebrated the law's defeat as a victory of their own, just as they celebrated low voter turnout in elections. They seemed to understand that their fortunes rose to the degree that the state was disengaged from social and labor relations and committed to political exclusion, although they did not grasp that the state's relationship to society was in the midst of a profound transformation, one that they had helped to generate.

As noted, the Argentine state consolidated itself through the expansion of the public school system during the initial years of the twentieth century. Something similar occurred in the arena of public health. The state also bolstered its presence in other, more conflicted and emergent spheres of local society. For instance, the Obligatory Military Service Law, approved in 1902, complemented schools' integrative function and fostered nationalist sentiments. And there were various additional legislative initiatives (some approved, others defeated) that, along with González's labor law, indicated the government's determination to intervene in labor and social conflicts. Finally, there was the Sáenz Peña Law: passed in 1912, it compelled all Argentine men above the age of eighteen to vote (using a free and secret ballot), which greatly expanded citizen participation in the electoral process. Deliberately or not, all of these measures led to the integration of broad swaths of the population and the marginalization of oppositional groups among workers. Of course, the process was highly uneven—women remained excluded and had only just begun to travel the path of social rights—but, for our purposes, what is important to note is that the state had started to implement reforms.

In one of their few areas of consensus, Buenos Aires anarchists unanimously opposed authority and the state—the latter being the maximum expression of the former. The libertarian movement unequivocally challenged the state, defending the possibility of life without government. Individualists, collectivists, pro-organizationalists, and anti-organizationalists directed all of their theory and practice to this end. Man, they argued, is able to:

> live without laws, without regulations, without government or administration or bureaucracy; without the army, without green and blue books, without hierarchies, without mandarins; in a word, each individual can live freely; eating, drinking, sleeping, and working according to his needs and faculties, satisfying amorous requisites through the manifestation of free impulse.[3]

They demanded life without government. The government, said *La Protesta Humana*, "does not contribute anything to the progress of the people or their well-being. It produces nothing."[4] Libertarians believed that it destroys individuals' innate tendency toward cooperation and violates society's nature because it relies on command and obedience, which constitute the essence of government and are also:

> the source of its own limit, because to sustain itself it must in the first place issue a command, which implies the need to act, and that is a limitation; in the second place, the government undermines itself because it needs obedience to satisfy its commands, which restrains the freedom of the one who is commanded, who naturally resists and rebels, and that is another, continuous limit.[5]

Anarchists rejected the claim that the state was necessary to maintain order and guarantee freedom. They asserted that its origins lay in class and social inequality, and that it must, by definition, preserve the dominant minority's dominance: "tyranny, inequality, injustice, and immorality are the foundation of government."[6]

Local anarchists embraced Kropotkin's view of the state. They frequently gave lectures on his work and printed innumerable articles by him on the state's uselessness and perversity. For instance, in 1901, *The Rebel* published his long essay, "The Scientific Bases of Anarchy," in which he argued for forms of social organization that protect individual freedom from statist oppression. Accepting Spencer's argument that the state restricts progress and concentrates power while it regulates society, he demanded a distribution of public functions that would encourage the initiative of freely constituted groups of individuals. This would guarantee the progress of social life after the state's collapse.[7]

Anarchists believed that the state's purpose was to protect ruling-class interests and restrict individual freedom. It was a perversion whose roots lay in the distant era of the clan when, due to the individual's weakness, the chief emerged to serve the stronger, thereby rupturing the natural order. The authoritarian, repressive functions of the chief evolved until they took on the form of the modern state and, from then on, society, a natural institution par excellence, and the state, an artificial institution, strained to coexist. The state annulled the individual legally and politically, eliminating his rights and psychologically undermining his capacity for freedom. Far from protecting freedom, the state was fundamentally incompatible with it: "it does not represent rights, but rather the privileges of those who operate and sustain it, the parasites of power and capital. It doesn't grant freedom to the individual but multiplies servitudes and subjugations."[8]

Champions of individual will, anarchists confronted a state that arrogated defense of the common good to itself and also, after the French Revolution, the representation of the general will. They built a great deal of their social, political, and cultural initiatives upon a foundation of anti-statism. In very concrete terms, they challenged three pillars upon which the state rested: the law or legal system, the fatherland and the army, and democracy and parliamentary politics.

2. THE LAW

Anarchists believed that the law was vital to the state's survival and to its ability to dominate individuals and regulate society. In their view, written law merely codified customs that had emerged spontaneously and thereby prevented their natural evolution. This led to "the decline of public action, since men, coming to rely on the law's efficacy and the power of those entrusted with enforcing it, cease to exercise social sanction, which has tremendous moralizing effects."[9] Through the law, individuals cede their responsibilities to the legal system and authorities, which are infinitely less effective than collective intervention. "Law and authority, however conscientiously managed, are utterly inflexible and therefore regressive; man must be an automaton to avoid conflicting with them."[10] That is, in addition to curtailing popular struggles, the law fossilizes social relationships and subverts progress, which anarchists understood as the emancipation from all forms of exploitation. For this reason, and with few nuances, anarchists saw legislation as an assault upon individual freedom and a sinister consequence of dominant groups' attempt to preserve their power.

The law defended dominant groups from mobilizations of the dispossessed. "[It] was established," Rafael Barrett said, "to preserve and strengthen the dominant minority; thus, at a time when the minority's weapon is money, the law's principal goal is to keep the rich, rich and the poor, poor."[11] Legislation, along with the magistracy and the police, safeguards the dominant order: "Though supposedly guaranteeing justice and protecting order, the law is unconditionally at the service of robbery enthroned and justice eviscerated."[12] The state, an instrument of domination and a foe of the masses from time immemorial, had benefited the dominant classes for centuries, a reality that only grew more pronounced under capitalism, when the bourgeoisie legally sanctioned private property, thereby underwriting exploitation and the appropriation of surplus value from the poor, who were prevented from enjoying the products of their labor and whose personal freedom was increasingly restrained. "Man, who ought to have the freedom to come and go, to see, to feel, to speak, to work, to study, to nourish himself, and intelligently satisfy his needs in nature and in society, as Spencer would have it, is trammeled by capital and law, by the organization of social life."[13] The law's mission was not to protect individuals but to preserve property and a state that safeguards bourgeois exploitation.

Moreover, anarchists believed laws to be ineffective. For instance, they questioned the utility of the labor law proposed by Joaquín V. González in 1904, which cast prostitution as a job: even though it tried to regulate it, it was meaningless "if women continue to be victimized by that social gangrene."[14] The real solution, libertarians argued, is social and economic. They also argued that the law does not stop crime: criminals as well as corrupt judges, policemen, jailers, politicians, and bureaucrats can easily evade it if they want to. "We oppose all legislation," declared La Protesta.[15] Anarchists even rejected sanitation laws, which many progressives thought indispensable to the prevention of epidemics and illness. For anarchists, such laws were tools of social control. Instead of approving such "brutal" laws, anarchists argued that those concerned with hygiene ought to focus on promoting healthy practices through education. "The law is never good and never will be," said Gleam, "because it rests upon a bad principle: the principle of imposition, which doesn't even work as a means of education."[16] Anarchists' alternative to the law was social consensus.

In addition to their abstract critique of the law, anarchists also advanced a concrete attack on parliamentarian action. Although they paid scant attention to legislative affairs—and did not do so at all throughout the 1890s—their attitude changed as the government began addressing workers' issues. This was the case with labor legislation, which appeared on the agenda after the conflicts in 1902 and especially following the National Labor Law debate in 1904. After that time, legislation became a consistent feature of public discourse, engaging the workers and political tendencies linked to them. Anarchists saw labor legislation as nothing more than state interference in an arena that it had previously ignored (except, of course, when it sent in the police).

Anarchists argued that labor laws' main purpose was to tame social conflicts and discipline workers through labor codes. They also alleged that it favored the bosses, "with the deliberate aim of preventing any rebellions, any explosions of the unfortunate, while eternalizing the regime of endless pain for the abused, enslaved masses."[17] It was a form of social control: for example, hygiene inspectors were thought to be state spies who pried into people's private lives, thus violating individual freedom. They saw something similar in Article 14 of Minister González's labor law, which treated foreigners' activity. The very possibility of controlling people's conduct, whether private or public, outraged libertarians: "We already have the inquisition here ... observing everything, scrutinizing everything ... they are ready to hurl themselves upon any foreigner, on his most meager liberty, on the slightest protest, because the watchful eye of the executive power" is attentive to "what a foreigner thinks, does, and says; what he reads and writes; the hours that he sleeps and works."[18] For them, laws of this type undermined individual freedom and thwarted the possibility of anarchy.

Rejecting socialists' gradualist view of progress, they insisted that the reduction of the working day, the weekly day off, and the regulation of women's and children's labor were not fundamental changes. For anarchists, the only solution was to eliminate unproductive groups: this included bosses, businessmen, politicians, the clergy, soldiers, clerks, and public functionaries, the "new employees of the government, the new budget eaters freeloading on everyone else ... new authoritarians who have sold out to capital."[19] They also accused politicians of being out of touch with the world of labor: in 1904, just before the government passed a law mandating a weekly day off, columnists from *La Protesta* voiced skepticism about how much deputies and senators could really know about workers' needs. The state's distance from the world of labor vitiated its ability to act there.[20]

"What does labor legislation contribute," they asked? "It creates nothing new," because when the state and bourgeoisie translate workers' demands into law, they are merely codifying something that workers had already obtained through collective action. The state has no choice but to recognize and legalize the consequences of their agitation. "Legislation limits itself to sanctioning the results of social struggle,"[21] said one writer, citing the approval of the weekly day off as an example. Beneficiaries of the law had the day off because workers had organized, not because of state intervention. Anarchists did not consider the possibility that the law could, in the future, protect workers who had not fought for it themselves. They challenged the law as such and its utility in every context, contending that people could establish norms of conduct without needing an entity (the state) to oversee and guarantee them.

Anarchists' rejection of the state and law raised some irresolvable problems. How could workers secure the eight-hour day, the weekend, or better working conditions without legislative sanction or the participation of the state in any capacity? Anarchists saw such demands as temporary improvements that were important to the long-term revolutionary process, but argued that there was no need for the government to manage agreements between workers and bosses, even if either side could unilaterally violate an arrangement. Anarchists did not accept state arbitration or regulation of labor relations. Convinced that the state only represented and defended the privileged, they opted to continue fighting through direct action and refused to utilize the state in negotiations.

Anarchists' repudiation of any form of state ratification made them unable to secure improvements obtained through mobilization. While it is true that the state had a minimal presence in labor relationships prior to the new century, it grew gradually more involved between 1902 and 1910 (from the approval of the Residency Law to the Social Defense Law), passing several labor laws and creating the National Department of Labor in 1907, which laid the foundation for the state's much more active presence in ensuing decades.[22] Faithful to their principles, libertarians' attitude toward the state did not change, which was surely one of the many causes of their rapid decline as a movement not long after.

But the movement's position even caused problems for it at the very beginning of the century, when it was on the upswing. Some workers found it contradictory to fight for the eight-hour day, the weekend, workplace safety, and the prohibition of children's and women's labor while also rejecting parliamentary sanction. Who would enforce labor accords and how? Anti-statism and an exaggerated self-confidence led the Argentine Workers' Federation to assert in 1901—paraphrasing Marx—that workers' emancipation ought to be accomplished by the workers themselves: given that the "law always favors capitalists, who can evade it, [the federation] resolves that workers ought to expect everything from their consciousness and their union, and not solicit any assistance from public authorities."[23] This position would reappear in practically every anarchist-led workers' congress during the first ten years of the century; the entire libertarian movement endorsed it.

Anarchists understood that the state responded to workers' pressure—their efforts, said *La Protesta*, had "brought the Residency Law, but also the Labor Law."[24] They asserted that the state's real goal was to muzzle conflicts and arrest the growth of revolutionary tendencies, which were emerging precisely because of state oppression. "The power of new ideas," said *La Protesta*, "is proportionate to the state's coercive force: when there is greater tyranny, protest is more virile and violent.... The state only worries about workers when their movement is powerful and proletarian forces are mobilized."[25] For them, legislation promising to improve workers' lives was a trap. FORA leader Francisco Jaquet argued that the passage of labor laws did not indicate the state's evolution but simply its engagement with the sociological principles of the time, to which "it must adapt itself in order to survive." No law, he said, could possibly put an end to the class conflict. Anarchists must never tolerate negotiation; on the contrary, they should focus on emancipating themselves from wage labor and stop "working for another's profit and charging a salary in return. For attaining that goal, legislation will never be of any use and will always fail."[26]

3. THE FATHERLAND AND THE BARRACKS

In addition to the legal system, anarchists thought the state legitimated itself through the idea of the fatherland. In their view, it needed the idea to furnish itself with an identity and thus laid down borders and invented nations, separating people not only by class but also by nationality. Cognizant of nationalism's growing influence, Rafael Barrett said: "Patriotism is too narrow a mold for our future. By delimitating our nature, it homogenizes us. Patriotism is division. We will not be victorious if divided."[27] At a time when nations and nationalist sentiments were growing rapidly, anarchists, again running against the current, called for a society without borders and a world without nationalities.[28] "It is necessary to replace the idea of the fatherland with the idea of humanity and to found it on the common interest, not on the particularities of class," wrote an author in *La Protesta*.[29]

Anarchists condemned the idea of the fatherland for its high degree of abstraction and for the innate difficulty of determining who belonged to it, whether the common denominator was birthplace, custom, or language. Anarchists charged that the dominant classes articulated the idea of the fatherland around precisely these elements, then goaded the people into embracing a national flag. For libertarians, the fatherland was a meaningless abstraction whose real goal was to mobilize people to attack other, foreign peoples or for the purposes of domestic repression. It was irrational, too: why should humans kill one another in the name of the fatherland? It is foolish to suppose a coherent collectivity on the basis of an arbitrary trait. Nation-states linked and mixed, sometimes forcibly, individuals with the most diverse identities, who often felt no real solidarity with one another. For instance, anarchists found it absurd to imagine a binding community among Galicians, Catalans, and Basques, all of whom lived within the abstraction known as "Spain." And what affinities, they asked, could possibly exist among the endless, different groups in Argentina?[30] None, they answered: "Spanish and German bankers have more in common with each other than they do with the workers from their own countries."[31] The fatherland was a tool of the ruling class, which it used to vertically organize the rest of the population around its foreign and domestic goals.

Anarchists directed their anti-patriotic propaganda to the workers, asking them: What does the fatherland matter to you? If "you experience the same oppression in France as you do in England, Chile, Argentina, or Germany, why do you care about the nationality of your exploiters?"[32] The workers' fatherland was the world. However, insofar as the world was divided into nations, workers had no homeland: "We are foreigners in every country!" proclaimed the hero of a libertarian drama. "We are the rejects! The bastards!"[33]

Anarchists knew that much of the populace had strong patriotic sentiments—it was part of common sense—or prejudice, to use their term—and encouraged in homes and schools. "Patriotic prejudices are deeply rooted among a substantial part of the people,"[34] said one newspaper, especially the youth, in their judgment, who might hate the army if they were mistreated in it, but not because they questioned the fatherland, which was the essence of the army. Ignorance and nationalist education had fostered a passionate attachment to the fatherland among young people, who "don't believe and perhaps can't even imagine that one can live well without government, without the fatherland."[35]

The state used public rituals and other propagandistic ploys to inculcate an identification with nationalist symbols and the idea of the fatherland. And once the people accepted the idea, the state imposed an institution—the army—that was not at all abstract and whose object was to protect the nation's supposed interests. "The fatherland needs defenders, and this is why it forms armies.... It is every honorable patriot's duty to join."[36] Thus, the abstract notion of the fatherland took shape in an armed body organized around the pretense of external defense. It was "the arm of the savage power called the state" and its real function was repression.[37]

Argentine anarchists understood that elites needed an institution with which to cultivate nationalist attitudes in the country's heterogeneous population. The army played an important role in this, and libertarians began rallying against it as early as the 1890s. Resisting the army and militarism generally became a topic of considerable interest for libertarians, as it was a way that they could fight the state directly. Translated articles from the French libertarian press initially provided most of the inspiration for anti-militarist activism. Later, without cutting ties to France, anarchists began to criticize the Argentine National Guard and focus on issues of domestic militarism, particularly between 1898 and 1902, when tensions between Argentina and Chile were at a highpoint.[38] The problem of the army figured consistently in the press after 1901 due to the passage of the Obligatory Military Service law.

Although socialists also participated, anarchists were the principal anti-militarist force in Buenos Aires at the time, just as the army was becoming an issue in Argentine society. Conscription reflected more than the need to defend national borders or Chile's approval of a similar law one year earlier, the claims of some of its advocates notwithstanding. Some hoped that the army would facilitate the civic and moral edification of the youth, who were often suspected of being excessively cosmopolitan and influenced by advanced social ideas. Others believed that conscription would help Argentinize immigrants, socializing them as well as those born in the country. It would complement the education imparted in school, helping unite the country's diverse nationalities while fostering respect for patriotic symbols and a spirit of obedience.[39]

Anarchists understood that the purpose of obligatory military service was not only to serve the needs of the army and national defense but also to protect the state and preserve domestic order. This is why they constantly called on soldiers to abandon the military:

> Conscripts, the army is a vampire that sucks your blood, squeezes you, twists you, and then spits you out, impotent and useless, far, very far away, where you cannot disrupt their criminal feasts. And now, soldiers, think about it and do what best pleases you! Go and swell the ranks of the army; give up your personality to prostitute yourselves in the barracks and fire murderous rifles at your brothers, or work alongside them to prop up the foundation of the gigantic edifice of social injustice.[40]

The same year that this statement appeared, the Workers' Federation took up the anti-militarist cause.

The effort became increasingly important for libertarian publications and groups, who hoped to make workers aware of the "evils of the army." In addition to publishing abundant articles on the topic, they also distributed newspapers, pamphlets, and flyers in army barracks denouncing the treatment of soldiers. For instance, in 1906, after military authorities tried and executed a soldier for retaliating against a superior who had assaulted him, anarchists issued a statement blasting militarism and the death penalty:

> If it is true that this penalty was decreed by feeble-minded men of a darker age, then today, in the twentieth century, a century in which enlightenment has enabled men to dominate the seas, the earth, and the air ... today, when man has become a being full of culture ... we cannot under any circumstance permit such a barbaric law to continue hanging like a double-edged sword over the soldier in military trials in the name of a nefarious discipline.[41]

Anarchists encouraged soldiers to rebel: they urged them to desert and, when they were ideologically committed, to organize against the army from within. In both cases, they urged them to resist the state's repression of the workers: "Listen, conscript ... if you refrain from firing upon the people ... you will accomplish a crucial task."[42]

Anti-militarist organizing became more systematic after the formation of the Anti-Militarist Council in 1904, an initiative that had the backing of most libertarian groups and the Argentine Workers' Federation. One of its first measures was to start a fund for deserters. In addition to disseminating propaganda, it also set out to build ties with European and American anti-militarist groups and planned to send a contingent to an anti-militarist congress in France. In 1906, in response to the army's growing importance in the country, the FORA called for stepping up anti-militarist action:

> The Sixth Congress, recognizing that militarism is a breach of the laws of nature with manifestations in our midst, invites the Anti-Militarist Council formed in Buenos Aires to create a nation-wide Anti-Militarist Federation, and urges comrades active in societies to encourage both members and sympathetic nonmembers to join the army and contribute to anti-militarist endeavors therein.[43]

There is no evidence that anarchists formed an anti-militarist federation, but they did redouble their anti-militarist activity. In 1906, news of dynamic mobilizations against the army in Europe further inspired their efforts.

Anti-militarism had become an integral part of anarchist activism and nurtured utopian hopes for a world without borders and a future without war. Although the slogan "There won't be wars or borders bathed in human blood in the year 2000," seems naïve today, such views were an article of faith for anarchists at the time.[44]

In the context of this momentum, and an extensive network of libertarian circles, centers, and groups, anarchists formed two groups specifically to carry out anti-militarist propaganda specifically: The Conscript, which was founded in 1906 and did not last beyond the year, and Soldier's Enlightenment, which had a longer, more fruitful existence (1907–1913). Headquartered in the Belgrano neighborhood, the latter concentrated on anti-militarist propaganda in addition to disseminating anarchist ideas generally. It organized talks and lectures for conscripts; encouraged militants to start similar groups in other areas; and raised funds for deserters, victims of repression within the army, and for printing and distributing pamphlets and flyers denouncing the military.[45] Its most important contribution was the publication of the leading anti-militarist newspaper of the time: *Soldier's Enlightenment* (1907–1913), which had widespread backing in the anarchist movement.[46] Circles like Gentlemen of the Ideal, The Commune, Social Studies Center, Art and Freedom, The Free, Émile Zola, Seed, and Friends of the Worker as well as *La Protesta* and the paper's founding group distributed subscription lists and organized *veladas* to help finance it. This broad support indicates that *Soldier's Enlightenment* was not the work of an isolated group and that anarchists in Buenos Aires as a whole were dedicated to fighting militarism in a comprehensive, multifaceted way. The periodical's long life—unlike most partisan publications, which were extremely fleeting—and the manifold efforts made to maintain it also show that anarchists regarded anti-militarism as important.

The biweekly appeared at a time of active anti-militarist publishing. There was the newspaper *Gleam*, which was prominent in anti-militarist efforts.[47] In 1907, the Seed library published *De la patria* (*On the Fatherland*) by Augustin Hamon, doubtlessly the most authoritative anti-militarist voice of the period. That same year, the Blanca Library put out a pamphlet by the Dutch Domela Nieuwenhuis titled *El militarismo y la actitud de los anarquistas y socialistas revolucionarios ante la guerra* (*Militarism and Anarchists and Socialists' Attitude to War*), translated by Elam Ravel, *La Protesta*'s former editor-in-chief. Two years earlier, the Workers' Library in Montevideo translated and published the *Manual del Soldado* (*Soldier's Guide*), originally released by France's Bourses du Travail federation. José de Maturana's cultural magazine, *The New Paths*, published Laurent Tailhade's "Los carteles antimilitaristas" ("Antimilitarist Posters") in May 1906.

The newspapers exhibited two different registers. One was an abstract analysis of patriotism and militarism, framed by the anarchist doctrine and vision of the future. The other, more concrete, consisted of news about the abuse of authority, ill treatment of soldiers, and climate of moral degradation in the barracks. *Soldier's Enlightenment* described military life in the following terms:

> The continual petty thefts, the need to constantly lie to conceal the thousand little infractions that one inevitably commits … the frequency with which one hears rude talk or foul observations of depraved vices like sodomy, inebriation, gluttony, sensualism, etc., the need for a degraded environment; the regularity with which one witnesses cruel and even savage acts; the depression of the spirit caused by the continual fear of punishment and the ill-humor and antipathy that any officer can impose upon the hapless conscript; the denunciations, sadistic jokes, insults and injustices endured or witnessed daily: all of this loosens, perverts, and destroys the internal moral fibers that all youth—even those with just a bit of honesty—possess, cultivate, and love.[48]

Anarchists hoped to expose the military's unnatural, violent character with denunciations of this sort, which they thought an effective way to raise awareness among soldiers. After describing the "evils of the barracks," they urged servicemen to desert or militate within the army itself.

There is not much information about the circulation of *Soldier's Enlightenment*, but we know that it was most widely distributed in Buenos Aires and that it also found its way to cities in the province of Buenos Aires (La Plata, Mar del Plata, Chacabuco, Piñero, Salto, Ingeniero White, Tandil, and Bolívar among others) and to the provinces of Santa Fe and Tucumán. It had a print run of 2,000, except in the year preceding the Centenary, when the rate doubled.[49] These figures, the appearance of another anti-militarist periodical (*The Barracks*), the increase in *La Protesta*'s print run, and the publication of the evening paper (*The Battle*) point to the dynamism of anarchist-inspired agitation at the time. The preventative mobilization of some army battalions during the events of May 1909 reinforced anarchist convictions about the military: "The experience of the general strike has demonstrated the truth for us," wrote *The Barracks*. "The Argentine army, sustaining itself through enormous taxes, has become a guard dog for foreign interests while pretending to protect the nation's integrity."[50]

In sum, militarism was a concern for anarchists for multiple reasons. On the one hand, it promoted authoritarianism and submission and was a major obstacle to libertarians' principal demand: the absolute freedom of humanity. On the other, the military embodied the idea of the fatherland, which safeguarded the privileged groups represented by the state. To fight against the army was to fight against the state directly. Although there is no evidence that anarchist antimilitarism acquired much popular resonance—they stopped a few young men from enlisting and encouraged others to desert, but nothing more—their efforts were original. They were almost the only ones to advance these positions at the time, being a discordant voice in a society in which the notion of the fatherland was deeply rooted.

Though law and the fatherland were among the state's principal means of legitimizing itself, democracy was its most powerful weapon. Anarchists viewed democracy and its attributes—popular sovereignty, individual rights, and equality before the law—as contrivances meant to conceal oppression. Like the law and the fatherland, they saw democracy as an instrument in the service of the privileged (and as a "farce"). While linked to the republic as a political form, it offered nothing new to the dispossessed: a president's authority was not fundamentally different from that of a king, and with either ruler, the bourgeoisie still held political power. "The modern bourgeoisie is imperialist under an emperor, monarchist under a king, republican under a president, and always an exploiter of the people" proclaimed Gregario Inglán.[51] Whatever the form of the state, workers' situation remained fundamentally the same. "Why should Argentine workers care any more about the Republic," asked Inglán, "than Germans care about the Empire or Spaniards the monarchy?"[52] Democracy's primary underpinnings were the parliamentary system and party politics.

4. THE MEANINGS OF POLITICS

What did politics mean for anarchists? A writer in *The Rebel* defined politics as "the art of deceiving the masses, who produce everything and yet receive only table scraps from the exploiters in return." It is something that "men of sound minds" cannot countenance, he said, as it reflects the interests of the dominant classes and depends on popular ignorance.[53]

Anarchists saw politics as a comedy that violated the principle of natural equality found in evolution. For the author in *The Rebel*, anarchists were the "vanguard of progress" who legitimately represented the masses "on rigorously scientific foundations" and in defense of the "great principle of equality." They draw their "ideals from science," whereas "politics has never been, nor will it ever be, anything but arbitrary agreements between parties" based on falsehoods.[54] Libertarians' interpretation of politics is inseparable from their rationalist world-view: they replaced religion's revealed, metaphysical truths with science and reason, which would make the elimination of authority possible as well as the harmony and justice that they thought prevailed in nature.[55] The exploitation of man would give way to individual liberation and the scientific administration of things. The dictates of science—sociology, above all—would determine political decisions.

Their commitment to a rational and scientific analysis of society led to an ambiguous conception of politics. Anarchists regarded "politics" as synonymous with the bourgeois political system and believed that it represented the interests of the dominant class. However, they did not reject political action as such, but rather specific forms of political representation like parliamentarianism and elections. Although anarchists were fundamentally anti-political and anti-legalistic, their practices were essentially political insofar as they were oriented toward the conquest of power.[56] They yearned for power, not in order to exercise it in a modern sense, but in order to destroy that which controlled it—the state—and to impose a different order.

Anarchists believed that the state violated nature because it relied on command and obedience. Its very existence signified that one individual or collective entity governed while another, being subjugated, was obliged to obey it and therefore oppressed. Anarchists insisted that command and obedience were identical with servitude and inequality, which were the essence of the state and the falsity of the politics that sustain it. "Anarchist communists abhor and fight politics, resisting politicians who are in power as much as those who hope to acquire it…. Politics is the art of governing; anarchy is the abolition of government and, consequently, politics."[57]

They also condemned politics as an act of delegation in which individuals entrust their needs and desires to another. "Reclus said that to delegate power is to lose it," wrote González Pacheco, " but, oh, excuse me, it's much worse! It is to be the dog of a freedom belonging to others.... To delegate power is immoral and barbaric."[58] In the act of political representation, the represented subject loses his or her freedom because the representative assumes the authority and power to act autonomously on his or her behalf, substituting his or her will for that of the represented. "To vote is to abdicate," said *La Protesta*. "The man who puts his vote in the ballot box hands over his will and his rights to the person that he elects.... He hands over what he should protect fervently."[59] For libertarians, the problem of political delegation had roots in the concept of citizenship that emerged after the French Revolution, which undermined man's natural state (natural man precedes the citizen) and legalized privilege (citizenship connotes political privilege), converting political representation into a legal fiction or, as Proudhon argued, the illusion of universal representation. For anarchists, the crux of the problem lay in the fact that freedom is impossible to delegate.

Anarchists also believed that elections diverted the masses from the revolutionary path. In 1900, Argentine anarchists published a letter that Malatesta wrote in London that captured their opposition to parliamentarianism. Malatesta thought it generated false hopes in the people and cultivated the habit of waiting passively for the government to provide freedom and well-being, and also that "accepting that system implies, logically and psychologically, recognition of the principle of government, of law, and of authority, which is antagonistic to freedom and progress."[60]

Three years earlier, Malatesta and a former comrade, Saverio Merlino, had a long and interesting debate on the anarchist position on elections. Merlino, then more of a socialist, argued that dismissing politics and encouraging abstentionism alienated anarchists from the most active, militant sectors of the people. He thought it a mistake and pure dogmatism to scorn the use of elections, which were really means, not ends, and presented an opportunity to propagandize, agitate, and protest government abuses. In reply, Malatesta argued that abstentionism was not only a matter of tactics but also of ends and principles. In his view, parliamentary strategies transformed those who practiced them into parliamentarians and thus integrated them into the state, which violated anarchist principles. "The right to vote," he said, "is the right to renounce one's rights and therefore contradicts our goals."[61]

Anarchists sometimes assailed politics with irony, portraying it as a farce. In their depiction, the various political factions lived at peace between elections, battled fiercely when seats and offices were up for grabs, and then returned to peaceful coexistence once the election was over. Meanwhile, wrote *The Rebel*, "those who are trampled in such ceremonies (the people), humbly bow their heads, hoping that the triumphant candidates will toss them a few crumbs and privileges from their altars to the fatherland and the good of the people. The farce, the endless farce!"[62]

They also represented politics as theater: "A party is highly theatrical. One could say that the country is a stage; the party boss, an impresario or financier; the people, an audience; the events, performances; the politicians, comedians." Among the latter, there were all types of actors: bosses, great men, poseurs, and employees. Politicians' popularity fluctuated just like that of actors; a politician fell out of favor when he made an unwelcome move, just as a bad performance causes a thespian's prestige to drop. Anarchists extended the analogy to comebacks: both actors and politicians could recycle their theatrical-political roles in other spheres (i.e., on other stages). For the political comedy to be possible, the people-audience have to be present, who, like extras, uncritically follow the politicians-actors and, with their votes, convert them into statues at the end of their careers. In this

> metamorphosis into a statue ... [the politician] usually has to purify his vices and redeem himself through civic virtue. While organisms ultimately exhaust themselves in the natural course of their physiological trajectory, social life evolves unceasingly and dramatically expands the public's moral capacities in a way that consumes the body in which it takes root. But politics dilate the growing soul and easily prompt an ambitious egoist to portray himself as a dedicated altruist.[63]

They also polemicized against the socialists. Rejecting Marxists' claim that suffrage was a positive step toward the conquest of class power, anarchists argued that the right to vote was actually the right to renounce one's own rights and accustomed people to passivity, neglecting their interests, and handing their hopes over to the bourgeoisie.[64] Anarchists accused socialists of being mere parliamentarians and, as early as 1898, posed a challenging question: What would happen if Socialists won a parliamentary majority and tried to abolish private property? Would the bourgeoisie allow this? No, it would not, said Gilimón in reply, who had once been active among socialists and described the idea that this could happen as one of the "sublime absurdities of contemporary Marxism." He argued that it is impossible to destroy the bourgeois regime through parliamentarian action.[65] Also in 1898, publishers of *The Future* newspaper asked why Socialists wanted to participate in a fraudulent, perverse, and limiting electoral system. In their view, the legal path made more sense in Europe, where "the illusion of respect for legal procedures may be deceptively appealing," but "such hopes are childish" in Argentina, where politics was almost a matter of brute force.[66] Although some Europeans had been optimistic about the results of workers' participation in elections, nothing had been achieved. Where could one find a positive example? Take Germany, for instance. In that country, with its endless deputies and millions of voters, the government still passed repressive, reactionary, and anti-worker laws. In light of that experience, libertarians saw Deputy Palacios's lone presence in the Argentine Congress as an absurdity and more of a concession to the bourgeoisie than a triumph for the proletariat.[67]

Libertarians published articles every election reviling the electoral system in general and socialists in particular. For their sake, Socialists were reluctant to participate in the elections, although not because of anarchist opposition so much as the apathy that Argentina's restricted system elicited and the lack of democratic political habits among workers. It is worth recalling that Spain and Italy—the countries from which most immigrants had come—also had restrictive political regimes. Fraud, caciquism, and electoral clientelism were pervasive in Spain, and in Italy, where there was no suffrage until 1913 (and even then, it was limited to adult, literate males), patterns of political participation there generally formed a close parallel to those in Argentina.[68] Despite the popular disinterest in elections, anarchists saw the Socialists as a serious threat. For them, "progressive" political parties were more dangerous than moderate ones: "The more good men they have in their ranks, the more damage they can do."[69] This is why they did not passively accept Socialist proselytizing and, in fact, made interrupting Socialist rallies a major part of their anti-electoral agitation. Enrique Dickmann complained bitterly about this in his memoirs: "Anarchists regularly disturbed Socialist election rallies. They did not concern themselves with Argentine politics—*acuerdista* or *oficialista* or Radical—but instead directed their confused, sectarian aggression at Socialists."[70]

Anarchists occasionally made very lucid critiques of the electoral system, but generally their analyses were repetitive and bereft of nuance, like their mechanical analysis of society. In 1906, they pilloried the Socialist Party's electoral platform, which called for abolishing indirect taxes, democratizing the army, and separating the church and state. Libertarians disdained these reforms as mere refinements in the forms of exploitation. Why separate church and state or democratize the army if these institutions are obstacles that ought to be abolished? For anarchists, legal reforms would never suffice and socialist gradualism would never challenge the state's deeper structure.

Anarchists paid more attention to the elections in 1906 than they had to any held previously and published an unusually large number of articles criticizing the electoral system and exhorting workers to abstain. Their heightened interest was likely due to the election of Socialist Alfredo Palacios as a deputy two years earlier and the increase in voters, which had jumped from 18,208 in 1902 to 27,836 in 1904.[71] Although these numbers were still low in relation to the size of the population of Buenos Aires, anarchists were not primarily concerned with voter turnout or patterns. They were preoccupied by the electoral act itself and, in fact, did not analyze the lack of popular participation in elections or restrictions on voting. What mattered to them was the voters' attitude, especially because so many were workers.[72] They claimed that people voted because they had been seduced by political caudillos, who garnered votes by distributing handouts ("cash, beer, and jobs").[73] Anarchist analyses generally ended with fiery calls for abstention (or the "voters' strike," which was their term for active abstention). They also railed against voters: "There is no initiative, nothing of substance in those stultified people who go out to vote in the belief that they are exercising a sacrosanct right."[74] Anarchists made derisive, angry statements about the masses whenever they made decisions that they questioned, but turned laudatory when they found events more pleasing. Admiration for the people on the part of the libertarians was in inverse proportion to their apparent degree of loyalty to the system, fluctuating in correspondence with the changing attitudes of the masses.

Commenting on the limited voter turnout in the 1900 election, *The Rebel* made the following claim:

> This shows that the people understand, if only intuitively, that the masters will never let themselves be governed by their shoemakers or stable hands. The people know the siren songs of their disinterested protectors all too well now, and if they look upon politicians with disgust today, tomorrow they will hold them to account for all the crimes that they have committed.[75]

The workers' movement was anarchists' primary concern until the Centenary, if not later, and their remarks on elections did not go beyond proclamations of this type. If Palacios's election caused some agitation, Socialist's poor results and loss of votes between 1906 and 1910 calmed them.[76] Responding to Socialists' meager vote tallies in 1908, and to their attempt to explain it by pointing to corruption in the electoral system, anarchists declared that Socialists had no right to protest after they had knowingly accepted the rules of the electoral game. They noted that Palacios himself had been elected in 1904 by the La Boca electoral district thanks to an alliance with the Republican Party, which supported the dominant regime, and that the Socialists had also endorsed Emilio Mitre's senatorial candidacy.

Anarchist critiques of Socialist electoralism grew more scathing as the first decade unfolded. They disdained Socialists' attempt to represent popular sectors with "their miserable party, a hybrid product of the bourgeoisie and proletariat"; one that uses the prestige and valor of suffrage to deceive the people and "prolong the survival of an exhausted, corrupt system through farce and deception." The shared social space that they had constructed with Socialists years before fragmented as their differences over the electoral system and, especially, the type of society that they wanted, deepened. Anarchists judged the socialists with rancor: "They are hybrids, a political leprosy. Be on the alert. Don't vote for them."[77]

Seven thousand people voted in the Federal Capital in 1910, which was less than in 1906. Anarchists claimed the decline as a victory. They alleged that the political parties participating were responsible for the drop and that the magnitude of abstention showed the good sense gradually emerging among the people thanks to effective anarchist proselytizing: "Those who aspire to the political feeding trough, the electoralists who believe that ballot boxes will bring emancipation, have failed again. We anarchists chalk this up as another triumph."[78] In fact, at the time, most of the libertarian movement optimistically thought that the Argentine electoral system was on the verge of collapse. Prisoners of their rejection of the state, they made no concession to the political regime, and their analyses were rarely more than cavalier denunciations of state institutions, the parliamentary system, and political parties.

But anarchists were well suited to the restrictive social and political circumstances of the era. An exclusionary political regime, a society that incorporated but that also excluded, and Argentina's immense cultural heterogeneity were a gold mine for libertarians, who applied the anarchist principle par excellence: "direct action." The strategy of direct action presupposed a battle between conflicting forces; anarchists sought thereby the immediate, revolutionary destruction of the state and the inauguration of a just and free society. Anarchists set out to establish justice without the mediation of statist institutions of any sort, founding it upon a consensus within the workers' movement. Direct action included tactics that usually reinforced but sometimes contradicted one another. There were three primary forms of direct action: a) propaganda intended to win over the workers, specifically the dissemination of the press and the creation of a network of circles, groups, and centers from which to transmit alternative political and cultural messages; b) violence, or propaganda by deed (sabotage, terrorism, etc.); and c) the general revolutionary strike, which was usually peaceful, but which anarchists thought would lead to an insurrection in which acts of violence would necessarily occur.[79] I examined the first of these strategies in initial chapters; I explore the latter two below.

5. PROPAGANDA BY DEED: ANARCHISM AND ITS CONTRADICTORY CONCEPTION OF VIOLENCE

Anarchists in Buenos Aires never supported violence to the extent that their European counterparts did—particularly the French—during the last decade of the nineteenth century.[80] In practice, they were far from terrorist, even though they freely used violent rhetoric, which encouraged elites to become anxious and to see anarchism in highly negative terms. News of bombings and assassinations in Europe also stirred these fears, as did Lombrosian criminology, which defined anarchism as an inherited, psychophysical predisposition to crime and violence.[81]

Argentine anarcho-individualists celebrated terror in the movement's early period, as indicated by short-lived newspapers whose names paid homage to European anarchist terrorists—*Ravachol's Voice* (1895) and *Caserio* (1896)—but their enthusiasm remained rhetorical. There were no terrorist acts of note during those years, although anarchists discussed the topic constantly. Most justified violence as an unfortunate consequence of social ills and some small, fleeting, and markedly individualist groups defended violence as a revolutionary tool from an almost essentialist, Nietzchean perspective. "Anarchy means the destruction of all authority, no matter how minor it may be: therefore, if that is what anarchy means, anarchy means destruction," wrote some individualists.[82] In their definition, violence was important in its own right and caused "the spheres of propaganda to expand and the revolutionary seed to sprout among the proletariat." They saw violence and revolution as synonyms, although for them acts of violence were not the result of a moment of exaltation or hatred but entirely rational deeds that would lead to the destruction of bourgeois society, after which, "atop the smoking ruins of palaces and the blood of bourgeois corpses, anarchy will implant itself."[83]

The newspaper containing this maximalist statement ran an opposing article in the same issue outlining a conception of violence that was much more common among local anarchists and the Argentine left later on. It argued that anarchy is in no way synonymous with destruction and, in an ambiguous defense of violence, said that it was not anarchism that made rebellion violent, but social injustice: "It is not people's opposition to barbarism that arms the revolution, but those barbarities themselves."[84]

The rise of the pro-organizationalists at the turn of the century pushed "propaganda by deed" and terror even further off the agenda, although anarchists never tired of warning authorities that they might face a wave of bombings and assassinations if the oppression of the workers and their movement continued:

> In the Argentine Republic ... those of us who propagate ideas in opposition to the capitalist order are persecuted mercilessly. Accordingly, we must make it known that we will be obliged, if the police mob go down the path of torture and mistreatment, to put down the pen, push aside the paper, and study more inhuman [*sic*] but necessary tactics of defense.[85]

There were some isolated acts of terror, despite the predominance of the nonviolent tendency. Attempts were made on the lives of presidents Quintana and Figueroa Alcorta in 1905 and 1908, respectively. Enrique Nido, who had worked with Francisco Ferrer in Spain, tried to kill the Spanish consul in Rosario in retaliation for Ferrer's execution. In a deed that would have greater resonance than any of the others, a young Russian immigrant named Simón Radowitzky killed Police Chief Ramón L. Falcón in 1909. These sporadic incidents reveal the ambivalence in anarchists' stance on violence, although the most common attitude—among individualists and collectivists—was to justify it as a by-product of social injustice.

Framed in this way, anarchists construed individual acts of violence against representatives of the dominant institutions (the state, the legal system, the church, capital, etc.) as acts of justice. Such deeds often benefited the workers, too, given that the person sent to replace an executed member of the ruling class "would rethink the expediency of giving some reforms to the people, so that the curse of the oppressed—a bomb or a dagger—does not fall upon him."[86] A writer in *The Rebel* was emphatic: "I accept and applaud every act of rebellion, every violation of coercive, conservative, and prohibitive laws, every blow, direct or indirect, faithful or unfaithful, against any and all social institutions, and all protest actions that torpedo or threaten the present social order."

The author also polemicized against [Socialist Party leader] Juan B. Justo, who argued that bombings and assassinations were merely the expressions of poverty and ignorance. Justo, the anarchist writer protested, forgot that the bourgeoisie also uses violence and robbery in its struggle against the proletariat. If the worker demands the part of his salary taken by the boss, he is tossed out of work with the backing of authority:

> Nothing is more appropriate, at that moment and even later, than that he who is robbed and violated should take justice into his own hands, since justice under the law does not exist for him. He doesn't have enough money to pay for it, and even if he did, it would only sanction the boss's conduct, for that is the nature of the law.[87]

The writer thus asserted an unwritten, extralegal norm by which a worker could exact justice through his own deeds. As an example, he cited Italian anarchist Michele Angiolillo, who murdered the Spanish minister Antonio Cánovas in 1897, thereby avenging the oppressed workers of Spain and the casualties of the war with Cuba. In a similar vein, Félix Basterra said that Gaetano Bresci's assassination of Humberto I was vengeance for the repression that Italians had suffered in Naples in 1893 and Tuscany and Milan five years later. "This is why Bresci did what he did and that's what it was: justice for the martyrs." Bombing and assaults "are almost always revolutionary: the last-ditch effort of the dispossessed in their fight for life."[88] Put differently, libertarians thought that acts of individual violence had a certain rationality and that, in the absence of other mechanisms through which popular sectors could secure justice, it was logical and natural to resort to such deeds in extreme cases. "The violent act is a consequence of the state that rules society, not of any specific doctrines," said *The Rebel*.[89] Though uncomfortable defending terrorism per se, anarchists asserted that social injustice, inequality, and police and legal arrogance inevitably bred hatred of the dominant institutions and the men who represented them, whether they were ministers, presidents, or police chiefs.

It is no surprise that the libertarian community voiced its solidarity with Radowitzky after he assassinated Colonel Ramón Falcón. *La Protesta* described his deed as the "execution of a hangman and a gift of fear to a tyrant." The FORA also expressed its support for the "avenging brother," saying that while it does not encourage violence it defends the desperate acts of a person who watched impotently as the man responsible for the 1909 May Day massacre continued to hold his position with impunity.[90] However, even though Radowitzky became a symbol for anarchists, they did not imitate him. This ambivalent position on violence runs throughout the history of the movement. For instance, small pieces appeared in *La Protesta* titled "the scientific world" or "practical chemistry" describing how to make, handle, and detonate bombs and dynamite.[91] In 1904, there was a quasi-anarchist group known as the Mitin Club made up of pro-terrorist Russian expatriates who gave public lectures announcing the deeds of their compatriots: "The latest Russian attack, its implications, and the need for more of the same." Other lectures had very practical ends: "Simultaneous explosions in two or more preselected places," "Acids and how to handle them," and "Practical chemistry: nitroglycerin, potassium chloride, and guncotton."[92]

Despite libertarians' generally affirmative comments on bombings and assassinations and their defense of such actions, none encouraged deeds of that nature. Argentine anarchists firmly believed that individual acts committed in isolation from collective mobilizations against capitalism should only occur in exceptional cases. Malatesta, who was so favored by local libertarians, is the best exponent of this contradictory position. Though he acknowledged that such actions were "wrong in and of themselves," he claimed they are "justifiable when they are a means of defending oneself or others against a crime."[93]

If the issue of individual violence raised complicated issues, that was no less true of collective violence. The tragic denouement of the Paris Commune had demonstrated the limits of popular insurrections lacking a coherent organization. A writer in *La Protesta*, conscious of such limits, wrote: "We must not spread illusions. Today it is impossible to fight the state with arms. The large avenues cutting through cities, the technological advancement of weaponry, added to the working class's inability to get them, are among the many reasons that we must find a new method of struggle. That method is the general strike."[94] More than a few libertarian leaders were obsessed with the relation between mass movements and the strategic use of violence. Some argued that peaceful strikes were futile, given that the bourgeoisie still controlled the means of production and workers often exhausted their reserves and returned to work worse off than they had been before, with their leaders isolated from the movement. Many thought that workers ought to impose their demands through force but, cognizant of the difficulties of doing so, concluded disappointedly that "since we lack the force of arms, even if we evolve greatly, many years will have to pass, maybe even centuries, before we will know real justice."[95]

6. THE GENERAL REVOLUTIONARY STRIKE

The general strike seemed to be the solution. Anarchists saw it as a means of crossing a threshold in the battle against capitalism: it was not a tactic for winning material improvements, but a revolutionary weapon for radically changing society. "Revolutions have their girders and the general strike is the girder of the proletarian revolution," wrote Pascual Guaglianone, who, after criticizing the idea of mere economic demands, defined such a strike as a "masculine protest against capitalist exploitation, against state tyranny, against religious enthronement.... The triumphant general strike will mark the start of the proletarian revolution, the beginning of the era of destruction and reconstruction that we yearn for."[96] Anarchists embraced the general strike as the most practical strategy for the working class, although it was also useful for people at various levels of society.[97]

> The general strike consists of suspending work in every branch of production long enough to destroy exchange value and for the proletariat to take possession of the mines, the land, homes, and machines—in a word, to seize everything that contributes to the production of wealth.[98]

In anarchists' view, the general strike would drag the backward sectors of the populace into the fight. Socialists thought this implausible, arguing that such a strike would never have the support of the entire working class. Anarchists responded by acknowledging that, indeed, a conscious, advanced minority would have to lay its foundations. Once again, a certain elitist disdain for the masses manifested itself in anarchist discourse: "The majority has no real value," said *La Protesta*. "It doesn't do anything but enjoy and ratify the benefits that the minority, the vanguard of progress, has won for them."[99] This raised a difficult question: how could the "uneducated masses" participate in the revolution?

The general strike embodied anarchist revolutionary urgency; it did not seek gradual or partial reforms and would involve violence because of opposition from dominant groups, who would not allow revolutionaries to topple the state peacefully. Anarchists claimed that respect for bourgeois legality would disappear in the course of a rebellion, after which the people would socialize the means of production, expropriate capitalists' wealth and property, and inaugurate the era of anarchist communism. Unlike the Socialists and other political radicals (Jacobins, Blanquists, and Republicans), who hoped to occupy the areas of the state vacated in the revolutionary tumult, anarchists asserted that all individuals have a "right to live" and thus to the means of life. They were preoccupied first by people's "necessities" and would only later establish "duties." Such changes could not be realized by decree, but only through the direct, immediate expropriation of essential resources such as stores of foodstuffs, clothes, and housing.[100]

The general strike was a maximal revolutionary aspiration; partial strikes occupied a conditional, less-important place for anarchists. Many thought them useless because capitalists could easily raise the price of consumer goods and thereby undermine the value of victories like higher salaries and shorter working days. Some even argued that strikes were more beneficial to business owners than workers in periods of overproduction, because they gave them an opportunity to reduce surpluses without big losses. Furthermore, pointing to the example of the seventeen-month strike by English mechanics, which the workers lost and during which they exhausted their union's reserves, they alleged that strikes weakened workers' organization.

This is an ambiguous position that neither explicitly condemns nor explicitly supports strikes. With the exception of solidarity strikes, *La Protesta Humana* said that "these movements only have a minimal effect on the social question. While a strike may be useful at times, it is not the answer."[101] Of course, anarchists were not unanimous on the issue: some defended economic battles, partial strikes, and union action as means of fostering workers' practical, revolutionary education:

> The partial strike is effective whether victorious or not. Its merit is obvious in the first case; in the second, it activates forces that under other circumstances would have remained passive and convinced of their impotence, linked in disgrace and hatred, filled with thoughts of revenge; it communicates to the striking worker that he is significant as an individual force for change. Some get disheartened, but only a few, and insofar as their attitude makes them suspicious to capital, it rejects them, and they have no choice but to turn to our ranks.[102]

Despite these differences, anarchists were very flexible and encouraged and supported all types of contention, in workplaces and elsewhere. And it was here that they had the most success, since their hopes for the general revolutionary strike were chimerical: there was a gulf between popular sector's immediate, economic needs and libertarian militants' transformative aspirations. When this came into the open, so too did anarchist complaints about the "uneducated masses" and "ignorant people." Agnes Heller aptly captures this disconnection: "Political leaders are often obliged to fight tenaciously against the quotidian consciousness of their followers, who regard solutions to their particular problems as remedies to general ills."[103]

These tensions erupted repeatedly during the opening decade of the century, especially when the more explosive conflicts (the general strikes of 1902 and 1909, the 1904 May Day demonstration, and the 1907 renters' strike) deescalated and workers' interests and libertarian hopes went in opposite directions. Anarchists supported demands for short-term reforms not because of their inherent value, but as means of pushing the masses toward generalized revolt: "if it is to have any effect, the movement against the landlords must become insurrectionary," wrote *La Protesta* during the renters' strike.[104] Excited by the magnitude of the confrontation, they believed that "the proletarian discontent could mark the start of a social revolution,"[105] noting that the people had begun to lose respect for the sanctity of private property. But when the conflict took a different course, anarchists' view of the people also changed. Popular consciousness was no longer the harbinger of a new era but instead defined by the "imbecility" of the masses who "drop their flags and demands and humbly and tearfully" accept the imposition of authority.[106]

Shortly after the Centenary, a writer in *The Libertarian* assessed the use of the general revolutionary strike during the first ten years of the century. With some bitterness, he acknowledged that it was only during the May 1909 strike that the Argentine proletariat had come close to fulfilling libertarian hopes, "when it responded to Falcón's collective assault on a peaceful demonstration with a general revolutionary strike," although, by contrast, workers' had passively accepted the repression in 1910. He concluded by complaining that "no one raised a voice in protest" then, and that they "put up with the foulest slavery, the most disgusting tyranny, just to earn some cash."[107]

Notwithstanding these ruptures, anarchists sank deep roots among Buenos Aires workers during the opening decade of the century. Evidence of their popularity and representativeness abounds, even if anarchists' "success" was ephemeral. One reason for their evanescence can be found in their conception of politics.

7. THE EXPANSION OF POLITICAL REPRESENTATION AND THE LIMITS OF ANARCHISM

Bound to a view of the state and political participation that was more appropriate to the nineteenth than twentieth century, libertarians were unable to respond effectively to the expansion of the electoral system or the state's increased involvement in society. Anarchists represented a significant segment of the workers during the momentous period of social change between the mid-1890s and the Centenary—the latter date could be extended to 1912, 1916, or even to the "Tragic Week" of 1919. But when examined in the context of the years between the organization of the nation-state and the country's incorporation into the world market and the crisis of the agricultural export model that occurred after the 1930s, one can observe profound transformations of society and the state that clearly contributed to the libertarian movement's marginalization, which was trapped by the limitations of its own doctrine and soon to become a minority force among popular sectors.

One could argue that the political crisis of the conservative order was the political crisis of the libertarian movement, that anarchism was only functional for a restrictive regime, occupying public spaces that the state neglected. The expansion of the electoral system in 1912 transformed many workers into citizens, and political parties altered their demands and approaches to politics as a result. While changes in the political system modified workers' political habits slowly, especially because many, as foreigners, still lacked suffrage, there is no doubt that political parties changed their discourse.[108] Anarchist discourse, however, remained the same. The passage of the Sáenz Peña Law, the increase in voters thanks to the events of 1912, and the number of Socialist representatives, who obtained seven deputies in the Capital in 1914, shook the anarchist movement, which the repression of the Centenary had left in a weakened state. *La Protesta* repeatedly lamented that workers had let themselves be dragged to the ballot box by the Radical Party and Socialists. Teodoro Antilli, one of the principal libertarian leaders in 1913, threw the movement's impotence into relief when he said: "There are so many anarchists in Argentina and yet we do so little!"[109] Of course, the historian may ask: was the number so large or was he simply recalling a recent and much more promising past?

In addition to the shrinking number of activists, the Sáenz Peña Law presented the libertarian movement with a serious problem when it made voting mandatory. Anarchists, who saw voting as an act of delegation that compromised individual freedom, were outraged by its compulsory nature: "The obligatory vote is an attack upon individual freedom and an indignity for the country that endures it. It's disgraceful to force citizens to go to the polls and choose the individuals that will oppress them tomorrow."[110] The Sáenz Peña Law brought more people into the political process, boosted the Socialists' electoral fortunes, and shrank the space for political action available to anarchists. The latter responded to these changes with defiance: "Among the forces in battle, only the anarchists remain pure. We have never lowered our flag."[111] In fact, during the process inaugurated in 1916, anarchist strategies and tactics (electoral abstention or the voters' strike) were identical to those that they had used in 1902 and 1906.

Anarchists discounted electoral politics with the same arguments they had made a decade earlier. This created multiple problems for them, leading to a large number of splits and a loss of confidence, prompting many activists to join other groups. However, it should be noted that only a small portion, in the course of this bloodletting, turned to the Radical Party, notwithstanding the unconfirmed suspicions raised by historians about anarchists joining the party. Anarchists did not participate in the 1905 rebellion, although doctrinal purists, amid battles for control of the anarchist movement, claimed that some had. I believe that this is the source of the perseverance of allegations of anarchist-Radical collaboration. With the exception of Julio Barcos and a small group of less-important militants who joined the party, Buenos Aires anarchists lost few to the Radicals who, with their Krausism and unblemished Catholicism, alien-ated far more than they attracted, which is not to say that the Radical Party's impact on the sectors that supported anarchism has been fully explored.[112] Years later, the *Última Hora* newspaper reported that Ghiraldo might be a candidate in the 1912 elections, which prompted him to categorically deny, once again, sus-picions about his pro-Radical Party sentiments. "Me, the anti-parliamentarian, me, the staunch advocate of direct action, today on a quaint list of candidates, naïve and daring saviors of opinion, unconditional, magnanimous defenders of legislative representation! Please, no!"[113]

The influence of Uruguayan President Batlle y Ordóñez is a different mat-ter. Batlle y Ordóñez, who was more progressive than the Radical Party, but also more statist, modernized Uruguay and led a process of political and social democratization unprecedented in South America.[114] Tolerant of labor organiza-tions, an opponent of rural caudillos, and vigorously anti-clerical, his politics tempted more than a few anarchists, who were also seduced by his charisma and patience with deportees from Argentina who carried out their activity on Uru-guayan shores.[115] Indeed, many of those exiled from Argentina to Europe ended up in Montevideo, where they enjoyed significantly more freedom than they had had in Buenos Aires. Some issues of *La Protesta* were even published there after the Argentine government shut it down during the Centenary. *The Libertarian*, which briefly replaced *La Protesta*, openly praised Batlle's respect for individual liberties and abolition of the Social Order branch of the police. "Today it is Uru-guay, where a people of unique and superior conditions live, that is the loving mother of the heroes and martyrs of social justice in the Americas; this is largely the result of the impact of an unusual man named José Batlle y Ordóñez."[116]

In 1912, a group of distinguished libertarian militants who had been expelled from Argentina—Adrián Zamboni, Virginia Bolten (the foremost female anarchist activist of the time), F. Clérici, Francisco Berri, and Adrián Troitiño among others—provoked a notorious rupture in the movement.[117] All had been active for more than a decade and were part of the historic core of Argentine anarchism: some had participated in the creation and consolidation of the FORA, others had served on *La Protesta*'s editorial board, and all had sacrificed countless hours to daily propagandistic labors. The group, later denominated "anarcho-Batllists," settled in Uruguay and critically supported Batlle y Ordóñez in their active propaganda efforts, including through the publication of a paper, *The Free Idea*.[118]

There was another breach in March of the same year. This one was the work of Bautista Fueyo (bookseller, importer, and publisher of many anarchist texts that circulated in the country) and Santiago Locascio. Like those just mentioned, both were distinguished militants and part of the movement's historic foundation, although neither were active organizationally at the time. Santiago Locascio's case is paradigmatic. He had traveled much of the journey of the Argentine anarchist movement and had been a militant in various internal currents. He was an active member of *The Rebel*'s editorial staff from its first issue, where he battled pro-organizationalists and argued fiercely with Pietro Gori. He joined the Argentine Workers' Federation four years later and then began fighting tirelessly for workers' organization. He secured the adhesion of the longshoremen and helped lead the 1902 strike, a year in which he also put out *New Era* monthly. These exertions prompted the Argentine government to apply the Residency Law to him and deport him to his native Italy. His case caused a stir, and socialist lawyer Del Valle Iberlucea played a role in his legal defense. He distanced himself from the anarchist movement when he returned to Argentina and slowly turned toward the "political" position that he would assume after 1912. Locascio and Fueyo, motivated by the imminent approval of the Sáenz Peña Law, set out to form a workers' party and to compete in the general elections. Although the party never materialized, their efforts confirm that there was some dissatisfaction among anarchists who, without ceasing to profess their libertarian faith, wanted a new approach to politics.

Locascio launched an interesting critique of the movement when he assailed the extreme revolutionary heroism that anarchists were so fond of promoting. He argued that anarchists should not follow the revolutionary tradition blindly and, taking an unusually pragmatic posture, he called for embracing traditions that were more relevant to contemporary battles. He claimed that the course of events had demonstrated that one could no longer think in Bakunin's terms and hope to effect a revolutionary transformation of capitalist society in a single stroke. The presence of an increasingly strong state, which belied libertarian predictions, was evidence of this, he said. He challenged anarchists to abandon their outmoded tactics and revolutionary urgency: "Instead of obstinately perpetuating a tactic without any practical result, we should find one that is more adequate to the times and more consonant with the facts of the historical moment."[119] The "tactic" that he was referring to here was the general strike: in his view, and in accord with positivist principles, change would be slow and progressive.

Years later, impacted by the Russian Revolution, he disparaged his former comrades: "Many of you seem to live in a fantasy world.... Anarchism is not simply savage rhetoric and catastrophic action.... It is a variant of socialism."[120] He called for the creation of a party that would be an amalgam of communism and anarchism. The synthesis, which he termed maximalism, garnered little enthusiasm, especially as anarchists came to understand the state's centrality in Russia's post-revolutionary society, causing their initial excitement for the Russian Revolution to chill.

The fate of these factions is less important than the dispersion that they likely provoked within the libertarian movement. Santillán's comments seem evasive when he argues that "the aura surrounding the anarchist movement had attracted numerous activists who had failed to understand the ideas and who were propitious candidates for deviations of all sorts; without the anchor of an ever-vigilant movement, the most outlandish extravagances naturally sprouted in anarchist ranks. It was necessary to establish a solid orientation."[121] Fighting for that orientation, as Gilimón and other doctrinal purists had done in the previous decade, would now be the task of others, who were working in a political movement that was in retreat.

The red flags fluttered above the immense expanse of proletarian agitation. They were flags of dreams, symbols of combat, heralds of justice and freedom.

—*La Protesta*, May 2, 1906

CHAPTER VIII

Anarchist Rites and Symbols

ANARCHISM WAS THE dominant political tendency among urban workers in Argentina between 1900 and 1910. Anarchists led many of the resistance societies, secured predominance in the FORA in 1905, built an extensive network of circles, study centers, libraries, schools, drama groups, and other cultural institutions, and published an enormous quantity of newspapers, books, and pamphlets. In addition to all of this, they created a well-defined symbolic and ritualistic framework with clear ties to the world of labor.

Radical political vanguards—anarchist and otherwise—used symbols and rituals to affirm their identity to the workers, and hoped that workers would assume these symbols and rituals as their own. They "understood that a symbolic apparatus was an effective means of influencing and orienting collective sensibilities," wrote Bronislaw Baczko, and endeavored to construct and disseminate one that would counter the dominant symbolic structure. What they needed, said Baczko, was "clothing": that is, "signs and images, gestures and figures" that would allow them to communicate with others and recognize themselves as political and social actors.[1]

Almost all political and social groups active in this formative period of modern Argentine history regarded the elaboration of a historical tradition as an elemental necessity. Their concerns emerged logically in the context of the times. On the one hand, pressures were exerted by the state, which poured all of its educational and propagandistic energies into the invention of an Argentine historical tradition as it urgently attempted to forge a common identity out of the country's heterogeneous population. On the other hand, socialists and anarchists introduced stresses as well, disseminating their own symbolic framework as they endeavored to organize workers around a specific identity and social imaginary. There is no doubt that libertarians tried to invent a historical tradition of their own, with its own content, boundaries, allies, and adversaries. Eric Hobsbawm defines an "invented tradition" as "a set of practices, normally governed by overt or tacitly accepted rules and of a ritual or symbolic nature, which seeks to inculcate certain values and norms of behavior by repetition, which automatically imply continuity with the past." The creation of new traditions was a common feature of political life in the last third of the nineteenth century; in Hobsbawm's view, they were "response[s] to novel situations which take the form of reference to old situations, or which establish their own past by quasi-obligatory repetition." Such was the case in Argentina, where anarchists created an alternative symbolic space that they hoped workers would embrace, just as the state was feverishly elaborating its own rituals and icons in hopes of incorporating all social classes into its invented national tradition.[2]

Anarchists built their symbolic structure primarily by re-signifying elements received from European social and political movements. This is another reflection of the cosmopolitanism of Argentine workers, who were multi-national and multi-linguistic. Indeed, in 1895, there were 4.5 times more foreigners employed in manufacturing than native-born Argentines in Buenos Aires and three times more in 1914, when they were also a majority in the service industry, especially commerce.[3] Joaquín V. González commented on this: "Buenos Aires functions as an extension of Europe … it is no surprise that the modalities that shape the urban centers from which the immigrant masses in this country initially came are also visible here."[4]

The emerging workers' tradition in Argentina drew from the diverse cultural, political, and ideological material that workers brought with them to the Río de la Plata region. This included anarchism, which, as seen throughout this work, became an important presence among Buenos Aires workers and whose affirmation of proletarian internationalism resonated with local diversity. Taking these two characteristics into account—local cosmopolitanism and anarchist internationalism—I argue in this chapter that anarchists created a symbolic space in 1890s and especially the 1900s that was linked to urban workers and whose principal symbols (heroes, martyrs, flags, banners, and mobilizing rituals) were identical to those circulating in Europe.

But adopting and deploying these international cultural references did generate some tension among militants. For instance, the need to appeal to the Argentina born (particularly rural workers and conscripts) prompted some libertarians to utilize specifically Argentine symbols and elements. This was the case with the writers that celebrated the gaucho, a figure that anarchists typically construed in negative terms but who came to represent libertarians' cherished instincts for justice, social struggle, and independence. As noted in Chapter Two, Alberto Ghiraldo was among the few propagandists who understood the need to synthesize European and Argentine traditions. He tried to incorporate the gaucho by using "Martín Fierro" as the name of *La Protesta's* supplement between 1904 and 1905 and by evoking the gaucho as an archetype of rebellion. For Ghiraldo, the gaucho represented "the cry of the laboring class against the upper strata of society that oppresses it, a protest against injustice."[5] Nonetheless, specifically Argentine icons and rituals did not occupy a prominent place in libertarians' symbolic world, if one judges from the cultural framework utilized in strikes, public gatherings, recreational activities, and the press.[6] Indeed, the use of international insignia was a defining characteristic of the Argentine anarchist movement and helped endow the workers' movement with its oppositional, confrontational character.

1. ANARCHISM INVENTS ITS IMAGE

Anarchists and socialists invented a workers' tradition and a body of alternative symbols and rituals in the common space that they occupied at the turn of the century, although tensions in their views of social transformation made coexistence difficult. Symbols like the red flag or rites like the May Day commemoration had much of the same content for activists of either stripe, but they used them differently and invested them with different aspirations. Their differing presentations showed dominant groups two sides of the same coin: one, rational and peaceful, and the other, rational but also violent and unruly.

Socialists heeded the legally defined parameters of public behavior and did not try to displace the national flag in their mobilizations: they demonstrated peacefully during May Day celebrations and other events, flew their flags respectfully, obeyed police directives and municipal ordinances, and sang revolutionary hymns without being shrill. Their events were fundamentally disciplined.[7] As a political party, Socialists operated in the legal, constitutionally circumscribed space provided by the state for contestation, and their goal was to transform workers into citizens and to represent them in parliament. They flatly rejected libertarians' "revolutionary gymnastics." Socialist leader Enrique Dickmann wrote: "Anarchists expected the Social Revolution to arrive as some catastrophic event, which is why they called general strikes for an indeterminate time, without rhyme or reason.... All of this was in total opposition to the Socialist Party's methods, which sought the demonstrable, increased well being of working people over the long haul."[8] Socialists wanted the government to listen to them and to serve as its interlocutor. They intended to peacefully reform—not destroy—the prevailing social order, and all of their symbols and rites reflected that desire.

Anarchists used the same symbols and rituals for a different end—as weapons and battle cries in their struggle to radically change society, and as substitutes for national symbols. They hoped that these rituals and symbols would galvanize those who were discontented with a system that they deemed fundamentally unjust and communicate anarchism's viability as an alternative. They intended to eliminate the state as interlocutor, though they were far from achieving that goal. Anarchist symbols and rites were a source of fear for some, especially dominant groups. Indeed, libertarians wanted their impassioned, combative rhetoric to scandalize and frighten their enemies. A depiction of the 1909 May Day. mobilization in Buenos Aires conveys this: "The groups didn't arrive quietly. On the contrary, their members let loose all types of shouts: 'Down with the police!' 'Death to the Cossacks!' 'Death to Colonel Falcón!' 'War on the bourgeoisie!' These cries rang out all through the raucous assembly."[9] This account underscores anarchists' ardent hostility to the system. Participants damned the bourgeoisie and the police—the latter being the institution that, in their view, safeguarded the interests of the former. These and related motifs could be found at all libertarian rallies.[10]

Elites also cultivated anti-anarchist anxieties. Under the influence of Cesare Lombroso's criminology and prevailing ideas about public order and social defense, they viewed anarchism as a pathology. The perspective had been latent since the 1890s, more because of European assassinations and bombings than anarchist activity in Argentina, but grew pronounced after the strikes in late 1901 and early 1902 and as the anarchist movement expanded during the first decade of the twentieth century. A consensus emerged among government figures concerning the need to excise anarchism from the social and political realm. Miguel Cané, Joaquín V. González, and Ernesto Quesada—three figures who approached social problems in very different ways—all agreed on the need to bar anarchism.[11]

Local anarchist iconography typically reproduced what was circulating in Europe and tended to be replete with images of violence and references to the destruction of capitalism. An image that circulated widely in the libertarian press titled "The collapse of bourgeois society"[12] showed a woman, a symbol of freedom, holding aloft a torch to guide the proletariat to redemption. She stands on rubble of emblems typifying the system: the cross and the papal miter, the sword and military regalia, and a bourgeois top hat and walking stick. On either side of her lay the wreckage of prisons and courts, completing the allegory. The message was unambiguous: the social revolution would soon raze anarchists' most hated adversaries. This image is a secular re-signification of one used in Christian iconography, in which a heroine stands upon a man, serpents, or dragons in an allusion to the triumph of good over evil. In our image, woman/liberty (good) is perched upon the symbols of capitalist society (evil).[13]

Anarchists hoped that their rites and symbols would encourage rebellion among Buenos Aires workers and awaken feelings of belonging to an exploited class. They wanted workers to embrace an identity formed around proletarian not capitalist values. Their symbolic, ritualistic arsenal was broad, including more than just the red flag and May Day commemorations: there was also a large and heterogeneous gallery of anarchist and anarchist-related heroes, a pantheon of revolutionary martyrs, funeral rites, almanacs replacing the calendar of Catholic saints' days with events of note for revolutionaries, hymns and songs, and even a new approach to naming children. Anarchists tried to furnish workers with a sense of connection to the universal values of the proletariat: the red flag (or black and red flag) was the workers' emblem, May Day was the workers' celebration, and the martyrs and heroes of the revolutionary pantheon had sacrificed themselves to the cause.

In an environment awash with political, nationalist, secular, and religious symbols circulated by the church, school system, and other powerful institutions, at least some Argentine workers adopted anarchist symbols. Anarchists drew many of their images from the French republican tradition, such as the pike, the torch, the sun, liberty, and the Phrygian cap, all of which had also become important nationalist symbols after the 1810 May Revolution.[14] Anarchists fought for influence in this conflicted symbolic sphere, a vigorous battle waged in other countries that, like Argentina, were in the midst of historic transformations. The new social actors were responsive to anarchists' cultural interventions, especially immigrants, who lacked a strong attachment to Argentine symbols. To note this, however, is not to deny workers' other symbolic loyalties, whether they were religious, regional, or national in character, or those coming from creolism, promoted by the church and the various Creole and national associations active at the time. Indeed, commentators often mention the broad array of images—kings, presidents, national heroes, saints, and portraits by popular artists—that decorated the walls of workers' homes. One observer notes that their walls were commonly adorned "with images of Madonnas or pictures of kings, generals, or well-known caudillos."[15] Anarchists intervened in this space of popular iconography.

Anarchists and socialists understood the propaganda value of symbols and ceremony, and attempted to counteract the heterogeneous symbolic forces operating on workers. They tried to forge an alternative collective identity for that dispersed mass of individuals making up the Argentine proletariat at the turn of the century. Many of their symbols and rituals were appropriations and re-significations of those already in existence—"all symbolism," writes Castoriadis, "is built on the ruins of proceeding symbolic edifices, which it uses as material."[16] Anarchists endowed these symbols with new meaning and expanded their reach; Marianne, the emblematic female representative of bourgeois freedom, could also represent human freedom and of course proletarian freedom. It had universal value and spoke to all Argentines, including workers.

Anarchists' drew their symbolic system from elements derived from the bourgeois revolutions as well as Greek myth. They stripped these symbols of their original content, making them "empty forms," and injected them with new and different content, or re-signified them. Since the French Revolution, and especially during the nineteenth century, political activists frequently secularized—and sometimes made revolutionary—traditional images, filling these "empty forms" with their own political and social content. Anarchists and the rest of the socialist camp engaged in this re-signification.[17] For example, the symbol of the sun, which numerous civilizations and social and political groups have used, was one of libertarians' favorites—representing the source of energy and life, it also signified the path to the future and was an emblem of the proletariat's historic challenge. "A revolutionary hurricane," wrote *La Protesta*, "will soon shake the world's foundations and out of this a new one will emerge, strengthened by the sun of justice, whose warmth and well-being the wage slave has dreamed of, and whose powerful rays of light will illuminate the intellect."[18]

The torch was another staple of the anarchist imaginary, which was sometimes replaced with the ax. It often appeared in the raised, left hand of libertarians' Marianne (Liberty, re-signified), marking the road to revolution and revealing the path that the exploited had to follow—"which the torch of truth will illuminate with its purifying rays."[19] The torch, closely linked to the sun and a life cleansed through illumination, was also an emblem of truth that has figured in countless allegories since it first appeared in Greek myth, when Hercules used it as a weapon in his battle against the Hydra.[20] In the more concrete arena of mobilizing practices, the red flag performed the torch's guiding function, and always led libertarian demonstrations.

2. RED FLAGS OF DREAMS

As the workers' movement grew, the red flag and emblems related to it (rosettes, coats of arms, placards, etc.) became potent symbols in the world of labor, ubiquitous at public rallies and meetings. Disparate civilizations have used flags, and flying them on a flagpole represents the flag bearer's spirit raised above the normal level, symbolizing unity, victory, identification, recognition, and self-affirmation. Though important for peoples of antiquity and the Middle Ages, flags became national symbols after the bourgeois revolutions, when citizens began performing binding rituals around them through which they articulated feelings of national connectedness. Likewise, members of labor and anarchist groups assembled around their flags, which identified them and gave them a sense of belonging. Take the following account from *La Nación*: "They pulled together the demonstration. There were societies from the Argentine Workers' Federation, and the shoemakers, mechanics, builders, hatters, graphic arts, and barbers' societies, etc. Each of these groups carried a red flag with a black stripe or band."[21]

The red flag was the most conspicuous symbol of the workers' movement, representing revolutionary unity against the bosses and the state. Argentines started using it just as the first anarchist and socialist groupings began to appear. And, unlike in Europe, where, says Hobsbawm, workers spontaneously adopted the red flag and it was only embraced by socialists later, Argentine left groups actively encouraged workers to use it, although of course the Argentine workers' movement and its political vanguards had direct ties to the European Left.[22] The use of the red flag reflected the fact that the dispersed, heterogeneous body of individuals making up the local working class at the end of the nineteenth century needed a symbol of their own. Indeed, it remained the symbol of the Argentine workers' movement over the years, whether led by socialists, anarchists, syndicalists, or communists.

Its meaning was straightforward. The red flag was the banner and guide for proletarians and the poor. It signified joy and liberation from the injustices of capitalism, the promise of a better world, and identification with the anarchist ideal:

> The flag flutters in the wind
> It is the dawn of new redemptions
> It has songs in its symbols
> Of a sublime and advanced idea
> Oh! Red and shinning emblem
> Of the dispirited, of the dispossessed
> You are light! For the ruthless slaves
> Who are inspired by love for you.[23]

By lining up behind the red flag, militants also differentiated themselves from others, such as those who identified with patriotic or religious symbols. They were making a statement about their unique identity. Just as nationalists pledged their lives to the fatherland, those following the red flag made it known that they would give their lives to the cause that it embodied:

> This is why my soul venerates you so!
> it is my greatest wish, my dearest flag,

to join the red division
and in a sublime moment, flag of my loves,
tragically spurring on my anarchic rages,
to throw my bloody heart to the tyrants![24]

The red flag was a symbolic focal point during confrontations with police. In its account of the 1904 anarchist May Day mobilization in Buenos Aires, *La Nación* reported that police charged demonstrators in an attempt to disperse them and that "some dropped their flags in the tumult ... [but they] reassembled around those who held onto theirs and began to throw rubble at the authorities."[25] The flag had unmistakable rallying power—it was a battle cry against the system. Shouts of "Viva anarchy!" "Death to the bourgeoisie!" rang out during the May Day rally in Rosario in 1900; at the head of the protesters there was a "red flag that said, in black letters, '*Viva* the social revolution!' and in whose center a new dawn is outlined; they set out to the street with it held aloft."[26] The flag's color was meaningful, as were the allegories depicted upon it, which typically referenced anarchists' central claims. In the May Day event just mentioned, *La Nación* noted that "a group of rascals held aloft a small banner portraying representatives of the military, clergy, and bourgeoisie; words above them read, 'The vampires of the people.'"[27]

The red flag's potency was not limited to those who rallied behind it: ruling groups and especially the police saw it as a subversive symbol that incited rebellion and violence. This is why they tried to prevent demonstrators from using it, and often provoked conflicts in the process. The flag's symbolism was so charged that during a 1901 mobilization in Mar del Plata, police only agreed to allow demonstrators to march if they did not fly their red flags.[28] Militants postponed the May Day commemoration in 1905—a particularly combative year—until the government lifted martial law, which had been decreed during the Radical Party's rebellion. Authorities permitted the commemoration days later but banned the flying of the red flag. *La Nación* criticized the measure for exasperating demonstrators and also pointed out that the ban was ineffective: "It was easy enough to get around the prohibition by inventing another symbol: though yesterday's demonstrators were deprived of red flags, they wore red ties, whose points fluttered in the wind, and thereby made an even more poignant statement than they would have made just by hoisting a piece of cloth up onto a pole."[29] Demonstrators ultimately disregarded police orders and flew a red banner, which elicited a brutal police response that resulted in two deaths and dozens of injuries and arrests. Workers pressed for the right to use their symbols, and police attempted to deny them this right. In this back and forth, anarchists nurtured the tradition of a combative May Day. Given the gravity of the events that May Day, Interior Minister Rafael Castillo spoke to the National Congress in response to an interpellation by Socialist deputy Alfredo Palacios. He defended the police's actions and the government's right to outlaw the red flag, which he described as an emblem of "war and bloodshed" and, even worse, a substitute for the national flag: "On what grounds can we embrace this collision of colors, in which some assert that the red flag represents their demands and rights, while their children need simply to recognize the flag of the Fatherland?"[30]

Rituals involving the red flag took shape during such events. It was a battle cry, a sign of a more propitious future, but it also communicated mourning and grief. This is why anarchists added black to it, the color of death and suffering. Libertarians encouraged the ritual of the funeral retinue, when they draped red flags over coffins bearing proletarians killed by police and displayed them prominently in funeral processions. This was another important symbolic innovation, in which anarchists transformed mourning into a public declaration and fought with authorities over the right to exhibit their dead, celebrate revolutionary commitment, and voice outrage over the murder of a comrade. The demand to keep vigil, to demonstrate with a funereal retinue, and to bury their dead became a constant for left-wing parties and groups from the moment that anarchists introduced them, persisting at least into the 1970s.

From the very first casualty of police repression (Cosme Budeslavich, an Austrian worker killed in Rosario in 1901), Argentine police and demonstrators fought pitched battles over public funerals.[31] These were part of a broader war for the control of public space and, for anarchists, a means to reach people outside of their networks. A Buenos Aires newspaper ran a compelling description of the internment of Miguel Pepe, a youth killed by police during the 1907 renters' strike:

> The strike commission took his body to the street at about 8:00 AM. They pulled a procession together at once and set off along San Juan Street, then went on Buen Orden, Avenida de Mayo, and Callao up to Córdoba. It was an impressive spectacle—complete order reigned during the entire march, not even a whistle broke the silence. The carriage was at the head, followed by the coffin, which eight women carried by hand, taking turns with others as the march proceeded. Eight hundred to a thousand women followed the casket.... Approximately 2,500 workers came up behind. There was a surfeit of red rosettes and three flags of the same color.[32]

This account underscores the importance of the funeral ritual. Participants' disposition, their funeral attire, and the insignias that they carried made it a show of force. The procession appropriated the physical space of the city, as mourners pushed back the police, putting then on the defensive, as they traveled through Buenos Aires's main thoroughfares, displaying the martyr's coffin, an expression of outrage and a righteous example to others. It was a working class demonstration, and an angry statement potentiated by the solemnity of grief. Anarchists, comfortable in such situations, struck a belligerent pose toward authorities, who usually permitted such funerals to occur when they were held indoors but, on the pretext of preserving public order, tried to prevent outdoor funerals. For instance, police took the body of a port worker killed during the 1904 May Day rally in Buenos Aires from the Argentine Workers' Federation building, where he had been laying in wake, and furtively buried him in a common grave.[33] Undeterred, the Workers' Federation and *La Protesta* immediately raised enough money to pay for his interment in a private grave. The burial ritual was also remarkable to the degree that anarchists stripped the ceremony of religious connotations and made it into a secular affair. This was highly symbolic, as anarchists transformed a fallen comrade into a martyr. Funereal rites were clearly a matter of importance for libertarians, who believed that they encouraged people to join the ranks of revolutionaries.

3. HEROES AND MARTYRS OF THE PROLETARIAT

Typically, revolutionaries decreed a period of mourning in the days immediately following a funeral; the Argentine Workers' Federation and *La Protesta*, two of the mainstays of Argentine anarchism, flew their flags at half-mast. This marked the beginning of the ritual worship of the martyrs, whose graves became pilgrimage sites for libertarians, who paid homage to them on the anniversaries of their deaths.[34] Anarchists transformed a worker shot down by police into a revolutionary hero. The revolutions of 1848 as well as Christian theology supplied the rites surrounding the dead worker, and the image of him as a hero. The slain proletarian evolved into a potent symbol in left iconography, most famously depicted in Daumier's *Rue Transnonain*, a painting that presents the body of a murdered worker in a Christ-like pose.[35]

Anarchists turned the unknown worker into a "victorious hero" and brave revolutionary who "fell like a lion." With abundant hyperbole but saying little about the worker's actual biography, anarchists constructed a solemn obituary of their fearless combatant: "Flying like an eagle, the valiant conqueror of bread pitched his tent in the heart of the city where hyenas and vultures forge their malignant consortium." No longer an anonymous plebian, he became a quasi-mythical warrior: "a Centurion's mane crowned the proud head of this child of labor. He fell like a lion, and lions need no words."[36] Two interesting elements appeared in the mourning of this particular worker. First, the libertarian press emphasized that he hailed from the interior of the country, implying that anarchists had roots among the entire working class, not only among foreigners as some alleged. Second, they deployed the allegory of the lion, which has denoted strength and nobility of spirit from time immemorial. Anarchists' use of the image of the lion and his mane was a common element in the iconography of heroic figures at the time.

The entire left participated in the creation of a pantheon of revolutionary heroes and martyrs. The practice had roots in the political tradition dating back to the French Revolution.[37] The construction of a cult of revolutionary heroes—often paradoxically recruited from the same sources as official heroes—was a compelling propaganda weapon, a means of legitimizing an alternative value system. Although anarchists used a rhetoric of glorification and redemption similar to that found in the Republican and national pantheons, they celebrated different protagonists and a different cause. Instead of venerating martyrs to the fatherland or the Republic, they exalted victims of capitalism and sacrifices to the proletariat. And they presented such sacrifices as inevitable: writing about the death of Budeslavich, a libertarian paper said, "This beautiful movement, which must lead this country's working masses, had to be soaked in martyrs' blood."[38]

Anarchists not only memorialized victims of murder and repression but also those who suffered everyday exploitation. For them, the mere fact of daily labor was heroic and exemplary, and they presented an epic of visible work in all of their iconography, one that, in their Manichaean perspective, awarded all the laudatory attributes to workers, who toiled and endured mistreatment, and all the negative characteristics to the allegorical trinity of capitalism—the priest, the bourgeois, and the soldier.[39] Anarchists habitually exalted the heroes of daily life, workers fleeced by the bourgeoisie and the state. The images were consistent: workers with haggard faces and malnourished bodies counterposed to obese, lecherous, and sadistic representatives of the system. The workers, anonymous victims and collective heroes, had to be defended, especially when they rebelled and faced repression. Anarchists intended their discursive scheme to stir the masses and ready them for battle. The agenda was simple: glorify the fallen, cultivate contempt for the dominant class, appeal to international proletarian unity, urge workers to remember their martyrs, and envision a just society created under anarchist stewardship:

HOMAGE TO THE MARTYRS OF THE COMMUNE
ETERNAL HATRED FOR THE EXECUTIONERS
Proletarians of all countries, remember!
Ready yourself for vengeance and let the torch
of regeneration encircle everything that you encounter
in your fight to liberate the world from all this foul misery

Rebel, modern slaves! Rebel, pariahs
of the world, shout out
your well-being, your happiness
Anarchist communism will emancipate you
from all oppression
THERE WILL BE NEITHER MARTYRS NOR VICTIMS
WHEN THE EXECUTIONERS DISAPPEAR.[40]

Anarchists often published exaggerated biographies and portraits of their heroes in their effort to nurture the incipient tradition of working-class radicalism, thereby appropriating another strategy used by power. Instead of national heroes, they depicted libertarian and popular heroes, supplanting scenes of battle and great military deeds with mass rebellions and clashes with authorities. They tried to move readers by running allegorical images in newspapers and magazines that showed how acts of flagrant injustice had cost martyrs their lives: images of the dead from the Commune, those executed in Barcelona's Montjuich castle, and those killed during the repression of May Day 1909 in Buenos Aires. The most widely circulated image was that of the Chicago martyrs, whose drama, which was so close temporally, had an immense impact on workers and elicited strong sentiments of solidarity from them. Such portrayals also served a didactic end: they explained the trial, called for the preservation of the memory of what had occurred, celebrated the martyrs' example, and appealed to people's sense of justice and freedom.

Heroes and martyrs in libertarian mythology were mostly foreigners, reflecting the internationalism of the local workers' movement and its novelty in Argentina. Bakunin and Reclus were among the heroes; among the martyrs, one found Ferrer, "the martyr of science"; Caserio, "the warm-hearted, good youth"; Angiolillo, "the poet of justice"; Vaillant, "the stoic"; Ravachol, "the avenger of bourgeois society," among other fallen militants.[41] And some of the martyrs were still alive: libertarians elevated Radowitzky to the status of a "living martyr" for having killed Colonel Falcón and then enduring a long incarceration in the province of Tierra del Fuego; something similar occurred in the case of Salvador Planas, the Spanish anarchist who tried to assassinate President Quintana in 1905. Anarchists applauded his act and celebrated him: "Planas is the ideal type of redeemer," who, like Radowitzky, had "disinterestedly" risked his life in pursuit of a better world. The vindicating hero was a model for others. A writer in *Gleam* effusively asserted that "the Planases of the world haven't disappeared and, thanks to them, we won't have to wait long for anarchy's beautiful sun to rise."[42]

Anarchists integrated these men into their revolutionary pantheon and hoped that they would provide workers with a sense of class identity. Such figures also represented the individual concretion of the libertarian ideal, which, as Litvak argued, "accentuated the ideology's material elements and credibility. The individual's experience was, in effect, always more real and alive than ideological abstractions."[43] This is why militants decorated their homes with portraits and images of their heroes and martyrs—icons and artworks that competed for space in workers' small, motley homes with paintings by popular artists and depictions of national heroes, saints, and kings. Libertarians promoted the pantheon in their fundraising efforts and frequently awarded raffle winners paintings depicting the Haymarket affair and portraits of Reclus, Bakunin, Proudhon, Zola, and Victor Hugo, among others. For instance, anarchists held a "popular lottery" to benefit libertarian publications in which they gave out the following items: a portrait of Élisée Reclus, a painting of the Haymarket martyrs, and "an artistic drawing by comrade Marino representing 'The Collapse of the Present Society,' in a rich cedar frame."[44]

Some militants were frustrated with the new cult of revolutionary martyrs and questioned, from a rational and somewhat puritanical perspective, what they interpreted as the emergence of a new hagiography. Celebrating martyrs was clearly an elemental part of anarchist (and left) discourse, despite the movement's professed rationalism. Pierre Ansart wrote:

> Rationalist philosophers believed that renouncing religious iden-
> tifications and passionate attachments to the irrational would
> make social relationships more pacific, but experience shows that
> political values linked to ideologies are as emotionally charged as
> religious ones. The ideological verb does not offer the subject a
> range of possibilities from which to choose, but rather a *singu-*
> *lar truth* from which it would be humiliating and degrading to
> withdraw.[45]

Anarchists tried to provoke enthusiastic adherence to their ideals, but their passion for ideological ends generated strong doses of irrationality.

One of the most lucid writers in the Buenos Aires anarchist movement, Mariano Cortés (Altair), noted deep contradictions between anarchists' hero worship and their rational philosophy, and also worrisome parallels to religious, specifically Catholic, mysticism. "We have an hagiography, too," he said, "just like the Catholics, and we expand it daily. Who cares if we don't burn candles or shoot off fireworks to honor the miraculous Saint Anthony or some other dubious figure if we are about to inscribe a Saint Ravachol into our catalog of idols?"[46] This was a shrewd critique and, though applicable to the entire libertarian camp, his focus was on prominent libertarian publications that published veritable elegies—with images included—of individualist terrorists who had attacked kings and well-known politicians. In their depictions, these "vindicating martyrs" had angelic qualities and the familiar attributes of heroes and saints.

4. REVOLUTIONARY CALENDARS AND ALMANACS

Anarchists did not construct their symbolic apparatus with new materials but rather endowed existing ones with new meaning. Their secular *Popular Almanac*, published by *The Social Question,* an Italian-and-Spanish-language libertarian newspaper, exemplifies this. Libertarians did not expect it to supplant the dominant calendar but to indicate the possibility of an alternative registry of holidays and heroes. Released in 1894, the subtitle of the first edition stated: "Contains a socialist calendar and various writings of use for proletarians." It came out at the beginning of each year until at least 1902. The release schedule, in fact, points to anarchists' acceptance of the structure of the prevailing calendar, which they probably did not consider challenging and, in any case, would not have been influential enough to displace if they had.

Anarchists embraced calendar reforms introduced during the French Revolution, particularly the secularism and appeal to natural cycles, but did not put forward more radical modifications. They used the calendar for the purposes of propaganda without altering its formal structure. The changes that they advanced were limited to the Gregorian hagiography, which they replaced with secular and revolutionary historical anniversaries. The first edition *Popular Almanac* explained:

> *The Social Question*'s *Popular Almanac* for 1895 is the antithesis
> of the Gregorian calendar: instead of saints, it records the great
> deeds, notable events, discoveries and inventions, and the names
> of the men whose virtues and talents have enabled them to win the
> sympathies and esteem of peoples worldwide.[47]

Anarchists' substitution of religious with secular holidays, and articulation of a different concept of history, made their alternative almanac a significant innovation. Their history was a history of workers' battles for freedom, which was the foundation of their attempt to invent a proletarian tradition. Indeed, the anarchist calendar assumed an internationalist history by and about workers and built around their struggles, thinkers, and those who had contributed to the rational progress of humanity or—and this was the same thing for them—workers' well-being.

Like the Gregorian calendar, the anarchist almanac recorded a different event on each day of the year. The anniversaries that they selected reflected diverse concerns, though all commemorated popular struggles and principles dear to anarchists and the left generally.[48] Sometimes the references went beyond the socialist tradition and pointed to anarchism's deeper philosophical roots (in rationalism and the Enlightenment, specifically). Figures whose births or deaths were noted indicate anarchist sources of inspiration: alongside revolutionaries like Blanqui, Proudhon, Owen, Fourier, Marx, Bakunin, Saint Simon, and Louis Blanc, there were symbols of modern rationalism like Galileo, Descartes, Voltaire, Gutenberg, Newton, Franklin, Humboldt, and Kepler. Representatives of the arts included Cervantes, Victor Hugo, Renan, Lamennais, Bocaccio, and Lord Byron. Some of the figures that anarchists included were surprising, such as Martin Luther, for instance, although perhaps he owed his presence to the schism that he had caused in the Catholic Church, and Mazzini, whom anarchists criticized for his nationalism but who may have earned his place through his battles against the Vatican.

Many of the dates that anarchists memorialized testified to their opposition to religion and the church. They vehemently opposed religious obscurantism, which they blamed for impeding the development of culture, keeping the masses in ignorance, and ensuring that power remained in the hands of the privileged. Anarchists drew dates from European, not Argentine, history: January 6 recalled "the first victims of the Inquisition, who died in Seville" (in 1481); on January 17, they remembered the day in 1836 when "all the religious communities of Madrid were suppressed, because they were at the center of a conspiracy against progress"; on February 16, anarchists marked the day in 1600 when "the despicable sectarians of the Inquisition burned the immortal astronomer Giordano Bruno alive in Rome." More than antagonism to religion per se, these commemorations bespoke an anger at the church, which they believed was an impediment to progress and had committed injustices against freethinkers.

Anarchists highlighted other dates that voiced their disdain for well-known representatives of the nobility and bourgeoisie: the "rickety little tyrant Louis Adolphe Thiers, known as the hyena of the proletariat, was born in Marseilles" on April 16 (in 1779); "France's Louis XIV, the most repugnant of the Royal type, was born in Paris" on September 5 (of 1638). Anarchists also celebrated the executions of Louis XVI and England's Charles I, as well as anarchist attacks upon kings, presidents, and ministers. This was another instance in which they counterposed revolutionary to traditional justice.

Above all, anarchists commemorated events related to the workers' movement and their role within it. They marked a series of days in January recalling an 1894 workers' rebellion in Italy: the dates on which the conflict erupted, the repression and then the uprising that followed, the imposition of martial law, the intensification of the strife, and the use of a war crimes tribunal against anarchists and their incarceration. There were a number of sequences of this type, like the 1892 peasant rebellion in Andalusia, the Paris Commune of 1871, and of course the events that took place in Chicago in 1886 that would turn May 1 into a universal day of proletarian jubilation—doubtlessly the most important date in the anarchist calendar. The internationalism of these commemorations was significant, and a clear response to the First International's call to workers to organize themselves without regard for nationality.

Anarchists' attempt to differentiate themselves and assert their identity in the broader socialist camp is also pertinent. Although they were fairly ecumenical, they privileged anarchist struggles and events in their selection of dates—the founding of newspapers and groups, the birthdates and deaths of their luminaries, conflicts in which they had been pivotal, etc.

5. MAY DAY: THE WORKERS' EASTER

May Day was a major event in the revolutionary calendar. The commemoration was anarchists' most significant ritual and one heavily laden with symbolism, surely because it was the only anniversary linked exclusively to the proletariat. On that date, militants recalled the labor activists executed in Chicago in 1887, even though May 1 was the day of the demonstration that precipitated the tragic events in 1886, not the day that authorities actually took their prisoners to the scaffolds (that occurred on November 11, 1887). Anarchists recalled the two dates indiscriminately.[49] The commemoration was an assertion of working-class identity and an example of the willed construction of that identity, insofar as it was organized in response to directives issued by the Second International in 1889. From that moment onward, it became the official ceremony for workers around the world, led by diverse tendencies that attempted to endow it with meaning in their own ways. In Argentina, May Day emerged as a celebration of the workers' movement in reply to the Second International's call and a decision by some leading socialists. It was synonymous with the global proletarian struggle and a ritualized combination of workers' demonstration and celebration. As Hobsbawm argued, on that date there was a regular, public self-representation of a class, "an affirmation of its power and, in fact, its invasion of the social space of the system, a symbolic conquest."[50]

Argentine anarchists saw the May Day celebration as an event that united workers and articulated their political, social, cultural, and economic demands. Anarchist discourse, deployed in a climate overloaded with emotionalism, contained a mix of fervor and rationalism that occasionally took on religious overtones, despite their undeniable anti-clericalism and rationalism. They even appropriated some social elements of Christianity when they adopted oratorical rituals derived from the church, which they secularized and rationalized.[51] The anarchist variant of the Apostles' creed is a good example: man replaces God and the principal values of the libertarian philosophy replace Christian moral strictures—nature, scientific progress, individual freedom, justice, the disappearance of privilege, the critique of the state and religion, and, of course, social redemption under anarchist stewardship.

> I believe in man, a powerful being, creator of progress and foundation of all earthly pleasures, who, in individual freedom, his only medium, our motive achieved through the work of the human organism, born of the primitive anarchist virgin, he suffered under the weight of religion and the state; crucified, killed, and buried in the person of the propagandists; he descended to the hells of feudalism and in the third century was raised from the dead among the oppressed, rose to the skies of the mesocratic governments, he is seated to the right of the all-powerful bourgeoisie and from there came to judge and put an end to abuses and privileges; I believe in the spirit of incessant progress, in the sociological school, anarchic reforms, in the disappearance of every privilege and the resurrection of justice and in lasting human well-being, by virtue of my anarchist principles. Amen.[52]

Anarchists also appropriated and re-signified Easter. Although Italian socialist Andrea Costa was the first to make the analogy between May Day and Easter, libertarians assimilated the importance and meaning of the Christian holiday to May Day from very early on. Terms like "Workers' Easter" and "Red Easter" were common in the anarchist press, especially after a local paper published Pietro Gori's short poem, "Workers' Easter."[53] May Day became the definitive celebration of workers' culture, and competed with secular as well as religious commemorations.

Celebrating the day at rallies and publishing articles about it facilitated a moment of recognition and identification in which orators and authors related an alternative vision of history. Its narrative thread centered on social struggles and popular resistance, and it was led primarily by the workers of the world. In anarchists' view, the progressive evolution of reason and science—which they thought would parallel the workers' revolutionary struggle—bolstered social battles.

Libertarian efforts to invent a tradition are apparent in their newspapers' uniform accounts of May Day's origins. Every year, they mechanically recounted the events that led to it, portraying it not just as a moment in working-class history but in epic terms. Anarchists' goal was to fix these incidents in proletarian memory. For instance, in a meeting that occurred in the Doria Theater in 1900, "Comrades Montesano, Gori, and others took the stage to tell the story of the legalized murder committed by the North American bourgeoisie."[54] The account recalls the circumstances that ended with the execution of the five proletarian leaders (Fischer, Engel, Parsons, Spies, and Lingg) in 1887.[55] For Argentine anarchists, the significance of the affair lay in a wave of solidarity that workers around the world expressed toward the martyrs, a solidarity called for since the First International and that was palpable for the first time. The reception of these events in Argentina reinforced workers' class identity and provided them with a commemoration that was exclusively their own. The May Day celebration crystallized the construction of a workers' tradition.

In their highly emotional commemorations, anarchists' speeches culminated in eulogies to the Chicago martyrs' bravery and courage:

> In human history, one finds incrustations of luminous rubies, deeds that presage.... There are martyrs and sacrifices; red gleams from the past, irradiations that surround and illuminate figures such as Bruno, Bresci, Huss, Coligny, the martyrs of Saint Bartholomew's night and Chicago. Preachers of freedom, heralds of liberty all of them ... the ideal of the weak advances serenely and gallantly. This is why November 11 is a glorious day that recalls a great and solemn moment.[56]

Anarchists invested May Day with motifs of martyrdom, sacrifice, pain, mourning, rebellion, and conflict, rendering it combative, tragic, and anti-celebratory. They linked it to the general strike and ascribed a spirit of mass confrontation to it. As early as 1890, when the first May Day celebration in Argentina occurred, it was clear that libertarians had a very different approach than socialists.[57] These two sides of the workers' movement endowed the day with different content, and their competing orientations reflected their disagreements over how to mold a workers' tradition and historical memory.[58] This was an important matter: the group that shaped May Day commemorations would score a major victory in its effort to lead the labor movement. The state and dominant sectors had good reason to try to reshape the day around their own terms.[59]

Socialists and anarchists appealed to the same audience, but their different goals led to clashes in their approach to May Day from the outset. Socialists saw the commemoration as a means of petitioning the state for reforms that would occur in the framework of the established system; for instance, they were the main force behind mobilizations for the eight-hour working day (although anarchists were also involved). This is why their processions and events were so orderly and peaceable. For them, it was not a day for tumult or provocation, but a celebratory show of self-confidence: there was no reason for workers to take a day off to fight with police. They executed their mobilizing ritual in perfect order: they marched with their flags and insignia, sang hymns to the rhythms marked out by the bands, listened to orators, dispersed peacefully, and then treated the remainder of the day as a holiday. They demanded the right not to work and time for rest on May Day, which is why they organized recreational *veladas* and social gatherings. Socialists defended their approach from the very first commemoration of the day in Argentina, and their commitment to it only deepened over the years. In a lecture delivered in 1900, José Ingenieros said:

> May Day is a human and social festival. It celebrates everyone who works and produces, whether with muscle or pen, plow or paintbrush, needle or book. It is a day of expansion for those who have faith in the progressive increase in human well-being.[60]

Anarchists rejected socialists' celebratory and reformist conception of May Day. From their point of view, May Day should not be thought of as a celebration: that obscured "the real concept, the real significance of the day, which is a day of protest and rebellion."[61] They saw it as a moment to mourn all those killed, injured, and detained during protests and everyone whose lives had been thwarted by the capitalist system. It was a day to grieve workers' victimization and exploitation. Its purpose, said *The Rebel*, was to express "the sadness, despair, and pain engendered by years of suffering and ill-treatment at the hands of the boss, the tyrant."[62] Anarchists believed that socialists betrayed workers' spirit and alienated themselves from proletarian interests in order to reconcile with the bourgeoisie, who, thanks to socialists' efforts, "began to breathe easily, as fears that had terrorized them years ago started to dissipate." This is why, anarchists alleged, the dominant class tolerated the Socialist Party, and "hoped to convince workers that there would soon be harmony between capital and labor."[63]

The conflict between anarchists and socialists over the meaning of May Day reflected their political differences. Socialists' commemorative rituals cohered with their gradualist conception of social change, faith in electoral politics, and belief that the working class should fight for improvements within the prevailing system (such as the passage of progressive labor laws, for instance). Anarchists, by contrast, saw May Day as a day of struggle and protest epitomized by the general strike. It was a moment in which workers would come together in a voluntary, conscious way, "without indulgences, trepidation, or half measures; our mobilization," said *La Protesta*, "the fact that we took off of work that day, has to mean, has to indicate, a manly, energetic protest that shows the bourgeoisie that we matter and fight for something of importance."[64] Their outlook was straightforward: the workers had to improve their lot by their own efforts, without the mediation of the state or any political party. They had to take from capital what was rightfully theirs. It was not a date to launch the revolution but one on which workers would recognize themselves as a historical force, strengthen their bonds of solidarity, reaffirm and assert their rights and demands, and proclaim their dedication to revolution. It was a qualitative step in the working class's self-education and maturation.

Anarchist groups and the Argentine Workers' Federation released a manifesto convening the 1902 May Day mobilization that conveyed these aspirations. Based on their presupposition of natural human equality, they asserted that all workers have equal right to possess and enjoy natural and social wealth. To secure it, workers had to tear it out of capitalists' hands through the general strike.

> Workers! Those who suffer the weight of capitalist exploitation; those victimized by the present social order; those who are conscious; those who rebel; all those who fight today's confusion; assert your right to exist, demand to partake in life's pleasures, protest all the existing injustices and wrongs. Today, May Day, is the day of our demands, our freedom, our emancipation; today, you should leave the industrial prisons and fill the ranks of Argentine Workers' Federation.[65]

More combative and anti-celebratory, anarchists' May Day events also had an underlying but unmistakable aura of violence. This is evident when we contrast socialist and libertarian discourse as well as their respective practices. While historian Aníbal Viguera notes no great difference between their rallies, other than anarchists' "more inflamed orators and more oppositional speeches," and argues that police, not libertarians, provoked the violence, it is a fact that violence occurred at anarchist but not socialist demonstrations and, while police triggered it, it is likely that they were agitated by anarchists' belligerent discourse.[66] Police saw libertarians as a menacing, violent enemy, a view that anarchists encouraged to a degree. For instance, in a call for the 1902 May Day rally, a libertarian periodical proclaimed: "We hate! Hate engenders struggle and he who struggles hates! How noble and human it is to fight for an ideal that synthesizes truth!"[67] In an account of the clashes that occurred at the 1904 May Day rally, a journalist from *La Nación,* though he did not spare police from criticism, whom he held responsible for the strife, identified the origin of the incidents: "After twenty blocks of licentious words and gestures, the demonstrators were tied to a train of exaltation that made a conflict possible and even likely."[68]

Annual reports issued by the Interior Ministry of the Capital underscore the police's hostility toward anarchists. For instance, Police Chief Colonel Falcón released a report blaming all of the conflicts during the May 1909 "Red Week" on anarchists, who, he said, had committed "every type of outrage, as they attacked streetcars and motorists." Without a hint of self-criticism, he defended the police's response to the "epithets of 'Cossacks' and 'hired assassins' shouted out during the shooting," saying that it was "only their firm spirit of discipline that allowed them to endure so many provocations." In fact, for Falcón there was more than just a problem of public order: there was also a conspiracy. "Police were well aware" he said, "that sectarian forces had been patiently devising a plan for revolt, for social revolution.... "[69]

Similar though slightly more nuanced attitudes were common among political elites. One can find traces of them in Joaquín V. González's labor bill as well as speeches by Labor Department functionaries and politicians. They were also evident in the press and even encouraged by socialists.[70] These men thought that legislation could contain social conflicts generally, but feared that anarchists would encourage class war. And anarchists did not have to hurl bombs to seem violent: slogans like "May Day will arrive with the flames of a redemptive revolution," "Undying hatred for the bourgeoisie," and "Death to police henchmen" were enough to elicit feelings of alarm. Organizers of anarchist rallies, who were cognizant of this and hoped to avoid a police crackdown, often asked attendees for order and discipline.[71] Calm and rationality were desired characteristics of behavior for anarchists as well as socialists—they suggested a deeper knowledge of the cause and a degree of awareness. This does not contradict anarchists' defense of mass spontaneity or incitements to action. The purpose of the violent rhetoric was to galvanize workers and arouse their indignation about injustices committed by the dominant class, which, for its part, saw libertarian activity as a clear index of subversion.

Elites grew more afraid of anarchists between 1901 and 1910, as they laid roots among workers. May Day commemorations during the period often ended with heavy confrontations with the police as well as death and injury. In fact, anarchist militants frequently brought firearms to demonstrations and occasionally used them to repel police attacks.[72] It is undeniable that there was violence at anarchists' May Day commemorations, which does not disprove Viguera's assertion that orderliness was typical of their rallies. Order and violence are not always mutually exclusive.

These events evolved along with the libertarian movement. Initially very small, they grew quite large as the labor movement expanded, as workers became more assertive, and as anarchists' resolve to organize and lead them deepened. Indeed, in the 1890s, when libertarians had a limited presence among workers, they barely marked the day beyond running articles about it in their papers. And yet, even so, anarchists' sharp differences with socialists were already evident at the time, as they claimed that socialists' festive approach distorted the true meaning of the date. Socialists were then the primary conveners of May Day rallies, and anarchists were largely content to criticize their rivals.[73]

Libertarian groups began marking the event with indoor ceremonies just before the turn of the century. In 1900, they tried to participate in the socialists'

May Day rally in Rodríguez Peña Plaza, but event coordinators prevented anarchist speakers from addressing the crowd, for fear of disturbances. The following year, anarchists organized their first outdoor commemoration of the day, which inaugurated the ritual of their annual May Day rallies, which would continue at least until the Centenary. The rally took place in the Lorea Plaza, located at Avenida de Mayo and San José, which became a highly symbolic space and anarchists' preferred site for their mobilizations. Demonstrators marched along Avenida de Mayo up to Once Plaza. "The column of marchers was extremely long and densely packed," said *La Protesta Humana*. "One newspaper estimated that there were five thousand people present, another guessed six."[74] As an instance of an allegory taken from images of the French Revolution, two women bearing red flags led the marchers, while behind them the Height of Disgrace musical band played revolutionary songs ("Sons of the People," "The Anarchist Hymn," and "To the People") as the crowd sang along. Militants following them carried an enormous white banner bearing this inscription: "Workers' societies salute the universal proletariat. May Day is not a celebration, but a day of protest."[75]

Another group with flags followed further behind, before the bulk of the crowd, among which banners representing unions and libertarian centers flew. When they arrived at Once Plaza, marchers distributed themselves around an improvised stage, where close to a dozen orators let loose with their speeches and harangues. The crowd dispersed as the event came to a close, "amidst thunderous applause, delirious acclamations, and *vivas* for anarchy and social revolution echoed by hundreds of voices."[76]

Anarchists repeated the May Day ritual annually throughout the decade and managed to assemble a sizable crowd at times.[77] From 1902 onward, the Argentine Workers' Federation was the main convener. Its centrality emphasized the union character of the commemoration without losing anarchist influence. That year, libertarian centers marched alongside the builders of Lomas de Zamora; bakers from La Boca, the Capital, Belgrano, and San Martín; coachmen; united artisans; bread distributors; mechanics from Sola; workers from the Compañía General de Fósforos; and longshoremen from the port; among other unions. More than ten thousand anarchist newspapers were distributed.[78]

As noted, Lorea Plaza was the site where participants gathered to begin the mobilization, typically dressed in their best clothes. "As for the demonstrators," wrote *La Nación*, "there was a prodigious quantity of young men, a number of women including some old ones, and men of diverse nationalities. All sported anarchist emblems: red ties, rosettes, flowers, and berets."[79] Although anarchists rejected the festive conception of the event, their rallies had festive elements. They waved red flags, sang revolutionary songs, and cheered and applauded as columns arrived from various parts of the city: "Each association poured in through different points of Lorea Plaza, depending on what part of the city they were from," wrote *La Prensa*.[80] Once all the columns were arrayed in the designated order, they set off, slowly and with a defiant attitude toward watching police, against whom they shouted abuse and who charged at them unceremoniously.[81] The march through the city was a show of strength that went to different destinations every year: they took Rivadavia Avenue if they were marching to Once; or, if the endpoint was Constitución, the parade went through Rivadavia, Entre Ríos, Chile, Buen Orden (Bernardo de Yrigoyen), and Brasil to enter the wide plaza; other times they marched to Mazzini Plaza along Rivadavia, Callao, and Corrientes. They changed routes to show themselves to different parts of the population and symbolically occupy an increasingly larger part of Buenos Aires, affirming that they, too, were part of its symbolic framework.

In addition to the main demonstration, secondary demonstrations proceeded from different areas of the city. For example, anarchists commemorated the event in Lorea Plaza in 1904, with participants initially meeting in various places, depending on their neighborhood or union. The Pro-May Day Committee of the La Boca and Barracas Resistance Societies met at Suárez and Patricios, marched from there along Brasil, Perú, Venezuela, and Lorea until they reached the plaza. The resistance societies of Villa Crespo took Corrientes, Callao, and Avenida de Mayo. Societies from the Worker House concentrated at Pozos and Independencia and, passing through Entre Ríos and Avenida de Mayo, arrived at the terminus. When the event was over, all the marchers followed Avenida de Mayo to Mazzini Plaza.[82] Libertarian demonstrators invaded a sizable portion of Buenos Aires.

The arrival at the destination site was a climactic moment: "The demonstration flooded Mazzini Plaza, which rang with revolutionary chants and '*Vivas!*' for anarchy … it was full of agitated men, worked up by the excitement and success of the mobilization."[83] Sometimes militants introduced theatrical elements: for instance, on May Day 1902, demonstrators reenacted the storming of the Bastille as they entered Constitución Plaza, simulating an assault on a tower/rock placed in the middle of the square. Militants planted a red flag on its summit and orators addressed the crowd from there.

The years preceding the Centenary marked a peculiar moment in the evolution of Argentine workers' identity. The intense social turmoil, workers' internationalism, the need to mark off a space of contention and to create workers' institutions, and the state's absence from social affairs gave these years an embattled character that helped anarchists lay deep roots. They deployed rituals and symbols that corresponded to the conflicted nature of social relations and contributed to the emergence of a combative class identity that was visible in any of the major mobilizations of the period.

Anarchists' utilized their May Day rituals and symbolic apparatus in the short lapse of time during which they dominated the workers' movement. In 1910, when memories of the tragic events that had occurred during the previous year's "Red Week" were still fresh (whose ultimate aftershock was the assassination of the police chief who had led the repression), the government decided to suppress all protest during the Centenary celebrations. It hoped to prevent any conflict that might tarnish the events and to impose patriotic and religious symbols over the combative ones that emerged under anarchist influence. The state cracked down viciously on libertarians—preventing them from marking May Day—and mandated that all those in the national territory commemorate May 25. Its actions were a symbolic victory of a heroic national rite over a heroic workers' rite.

Libertarian symbols increasingly disappeared from public life a decade later, although the specter of anarchist influence endured in the collective imagination long after anarchists represented a popular alternative. Elites continued to worry over anarchists even after they had been displaced by syndicalists and later communists. The rites and symbols used by these groups may have seemed the same, but their meaning was very different.

CONCLUSION

It happened in a matter of seconds. A plume of white smoke shot into the calm blue skies ... and red flames engulfed the entire building immediately. It was as if they had scored a heroic victory, as if they had put a man-eating monster to death. The well-to-do crowd sang and danced around the enormous bonfire that devoured the printing press of that newspaper—*La Protesta*—which had been set up at the cost of untold exertions and workers' tears. "We've torched it!" "We've avenged Falcón!" It was like they had killed a mythical beast.[1]

ALTHOUGH THE "BEAST" was not dead, it was mortally wounded and would never again play the role in Argentine social and political life that it had played during the century's tumultuous first decade. A few months after the Centenary, the Italian consul in Argentina made a comment that captured anarchists' paralysis: "The press muzzled, every attempt at propaganda persecuted, even conventional newspapers banned from using the word 'anarchy'—the sect has been reduced to silence. Apparently, the Social Defense Law has achieved its goal."[2] He also mentioned that anarchists had been forced underground and feared that anyone who approached them was acting on behalf of the Social Order unit of the police. Their trepidation compounded their isolation.

The consul's depiction contrasts sharply with worries that Miguel Cané had voiced about anarchists just nine years earlier. At that time, influenced by Lombroso's criminology, most government men saw anarchism as a disease of the social body. Buenos Aires's police chief described the movement as "the focal point of a social pathology that our collective personality cannot assimilate."[3] It was on the basis of the same ideas that the government escalated its attacks on anarchists, culminating in the preventative application of martial law in May 1910 and the approval of the Social Defense Law shortly thereafter. These legal instruments, and a consensus about anarchism among the middle class, enabled the government to expel dozens of foreign and naturalized activists, lock up numerous Argentine-born leaders for long periods in the Ushuaia penitentiary (Rodolfo González Pacheco, Apolinario Barrera, and Teodoro Antilli among others), silence the libertarian press, stop public meetings, and shut down libertarian groups, centers, and circles.

The severity and duration of the repression were unprecedented and a shock to anarchists: "The mass detention of propagandists and active elements in the workers' movement was a surprise to us across the board," wrote Eduardo Gilimón.[4] Even more novel was civilian participation in the attacks on socialists and anarchists, foreigners, and particularly Jews, all of which the government not only permitted but also encouraged. Interior Minister José Gálvez justified the crackdown: "The youth are getting ready to begin," he declared. "Only minutes ago, the nationalist students' union informed me that they are going to hold a rally to defend their honor, which they believe has been offended."[5] These groups attacked workers' centers, torched the editorial offices and printing machines of *La Protesta*, *The Battle*, and *La Vanguardia*, stormed bookstores, cafés, brothels, shops in the Jewish neighborhood Once, and physically assaulted activists and people suspected of being foreigners. The government and right-wing civilians had launched a war against an opponent that was neither prepared for it nor able to respond. The magnitude of the crackdown had far less to do with actual size of the anarchist movement than the perception of its social danger among those who unleashed it.

The prolonged imposition of martial law inflicted serious damage on the continuity of libertarian activities. *La Protesta* was still banned a year after the Centenary and only resumed daily publication in 1913. Public events were prohibited, and even after restrictions became less onerous, anarchists were required to secure police authorization before holding a gathering or rally of any sort, which of course they were unlikely to receive.[6] The few anarchist publications that managed to come out during this time speak of a climate of crisis and defeat:

> Innocents are imprisoned … women are attacked … workers are deported, clothes and money are stolen from children, the elderly, and homemakers … peaceful strikers are persecuted and treated like they are rabid dogs, workers' institutions are raided and shut down, the circulation and sale of our press is undermined, armed

patrols go to cafés and homes and search them in ways that offend elemental standards of freedom and decency.[7]

As happened every time social struggles ebbed, anarchists inveighed against the populace, blaming it for its supposed materialism, passivity, and lack of solidarity with besieged activists. "All they cared about was their own economic well-being," complained *The Libertarian*. "Nobody moved, as if they were in a stupor."[8] Anarchist alienation from the workers became palpable and individualist and elitist tendencies among libertarians grew more pronounced.

Anarchist publishing came to an almost complete halt and the few publications that did come out strained to circulate underground. Libertarian groups fell apart, circles stopped functioning, and the parties, lectures, and theatrical performances disappeared. With the circles and groups inactive, the press mostly silent, and an environment of popular apathy, anarchists were hobbled and their ties to workers severed. The anarchist movement had changed by the time the more overt forms of repression dissipated in late 1913, and Buenos Aires itself was in the midst of a transformation that—while largely imperceptible to those living through it—would be a central factor in anarchism's decline.

The libertarian movement was confused and disoriented as its points of contact with workers disintegrated and the networks linking its institutions and the unions dissolved. Many anarchist writers, speakers, and other prominent figures—Alberto Ghiraldo and Eduardo Gilimón, for instance—withdrew from activism, and a large number of intermediate militants, who were really the backbone of libertarian institutions, were exiled, incarcerated, or simply disappeared from the scene.[9] More than a few joined the revolutionary syndicalists, whose pragmatism exercised a broad appeal. Others traveled surprising political paths: the aforementioned group of exiles in Uruguay (Clérici, Virginia Bolten, Adrián Troitiño, Francisco Berri, etc.) formed an anarchist, pro-Batlle y Ordóñez tendency in Montevideo. Others, such as Bautista Fueyo and Santiago Locascio, who were inspired by the universalization of male suffrage and the European left's parliamentarian experiences, attempted to form a workers' party and test their luck in the electoral arena. The Russian Revolution also had a powerful impact on libertarians, some of whom became maximalists and called for the creation of a workers' party. The Radical Party won over educator Julio Barcos, and Dr. Carulla followed a route that would ultimately lead him to the nationalist right. There were disparate escape routes from anarchism, and during the First World War, neither *La Protesta* nor the other surviving papers, circles, groups, or centers played the catalyzing role that they had during the previous decade.

The state's crackdown after 1910, and the absence of a unifying center (i.e., a party) that could forge a coherent strategy, made it extremely difficult for the dispersed militants to regroup. With their newspapers and institutions shuttered and their leading cadre absent, the anarchist moment fragmented and could not regain its footing. Internal disputes proliferated and grew more important than they had been during earlier times, when they were buried under the exigencies of the social conflict. In addition to the disagreement that distanced him from *La Protesta*, Alberto Ghiraldo was involved in a bitter polemic in 1914 related to his failed attempt to serve as a delegate to the anarchist congress in London (which was canceled due to the outbreak of WWI). In 1915, a debate in *La Protesta* prompted González Pacheco to break with the paper. A year later, Apolinario Barrera, who was a prominent leader, found himself implicated in a business scandal and González Pacheco and Teodoro Antilli became staunch enemies of the doctrinal purists. These internal battles dragged on for years.[10]

Government repression expedited the movement's decline, but the speed of its demise points to even more vexing, underlying problems. It deteriorated not only because it was out of tune with major developments in Buenos Aires's social structure but also because of more circumstantial changes. For instance, worker combativity decreased sharply around the start of WWI, just as the movement's internal disintegration was in full swing.[11] Anarchists lost their influence on the workers' movement to the revolutionary syndicalists, who had emerged as a tendency around 1905. The syndicalists were much more pragmatic and prioritized economic battles over anarchists' political objectives, which was more consistent with Buenos Aires workers' aspirations at the time. The labor structure was also becoming much more stratified and concentrated, and increasing numbers of workers acquired some job stability as well as debts linked to the purchase of land, homes, and building materials.[12] Tactics geared toward securing economic improvements became more attractive than those focused on inducing social rebellion—the latter were more appropriate to conflicts like the renters' strikes than those generated by workers worried about job security and purchasing power. Syndicalists also had an easier time recruiting native workers in the process of Argentinization that was taking place.[13]

Revolutionary syndicalists also pressed for national trade federations and union hierarchies, which anarchists, accustomed to decentralization and spontaneity, could not accept. Though syndicalists employed a discourse very similar to that used by anarchists (i.e., they were anti-statist and opposed parliamentarianism), they were quite different in practice. They had a class-based orientation, rejected anarchists' permanent confrontationalism, prioritized the union as a tactical tool (they were gradualists), and their support for the general strike was primarily rhetorical—they called them only reluctantly and preferred partial strikes. The solid organization of unions such as the Maritime Workers Federation and some successful strikes earned syndicalists a degree of prestige among workers and, as noted, even some adepts among libertarian workers. Syndicalists started to become a force around the Centenary, when they secured control of unions vital to the agricultural export economy such as those representing maritime, port, and rail workers. They seized control of the FORA during the ninth conference in 1915 and eliminated the clause placed in the statutes a decade earlier defining the federation as anarcho-communist.[14] Anarchists congregated in the FORA of the Fifth Congress, but only managed to organize the cart drivers, bakers, some port workers, and other small unions, and could never regain the influence that they had had just shortly before. Abad de Santillán claimed that the anarchist movement experienced a resurgence after 1918, but syndicalists were the main leaders of the big strikes of 1917 and 1919 (although libertarians spurred numerous partial and spontaneous conflicts).[15] Anarchist alienation from workers following their loss of control over the unions severed them from their main source of recruitment and made them a marginal force in social conflicts, which is not to deny their continued presence in the social imagination.

The decentralization of the city that began in the middle of the first decade of the century also intensified. The expansion of streetcar lines and the sale of plots of land through monthly installments enabled many workers to set up their own homes in urbanizing areas that were far from the city center. This facilitated the decentralization of the world of labor and a separation of the workplace from the home. Anarchists seem to have been better adapted to the workers' culture found in the cramped neighborhoods of El Centro, La Boca, and Barracas, where tenements and other types of transitory housing offered fertile ground for their propaganda.[16] Urban decentralization and neighborhood life mixed many workers with people from other social classes (office workers, store keepers, and some professionals) and they developed a shared identity as neighbors. An investment in neighborhood life, the separation of the home from the workplace, and the reduction of the workday changed social practices for some Buenos Aires workers and diluted working-class identity. Obviously there were still labor problems and disputes—demands for higher salaries and improved working conditions were as compelling then as they had been during the previous decade—but the range of demands now included neighborhood issues, and cultural arenas that had been oppositional became increasingly conformist and reformist, as images of successful social mobility undermined the coherence of an identity based primarily on the workplace. Furthermore, society and the state appeared too solid to confront successfully.[17] The Yrigoyen government's policy of rapprochement and negotiation with syndicalists also contributed to anarchists' isolation. Libertarians did not know how to respond to the state's practice of concessions and the emergence of a unique neighborhood culture, which centered attention on demands of a territorial character and presumed a permanent dialogue with municipal authorities. An old libertarian activist noted anarchists' incapacity to adapt to the social, cultural, and political transformation of Buenos Aires. He argued that anarchists had chosen a path riddled with obstacles and, in "a state of impotence," were unable to appeal to the "people and their institutions," primarily because they did not attend to new forms of association like the school cooperatives and, especially, *fomento* societies.[18] In his view, the *fomento* societies were perfectly consistent with anarchist federalism, and he faulted anarchists for continuing to prioritize a workers movement dominated by syndicalists.[19] It seems obvious that anarchists' Manichaenism, extreme confrontationalism, and refusal to heed social changes were huge barriers to the movement's survival.

The transformation of cultural practices, including some prefigured during the previous decade, also contributed to anarchists' marginalization. Parallel to the Argentinization of immigrants' children, the public education system consolidated itself, and the resulting growth in literacy among workers helped draw them into the rapidly expanding culture industry, whose offerings multiplied after the Centenary, when the amount of free time available to them also grew. Cinema, theater, and the mass press took their first steps and soccer became popular. These phenomena extended throughout the city, and although many of the cinema and theater halls were in El Centro, they quickly spread into the neighborhoods, where they acquired a unique local identity. The insufficiency of libertarians' cultural offering was transparent—it tended to satisfy only the movement's most faithful adepts, who were attached to their old ideas and doctrinal premises and who railed harshly and fruitlessly against a culture industry that overwhelmed and distanced them from workers. Anarchists increasingly withdrew into a self-enclosed, marginal world of their own, pursuing a "strategy of exile," as their spaces became sites for the idealistic representation of the working class and a utopian world of solidarity.[20] In contrast to the first decade, when the street was the primary arena for anarchist propaganda, in the years following the Centenary (with the obvious exception of the "Tragic Week") anarchists' public presence shrank dramatically, and their May Day celebrations and other public rituals ran out of steam. There is no doubt that the tendency toward self-marginalization, combined with their reluctance to analyze or even note domestic particularities, dramatically facilitated their separation from the workers.

Anarchists' use of direct action and proclivity for street violence, as well as their revolutionary urgency and predisposition to rebellion earned them prestige at the beginning of the century due to the character of social relations and because the state and the ruling groups had not yet fine-tuned certain mechanisms of political and social control. In this sense, anarchism can be seen as a reaction to the accelerated, tumultuous process of modernization that was underway and the state centralization that it entailed. Anarchists attempted to enlist workers in their tactic of permanent conflict and ambiguous rebellion, but the shortcomings of their political, social, and cultural alternatives would sooner or later prove insurmountable. The state's first steps in the arena of social policy, the expansion of the political system that occurred in 1912, and the other aforementioned transformations changed the relationship between society and the state and the role of political vanguards. For all of these reasons, anarchists were unable to advance an alternative that workers found attractive after the Centenary. Argentine anarchism was a striking but ephemeral phenomenon, immersed in a society in the midst of rapid changes: from the city's physical structure, which transformed at an impressive rate, to the social structure, which was in constant horizontal and vertical flux and whose social actors (immigrants and Argentine born) were determined to climb the social ladder. Anarchism was as international as Buenos Aires and reflected the diverse tendencies present in the European libertarian movement as well as—to an extent—local particularities.

Where did anarchism end? Speaking of the Spanish anarchist movement, one author says that "the movement was lost with the evolution of the times although its problems of freedom and equality were incorporated into European culture and, in that sense, touched the rest of the world."[21] Argentine anarchism was also lost in the course of the twentieth century and, like its Hispanic counterpart, installed the problems of freedom and equality in local society. It was almost the only oppositional current to defend individual freedom and the equality of men and women as supreme values: neither the state nor partisan interests ought to come between the individual and his or her freedom. This made it unlike any other left group or party. These ideas were inheritances from liberalism, but anarchists, unlike liberals, put them in practice (or attempted to) among the most oppressed social groups. Perhaps the contemporary human rights movements' defense of civil rights and individual liberties is an inheritance from the libertarian movement.

APPENDIX:

Spanish Names of Groups and Periodicals

Alberto Ghiraldo Philodramatic Group = Grupo filodramático Alberto Ghiraldo
The Almagro Libertarians = Los libertarios de almagro
Anarchic Communist Circle = Círculo comunista anárquico
The Anarchist Ideal = El Ideal anarquista
Anarchist Libraries = Bibliotecas ácratas
Anarchist Women's Center = Centro anarquista femenino
The Anarchos = Los ácratas
Anarchy = Acracia
Anti-Militarist Council = Consejo antimilitarista
Argentine Industrial Union = Unión industrial Argentina
Argentine Workers' Federation = Federación obrera Argentina
Art and Freedom = Arte y libertad
Art and Labor = Arte y labor
Art and Life = Arte y vida
Art and Solidarity = Arte y solidaridad
Art for life = Arte por la vida
Aspirants to the Ideal = Aspirantes al ideal
Awake = El despertar
Bakers' Union = Sindicato de obreros panaderos
Bakuninist Center for Workers' Propaganda = Centro de propaganda obrera bakuninista
The Barracas Anarchists = Los ácratas de barracas
The Barracks = El cuartel
The Battle = La batalla
Blue = Azul
Boca Popular Center for Education = Centro popular de enseñanza de la boca
The Bread Worker = El obrero panadero
Cart Drivers' Society = Sociedad de conductores de carros
Central Fruit Market = Mercado central de frutos
The Chicago Martyrs = Los mártires de chicago
Children of the Sun = Hijos del sol
The Conquest of Bread = Conquista del pan
The Conquest of Bread = La conquista del pan
The Conquest of the Ideal = La conquista del ideal
The Conscript = El conscripto
Creation = Creación
The Dawn = La aurora
Dawn Group = Grupo aurora
Dawn of the Future = Aurora del porvenir

The Dawn of the Twentieth Century = El alba del siglo xx
The Defenders of New Ideas = Los defensores de las nuevas ideas
The Deserters = Los desertores
Determination = La porfía
Did you notice? = ¿se dan cuenta?
The Dispossessed = Los desheredados
The Dynamiters =Los dinamiteros
Educational Centers = Centros instructivos
Emancipation = La emancipación
Émile Zola = Emilio zola
Emulators of Ravachol = Émulos de ravachol
Equality and Fraternity = Igualdad y fraternidad
Ermete Zacconi Drama Acadaemy = Academia filodramática ermete zacconi
Evolution = Evolución
Expropriation = La expropiación
Expropriation Is Necessary = La expropiación es necesaria
Federation of the Spanish Region = Federación de trabajadores de la región
    española
Floresta Education Center = Centro de instrucción de floresta
Forward = Adelante
The Free = Los libres
The Free Idea = La idea libre
Free Love = Amor libre
Freedom = Libertad
Freedom and Love = Libertad y amor
Freedom Lovers = Amantes de la libertad
Friend of the Worker = Amigo del trabajador
Friends of the Worker = Amigos del obrero
Friends of the Worker = Amigos del trabajador
The Future = L'Avvenire
The Gentleman of the Wilderness = El caballero del desierto
The Gentlemen of the Ideal = Los caballeros del ideal
Gleam = Fulgor
Glory to Art = Glorias al arte
Health and Strength = Salud y fuerza
The Height of Disgrace = El colmo de la desgracia
The Height of Misery = El colmo de la miseria
Heroines of the Future = Las heroínas del porvenir
The Hobos = Los atorrantes
The Honorable Delinquents = Los malhechores honrados
Human Emancipation = La emancipación humana
The Hungry = Los hambrientos
Illustrated Almanac = Almanaque ilustrado
Initiative = Iniciativa
International Social Studies Center = The centro internacional de estudios sociales
International Social Studies Circles = Círculos internacionales de estudios sociales
Iron = Hierro
Justice = La Giustizia
Labor and Science = Labor y ciencia

Land and Liberty = Tierra y libertad
Libertarian bookstore = Librería libertaria
Libertarian Choral Society = Orfeón libertario
Libertarian Dawn = Alba libertaria
Libertarian Federation of Socialist Anarchist Groups of Buenos Aires = Federación
 libertaria de los grupos socialistas anarquistas de buenos aires
Libertarian Social Studies Circle = Círculo libertario de estudios sociales
Libertarian Social Study Centers = Centros libertarios de estudios sociales
The Libertarians = Los libertarios
The Lie = La mentira
Life and Work = Vida y trabajo
The Light = La Luz
Light and Life = Luz y vida
Light and Progress = Luz y progreso
Los Corrales Libertarian Propaganda Group = Grupo de propaganda libertaria de los
 corrales
Los Corrales Libertarians = Libertarios de los corrales
Love = Amor
Love of Work = Amor al trabajo
The Martyrs = Los mártires
May Day = 1° de mayo
May First = Primero de mayo
The May Sun = Sol de mayo
The Mazzini Plaza Group = Grupo plaza mazzini
Misery = La miseria
Modern Art = Arte moderno
Modern Criminology Magazine = Revista de criminología moderna
Modern Dramatic Association = Agrupación dramática moderna
Modern School Bulletin = Boletín de la escuela moderna
Modern Schools = Escuelas modernas
Modern Theater = Teatro moderno
Modern Youth = Juventud moderna
National Federation of Port Workers = Federación nacional de obreros portuarios
The Natural = Lo natural
Nature = Natura
Nature Center = Centro natura
Neither God Nor Master = Né dio, né padrone
The New Civilization = La nueva civilta
New Dawn = Nueva aurora
New Directions = Nuevos rumbos
New Era = Nueva era
The New Era = La Nueva Era
The New Humanity = La nueva humanidad
New Light = Nueva luz
The New Paths = Los nuevos caminos
The New Rebels = Nuevos rebeldes
The New Roads = Los nuevos caminos
New Route = Rumbo nuevo
The New Times = Los tiempos nuevos

November 11 = 11 de noviembre
On March = En Marcha
The Oppressed = El oprimido
Pallás's Bomb = Bomba pallás
The Persecuted = El perseguido
Popular Almanac = almanaque popular
Popular Centers = Centros populares
Popular Committee for the Freedom of the Press = Comité Popular "pro libertad de imprenta"
The Popular School = La escuela popular
The Producer = El productor
The Proletariat = Il proletario
La Protesta Russian Group = Grupo ruso la protesta
Ravachol's Voice = La voz de ravachol
The Rebel = El rebelde
Rebellion = Rebeldía
Revenge = La revancha
The Revolutionary = El revolucionario
Revolt = La revuelta
Sandal Makers, Sign Makers, and Shoe Makers = Alpargateros, pintores de letras, y zapateros
The Scattered = Los dispersos
Science and Progress = Ciencia y progreso
The Seed = Germen
The Seed = Germinal
September 20 = XX Settembre
Slaves of the Counter = Esclavos del mostrador
The Slave's Voice = La voz del esclavo
Social Dawn = Aurora social
The Social Dawn = L'Alba sociale
Social Demand = La reivindicazione sociale
The Social Question = La questione sociale
The Social Revolution = La revolución social
Social Science = Ciencia social
Social Studies Center = Centro de estudios sociales
Social Studies Centers = Centros de estudios sociales
Social Studies Circle = Círculo de estudios sociales
Social Volcano = Volcán social
Sociological Bookstore = Librería sociológica
Soldier's Enlightenment = Luz al soldado
Solidarity = Solidaridad
Sons of the People = Hijos del pueblo
Spanish Choral Society = Orfeón español
Spanish Workers' Federation = Workers' federación de trabajadores españoles
The Struggle = La lucha
The Sun = El sol
Tailors = El obrero sastre
To Destroy and Build = Destruir y edificar
To Destroy Is to Create = Destruir es crear

The Torch = La antorcha
The Truth = la verdad
Universal Family = Familia universal
Universal Pain = Dolor universal
The Vagabonds = Los vagabundos
Vengeance = La venganza
The Voice of the Slave = La voz del esclavo
The Wake = El surco
White Magazine = Revista blanca
The Wretch = El descamisado
We Work = Lavoriamo
Without God or Country = Sin dios ni patria
The Woman's Voice = La voz de la mujer
Women's Labor Association = Unión gremial femenina
The Worker = El obrero
Worker's Shout = El grito del obrero
The Workers = Los obreros
Workers' Federation = Federación obrera
The Workers' Struggle = La lucha obrera
Workers' Union = Unión gremial de trabajadores
Young Lovers = Jóvenes amantes
Young Lovers of Art = Jóvenes amantes del arte
Zola's Disciples = Discípulos de zola

BIBLIOGRAPHY & SOURCES

I. DIRECT HISTORICAL SOURCES

I.1. PERIODICALS (NEWSPAPERS, WEEKLIES, BIMONTHLY, MAGAZINES)

Almanaque Popular de la Questione Sociale, annual (Italian and Spanish), Buenos Aires, 1895–1902.

Boletín de la Liga de Educación Racionalista, monthly, Buenos Aires, 1914–1915.

Ciencia Social, bimonthly, Buenos Aires, 1897.

El Cuartel, monthly, Buenos Aires, 1909 (issues 1 and 3).

El Rebelde, weekly, Buenos Aires, 1898–1903.

El Perseguido, weekly, Buenos Aires, 1890–1897.

Fulgor, bimonthly, Buenos Aires, 1896.

Germen, monthly, Buenos Aires, 1906–1907.

Germinal, bimonthly, Buenos Aires, 1897–1898.

Ideas y Figuras, Revista semanal de Crítica y Arte, Buenos Aires, 1909–1916.

La Autonomía Individual, bimonthly, Buenos Aires, 1897.

L'Avvenire, weekly (Italian language), Buenos Aires, 1896–1904.

La Batalla, daily, Buenos Aires, 1910.

La Questione Sociale, bimonthly (Italian language), Buenos Aires, 1895.

La Escuela Popular, Órgano de la Liga de Educación Racionalista, monthly, Buenos Aires, 1912–1914.

La Montaña, Periódico Socialista Revolucionario, bimonthly, 1897, Universidad Nacional de Quilmes, 1996.

La Nueva Era, monthly, Buenos Aires, 1901.

La Protesta Humana, weekly, Buenos Aires, 1897–1903.

La Protesta, weekly, daily from 1904, Buenos Aires, 1903–1916.

La Vanguardia, weekly, daily from 1905, Buenos Aires, 1894–1910.

La Voz de la Mujer, weekly, Buenos Aires, 1896–1897.

Los Nuevos Caminos, monthly, Buenos Aires, 1906.

Luz y Vida, bimonthly, Buenos Aires, 1908 (incomplete).

Luz al Soldado, monthly, Buenos Aires, 1908–1913 (incomplete).

Martín Fierro, Revista Popular Ilustrada de Crítica y Arte, weekly, Buenos Aires, 1904–1905.

I.2. CENSUSES, BOOKS, PAMPHLETS, MEMOIRS, TRAVELOGUES AND BROCHURES

AA.VV.: *Pascual Guaglianone*, La Plata, Homenaje de la Facultad de Humanidades y Ciencias de la Educación, Universidad Nacional de la Plata, 1960.

Abad de Santillán, Diego: *Memorias, 1897–1936*, Barcelona, Planeta, 1977.

Altair: *Fundamento y lenguaje de la doctrina anarquista*, Buenos Aires, Librería Sociológica, 1900.

Anónimo: *Anarquistas de Buenos Aires ¡Leed!*, pamphlet, Buenos Aires, 1898.

————: *Capacidad revolucionaria de la clase obrera*, Buenos Aires, Biblioteca de Propaganda Anárquica del grupo Los ácratas, 1897.

————: *Desagravio*, pamphlet, Buenos Aires, 1910.

————: *Manifiesto Comunista Anárquico: El 1º de mayo*, pamphlet, Buenos Aires, 1895.

————: *La Moral, su proclamación, su consecuencia*, Buenos Aires, Grupo de Propaganda Anárquica El Antiautoritario, 1897.

————: *No votamos ¿Por qué?*, pamphlet, Bahía Blanca, 1907.

Antilli, Teodoro: *Comunismo y Anarquía*, Buenos Aires, Acracia, 1919.

————: *Federalismo y centralismo*, Buenos Aires, 1924.

————: *Los males sociales*, Rosario, Ciencia y Progreso, 1901.

————: *La medicina y el proletariado*, Rosario, Ciencia y Progreso, 1899.

————: *La mujer y la familia*, Rosario, Ciencia y Progreso, 1897.

————: *Salud a la anarquía*, Buenos Aires, La Antorcha, 1924.

————: *Las secciones económicas de trabajadores y las organizaciones obreras*, Buenos Aires, 1924.

Arana, Emilio Z.: *La sociedad, su pasado, su presente·y su porvenir*, Rosario, Ciencia y Progreso, 1897.

Arraga, Julio: *Reflexiones y observaciones sobre la cuestión social*, Buenos Aires, 1910.

Avellaneda, Marco: *Del camino andado (economía social argentina)*, Buenos Aires, Cooperativa Editorial Limitada, 1919.

Barcos, Julio: *La felicidad del pueblo es palabra suprema*, Buenos Aires, 1915.

Barrett, Rafael: *Escritos: el terror argentino, Lo que son los yerbales y otros*, Buenos Aires, Proyección, 1971.

————: *Obras Completas*, Américalee, Buenos Aires, 1943.

————: *El terror argentino*, Asunción, 1910.

Basterra, Félix: *Asuntos Contemporáneos*, Buenos Aires, 1908.

————: *El crepúsculo de los gauchos*, Paris, Les Temps Nouveaux y Montevideo, Librería de la Universidad, 1903.

————: *Sobre Ciencia Social*, Buenos Aires, La Protesta Humana, 1901.

Bianchi, Edmundo F.: *La Utopía*, Montevideo, Biblioteca de la Rebelión, undated.

Bilbao, Manuel: *Buenos Aires. Desde su fundación hasta nuestros días*, Buenos Aires, Imprenta de Juan Alsina, 1902.

Carulla, Juan E.: *Al filo del medio siglo*, Buenos Aires, Editorial Llanura, 1951.

Castro, Alberto J, and C. García Balsas: *Críticas al proyecto González*, Montevideo-Buenos Aires, edición del grupo Aurora, 1904. *Ciudad de Buenos Aires*: Censo general de la

ciudad de Buenos Aires de 1910,
Buenos Aires, Compañía Sudamericana de Billetes de Banco, 1910.

Costa-Iscar: *Crítica y concepto libertario del naturismo*, Buenos Aires, Bautista Fueyo, 1923.

Crusao, Juan: *Carta Gaucha*, Buenos Aires, Editorial La Protesta, 1922.

Dickmann, Enrique: *Recuerdos de un militante socialista*, Buenos Aires, La Vanguardia, 1949.

Fernández, Serafín: *Recuerdos de la vida pampera (La semana trágica de 1919)*, Paris, Umbral, 1922.

Freda, Carmelo: *La superioridad de la lucha de clases*, Buenos Aires, La Palestra,1927.

Gálvez, Manuel: *Amigos y maestros de mi juventud. Recuerdos de la vida literaria (1900–1910)*, Buenos Aires, Guillermo Kraft, 1944.

García, E.: *El contraste social*, Buenos Aires, Bautista Fueyo, 1908.

García Velloso, Enrique: *Memorias de un hombre de teatro*, Buenos Aires, Eudeba, 1963.

Ghiraldo, Alberto: *Alma Gaucha*, Buenos Aires, 1906.

————: *Crónicas Argentinas*, Buenos Aires, 1912.

————: *Humano Ardor*, Editorial Lux, Barcelona, 1928.

————: *La Ley Baldón*, Buenos Aires, Fontanillas y Compañero, 1915.

————: *Los Nuevos Caminos*, Madrid, 1908.

————: *La tiranía del Frac*, Buenos Aires, Bublioteca Popular Martín Fierro, 1905.

Gilimón, Eduardo: *El anarquismo en los gremios*, Buenos Aires, 1921.

————: *Hechos y Comentarios*, Buenos Aires-Montevideo, Imprenta B. Puey, 1911.

————: *Para los que no son anarquistas*, Buenos Aires, 1920.

González Arrili, Bernardo: *Buenos Aires 1900*, Buenos Aires, CEAL, 1967.

González Pacheco, Rodolfo: *Carteles*, Buenos Aires, Américalee, 1956, two volumes.

————: Ordaz, Luis (editor), *El drama rural, "Las víboras,"* Buenos Aires, Hachette, 1959.

————: *Rasgos*, Buenos Aires, 1907.

————: *Teatro completo*, Buenos Aires, Américalee, 1953.

Gustavo, Soledad: *A las proletarias*, Buenos Aires, Biblioteca La Questione Sociale, 1896.

Gutiérrez, Federico (Fag Libert): *Noticias de policía*, Buenos Aires, 1907.

Herrera, Julio: *Anarquismo y defensa social*, Buenos Aires, 1917.

Lallemant, Germán Ave: *La clase obrera y el nacimiento del marxismo en la Argentina*, Anteo, Buenos Aires, 1974.

Lazarte, Juan: *Socialización de la medicina*, Buenos Aires, Imán, 1934.

Locascio, Santiago: *Maximalismo y Anarquismo*, Buenos Aires, Vicente Bellusci Editor, 1919.

Maturana, José de: *Canción de primavera*, Buenos Aires, Administración General Casa Vaccaro, 1920.

————: *La flor de trigo*, Buenos Aires, 1907.

————: *Gentes honradas*, Buenos Aires, Centro de Educación Popular, 1907.

Monzoni, Ana María: *A las Hijas del Pueblo*, Buenos Aires, Biblioteca La Questione Sociale, 1895.

————: *A las muchachas que estudian*, Buenos Aires, Biblioteca La Questione Sociale, 1895.

Nido, Enrique: *Informe general sobre el movimiento anarquista en Argentina*, Buenos Aires, 1923.

————: *El pensamiento filosófico y el anarquismo*, Rosario, 1921.

Pellicer Paraire, Antonio: *Conferencias Populares de Sociología*, Buenos Aires, Imprenta Elzaviriana, 1900.

Quiroule, Pierre: *La ciudad anarquista americana*, Buenos Aires, La Protesta, 1914.

————: *Orientación social. Para alcanzar la suma máxima de bienestar y libertad individuales*, Buenos Aires, 1920.

————: *Para meditar: al obrero y obrera huelguista*, Buenos Aires, edición de la Agrupación Anarquista Regeneración, 1922.

————: *Sobre la ruta de la anarquía*, Buenos Aires, Bautista Fueyo, 1911.

República Argentina: *Tercer Censo General de 1914*, Buenos Aires, Talleres Gráficos de L. J. Rosso y Cía, tomo IX, 1917.

Ricard, F.: *Fundamentos Biológicos de la Anarquía*, Buenos Aires, 1921.

Rouco Buela, Juana: *Memoria de un ideal vivido por una mujer*, Buenos Aires, Reconstruir, 1964.

Rusiñol, Santiago: *Un viaje al Plata*, Madrid, 1911.

Sux, Alejandro: *Bohemia Revolucionaria*, Buenos Aires, Biblioteca de la Vida Editorial, 1909.

I.3. THEORETICAL WORKS OF INTERNATIONAL ANARCHISM

Bakunin, Miguel: *Estatismo y anarquía*, Buenos Aires, Hyspamérica, 1984.

————: *La Instrucción Integral*, Barcelona, Pequeña Biblioteca Calamvs Scriptorius, 1979.

Berkman, Alexander: *El ABC del comunismo libertario*, Madrid, Júcar, 1981.

Brown, W, and others: *Estudios Educacionales*, Buenos Aires, Biblioteca de la Liga de Educación Racionalista, 1918.

Cortiella, Felip: *El teatro y el arte dramático en nuestro tiempo*, Barcelona, 1904.

Fabbri, Luigi: *La crisis del anarquismo*, Buenos Aires, Argonauta, 1921.

————: *Influencias burguesas sobre el anarquismo*, México, Antorcha, 1980.

Faure, Sebastián: *Hacia la dicha*, Barcelona, 1904.

————: *Malatesta. Su vida y pensamiento*, Buenos Aires, Américalee, 1945.

Federación de Bolsa de Trabajo de Francia: Manual del soldado. Paria-Ejército-Guerra, Montevideo, Edición Librería La Aurora, 1905.

Ferrer y Guardia, Francisco: *La escuela moderna*, Barcelona, Tusquets, 1978.

Girard, Andrés: *Educación y Autoridad Paternal*, Buenos Aires, Biblioteca del Grupo Los ácratas, 1898.

Gori, Pedro: *La anarquía ante los tribunales seguido de vuestro orden y nuestro desorden*, Barcelona-Palma de Mallorca, Olañeta editor, 1978.

Grave, Juan: *La sociedad moribunda y la anarquía*, Buenos Aires, 1895.

Hamon, A.: *De la patria. Estudio filosófico*, Buenos Aires, Biblioteca Germen, 1907.

Kropotkin, Pedro: *El apoyo mutuo*, Buenos Aires, Américalee, 1946.

————: *Conferencias: el Estado y su rol histórico*, s.i.p., 1923.

————: *La conquista del pan*, Barcelona, Editorial Mateu, 1971.

————: *Folletos Revolucionarios II. Ley y Autoridad*, Barcelona, Tusquets, 1977.

————: *La moral anarquista*, Madrid, 1903.

————: *Panfletos Revolucionarios*, Madrid, Edición a cargo de José Alvarez Junco, Editorial Ayuso, 1977.

Lorenzo, Anselmo: *El proletariado militante*, Barcelona, 1902.

Malatesta, Errico: *Anarquismo y anarquía*, Buenos Aires, Tupac Ediciones, 1988.

————: *Al Café, Conversazioni Sul Comunismo Anarchico*, New Jersey, Tipografía della Questione Sociale, Paterson, 1902.

Malatesta, Merlino, *Bonano: Anarquismo y elecciones*, Colección A, Barcelona.

Mella, Ricardo: *El ideal anarquista*, Barcelona, undated.

————: *La lucha de clases*, Buenos Aires, B. Fueyo Editor, undated.

————: *Sindicalismo y anarquismo*, Buenos Aires, B. Fueyo Editor, undated.

Miró, Fidel: *Anarquismo y anarquistas*, Madrid, Móstoles, 1979.

Nettlau, Max: *Esbozo de historia de las utopías*, Buenos Aires, Imán, 1934.

Niuwenhuis, Domela: *El militarismo y la actitud de los anarquistas y socialistas revolucionarios ante la guerra*, Buenos Aires, Biblioteca Blanca, 1907.

Pelloutier, Fernando: *Historia de las Bolsas de Trabajo*, Madrid, Editorial Tero, 1978.

Plejanov: *Anarquismo y socialismo*, Buenos Aires, Editorial Sudam, undated.

Proudhon, Pierre: *El principio del arte y su destino social*, Barcelona, 1905.

————: *La sanción moral*, Valencia, Sempere, 1909.

————: *El principio federativo*, Madrid, Sarpe, 1985.

————: *La capacidad política de la clase obrera*, Madrid, Ediciones Júcar, 1977.

————: *La educación. El trabajo*, Valencia, Sempere.

————: *Idea general de la revolución en el siglo XX*, Barcelona, Montaner, 1968.

Reclus, Eliseo: *Evolución y revolución*, Madrid, 1891.

Rocker, Rodolfo: *Artistas y rebeldes: escritos libertarios y sociales*, Buenos Aires, 1923.

Tolstoi, León: *¿Qué es el arte?*, Barcelona, 1908.

II. GENERAL AND SPECIFIC WORKS (BOOKS AND ARTICLES)

II.1. GENERAL WORKS

Agulhon, Maurice: "Clase obrera y sociabilidad antes de 1848" in *Historia Social*, No 12, Valencia, invierno de 1992.

————: *Marianne au Combat. L'imaginerie et le symbolique republicaines de 1789 a*

1880, Paris, Flammarion, 1979.

Altamirano, Carlos and Sarlo, Beatriz: "La Argentina del centenario: campo intelectual, vida literaria y temas ideológicos," in C. Altamirano and B. Sarlo, *Ensayos argentinos. De Sarmiento a la Vanguardia*, Buenos Aires, CEAL, 1983.

Álvarez, Jesús Timoteo: *Historia y modelos de la comunicación en el siglo XX. El nuevo orden informativo*, Barcelona, Ariel Comunicación, 1987.

Ansart, Pierre: "Ideologías, conflictos y poder," in Eduardo Colombo (editor*), El Imaginario social*, Montevideo, Tupac Ediciones, 1989.

Araujo, Ángela M. C. (editor): *Trabalho, Cultura e Cidadanía*, San Pablo, Ediçoes Sociaes Ltda, 1997.

Aricó, José: *La hipótesis de Justo. Escritos sobre el socialismo en América Latina*, Buenos Aires, Sudamericana, 1999.

Armus, Diego: "La idea del verde en la ciudad moderna, Buenos Aires, 1870–1940," in *Entrepasados*, No 10, Buenos Aires, comienzos de 1996.

————: *Mundo urbano y cultura popular. Estudios de Historia Social Argentina*, Buenos Aires, Sudamericana, 1990.Baczko, Bronislaw: *Los imaginarios sociales. Memorias y esperanzas colectivas*, Buenos Aires, Nueva Visión, 1991.

Baily, Samuel: "Las sociedades de ayuda mutua y el desarrollo de una comunidad italiana en Buenos Aires, 1858–1918," in *Desarrollo Económico*, vol. 21, No 84, enero-marzo de 1982.

Bajtin, Mijail: *La cultura popular en la Edad Media y en el Renacimiento. El contexto de F., Rabelais*, Barcelona, Seix Barral, 1974.

Barrancos, Dora: *La escena iluminada. Ciencias para trabajadores, 1890–1930*, Buenos Aires, Plus Ultra, 1996.

————: "Las lecturas comentadas: un dispositivo para la formación de la conciencia contestataria entre 1914 y 1930," *Boletín*, Buenos Aires, CEIL, No 16, 1987.

Belaval, Ivon: *La Filosofía en el siglo XIX*, Madrid, Siglo XXI, 1980.

Belloni, Alberto: *Del anarquismo al peronismo. Historia del movimiento obrero argentino*, Buenos Aires, Ediciones Documentos, 1960.

Bergeron, J.: *Niveles de cultura y grupos sociales*, Madrid, Siglo XXI, 1977.

Bertolo, Amadeo: "El imaginario subversivo," in Eduardo Colombo (editor), *El imaginario social*, Montevideo, Tupac Ediciones, 1989.

Bertoni, Lilia Ana: "Construir la nacionalidad: héroes, estatuas y fiestas patrias. 1887–1891," in *Boletin del Instituto de Historia Argentina y Americana Dr. Emilio Ravignani*, tercera serie, primer semestre de 1992.

————: "Nacionalidad o cosmopolitismo: la cuestión de las escuelas de las comunidades extranjeras a fines del siglo XIX" in *Anuario*, Tandil, IEHS, No 11, 1996.

Bialostocki, Jan: *Estilo e iconografía. Contribución a una ciencia de las artes*, Barcelona, Barral, 1973.

Bilsky, Edgardo: "Campo político y representaciones sociales: estudio sobre el sindicalismo revolucionario en Argentina (1904–1910)," Paris, mimeo, 1988.

Bobbio, Norberto, Nicola Matteucci, and Gianfranco Pasquino: *Diccionario de Política*, México, Siglo XXI, 1983, two volumes.

Botana, Natalio: *El orden conservador. La política argentina entre 1880 y 1916*, Buenos

Aires, Sudamericana, 1985.

Bourdieu, Pierre: *Cosas dichas*, Barcelona, Gedisa, 1987.

————: *La reproducción. Elementos para una teoría de la enseñanza*, Barcelona, Laia, 1977.

————: *Sociología y cultura*, México, Grijalbo, 1990.

Brake, L., Jones, Aled and Madden, Lionel: *Investigating Victorian Journalism*, Londres, Mac Millan, 1990.

Burke, Peter: *La cultura popular en la Europa moderna*, Madrid, Alianza, 1991.

Cantón, Darío: "Notas sobre las fuerzas armadas argentinas," in Torcuato S. Di Tella y Tulio Halperín Donghi, *Los fragmentos del poder*, Buenos Aires, Editorial Jorge Álvarez, 1969.

Castoriades, Cornelius: *La experiencia del movimiento obrero*, Barcelona, Tusquets, 1979, two volumes.

Cernadas, Jorge; Pittaluga, R. y Tarcus, H.: "Para una historia de la izquierda en la Argentina. Reflexiones preliminares," in *El Rodaballo*, No 6/7, otoño-invierno de 1997.

Cerroni, Umberto; Magri, Lucio and Johnstone, Monty: *Teoría marxista del partido político/*I, México, Pasado y Presente, 1987.

Chartier, Roger: *El mundo como representación. Historia cultural: entre práctica y representación*, Barcelona, Gedisa, 1992.

Clark, T. J.: *Imagen del pueblo. Gustave Courbet y la revolución de 1848*, Barcelona, Ediciones Gustavo Gilli, 1981.

Da Matta, Roberto: *Carnavais, malandros e herois. Para uma sociologia do dilemma brasileiro*, Río de Janeiro, 1979.

Devoto, F. and Rosoli, Gianfausto: *La inmigración italiana en la Argentina*, Buenos Aires, Biblos, 1985.

Dommanget, M.: *Le Drapeau rouge et la revolution de 1848*, Paris, 1948.

————: *Histoire du Premier Mai*, Paris, 1953.

Eagleton, Terry: *Ideología. Una introducción*, Barcelona, Paidós, 1997.

Egbert, D. D.: *El arte y la izquierda en Europa. De la Revolución Francesa a mayo de 1968*, Barcelona, Gustavo Gili, 1981.

Eley, Geoff: "Edward Thompson, Historia Social y Cultura Política: la formación de la esfera pública de la clase obrera, 1780–1850," *in Entrepasados*, No 6, comienzos de 1994.

Escudé, Carlos: *El fracaso del proyecto educativo argentino. Educación e Ideología*, Buenos Aires, Editorial Tesis, 1990.

Eujanian, Alejandro C.: *Historia de revistas argentinas. 1900/1950, la conquista del público*, Buenos Aires, Asociación Argentina de Editores de Revistas, 1999.

Falcón, Ricardo: *El mundo del trabajo urbano (1890–1914)*, Buenos Aires, CEAL, 1986.

Falcón, Ricardo; Macor, Darío, and Monserrat, Alejandra: "Obreros, artesanos, intelectuales y actividad político sindical. Aproximación biográfica a un perfil de los primeros militantes del movimiento obrero argentino," in *Estudios Sociales*, Santa Fe, No 1, segundo semestre de 1991.

Ford, Aníbal; Rivera, J. B. y Romano, E.: *Medios de comunicación y cultura popular*, Buenos Aires, Legasa, 1985.

Foster, John: *Class Struggle and the Industrial Revolution*, London, Methuen and Co Ltd, 1977.

Franco, Lily; Seibel, Beatriz and Terrero, Patricia: *Artistas y espectáculos*, Buenos Aires, CEAL, 1982–1985.

Fraser, Nancy: "Reconsiderando la esfera pública: una contribución a la crítica de la democracia realmente existente," in *Entrepasados*, No 7, Buenos Aires, fines de 1994.

Frydemberg, Julio and Irene: "Anatole France en Buenos Aires," in *Todo es Historia*, No 291, septiembre de 1991.

García, Germán: *Roberto Payró. Testimonio de una vida y realidad de una literatura*, Buenos Aires, Nova, 1961.

Gayol, Sandra: "Ámbitos de sociabilidad en Buenos Aires: despachos de bebidas y cafés, 1860–1930" in *Anuario*, IEHS, No 8, Tandil, 1993.

Gilliespie, Richard: *Soldados de Perón. Los Montoneros*, Buenos Aires, Grijalbo, 1987.

Ginzburg, Carlo: *El queso y los gusanos*, Barcelona, Muchnik Editores, 1986.

Giusti, Roberto: "La restauración nacionalista," in *Nosotros*, Buenos Aires, año IV, No 26, febrero de 1910.

González, Ricardo: *Los obreros y el trabajo. Buenos Aires, 1901*, Buenos Aires, CEAL, 1984.

Gramsci, Antonio: *Notas sobre Maquiavelo, sobre la política y sobre el Estado moderno*, Buenos Aires, Nueva Visión, 1984.

Grignon, Claude and Passeron, Jean-Claude: *Lo culto y lo popular. Miserabilismo y populismo en sociología y literatura*, Buenos Aires, Nueva Visión, 1991.

Gubern, Roman: *Mensajes icónicos en la cultura de masas*, Barcelona, 1974.

Gutiérrez, Leandro and Romero, Luis Alberto: *Sectores populares, cultura y política. Buenos Aires en la entreguerra*, Buenos Aires, Sudamericana, 1995.

Gutiérrez, Leandro and Zaida Lobato, Mirta: "Memorias militantes. Un lugar y un pasado para los trabajadores argentinos," in *Entrepasados*, Buenos Aires, No 3, fines de 1992.

Gutman, Herbert and Bell, Donald (editor): *The New England Working Class and the New Labor History*, Chicago, University of Illinois Press, 1987.

Guy, Dona: *El sexo peligroso. La prostitución legal en Buenos Aires, 1875–1955*, Buenos Aires, Sudamericana, 1994.

Habermas, J.: *Historia y crítica de la opinión pública*, México, Ediciones G. Gilli, 1986.

Hall, Stuart: "Notas sobre la desconstrucción de lo popular," in Raphael Samuel (editor), *Historia popular y teoría socialista*, Barcelona, Crítica, 1984.

Halperín Donghi, Tulio: "Una ciudad entra en el siglo XX," in Margarita Gutman and Thomas Reese (editores), *Buenos Aires 1910. El imaginario para una gran capital*, Buenos Aires, Eudeba, 1999.

————: *El espejo de la historia. Problemas argentinos y perspectivas latinoamericanas*, Buenos Aires, Sudamericana, 1987.

Haupt, Georges: *El historiador y el movimiento social*, México, Siglo XXI, 1986.

Heller, Agnes: *Sociología de la vida cotidiana*, Barcelona, Península, 1977.

Hobsbawm, Eric: *La era del imperio*, Barcelona, Crítica, 1990.

————: *El mundo del trabajo. Estudios históricos sobre la formación y evolución de la clase obrera*, Barcelona, Crítica, 1987.

Jones, Gareth Stedman: *Lenguaje de clase. Estudios de historia de la clase obrer inglesa*, Madrid, Siglo XXI, 1989.

Le Goff, Jacques: *El orden de la memoria*, Barcelona, Paidós, 1991.

Lenín, V. I.: *Acerca de la prensa y la literatura*, Buenos Aires, Anteo, 1965.

Liernur, Jorge F.: "El nido de la tempestad," *in Entrepasados*, No 13, fines de 1997.

Liernur, J. and Silvestri, G.: *El umbral de las metrópoli*, Buenos Aires, Sudamericana, 1993.

Linden, Marcel van der and Thorpe, Wayne: "Auge y decadencia del sindicalismo revolucionario," in *Historia Social*, Valencia, No 12, invierno de 1992.

Manhein, Karl: *Ideología y utopía*, México, Fondo de Cultura Económica, 1987.

Marrast, Roberto: "La prensa española del siglo XX: algunos problemas de investigación," in AA.VV., *Prensa y Sociedad en España (1820–1936)*, Madrid, Cuadernos para el diálogo, Edicusa, 1975.

Martín-Barbero, Jesús: *De los medios a las mediaciones. Comunicación, cultura y hegemonía*, Barcelona, Ediciones Gustavo Gilli, 1993.

Masiello, Francine: *Lenguaje e ideología*, Buenos Aires, Hachette, 1986.

Moya, José: *Cousins and Strangers. Spanish Immigrants in Buenos Aires, 1850–1930*, Los Angeles, University of California Press, Berkeley, 1997.

Nahum, Benjamín: "La época Batllista, 1905–1929," in *Historia uruguaya*, tomo 6, Montevideo, Editorial de la Banda Oriental, 1993.

Ozouf, Mona: *La fete revolutionnaire, 1789–1799*, Paris, Gallimard, 1976.

Pellarolo, Silvia: "La profesionalización del teatro nacional argentino. Un precursor: Nemesio Trejo," *Latin American Theatre Review*, vol. 31, No 1, fines de 1997, pages 59–70.

Perrot, Michelle: "Formas de habitación," in Philippe Ariès and George Duby, *Historia de la vida privada. Sociedad burguesa: aspectos concretos de la vida privada*, Madrid, Taurus, 1990, tomo 8.

————: *Os excluidos da historia. Operarios, mulheres, prisioneros*, San Pablo, Paz e Terra, 1988.

Plotkin, Mariano: *Mañana es San Perón*, Buenos Aires, Ariel, 1994.

Prieto, Adolfo: *El dicurso criollista en la formación de la Argentina moderna*, Buenos Aires, Sudamericana, 1988.

Puiggrós, Adriana: *Sujetos, disciplina y currículum en los orígenes del sistema educativo argentino*, Buenos Aires, Galerna, 1990.

Puiggrós, Adriana (editor): *Sociedad civil y Estado en los orígenes del sistema educativo argentino*, Buenos Aires, Galerna, 1991.

Puiggrós, Rodolfo: *Las izquierdas y el problema nacional*, Buenos Aires, Editorial Jorge Álvarez, 1967.

Pujol, Sergio: *Historia del baile, de la milonga a la disco*, Buenos Aires, Emecé, 1999.

Radford, Jean (editor): *The Politics of Popular Fiction*, London, History Workshop Series, 1989.

Ramos, Julio: *Desencuentros de la modernidad en América Latina. Literatura y política en el siglo XIX*, México, Fondo de Cultura Económica, 1985.

Rivera, J. B.: *La forja del escritor profesional (1900–1930), los escritores y los nuevos medios masivos*, Buenos Aires, CEAL, 1986.

Romero, Luis Alberto: "Los sectores populares en las ciudades latinoamericanas del siglo XIX: la cuestión de la identidad," in *Desarrollo Económico*, No 106, vol. 27, julio-septiembre de 1987.

Rosenzweig, Roy: *Eight Hours for What We Will. Workers and Leisure in an Industrial City, 1870–1920*, New York, Cambridge University Press, 1983.

Rossel, Andre: *Premier Mai, Quatre-vinght-dix ans de luttes populaires dans le monde*, Paris, 1972.

Rossi, Vicente: *Teatro Nacional Rioplatense*, Buenos Aires, Solar/Hachette, 1969.

Rouquié, Alain: *Poder militar y sociedad política en Argentina*, Buenos Aires, Emecé, 1979, two volumes.

Sábato, Hilda and Cibotti, Ema: "Hacer política en Buenos Aires: los italianos en la escena pública porteña, 1860–1880," in *Boletín*, Instituto de Historia Argentina y Americana Dr. Emilio Ravignani, No 2, primer semestre de 1990.

Samuel, Raphael et al: *Workers Theatre Movements in Britain and America*, London y NewYork, History Workshop Series, 1990.

Sarlo, Beatriz: *El imperio de los sentimientos*, Buenos Aires, Catálogos, 1985.

Sartori, Giovanni: *Partidos y sistemas de partidos*, Madrid, Alianza Universidad, 1994.

Schultz, Uwe: *La fiesta. Una historia cultural desde la antigüedad hasta nuestros días*, Madrid, Alianza, 1993.

Scobie, J. R.: *Buenos Aires del centro a los barrios, 1870–1910*, Buenos Aires, Solar/Hachette, 1977.

Shorter, Edward and Tilly, Charles: *Las huelgas en Francia, 1830–1968*, Madrid, Ministerio de Trabajo y Seguridad Social, 1985.

Solomonoff, Jorge: *Ideologías del movimiento obrero y conflicto social*, Buenos Aires, Proyección, 1971.

Suriano, Juan: *La huelga de inquilinos de 1907*, Buenos Aires, CEAL, 1983.

————: "La huelga de inquilinos de 1907 en Buenos Aires," in AA.VV., *Sectores populares y vida urbana*, Buenos Aires, Clacso, 1984.

————: "El Estado argentino frente a los trabajadores: política social y represión. 1880–1914," in *Anuario*, No 14, Rosario, Universidad Nacional de Rosario, 1989–1990.

————: "Vivir y sobrevivir en la gran ciudad. Hábitat popular en la ciudad de Buenos Aires a comienzos del siglo," in *Estudios Sociales*, No 7, Santa Fe, segundo semestre de 1994.

Suriano, Juan (editor): *La cuestión social en Argentina, 1870–1943*, Buenos Aires, La Colmena, 2000.

Tedesco, Juan C.: *Educación y sociedad en la Argentina (1880–1900)*, Buenos Aires, Pannedille, 1970.

Terán, Oscar: *Positivismo y nación en la Argentina*, Buenos Aires, Puntosur, 1987.

————: *Vida intelectual en el Buenos Aires fin-de-siglo (1880–1910). Derivas de la "cultura científica,"* Fondo de Cultura Económica, Buenos Aires, 2000.

Thompson, E. P.: *La formación histórica de la clase obrera,* Inglaterra: 1780–1832, Barcelona, Laia, 1977.

————: *Tradición, revuelta y conciencia de clase. Estudio sobre la crisis de la sociedad preindustrial*, Barcelona, Crítica, 1984.

Tuñón de Lara, Manuel: "Prensa e historia," in AA.VV., *Prensa obrera en Madrid*, Madrid, Alfoz-Cidur, 1987.

Viñas, David: *La crisis de la ciudad liberal*, Buenos Aires, Siglo Veinte, 1973.

————: *Literatura argentina y política. De los jacobinos porteños a la bohemia anarquista*, Buenos Aires, Sudamericana, 1995.

Vovelle, Michel: *Ideologías y mentalidades*, Barcelona, Ariel, 1985.

————: *La mentalidad revolucionaria*, Barcelona, Crítica, 1989.

Williams, Raymond: *Marxismo y literatura*, Barcelona, Península, 1980.

Williams, Raymond (editor): *Historia de la comunicación*, vol. 2 "De la imprenta a nuestros días," Barcelona, Bosch Comunicación, 1992.

————: *Palabras clave. Un vocabulario de la cultura y la sociedad*, Buenos Aires, Nueva Visión, 2000.

Zimmermann, Eduardo: *Los reformistas liberales. La cuestión social en la Argentina, 1890–1916*, Buenos Aires, Sudamericana-Universidad de San Andrés, 1995.

II.2. SPECIFIC WORKS

II.2.1. ON ANARCHISM INTERNATIONAL

AA.VV.: *Escritos anarquistas sobre educación*, Madrid, Zero, 1986.

Abad de Santillán, Diego: Estrategia y táctica, Madrid, Júcar, 1976.

Adsuar, Josep: "Algunas ideas básicas sobre anarquismo" in *Anthropos, Revista de documentación científica de la cultura*, Suplemento No 5, Madrid, marzo de 1988.

Alvarez Junco, José: "Los dos anarquismos," in *Cuadernos del Ruedo Ibérico*, Paris, No 55/57, enero-junio de 1977.

————: *La ideología política del anarquismo español (1868–1910)*, Madrid, Siglo XXI, 1976.

————: "La subcultura anarquista en España: racionalismo y populismo," in AA.VV., *Culturas populares*, Madrid, Complutense, 1986.

Ansart, Pierre: *Marx y el marxismo*, Barcelona, Barral, 1972.

————: *El nacimiento del anarquismo*, Buenos Aires, Amorrortu, 1973.

Apter, David and Joll, James: *Anarchism Today*, Doubleday and Company, Garden City, 1972.

Arnoni Prado, Antonio: *Libertarios no Brasil, memorias, luta, cultura*, San Pablo, Editora Brasiliense, 1986.

Arvon, H.: *El anarquismo*, Buenos Aires, Paidós, 1971.

Avrich, P.: Los anarquistas rusos, Barcelona, Anagrama, 1972.

————: *Anarchist Portraits*, New Jersey, Princeton University Press, 1988.

————: *Anarchist Voices. An Oral History of Anarchism in America*, New Jersey, Princeton University Press, 1996.

Baldelli, Giovanni: *Social Anarchism*, London, Penguin Book, 1971.

Bloch, Gerard: *Marxismo e anarquismo*, San Pablo, Kairos, 1981.

Brenan, Gerald: *El laberinto español*, Paris, Mundo Ibérico, 1962.

Burga, M. and Flores Galindo, A.: *Apogeo y crisis de la república aristocrática*, Lima, Rikchay, 1979.

Carr, E. H.: *Bakunin*, Barcelona, Grijalbo, 1970.

Castoriades, Cornelius: "La institución imaginaria de la sociedad," in Eduardo Colombo (editor), *El imaginario social*, Montevideo, Tupac Ediciones, 1989.

Cole, G.: *Historia del pensamiento socialista. II Anarquismo y marxismo*, México, Fondo de Cultura Económica, 1958.

Crensanz, Aurelio: *Anarquía y cristianismo*, Madrid, 1978.

Cohn, F.: En pos del milenio, Barcelona, Seix Barral, 1972.

Culla, J. B.: *El republicanismo lerrouxista a Catalunya (1901–1923)*, Barcelona, 1986.

Delgado, B.: *La Escuela Moderna de Ferrer i Guardia*, Barcelona, CEAC, 1979.

Díaz, Carlos: *El anarquismo como fenómeno político moral*, Madrid, Zero, 1978.

Dommanget, M.: *Les grands socialistes et l'education*, Paris, Colin, 1970.

Ermolaiev, Vasilij: "Le mouvement ouvrier et comuniste en Amérique Latine" in *Recherches Internationales, La lumiere du marxisme*, No 32, Paris, julio-agosto de 1962.

Fausto, Boris: *Trabalho urbano e Conflicto Social, (1890–1920)*, San Pablo, DIFEI, 1976.

Foot Hardman, Francisco: *Nem patria, Nem patrao, vida operaria e cultura anarquista no Brasil*, San Pablo, Editora Brasiliense, 1983.

Gabriel, Pere: "Historiografía reciente sobre el anarquismo y el sindicalismo en España, 1870–1923," in *Historia Social*, No 1, Valencia, primavera-verano de 1988.

Giroud, Gabriel: Paul Robín: *sa vie, ses idees, son action*, Paris, E. Mignolet y Atoy, 1937.

Gómez, Freddy: "Los puntos de ruptura entre Marx y Bakunin," in *Cuadernos del Ruedo Ibérico*, Paris, No 55/57, enero-junio de 1977.

Gómez Tovar, Luis and Paniagua, Javier: *Utopías libertarias españolas. Siglos XIX-XX*, Madrid, Ediciones Tuero, 1991.

Gómez Tovar, Luis and Delgado Larios, Almudena: *Utopías libertarias*, Madrid, Ediciones Tuero, 1991.

Goodway, David (editor): *History, Theory and Practice*, History Workshop Series, London y New York, 1990.

Guerin, Daniel: *El anarquismo*, Buenos Aires, Proyección, 1973.

Harich, Wolfgang: *Crítica a la impaciencia revolucionaria*, Barcelona, 1988.

Joll, James: *Los anarquistas*, Barcelona, Grijalbo, 1968.

Hart, J. M.: *El anarquismo y la clase obrera mexicana (1860–1930)*, México, Siglo XXI, 1980.

Hermosillo, F. and Hernández, S.: "De la dictadura porfirista a los tiempos libertarios," in *La clase obrera en la historia de México*, México, Siglo XXI, 1980, vol. 3.

Heblimg Campos, Cristina: *O sonhar libertario*, Campinas, Pontes Editores, 1988.

Horowitz, Irving Louis (editor): *Los anarquistas*, Madrid, Alianza, 1979.

Hobsbawm, Eric: *Rebeldes primitivos*, Barcelona, Ariel, 1974.

————: *Revolucionarios. Ensayos contemporáneos*, Barcelona, Ariel, 1978.

Kaplán, Tema: *Orígenes sociales del anarquismo en Andalucía*, Barcelona, Crítica, 1977.

Lichteim, George: *Breve Historia del Socialismo*, Madrid, Alianza, 1975.

Lida, Clara: *Anarquismo i Revolución en la España del XIX*, Madrid, Siglo Veintiuno, 1971.

————: "Educación anarquista en la España del 900," in *Revista de Occidente*, 97, 1971.

Litvak, Lily: *A Dream of Arcadia: Anti-Industrialism in Spanish Literature, 1895–1905*, Austin, University of Texas Press, 1975.

————: *España 1900. Modernismo, anarquismo y fin de siglo*, Barcelona, Anthropos, 1990.

————: *La mirada roja: estética y arte del anarquismo español (1880–1913)*, Barcelona, Ediciones del Serbal, 1988.

————: *Musa libertaria, arte, literatura y vida cultural del anarquismo español* (1880–1913), Barcelona, Antoni Bosch Editor, 1981.

————: "La sociología criminal y los escritores españoles de fin de siglo," in *Literature compares*, 1, enero-marzo de 1974.

López D'Alesandro: *Anarquistas y socialistas (1838–1910)*, Montevideo, Carlos Álvarez Editor, 1994.

Lubac, Henry de: *Proudhon y el cristianismo*, Madrid, 1965.

Masini, Pier Carlo: *Stori degli anarchici italiani da Bakunin a Malatesta, 1862–1892*, Milano, Rizzoli, 1969.

Meltzer, Albert and Christie, Stuart: *Anarquismo y lucha de clases*, Buenos Aires, Proyección, 1971.

Mintz, Frank and Fonatanillas, Antonia: "Diegos Abad de Santillán. Historia y vigencia de la construcción social de un proyecto libertario," *Suplementos. Materiales de Trabajo Intelectual*, Barcelona, Anthropos Editorial del Hombre, No 36, enero de 1993.

Nataf, Pierre: *La vie quotidienne des anarchistes en France, 1880–1910*, Paris, Hachette, 1986.

Nettlau, Max: *La anarquía a través de los tiempos*, Madrid, Júcar, 1977.

————: *Breve Historia de la Anarquía*, Buenos Aires, Cenit, undated.

Nuñez Florencio, Rafael: *El terrorismo anarquista. 1888–1909*, Madrid, Siglo XXI, 1983.

Olivé Serret, Enrique: *La pedagogía obrerista de la imagen*, Barcelona, José de Olañeta, 1978.

Pani, Filippo and Vaccaro, Salvo: *Il pensiero Anarchico*, Verona, Demetra, 1997.

Paniagua, Xavier: *Anarquistas y socialistas*, Madrid, Historia 16, 1989.

————: "Una gran pregunta y varias respuestas. El anarquismo español: desde la política a la historiografía," in *Historia Social*, No 12, Valencia, invierno de 1992.

————: *Libertarios y sindicalistas*, Madrid, Anaya, 1992.

————: *La sociedad Libertaria*, Barcelona, Crítica, 1981.

Peirats, José: *Diccionario del anarquismo*, Barcelona, Dopesa, 1977.

Pessin, Alain: "El sueño anarquista," in Eduardo Colombo (editor), *El imaginario social*, Montevideo, Tupac Ediciones, 1989.

Rama, Carlos M.: *Fascismo y anarquismo en la España contemporánea*, Barcelona, Bruguera, 1979.

————: *Mouvements ouvriers et socialistes (chronologie et bibliographie): l'Amerique Latine (1492–1936)*, Paris, Ouvrieres, 1959.

Reszler, Andre: *La estética anarquista*, México, Fondo de Cultura Económica, 1974.

Richards, Vernon: *Malatesta, vida e ideas*, Barcelona, Tusquets, 1975.

Rodríguez, Edgar: *Anarquismo: na escola, no teatro, na poesía*, Río de Janeiro, Achiamé, 1992.

Romero Maura, J.: *La rosa de fuego*, Madrid, 1974.

Roussopoulos, Dimitrios (editor): *The anarchist papers*, Montreal-New York, Black Rose Books, 1990.

Saña, Heleno: *El anarquismo. De Proudhon a Cohn Bendit*, Madrid, Índice, 1970.

Senabre Llabata, Carmen: "La estética anarquista a través de la Revista Blanca," in *Anthropos, Revista de documentación científica de la cultura*, Madrid, Suplemento No 5, marzo de 1988.

Sola, Pere: *Las escuelas racionalistas en Cataluña, 1909–1939*, Barcelona, Tusquets, 1978.

Trilla, J.: "Aportaciones pedagógicas de P. J. Proudhon," Universidad de Barcelona, 1976 (unpublished thesis).

Turin, Ivonne: *La educación y la escuela en España, 1874–1912*, Madrid, Aguilar, 1967.

Tomassi, Tina: *Breviario del pensamiento educativo libertario*, Madrid, Ediciones Madre Tierra, 1978.

Ullman, J. C.: *La semana trágica*, Cambridge, 1968.

Vernon, Richard: *Malatesta, pensamiento y acción revolucionaria*, Buenos Aires, Proyección, 1974.

Woodcock, George: *El anarquismo*, Barcelona, Ariel, 1979.

II.2.2. ON ARGENTINE ANARCHISM

Abad de Santillán, Diego: "Bibliografía anarquista argentina" in *Timón*, Barcelona, septiembre de 1938.

Ainsa, Fernando: "La ciudad anarquista americana. Estudio de una utopía libertaria," in *Caravelle*, Toulouse, 46, 1988.

————: *La FORA (1933): ideología y trayectoria*, Buenos Aires, Proyección, 1971.

————: *El movimiento anarquista en la Argentina desde sus comienzos hasta 1910*, Buenos Aires, Argonauta, 1930.

Andreu, Jean: "Contracultura libertaria en el Río de la Plata y Chile (1890–1914)," in AA.VV., *Hacia una historia social de la literatura*, Actas Giessen, Tomás Bremer y Alejandro Lozada Editores, 1985.

————: and others, *Anarkos, literaturas libertarias de América del sur, 1900*, Buenos Aires, Corregidor, 1990.

Armus, Diego: "Salud y anarquismo. La tuberculosis en el discurso libertario argentino," in Mirta Z. Lobato (editor), *Política, médicos y enfermedades. Lecturas de historia de la salud en la Argentina*, Buenos Aires, Biblos, 1996.

————: An autonomous anarchist subculture? The anarchist press in Argentina, Conference, Duke University, April 1994.

Barrancos, Dora: *Anarquismo, Educación y Costumbres en la Argentina de principios de siglo*, Buenos Aires, Contrapunto, 1990.

————: "Cultura y educación en el temprano sindicalismo revolucionario," in *Anuario*, No 14, Rosario, 1989–1990.

————: "La modernidad redentora: difusión de la ciencia entre los trabajadores de Buenos Aires," in *Siglo XX. Revista de Historia*, México, Segunda Época, No 12, julio–diciembre de 1992.

————: "Participación de españoles en la educación racionalista difundida en la Argentina a principios de siglo (1900–1912)," in F. J. Devoto and E. J. Miguez (editors), *Asociacionismo, trabajo e identidad étnica*, Buenos Aires, CEMLA- CSER-IEHS, 1992.

Basterra, Félix: *Una lectura crítica de la modernización argentina*, Buenos Aires, mimeo, 1990.

Bayer, Osvaldo: *Los vengadores de la Patagonia trágica*, Buenos Aires, Galerna, 1973.

Bertolo, Maricel: *Una propuesta gremial alternativa: el sindicalismo revolucionario (1904–1916)*, Buenos Aires, CEAL, 1993.

————: "El sindicalismo revolucionario en una etapa de transición (1910– 1916)," in *Estudios Sociales*, Santa Fe, año 3, No 4, primer semestre de 1993.

Bettini, Leonardo: *Bibliografia dell'anarchismo*, tomo 2 "Periodici e numeri unici anarchici in lingua italiana pubblicati all'estero (1872–1971)," Firenze, Cp editrice, 1976.

Bilsky, Edgardo: *Contribution a l'histoire du mouvement ouvrier et social argentin*, Paris, Nanterre, 1983.

————: *La FORA y el movimiento obrero (1900–1910)*, Buenos Aires, CEAL, 1985.

Bitlloch, Ruben: *La theorie de la violence dans l'anarchisme argentin, 1890–1910*, Paris, 1982.

Bordi de Ragucci, Olga: "Los primeros anarquistas en la Argentina," in *Historia*, No 28, 1987.

Borrero, José María: *La Patagonia trágica*, Buenos Aires, 1928.

Campo, Hugo del: *Los anarquistas*, Buenos Aires, CEAL, 1971.

————: *El "sindicalismo revolucionario" (1905–1945)*, Buenos Aires, CEAL, 1986.

Ciafardo, Eduardo and Espesi, Daniel: "Patología de la acción política anarquista. Criminólogos, psiquiatras y conflicto social en Argentina, 1890–1910," in *Siglo XX. Revista de Historia*, México, Segunda Época, No 12, julio–diciembre de 1992.

Cordero, H. A.: *Alberto Ghiraldo, precursor de nuevos tiempos*, Buenos Aires, Claridad, 1962.

Cuneo, Dardo: "Las dos corrientes del movimiento obrero," in *Revista de Historia*, Buenos Aires, No 1, 1957.

————: *El periodismo de la disidencia social (1858–1900)*, Buenos Aires, CEAL, 1994.

Díaz, Hernán: *Alberto Ghiraldo: anarquismo y cultura*, Buenos Aires, CEAL, 1991.

Falcón, Ricardo: "Izquierdas, régimen político, cuestión étnica y cuestión social en Argentina (1890–1912)," in *Anuario*, No 12, Rosario, 1986–1987.

Frydenberg, Julio and Ruffo, Miguel: *La semana roja de 1909*, Buenos Aires, CEAL, 1992.

Gameno, Carlos: "La gauchesca anarquista," in *Filología*, año XXIV, 1–2, 1989.

Geli, Patricio: "Los anarquistas en el gabinete antropométrico. Anarquismo y criminología en la sociedad argentina del 900," in *Entrepasados*, año II, No 2, comienzos de 1992.

Giustachini, Ana Ruth: "La dimensión verbal en el teatro anarquista: la columna de fuego de Alberto Ghiraldo," in *Espacio de crítica e investigación teatral*, Buenos Aires, año 4, No 8, octubre de 1990.

Giusti, Roberto: *Florencio Sánchez, su vida y su obra*, Buenos Aires, 1920.

Godio, Julio: *Historia del movimiento obrero argentino: inmigrantes, asalariados y lucha de clases, 1880–1910*, Buenos Aires, Tiempo Contemporáneo, 1973.

————: *La semana Trágica de enero de 1919*, Buenos Aires, Hyspamérica, 1985.

Golluscio de Montoya, Eva: "Círculos anarquistas y circuitos contraculturales en la Argentina de 1900," in *Caravelle*, Toulouse, 46, 1986.

————: "Elementos para una teoría teatral libertaria (Argentina 1900)," in *Latin American Theatre Review*, late 1987.

————: "Un manuscrito libertario: la versión maestrini de ¡Ladrones! (1987) de Florencio Sánchez," in AA.VV., *Reflexiones sobre el teatro latinoamericano del siglo veinte*, Buenos Aires, Galerna/Lemcke Verlag, 1989.

————: "Sobre ¡Ladrones! (1897) y Canillitas (1902–1904): Florencio Sánchez y la delegación de poderes," in *Gestos*, No 6, noviembre de 1988.

Gómez, Alfredo: *Anarquismo y anarcosindicalismo en América Latina. Colombia, Brasil, Argentina y México*, Ruedo Ibérico, Madrid, 1980.

Gómez Tovar, Luis; Gutierrez, Ramón, and Vázquez, Silvia A.: *Utopías libertarias americanas: La ciudad anarquista americana de Pierre Quiroule*, Madrid, Ediciones Tuero, 1991.

Gordon, E.; Hall, M. and Spalding, H.: "A survey of Brazilian and Argentine Material at the International Instituut voor Sociale Geschiedenis in Amsterdam," in *Latin American Research Review*, VIII (3), late 1973.

Larroca, Jorge: "Un anarquista en Buenos Aires," in *Todo es Historia*, Buenos Aires, No 47, marzo de 1971.

López Arango, E. and Abad de Santillán, Diego: *El anarquismo en el movimiento obrero*, Barcelona, Cosmos, 1925.

Molineux, Maxine: "No God, No Boss, No Husband: Anarchist Feminism in Nineteenth Century Argentina," *Latin American Perspectives*, No 48, winter 1986.

Monserrat, Alejandra: "El anarquismo rosarino y la cuestión de la organización (1880–1910)," in Adrián Escolani and Macor, Darío: *Historia del sur santafesino. La sociedad transformada (1850–1930)*, Rosario, Ediciones Platino, 1993.

Moreno, José L.: "A propósito de los anarquistas italianos en la Argentina, 1880–1920," in *Cuadernos de Historia Regional*, UNLU, vol. II, No 4, diciembre de 1985.

Nettlau, Max: *Contribución a la bibliografía anarquista de la América Latina hasta 1914*, Buenos Aires, Certamen Internacional de La Protesta, 1927.

Ordaz, Luis: "Florencio Sánchez," in AA.VV., *Historia de la literatura argentina*, Buenos Aires, CEAL, 1986.

Oved, Iaacov: *El anarquismo y el movimiento obrero en Argentina*, México, Siglo XXI, 1981.

————: "El trasfondo histórico de la Ley 4.144 de Residencia," in *Desarrollo Económico*, Buenos Aires, No 61, vol. 6, abril–junio de 1976.

Quesada, Fernando: "La Protesta, una longeva voz libertaria," in *Todo es Historia*, Buenos Aires, No 82, marzo de 1974 y No 83, abril de 1974.

Rama, Carlos: "Obreros y anarquistas" in *Enciclopedia Uruguaya*, vol. 3, Montevideo, 1968.

Rama, Carlos, and Cappelletti, Ángel: *El anarquismo en América Latina*, Caracas,

Biblioteca Ayacucho, 1990.

Ratzer, José: *Los marxistas argentinos del noventa*, Córdoba, Pasado y Presente, 1969.

Thompson, Ruth: "The Limitations of Ideology in the Early Argentine Labour Movement: Anarchism in the Trade Unions, 1890–1920," in *Journal of Latin American Studies*, vol. 16, parte I, mayo de 1984.

Sapriza, Graciela: *Memorias de rebeldía. Siete historias de vida*, Montevideo, Puntosur-Grecmu, 1988.

Solomonoff, Jorge: *Ideologías del movimiento obrero y conflicto social: de la organización nacional hasta las Primera Guerra Mundial*, Buenos Aires, Proyección, 1971.

Spalding, Hobart: *La clase trabajadora argentina (documentos para su historia, 1880–1912)*, Buenos Aires, Galerna, 1970.

Suriano, Juan: "El anarquismo," in Mirta Z. Lobato (editor), *El progreso, la modernización y sus límites, 1880–1916*, Buenos Aires, Sudamericana, 2000.

————: "Ideas y prácticas políticas del anarquismo argentino," *in Entrepasados*, No 8, comienzos de 1995.

————: "Las prácticas políticas del anarquismo argentino," in *Revista de Indias*, Madrid, vol. LVII, No 210, mayo–agosto 1997, pages 421–450.

————: *Trabajadores, anarquismo y Estado represor: de la Ley de Residencia a la de Defensa Social (1902–1910)*, Buenos Aires, CEAL, 1988.

Vázquez de Fernández, Silvia: "Semblanza del socialismo libertario argentino," in AA.VV., *Historia de los argentinos*, Premio Coca Cola en las Artes y las ciencias 1989, Buenos Aires, 1990.

Viñas, David: *De los mantoneros a los anarquistas*, Buenos Aires, Carlos Pérez Editor, 1971.

Warley, Jorge A.: (Selección de textos): *Rafael Barrett, anarquismo y denuncia*, Buenos Aires, CEAL, 1987.

Weimberg, Félix: *Dos utopías argentinas de principios de siglo*, Buenos Aires, Solar/Hachette, 1976.

Yerrill, P., and Rosser, L.: *Revolutionary Unionism in Latin America. The FORA in Argentina*, ASP, London and Docaster, 1987.

Yoast, Richard: *The development of argentine anarchism: a social ideological analysis*, Madison, The University of Wisconsin, 1975.

Zaragoza Ruvira, G.: *Anarquismo argentino (1876–1902)*, Madrid, Ediciones de la Torre, 1996.

————: "Anarquistas españoles en Argentina a fines del siglo XIX," *SAITABI*, Valencia, Facultad de Filosofía y Letras de la Universidad de Valencia, 1976.————: "Enrique Malatesta y el anarquismo argentino," in *Historiografía y bibliografía americanista*, Sevilla, vol. XVI, No 3, diciembre de 1972.

————: "Orígenes del anarquismo en Buenos Aires, 1886–1901," in *Anales de la Universidad de Valencia*, Valencia, 1972.

NOTES

INTRODUCTION

1 Cámara de Senadores, *Diario de Sesiones* (Buenos Aires: 1902), 658.

2 Ibid.

3 Among others: Edgardo Bilsky, *La FORA y el movimiento obrero (1900–1910)* (Buenos Aires: CEAL, 1985); Iaacov Oved, *El Anarquismo y el movimiento obrero en Argentina* (Mexico: Siglo XXI, 1978); Diego Abad de Santillán, *La FORA: ideología y trayectoria del movimiento revolucionario en la Argentina* (Buenos Aires: Nervio, 1933); Jorge Solomonoff, *Ideologías del movimiento obrero y conflicto social: de la organización nacional hasta la Primera Guerra Mundial* (Buenos Aires: Proyección, 1971); Gonzalo Zaragoza Ruvira, *Anarquismo Argentino (1876–1902)* (Madrid: Ediciones de la Torre, 1996).

4 Focusing on Buenos Aires has methodological advantages because it limits the object of study, which is by no means a minor concern, given the serious dispersion of archival resources. Studying anarchism requires using Amsterdam's International Institute of Social History, which doubtlessly holds the most important—though still incomplete—archives on the topic. There are several relevant collections of source materials in Argentina: the archives at the Federación Libertaria Argentina and the Biblioteca José Ingenieros are incomplete and uncataloged; the Biblioteca Nacional holds very little of relevance and what it does have is poorly preserved; police and judicial archives, in addition to lacking any logical criteria of classification, are inaccessible, in contrast to what occurs in other countries. The absence of a national policy for archival preservation has been and continues to impose formidable burdens on researchers, particularly those investigating left-wing movements. All of these problems make it difficult to reconstruct an exhaustive, national history of anarchism.

5 A wide range of sources indicate anarchists' very significant presence in fin-de-siècle Buenos Aires: articles and editorial statements in the big newspapers (*La Nación, La Prensa*), records of sessions of the House of Representatives [*Cámara de Diputados*], reports from the police and Interior Ministry, some university theses from the time, commentaries by census takers, and travelers' chronicles. There is a vast amount of relevant material, which is listed in the bibliography.

6 There are abundant studies on these topics. See: Edgardo Bilsky, *La FORA,* and *La semana trágica* (Buenos Aires: CEAL, 1984); Ricardo Falcón, *El mundo del trabajo urbano (1890–1914)* (Buenos Aires: CEAL, 1986); Iaacov Oved, *El anarquismo*; Juan Suriano, "La huelga de inquilinos en Buenos Aires en 1907" in Benjamin Nahum, et al., *Sectores populares y vida urbana* (Buenos Aires: CLACSO, 1984).

7 Report of the Italian Consul in Buenos Aires to the Italian Ministry of the Interior, May 8, 1910 in Archivo Centrale dello Stato (ACS), MI-PS, AA-GG-RR, 1910.

8 Ibid. Luis A. Romero noted the confrontational character of urban society in Argentina at the beginning of the century in "Los sectores populares en las ciudades latinoamericanas del siglo XIX: la cuestión de la identidad," *Desarrollo Económico*, 106, vol. 27 (1987).

9 Falcón aptly identified the conditions that made the emergence of the anarchist

movement possible, stressing ethnic, political, and social questions. See: Ricardo Falcón, "Izquierdas, régimen político, cuestión étnica y cuestión social en Argentina (1890–1912)," *Anuario* 12 (1986–87).

10 On the connection between workers and the state, see: Juan Suriano, "El Estado argentino frente a los trabajadores urbanos: política social y represión. 1880–1914," *Anuario*, Rosario, No. 14, Universidad Nacional de Rosario, 1989–90. For an analysis of Italian mutualism: Samuel Bayly, "Las sociedades de ayuda mutua y el desarrollo de una comunidad italiana en Buenos Aires, 1858–1918," *Desarrollo Económico* 21, no. 84 (January–March 1982). Also: Fernado Devoto, "Participación y conflictos en las sociedades italianas de socorros mutuos" in Fernando Devoto and Gianfausto Rosoli, *La inmigración italiana en la Argentina* (Buenos Aires: Biblos, 1985), 141–164. On the Spanish institutions in Buenos Aires: José Moya, *Cousins and Strangers: Spanish Inmigrants in Buenos Aires, 1850–1930* (Berkeley and Los Angeles: University of California Press, 1997), 277–331.

11 See: "Informe de A. G. Barrington to the Marquess of Salisbury" in Oved, *El anarquismo*, 286 and Ministerio del Interior, *Memoria, 12 de octubre de 1904 al 30 de abril de 1905* (Buenos Aires: 1905), 56.

12 "Banning the red flag is outrageous and accomplishes nothing," *La Nación*, May 22, 1905.

13 Cámara de Diputados, "Interpelación del diputado Alfredo Palacios al Ministro del Interior," May 21, 1905, *Diario de Sesiones*, vol 1 (Buenos Aires: 1905), 358.

14 See: José Alvarez Junco, *La ideología política del anarquismo español* (Madrid: Siglo XXI, 1976), 584; Javier Paniagua, "Una gran pregunta y varias respuestas. El anarquismo español: desde la política a la historiografía," *Historia Social*, Valencia, no. 12 (1992), 34–35.

15 Translator's note: "resistance societies" were trade union organizations with a specifically anarchist bent.

16 With respect to the Socialists, there are a few articles of interest on Juan B. Justo, but the only book on the party has not been translated into Spanish: Richard Walter, *The Socialist Party of Argentina, 1890–1930* (Austin, Texas: Institute of Latin American Studies, University of Texas, 1977). The most interesting reflections on socialism can be found in José Aricó: *La hipótesis de Justo. Escritos sobre el socialismo en América Latina* (Buenos Aires: Sudamericana, 1999). The historical vacuum on communism is greater still. For an exhaustive study of publications on the Argentine left, see J. Cernadas, R. Pittaluga, and H. Tarcus, "Para una historia de la izquierda en la Argentina. Reflexiones preliminares," *El Rodaballo*, no. 6/7 (1997), 28–38.

17 Diego Abad de Santillán, *El movimiento anarquista en la Argentina: Desde el comienzo hasta 1930* (Buenos Aires: Argonauta, 1930) and *La FORA*. Although Santillán is the first recognized historian of the Argentine anarchist movement, one should also mention Eduardo Gilimón, *Hechos y Comentarios* (Buenos Aires-Montevideo: Imprenta B. Puey, 1911), upon which Santillán based his discussion of libertarian activity prior to 1910.

18 Eric Hobsbawm, *Revolucionarios. Ensayos contemporáneos* (Barcelona: Ariel, 1978), 121–133.

19 Germán Ave Lallemant, *La clase obrera y el nacimiento del marxismo en la Argentina* (Buenos Aires: Anteo, 1974), 167–68 (the piece was originally published in Die Neue Zeit, vol I (1895–1896). This narrative was amplified by Enrique Dickmann, *Recuerdos de un militante socialista* (Buenos Aires: La Vanguardia, 1949), canonized by Jacinto Oddone, *Historia del Socialismo Argentino* (Buenos Aires: Talleres

Gráficos "La Vanguardia," 1934), and accepted by the communists: Rubens Iscaro, *Historia del movimiento sindical* (Buenos Aires: Fundamentos, 1973).

20 David Rock, *El radicalismo argentino* (Buenos Aires: Amorrortu, 1977), 93.

21 The clearest account of this perspective's origins is in Vasilij Ermolaiev, "Naissance du mouvement ouvrier" in *Recherches Internationales*, Paris, no. 32 (July–August, 1962) and J. Chavaroche's prologue to the Argentine edition of the book by Plekhanov, *Anarquismo y socialismo* (Buenos Aires: Sudamericana, n.d.).

22 Alberto Belloni, *Del anarquismo al peronismo. Historia del movimiento obrero argentino* (Buenos Aires: Ediciones Documentos, 1960). Likewise, Puiggrós argues that "neither the anarchists of the time, who led almost the entire workers' movement, nor the Socialists, when they won elections in Buenos Aires, broke through the wall dividing them from the real national-historical process." Rodolfo Puiggrós, *Las izquierdas y el problema nacional* (Buenos Aires: Editorial Jorge Alvarez, 1967), 42.

23 David Viñas, *De los Montoneros a los Anarquistas* (Buenos Aires: Carlos Perez Editor, 1971). [Translator's note: The Montoneros, also known as the Movimiento Peronista Montonero, were an organization of left-wing, Peronist insurgents active in Argentina during the 1960s and 1970s.]

24 Julio Godio, *La semana trágica de 1919* (Buenos Aires: Granica, 1972). For a thought-provoking critique of this perspective, see: David Rock, "La semana trágica y los usos de la historia," *Desarrollo Económico*, no. 45 (June 1972).

25 Osvaldo Bayer, *Los vengadores de la Patagonia trágica* (Buenos Aires: Galerna, 1974).

26 Julio Godio, *El movimiento obrero y la cuestión nacional. Argentina: inmigrantes, asalariados y lucha de clases, 1880–1910* (Buenos Aires: Erasmo, 1972); Oved, *El anarquismo*; Jorge Solomonoff, *Ideologías*, and especially Bilsky, *La FORA*. Oved's work is still the most complete and detailed study of the topic, although unfortunately it ends in 1904. An exception to analyses concentrating on anarchists' relation to the workers' movement is the little-read dissertation by Richard Yoast, *The Development of Argentine Anarchism: A Socio-Ideological Analysis* (Madison, WI: University of Wisconsin, 1975). Yoast focuses on activists' social backgrounds and the ideological content of the libertarian program.

27 Bilsky, *La FORA*, vol. 2, 121.

28 On the diminished role of confrontation in Buenos Aires between the wars and changes in sociability, see: Leandro Gutiérrez and Luis Alberto Romero, *Sectores populares, cultura y política. Buenos Aires en la entreguerra* (Buenos Aires: Sudamericana, 1995).

29 With respect to the Montoneros, there are at least two—admittedly indirect—links to anarchism: the appeal to the people (the oppressed as a whole) and the cult of the hero. For an analysis of the Montoneros, see Richard Gillespie, *Soldados de Perón. Los Montoneros* (Buenos Aires: Grijalbo, 1987).

30 In one form or another, this affirmation appears in: Eva Golluscio de Montoya, "Círculos anarquistas y circuitos contraculturales en la Argentina de 1900," *Caravelle* 46, (1986); Oved, *El anarquismo*; Zaragoza Ruvira, *Anarquismo Argentino*.

31 According to Raymond Williams: "The reality of any hegemony, in the extended political and cultural sense, is that, while by definition it is always dominant, it is never either total or exclusive," in Raymond Williams, *Marxismo y literatura* (Barcelona: Península, 1980), 135. On the cultural field as a field of tension, see Stuart Hall, "Notas sobre la deconstrucción de lo popular," in Raphael Samuels (editor), *Historia popular y teoría socialista* (Barcelona: Crítica, 1984).

32 Drawing on Raymond Williams, I see culture as a system of signs shaped by symbolic representations such as practices, discourses, and institutions that are, in turn, related to the social process of the creation and reproduction of a product, its circulation, and its ongoing consumption by individuals. Williams, *Marxismo y literatura*, 129.

33 Among other places, one can find this perspective in Dora Barrancos: *Anarquismo, educación y costumbres en la Argentina de principios de siglo* (Buenos Aires: Contrapunto, 1990).

34 Diego Armus, "*An Autonomous Anarchist Subculture? The Anarchist Press in Argentina*" (paper presented at Eleventh Latin American Labor History Conference, Duke University, April, 1994). By the same author, see "Salud y anarquismo. La tuberculosis en el discurso libertario argentino, 1890–1940," in Mirta Z. Lobato, *Política, médicos y enfermedades. Lecturas de historia de la salud en Argentina* (Buenos Aires: Biblos-Universidad Nacional de Mar del Plata, 1996). Although Armus's works are stimulating, I believe that they overemphasize the consensualist aspects of libertarian cultural discourse, erroneously minimizing its oppositional political stance.

35 Juan Suriano, *Trabajadores, anarquismo y Estado represor: de la ley de Residencia a la de Defensa Social (1902–1910)* (Buenos Aires: CEAL, 1987); "Ideas y prácticas políticas del anarquismo argentino," *Entrepasados*, no. 8 (1995); "Las prácticas políticas del anarquismo argentino," *Revista de Indias* vol. LVII, no. 210 (1997).

36 Although there was some concord with liberals on the issue of individual freedom, and they even shared elements of the critique of the state, the confluences ended there. On liberal philosophy's influence on anarchism, see Henri Arvón, *El anarquismo* (Buenos Aires: Paidós, 1971).

37 Gareth Stedman Jones, Lenguajes de clase. Estudios de historia de la clase obrera inglesa (Madrid: Siglo XXI, 1989), 90.

CHAPTER I

1 Translator's note: In Argentine parlance, *criolla /criollo* ("creole") refers to native-born Argentines of mixed European and South American ancestry, as opposed to newly arrived (typically European) immigrants. In this context, the terms *criollismo* and *criollista* refer to a kind of ethnic nativism and/or cultural nationalism.

2 José Luis Romero, *Las ideas políticas en Argentina* (Mexico: Fondo de Cultura Económica, 1946), 169. On the formation of modern Buenos Aires See: James Scobie, *Buenos Aires, del centro a los barrios, 1870–1910* (Buenos Aires: Solar/Hachette, 1977); Guy Bourde, *Buenos Aires: urbanización e inmigración* (Buenos Aires: Huemul, 1977); Jorge Liernur, "La ciudad efímera" in *El umbral de las metrópolis*, ed. Jorge Liernur and Graciela Silvestri, (Buenos Aires: Sudamericana, 1993).

3 On the early period of anarchist activity, see: Iaacov Oved, *El anarquismo*. Also: Gonzalo Zaragoza Ruvira, *El anarquismo argentino*.

4 Oved, *El anarquismo*. On the origins of the Argentine workers' movement, see: Ricardo Falcón, *Los orígenes del movimiento obrero (1857–1899)* (Buenos Aires: CEAL, 1984).

5 Between 1902 and 1906, monthly contributors to the FOA oscillated between 5,000 and 10,000, although there must have been significantly more members. Edgardo Bilsky, *La FORA y el movimiento obrero: 1900–1910*, volume 1 (Buenos Aires: CEAL, 1985), 73–76.

6 Iaacov Oved, "El trasfondo histórico de la Ley N° 4.144 de Residencia," *Desarrollo*

Económico, no. 61, vol. 6, (1976); Juan Suriano, *Trabajadores, anarquismo y Estado represor: de la Ley de Residencia a la de Defensa Social (1902–1910)* (Buenos Aires: CEAL, 1988).

7   In addition to the aforementioned conflict in 1902, the following general strikes occurred: December 1904, in response to a police crackdown on workers in Rosario; November 1905, as a reaction to the imposition of martial law due to the port strikes; January 1907, again in solidarity with the Rosario workers' movement; August 1907, as a reply to the massacre of workers in Ingeniero White; between May 3 and 9, 1909, the most important general strike of the decade in protest against the repression of the May Day demonstration, mobilizing more than 200,000 workers and galvanizing other sectors of the population. The last general strike, which lacked any mass support, took place on October 16, 1909 in response to Francisco Ferrer's execution in Spain. On turn-of-the-century labor conflicts, see: E. Bilsky, *La FORA*, volume 1, 67–108; Julio Godio, *Historia del movimiento obrero argentino: inmigrantes, asalariados y lucha de clases, 1880–1910* (Buenos Aires: Tiempo Contemporáneo, 1973). On the May 1909 strike, see: Julio Frydemberg and Miguel Ruffo, *La semana roja de 1909* (Buenos Aires: CEAL, 1992).

8   I understand propaganda as the deliberate, systematic transmission of messages directed to a determinate audience with the object of generating certain ideas and stimulating specific forms of behavior.

9   I regard ideology as a system of signifiers and values that constitute the expression or projection of a particular interest. See: Raymond Williams, *Marxismo y Literatura* (Barcelona: Península, 1980), 71–89. On the historical evolution of the concept of ideology, see: Terry Eagleton, *Ideología* (Barcelona: Paidós, 1997).

10 Italics in original. V. I. Lenín, *Acerca de la prensa y la literature* (Buenos Aires: Anteo, 1965), 9–17.

11 *La Protesta*, October 1, 1904. Dozens of anarchist and also socialist lectures on religion indicate this concern.

12 *La Protesta*, September 16, 1906. That same year, a group of Buenos Aires libertarians deemed it important to "ruin the clergy, which prevents us from influencing women, dominates public education, and, in alliance with the government, arms its Catholic circles so that they can murder us with the army when they get the chance," in *El caballero del Desierto*, Declaración de guerra al orden o La Acción Anarquista en la República Argentina, Buenos Aires, 1906, 31.

13 On spontaneity and the revolutionary party, see Umberto Cerroni, Lucio Magri, and Monty Johnstone, *Teoría marxista del partido revolucionario* (Mexico: Cuadernos de Pasado y Presente, 1987).

14 Pierre Quiroule. "La Ciudad Anarquista Americana," in *Utopías Libertarias Americanas*, ed. L. Gómez Tovar, R. Gutiérrez, and S. A. Vázquez, (Madrid: Tuero, 1991), 14.

15 On the formation of popular-revolutionary societies and the political and educational role that they played in France, see Albert Soboul, *Los sans-culottes, movimiento popular y gobierno revolucionario* (Madrid: Alianza, 1987), 180–203; also: Michel Vovelle, *La mentalidad revolucionaria* (Barcelona: Crítica, 1989), 153–168. On the earlier establishment of circles and workers' clubs, see M. Agulhon, "Clase obrera y sociabilidad antes de 1848," *Historia Social*, no. 12, (1992).

16 On the first steps of workers' associational life, see Ricardo Falcón, *Los orígenes del movimiento obrero*; Hilda Sabato, *La política en las calles. Entre el voto y la movilización Buenos Aires 1862–1880* (Buenos Aires: Sudamericana, 1998).

17 It is worth mentioning that this structure was not unique to anarchists but rather shared by the left broadly. Socialists embraced similar cultural patterns and their hymns, songs, theatrical works, and events in general were very similar to those put on by anarchists.

18 The question of workers' identity is complex and, although I will not tackle it here, it is worth noting that diverse groups more or less consistently sought to curtail workers' foreignness and excessive cosmopolitanism, to endow them (and especially their children) with a national spirit, and to integrate them into society as Argentine citizens. The public school, patriotic ceremonies, nationalist centers, and the church stood out in this respect. Such efforts had to ignore the European past or, as Halperín puts it, "to integrate [the workers] into a well-defined community on the basis of their future more than their past." See: Tulio Halperín Donghi, "Una ciudad entra en el siglo XX," in *Buenos Aires 1910. El imaginario para una gran capital*, ed. Margarita Gutman and Thomas Reese (Buenos Aires: Eudeba, 1999), 55. On workers' identity, see: Luis Alberto Romero, "Los sectores populares en las ciudades latinoamericanas del siglo XIX: la cuestión de la identidad," *Desarrollo Económico*, no. 1906, vol. 27 (1987).

19 According to Plekhanov, who regarded anarchism as a bourgeois ideology, Spencer was nothing more than "a conservative anarchist." Georgiï Plekhanov, *Anarquismo y socialismo* (Buenos Aires: Sudamericana, undated), 158.

20 Los Caballeros del ideal had a long career and, shortly before the group dissolved, it was criticized for its name. Taking the concept of equality to the extreme, a writer questioned whether an anarchist group should have the word *caballero* [gentleman] in its name: "in anarchy there won't be gentlemen or nobles, or people who exercise authority over others in any way, neither gentlemen nor people of lesser ancestry, which is why the noted name is entirely inappropriate for a group of anarchists," in *La Protesta*, February 7, 1907.

21 There is no direct, material evidence of the Bakuninist Center. José Ingenieros referred to it in the 1898 *Almanaque Socialista* and it was mentioned in the article "El anarquismo en el Río de la Plata," which *Caras y Caretas* published on August 11, 1900. Perhaps Abad de Santillán drew from these publications when he described the center as pioneering. See: Diego Abad de Santillán, "*La Protesta*: Su historia, sus diversas fases y su significado en el movimiento anarquista de América del Sur," in *Certamen Internacional de* La Protesta in (Buenos Aires: La Protesta,1927), 35.

22 On Malatesta's activity in the country, see: Gonzalo Zaragoza Ruvira, "Enrique Malatesta y el anarquismo argentino," *Historiografía y bibliografía americanista* vol. XVI, no. 3 (1972).

23 See Manuel Reguera, "De *El Perseguido* a *La Protesta*," in *La Protesta*, January 22, 1909.

24 See *La Protesta Humana*, July 15, 1897; March 6 and May 1, 1898. Also Oved, *El anarquismo*, 72.

25 *Capacidad revolucionaria de la clase obrera* (Buenos Aires: Biblioteca de Propaganda Anárquica, 1897), 10.

26 Ibid., 13.

27 Leandro Gutiérrez and Mirta Lobato, "Memorias militantes: un lugar y un pasado para los trabajadores argentinos" *Entrepasados*, no. 3, (1992): 29.

28 According to Pasquino, "a correct definition of a political movement ought to encompass both elements of the expression: a movement is distinct from a party, especially, and indicates the non-institutionalization of an idea, group, or activity.

Politics refers to the objectives of the movement, its action in the arena of collective decisions, its judgement upon those holding government power...." See: Gianfranco Pasquino, "Movimiento Político," *Diccionario de Política,* N. Bobbio, N. Matteucci, and G. Pasquino, vol. II (Mexico: Siglo XXI, 1994), 1014.

29 *La Protesta Humana,* July 15, 1897.

30 The government applied the Residency Law to Serantoni in late 1902 and deported him. Police raided the shop in the beginning of the following year and destroyed a large quantity of books, which forced the bookstore to close. The Libertarian Bookstore replaced it briefly and then Bautista Fueyo's bookshop. On the Librería Sociológica, see: *La Protesta Humana,* April 11, 1903 and Oved, *El anarquismo,* 70.

31 *The Rebel,* July 24, 1901.

32 *La Protesta Humana,* April 20, 1901.

33 *La Protesta Humana,* September 17, 1899.

34 *La Protesta Humana,* December 24, 1899.

35 *La Protesta Humana,* November 12, 1899.

36 *La Protesta Humana,* January 7 and 21, 1900. The writer intimates that political pressures caused the closure, but it appears that economic problems resulting from the high cost of maintaining the building were more decisive.

37 *La Protesta Humana,* April 15, 1900.

38 *La Protesta Humana,* April 23, 1900.

39 See: *La Protesta Humana,* January 12, 1901. [Translator's note: for explanation of the subscriptions, please see pages 138–141.]

40 *La Prensa,* May 27, June 2, and June 7 of 1902, and *La Protesta Humana,* May 23, 1902.

41 *La Protesta Humana,* September 27, 1902.

42 *La Protesta Humana* and *The Rebel* tracked the centers' activity that year.

43 See: *La Prensa,* January to December 1902; March to November 1903.

44 Doctor Emilio Arana, a Spanish immigrant, joined the anarchist movement in Rosario in 1896 and was intensely active until his death five years later. In addition to leading the cited circle and running the newspaper *Nueva Humanidad,* he gave countless lectures, many of which were published by the Ciencia y Progreso group in Rosario: for example, "La sociedad, su pasado, su presente y su porvenir" (1897), "La mujer y la familia" (1897), "La medicina y el proletariado" (1899), "Los males sociales" (1901). He was evidently extremely popular among militant anarchists, who attended his funeral in enormous numbers. See the obituaries section in *La Protesta Humana,* May 8 and 15, 1901.

45 My comments about anarchist groups in the interior rely on information published in *La Protesta Humana* between 1897 and 1903 and in its latter incarnation, *La Protesta,* between 1903 and 1910.

46 *La Protesta,* April 28, 1904.

47 May Day commemorations could not occur until martial law was lifted, and thus took place on May 21. See: Sebastián Marotta, *El movimiento sindical argentino, su génesis y desarrollo,* vol. I (Buenos Aires: Ediciones Lacio, 1960), 202.

48 Data about the circles' activity between 1904 and 1910 come primarily from *La Protesta* and, secondarily, more sporadic publications: *Seed,* Buenos Aires, 1906–1907; *Luz y Vida,* Buenos Aires, 1908; *Soldier's Enlightenment,* Buenos Aires, 1908–1910; *Martín Fierro,* Buenos Aires, 1904–1905.

49 *La Protesta* printed more than 10,000 copies every day on the eve of the Centenary.

The nightly, "anarchist evening newspaper," *The Battle*, was also coming out at this time. See: Max Nettlau, "Contribución a la Bibliografía anarquista de la América Latina hasta 1914," in *Certamen Internacional de* La Protesta (Buenos Aires: La Protesta,1927), 23. I analyze the anarchist press in chapter five.

50 Cámara de Senadores, *Diario de Sesiones de 1902*, vol. I (Buenos Aires, 1902), 657. This view would reappear throughout the decade. On the subject, see: J. Suriano, *Trabajadores, anarquismo y Estado represor.*

51 The Amigo del Trabajador group published the newspaper *La Vida Obrera* in Hebrew for several months, see: *La Protesta*, July 11, 1907.

52 For example, in 1906 the following theater groups were in operation: Amantes del Arte, Modern Art, Art for Life, Ibsen, Equality and Fraternity, Modern Youth, The Libertarians, The Truth, and the group organized by the Gentlemen of the Ideal. With respect to musical bands, at least two functioned consistently: Libertarian Choir and The Height of Disgrace.

53 *La Protesta,* February 12, 1907.

54 *La Protesta,* March 9, 1907.

55 For example, twelve anarchist groups and three union societies joined forces in 1908 and formed the Popular Committee for the Freedom of the Press to fight restrictions on the freedom of speech. See *La Protesta*, May 23, 1908. There were also conflicts here: the committee and two centers that did not join it (Nueva Luz and Evolution) organized an event supporting the freedom of the press on the same day, which confused the public and led to a long argument among anarchists. See *La Protesta*, May 23, 1908. On this matter, also see Chapter Five.

56 *Luz y Vida,* no. 6, September 9, 1908.

57 Juan Suriano, Trabajadores, anarquismo y Estado represor.

58 *La Protesta Humana*, November 17, December 1, 8, 15, 1900. Oved, *El anarquismo*, 150–157; Abad de Santillán, *El Movimiento anarquista en la Argentina*, 51–120. Iaacov Oved has studied the influence of Spanish anarchism on local libertarian militants: "Influencia del anarquismo español en el anarquismo argentino," in *Estudios Interdisciplinarios de América Latina y el Caribe* 2, no. 1 (1991). The topic is also addressed in José Moya, *Cousins and strangers. Spanish Immigrants in Buenos Aires, 1850–1930* (Berkeley: University of California Press, 1997), 307–314. On associationism in Spanish anarchism: José Alvarez Junco, *La ideología política del anarquismo español (1868–1910)* (Madrid: Siglo XXI, 1976), 453–479.

59 "Declaración de Principios Anarquistas," *The Rebel*, No 1, November 11, 1898, 1.

60 Here "socialist tradition" means the totality of the left at the turn of the century. I use the term in its broadest sense, encompassing all the tendencies that asserted the need to mobilize a political core to lead the workers' movement. Solomonoff has perceptively outlined socialism and anarchism's shared Hegelian roots and their break from "the theory of historical materialism and its consequent inversion in praxis: it is men, who by their action, produce history," in Jorge Solomonoff, *Ideologías del movimiento obrero y conflicto social* (Buenos Aires: Proyección, 1971), 187.

61 *The Rebel,* September 3, 1899.

62 *The Rebel*, February 2, 1901. And they would later add: "This decentralization that scares some and makes us extremely happy is the best possible tactic that can be used to get individuals accustomed to proceeding for its own sake, without the need for tiresome crutches." *The Rebel*, September 29, 1901.

63 *The Rebel*, February 2, 1901.

64 *The Rebel,* February 16, 1901.

65 Jean Grave, "Organización, Iniciativa, Cohesión," *The Rebel*, March 18, 1901. Jean Grave, a shoemaker who would become one of the most important propagandists of French anarchism, published and directed *La Révolte* and *Les Temps Nouveaux*. He supported the independence of the anarchist groups throughout the 1880s but later, in opposition to the individualists, actively supported libertarian participation in unions and involvement in union organizing.

66 This process has been analyzed in detail in Oved, *El anarquismo*, 66–173.

67 Speaking of European anarchists, George Woodcock said that libertarians had failed in this task: "even among themselves they have not often been able to achieve this reconciliation." George Woodcock, *El anarquismo* (Barcelona: Ariel, 1979), 221.

68 *La Protesta Humana*, April 2, 1901.

69 *La Protesta Humana*, September 3, 1897.

70 Ibid.

71 José Alvarez Junco, "Los dos anarquismos," *Cuadernos del Ruedo Ibérico*, no. 55/57 (1977): 141. Peter Kropotkin, *El apoyo mutuo* (Buenos Aires: Américalee, 1946).

72 *La Protesta Humana*, November 14, 1897.

73 Ibid.

74 *La Protesta Humana*, January 15, 1899.

75 Ibid.

76 *La Protesta Humana*, April 2, 1901.

77 Pascual Guaglianone, "La propaganda anarquista en la Argentina," *La Protesta Humana*, March 9, 1901.

78 Ibid.

79 It is interesting to note that Guaglianone was repeatedly accused of self-absorption and egoism, bringing anarchists' traditional distrust of intellectuals upon himself. One militant stated publicly that the working masses "do not admire his personality, but rather the greatness of the idea that he and everyone propagates" *La Protesta Humana*, December 19, 1903.

80 There was another unsuccessful attempt in 1907 to organize anarchists around the Almagro Libertarian Center. See *La Protesta*, February 12, 1907; February 16, 1907; and March 9, 1907.

81 On these incidents, see: *The Rebel*, *La Protesta Humana*, and *The Future* between November 1900 and June 1901.

82 See: Juan Suriano, *Trabajadores, anarquismo y Estado represor*; Oved, "El transfondo histórico."

83 *The Rebel*, July 15, 1900.

84 *La Protesta Humana*, April 24, 1901.

CHAPTER II

1 Translator's note: The Spanish title of the chapter is "La interpelación Anarquista," which could be translated as "The Anarchist Interpellation." I translated *interpelación* as "appeal" for the sake of comprehensibility, but readers should bear in mind that Suriano's term *interpelación* or "interpellation" generally means "calling," "addressing," or "hailing" somebody and is a key concept in the work of structuralist-Marxist Louis Althusser, who uses it to articulate a theory about how ideologies make us into the kinds of subject that they want us to be by "hailing" us *as* such-and-such (e.g., as a "woman," an "American," a "consumer," a "worker," etc.)—imposing a definition, an identity that the subject then accepts by answering to the "call." See Louis

Althusser, *On Ideology* (London: Verso, 2008), 48.

2   Iaacov Oved, *El anarquismo*, 228.

3   The militants themselves did not use these terms: they are my means of classifying the tangled fabric of the local anarchist movement.

4   Acknowledging Ghiraldo's heterodoxy, some authors argue that he was not a logical, systematic thinker and could appeal to Christ or Spartacus as easily as any of the major anarchist thinkers: emotions rather than ideas were more determinate in his views. See: R. Yoast, *The Development of Argentine Anarchism: A Social Ideological Analysis* (Madison: The University of Wisconsin, 1975), 335–340. Emotionalism was not unique to Ghiraldo or a particular sector of the local anarchist movement, but an important element of anarchism as such. On this topic in the context of Spain, see: Gerald Brenan, *El laberinto español* (Paris: Mundo Ibérico, 1962); Eric Hobsbawm, *Rebeldes primitivos* (Barcelona: Ariel, 1974); and Lily Litvak, *Musa Libertaria. Arte, literatura y vida cultural del anarquismo español (1880–1913)* (Barcelona: Antoni Bosch Editor, 1981).

5   I take the term "populism" from José Álvarez Junco, "Los dos anarquismos," *Cuadernos del Ruedo Ibérico*, no. 55/57 (1977): 139.

6   *The Rebel*, December 11, 1898.

7   *The Rebel* published "El concepto de revolución" from November 11 to November 27, 1898 and the "Bases Científicas de la Anarquía" over several months in 1902.

8   *La Protesta* published more articles by Kropotkin than any other European theorist. Between 1904 and 1910, it ran twenty-eight articles by Kropotkin; twenty-seven by Élisée Reclus, ten by Errico Malatesta, thirteen by Jean Grave (the last three authors had close theoretical and ideological ties to Kropotkin) and only three by Stirner, three by Bakunin, three by Herbert Spencer. On the publication of Kropotkin's books and pamphlets in the country, see Chapter Three.

9   José Álvarez Junco, *La ideología política del anarquismo español (1868–1910)* vol. I (Madrid: Siglo XXI, 1976), 182–183.

10   Gareth Stedmann Jones, Lenguajes de clase. Estudios sobre la historia de la clase obrera inglesa (Madrid: Siglo XXI, 1989), 91.

11   Gilimón, *Hechos y Comentarios*, 104.

12   Once again, the contradictions: these fervent defenders of progress applauded mechanization as a labor-saving innovation and saw machines as vital to humanity's well-being in the society of the future, but questioned the unemployment caused by the use of machines under capitalism, given that employers utilized them not to improve working conditions but to increase profits. Some anarchists argued that so long as these social relations of production exist, workers, in addition to using strikes, should destroy the machines that had put workers out of their jobs. See, for example, Carmelo Freda, "Dinamita a las máquinas," *Gleam*, no. 2, March 25, 1906.

13   Not only did they frequently publish anti-militarist pieces in the movement press, but they also published specifically pacifist newspapers like *El Cuartel* (1909) and *La luz del soldado* (1909–1914), which were widely distributed. I discuss libertarian anti-militarism in Chapter Seven.

14   This choice expression—"categorical directness"—comes from David Viñas, *Literatura argentina y política. De los jacobinos porteños a la bohemia anarquista* (Buenos Aires: Sudamericana, 1995), 219.

15   Pierre Quiroule, *La Ciudad Anarquista Americana* (Buenos Aires: Editorial La Protesta, 1914). For an analysis of this work, see: Félix Weimberg, *Dos utopías argentinas de*

principios de siglo (Buenos Aires: Solar/Hachette, 1987); Fernando Ainsa, "La ciudad anarquista americana. Estudio de una utopía libertaria," *Caravelle*, no. 46 (1988); Luis Gómez Tovar, Ramón Gutiérrez, and Silvia A. Vázquez, *Utopías Libertarias Americanas* (Madrid: Tuero, 1991).

16 Gómez Tovar, Gutiérrez, Vázquez, *Utopías Libertarias Americanas,* 37–43.

17 On anarchism's spontaneity and insurrectionalism, see Gian Mario Bravo, "El anarquismo," in *Diccionario de política*, ed. Norberto Bobbio, Nicola Matteucci, and Gianfranco Pasquino (Mexico: Siglo XXI, 1994), 29–36. Some historians of anarchism affirm the role of spontaneity and the lack of a clearly developed utopian perspective, such as George Woodcock, *El Anarquismo (Barcelona:* Ariel, 1979), 25. Marxists have often criticized anarchist immediatism. For instance, in the context of a discussion of the 1968 uprising in France, Wolfgang Harich recently defined it as a form of "revolutionary impatience." In a highly psychological and somewhat pejorative explanation, he argues that anarchists are (and were) impatient because they do not know how to wait for the right revolutionary conditions and imagine that revolution is always possible. See, Wolfgang Harich, *Crítica de la impaciencia revolucionaria* (Barcelona: Crítica, D.L, 1988).

18 *The Rebel,* January 12, 1902.

19 Diego Abad de Santillán, "Los anarquistas y la política colonial de los estados civilizados." *La Protesta* published this article in its weekly supplement on January 12, 1925. Taken from *Suplementos. Materiales de trabajo intelectual* (1993): 21.

20 Translator's note: "In its purest sense," Nicolas Shumway explains, "*gaucho* referred to the nomadic, often outlaw inhabitants of the great plains of Argentina, Uruguay, and Brazil," and the term has since come to designate "the rural working class in general"; gauchos have also, in part through their representation in works like José Hernández's epic poems *El Gaucho Martín Fierro* (1872) and *La Vuelta de Martín Fierro* (1879), functioned as "a national type, a popular figure with mythical overtones who in some sense embodies the real Argentina" (*The Invention of Argentina* [Berkeley: University of California Press, 1991], 12, 49).

21 Translator's note: Domingo Faustino Sarmiento Albarracín (1811–1888) and Juan Bautista Alberdi (1810–1884) were nineteenth-century Argentine liberals opposed to the *caudillo* (dictator) Juan Manuel de Rosas (who ruled Argentina from 1829 –1832 and 1835–1852). In contrast to Rosas, Julio Argentino Roca (president of Argentina from 1880–1886 and 1898–1904) might have appeared as a relatively benign modernizer, at least during his first presidency.

22 The appeal to Alberdi should be no surprise. His awkward position in the pantheon of official heroes endowed him with a certain legitimacy among Socialists, Communists (later), and anarchists, who appreciated his criticism of the Paraguayan war and his positivism. Basterra's reference is not the only instance: years later, although not without criticism, Rodolfo González Pacheco and Teodoro Antilli choose Alberdi's name for one of their publications. See *Ideas and Figures*, no. 40, December 31, 1910. One anarchist paper recognized Alberdi as "one of our ancestors, one of the few who intuitively grasped the inevitable social struggle of our time" in *The Libertarian*, March 2, 1911.

23 Félix Basterra, *El crepúsculo de los gauchos* (Paris-Montevideo: Les Temps Nouveaux y Librería de la Universidad, 1903), 94. On Basterra's intellectual history, see Patricio Geli, *Félix Basterra: una lectura crítica de la modernización argentina* (Buenos Aires: mimeograph, 1990).

24 Alberto Ghiraldo published nine volumes of poetry, ten works of theater, twenty-

four books of essays (in which he alternated between politics, social criticism, and autobiography). He founded and directed four publications, led *La Protesta* for almost two years, and published numerous articles. Eduardo Gilimón was a journalist and tireless contributor to *La Protesta* from 1898 to 1910. Between 1906 and 1910, he published 568 articles in the paper, which were mostly doctrinal in character. He also released various pamphlets and an autobiographical book.

25 Alberto Ghiraldo, *Humano Ardor* (*Barcelona:* Editorial Lux, 1928), 19.

26 *Martín Fierro*, no. 1, March 13, 1904.

27 David Viñas, *De los Montoneros a los Anarquistas* (Buenos Aires: Carlos Pérez Editor, 1971), 213.

28 Camilucho Tresmarías, "Crónica gaucha," *Martín Fierro*, no. 5, March 31, 1904. Much like Ghiraldo's perspective, although appealing directly to rural workers, there is the "Carta Gaúcha" by Juan Cruzao (Luis Woolands). On this see Ángel Cappelletti, "Anarquismo Latinoamericano," in *El anarquismo en América Latina*, ed. Carlos Rama and Ángel Cappelletti (Caracas, Biblioteca de Ayacucho, 1990), LII. On the use of the Gaucho-esque genre, see Carlos Gameno, "Gauchesca anarquista" *Filología* XXIV, no. 1–2 (1989): 133–164.

29 Alberto Ghiraldo, *Alma Gaucha* (Buenos Aires, 1906).

30 Delio Sánchez, "Tradición (A mis paisanos)," *Soldier's Enlightenment*, no. 62, September 7, 1913.

31 Ibid.

32 Rodolfo González Pacheco, "El gaucho," in *Carteles*, vol. I (Buenos Aires: Américalee, 1956), 150. The vindication of the persecuted gaucho, who had been stripped of his freedom and right to the land as a result of the advance of private property, ran throughout González Pacheco's work, both journalistic and theatrical. For instance, it is the central theme of one of his most celebrated plays: *Las víboras* [*The Vipers*], first performed by Enrique Muiño and Elías Alippi's company in 1916. In it, he celebrated the gaucho's rebellious spirit and his right to travel freely. Near the end of the work, one of the main characters, Evangelisto, exclaims: "Yes, man, yes! The fences are the prison bars of the Pampa! The gauchos' fate will shatter against them! Smash the fences with iron!" Rodolfo González Pacheco, *Las víboras*, in *El drama rural*, ed. Luis Ordaz (Buenos Aires: Hachette, 1959), 199.

33 Delio Sánchez, "Tradición (A mis paisanos)"

34 Basterra, *El crepúsculo de los gauchos*, 90, 95. There was no unanamimity on the question of the gaucho. Renowned playwright Florencio Sánchez, a clear supporter of anarchism, never finally pinned down the role of the native-born Argentine [*criollo*] in relation to the immigrant, despite the transparent *anti-moreirismo* [i.e., antagonism toward the glorification of gauchos such as the folk hero Juan Moreira, subject of a novel by Eduardo Gutiérrez] in a play like *La Gringa*, underscoring the difficult coexistence of the native-born and traditions. See Adolfo Prieto, *El discurso criollista de la Argentina moderna* (Buenos Aires: Sudamericana, 1988), 181–182.

35 On Alberto Ghiraldo's work, see Héctor A. Cordero, *Alberto Ghiraldo, precursor de nuevos tiempos* (Buenos Aires: Claridad, 1962); Hernán Díaz, *Alberto Ghiraldo. Anarquismo y Cultura* (Buenos Aires: CEAL, 1991).

36 Translator's note: When Suriano says that Gilimón "opposed the unity of the workers' movement," he means, specifically, that Gilimón rejected attempts to unite the Socialist-led Union General de Trabajadores and the FORA. For more information, see Robert Jackson Alexander, *A History of Organized Labor in Argentina* (Westport, CT: Praeger Publishers, 2003), 21–22. Also, Ricardo Melgar Bao, *El movimiento*

obrero latinoamericano: historia de una clase subalterna, vol I (Mexico City: Consejo Nacional para la Cultura y las Artes, 1988), 172.

37 Eduardo Gilimón, "El anarquismo revolucionario," in *Gleam*, no. 4, March 8, 1906.

38 In addition to his hundreds of articles in *La Protesta*, he summed up his ideas clearly in the pamphlet *Para los que no son anarquistas* (Buenos Aires, 1920) and especially in *Hechos y Comentarios*.

39 Translator's note: The Sáenz Peña Law extended voting rights to all male citizens in Argentina in 1912.

40 Javier Paniagua, "Una gran pregunta y varias respuestas. El anarquismo español: desde la política a la historiografía," *Historia Social*, no. 12 (1992): 39.

41 For a summary of these ideas, see Eduardo Gilimón, *El Anarquismo en los gremios* (Buenos Aires: Talleres Gráficos de La Protesta, 1921).

42 *Luz y Vida*, no. 3, July 6, 1908. This newspaper appeared for several months in 1908, representing the sectors of the libertarian movement linked to unionism. Without opposing them directly, it confronted *La Protesta's* doctrinaire leadership. Prominent activists like Esteban Almada, Mario Chiloteguy, and playwright José de Maturana were its most active writers and, while Ghiraldo's name did not appear, he clearly had an influence. The piece cited above ends with an invitation: "We believe that ideas are discussed, not imposed. Since imposition is contrary to ideas themselves, we repeat the same words that we stated in our first issue: *Luz y Vida* is an open forum for the free discussion of ideas within the revolutionary camp."

43 *New Route*, no. 1, April 22, 1906. Edmundo Calcagno and Pascual Guaglianone, ex-editors of *La Protesta*, led this newspaper. It came out for a few months, defending the anarcho-syndicalist line.

44 *Luz y Vida*, no. 6, September 9, 1908.

45 This debate can be followed in *La Protesta Humana* (May, June, and July 1903).

46 Juan E. Carulla, *Al filo del medio siglo* (Buenos Aires: Editorial Llanura, 1951), 80–81.

47 Ghiraldo directed *Ideas and Figures* between 1909 and 1916, using it as a platform from which to wage polemical battles. In 1914, he was selected to represent the local libertarian movement at the International Anarchist Conference scheduled to occur in London. The distrust toward him prevailing among libertarians, who were sure that he only wanted a trip to Europe, and his confused position, thwarted his participation in the Congress and reignited the debate about the role of intellectuals, which would ultimately lead Ghiraldo, Barcos, Carulla to leave formal structures. See Hernán Díaz, *Alberto Ghiraldo. Anarquismo y Cultura*, 86–95.

48 Abad de Santillán, "Suplemento Semanal de *La Protesta*," March 16, 1925, taken from *Suplementos. Materiales de trabajo intelectual* (1993): 15. This statement was a late confirmation of the durability of this perspective on syndicalism. For an understanding of revolutionary syndicalism, it is essential to read Marcel van der Linden and Wayne Thorpe, "Auge y decadencia del sindicalismo revolucionario," *Historia Social*, no. 12 (1992): 3–30.

49 Eduardo Gilimón, "La Anarquía," *La Protesta*, August 20, 1908.

50 Ibid.

51 Abad de Santillán, "Suplemento semanal de *La Protesta*," in *Suplementos. Materiales de Trabajo Intelectual* (1993): 14.

52 Ibid., 16.

53 On this matter, see: Hobsbawm, *Rebeldes primitivos*, Brenan, *El laberinto español*,

and Litvak, *Musa Libertaria.*

54 Rodolfo González Pacheco, *Carteles*, vol. I (Buenos Aires: Américalee: 1956), 108. Ghiraldo's discourse can be understood in similar terms. See, for example: Alberto Ghiraldo, *Humano Ardor* (Barcelona: Editorial Luz, 1928) and *La tiranía del frac* (Buenos Aires: Biblioteca Popular Martín Fierro, 1905).

55 Santillán argued that "Ghiraldo was not a theorist; he was a temperamental rebel, but mere subversionism is not enough to truly build a social movement." Diego Abad de Santillán, "*La Protesta*. Su historia, sus diversas fases y su significación en el movimiento anarquista de América del Sur," *La Protesta*, Buenos Aires, 1927, 51.

56 Ghiraldo, *Humano Ardor*, 319–320.

57 Ibid., 323.

58 Juan E. Carulla, "Los agitadores," *Ideas and Figures*, May 8, 1910, no. 33. Carulla's memoirs are interesting, although they should be read with a degree of skepticism given his enthusiastic support for Uriburu's coup and conversion to fascism. Nonetheless, the following statement is eloquent: "In the pleasant company of two excellent comrades [Julio Barcos and José de Maturana], I became deeply involved in that sector [the anarchist movement] and, though lacking in oratorical skills, participated actively in events of that nature. I typically read my pseudo-psychological speeches, in spite of the fact that I did not really believe in socialism or in any theory with a collectivist or communist character." Even so, he was active in the anarchist movement for nearly eight years: "Why, then, did I find myself dangerously mixed up in those movements? Why did I participate at the risk of ruining my studies and, even worse, prison? … It was a totality of circumstances that drew me into their web, just like countless youth of that generation, almost from infancy; socialist or advanced doctrines scented the air; books, magazines, and teachers spread them directly or indirectly; in those years the country itself reflected Europe ideologically and seemed on the verge of great social changes that would bring with them the installation of a new, collectivist regime," in Juan Carulla, *Al filo del medio siglo* (Buenos Aires: Editorial Llanura, 1951), 83–84. In contrast to his almost irresponsible account of his youthful activism, his articles from the period have a highly radicalized, polemical character and demonstrate his active participation in battles within the anarchist movement, in which he aligned himself with intellectuals like Ghiraldo, Maturana, and Barcos. In that context, he had a strong class perspective and supported direct action, criticizing the "comrades who, full of unction, insist on advancing the comprehensive emancipation of man, preaching more or less poetic doctrines that are circulated by newspapers and lectures these days that deny the class struggle in the name of an anarchism that does not represent all anarchists," from his article "Reflexiones," *Luz y Vida*, Buenos Aires, no. 3, July 6, 1908.

59 Eduardo Gilimón, "Lucha de clases," *La Protesta*, August 12, 1907.

60 Thus works like Mill's Libertad [On Liberty]; Spencer's El individuo frente al Estado [Man Versus the State]; Guyau's *Esbozo de una moral sin obligación ni sanción* [*A Sketch of Morality Independent of Obligation or Sanction*]; and Wagner's *Arte y Revolución* [*Art and Revolution*] could be appropriated by the anarchist camp. Also, authors like Herzen, Nietzsche, Thoreau, Ibsen, Walt Whitman, and, of course, Tolstoy and Zola were read frequently. See Peter Kropotkin, "Anarquismo," in *Folletos Revolucionarios*, ed. Roger N. Baldwin (Barcelona: Tusquets, 1977), 140–141.

61 Max Nettlau, *Breve Historia de la Anarquía* (Buenos Aires: Cenit, undated), 78.

62 *La Protesta Humana*, August 6, 1899.

63 Eduardo Gilimón, "Cómo concebimos la anarquía," *La Protesta*, July 18, 1909.

64 E. Malatesta, *Anarquismo y Anarquía* (Buenos Aires: Tupac Ediciones, 1988), 57.

65 E. Gilimón, *La Protesta*, July 18, 1909.

66 *Luz y Vida*, Buenos Aires, no. 4, July 20, 1908.

67 *Luz y Vida*, Buenos Aires, no. 6, November 9, 1908. As additional proof of the doctrinal diversity and heterogeneity, Ricardo Mella argued that "Socialists and anarchists have their principal core and most supporters among the bourgeoisie," and that "the revolution that we advocate goes beyond the interests of one class or another; it calls for the complete and comprehensive liberation of humanity." Ricardo Mella, *La lucha de clases* (Buenos Aires: B. Fueyo Editor, undated), 5, 8.

68 "Anarquismo y gremialismo," *La Protesta*, February 4, 1908.

69 Ibid.

70 The doctrinal purist wing of anarchism controlled the FORA from 1905 and was responsible for the insertion of a declaration of support for anarchic communism in the federation's statutes.

71 Of course, it was not the only paper committed to this campaign: *Gleam*, which came out for most of 1906, actively accompanied *La Protesta*. See, *Gleam*, no. 6, June 12, 1906; no. 7, July 8, 1906, and no. 10, September 9, 1906.

72 Máximo Aracemi, "Sobre agremiación," *La Protesta*, September 9, 1908.

73 A. Sotanetti, "Organización sindicalista y organización anarquista," *La Protesta*, September 10, 1908.

CHAPTER III

1 Nancy Fraser, "Reconsiderando la esfera pública: una contribución a la crítica a la democracia realmente existente," in *Entrepasados* IV, no. 7 (1994): 99.

2 In response to an eleven-year sentence given to a worker for attacking his boss, a group of well-known activists published a circular arguing that the anarchist movement could not turn a blind eye to such events: "Every good comrade must contribute … so that he does not have to suffer such injustice and iniquity.… We expect support from all comrades, confident that on this occasion the chord of anarchist solidarity will ring out among them." In *La Protesta Humana*, April 15, 1900.

3 Antonio Pellicer Paraire, *Conferencias Populares sobre Sociología* (Buenos Aires: Imprenta Elzeviriana, 1900), 43.

4 Peter Kropotkin, "La moral revolucionaria," en *Panfletos Revolucionarios*, ed. José Álvarez Junco (Madrid: Editorial Ayuso, 1977), 179–208. By the same author, *El apoyo mutuo* (Buenos Aires: Américalee, 1946). Works by Kropotkin in which he developed the concept of mutual aid had been circulating in Buenos Aires since the 1890s.

5 José Álvarez Junco, La ideología política del anarquismo español (1868–1910) (Madrid: Siglo XXI, 1976), 120.

6 Pellicer Paraire, *Conferencias Populares*, 94.

7 Most of the aid provided to the press went to *La Protesta*. Indeed, it probably would not have survived without this constant assistance.

8 On the "floating prisons," see Alberto Ghiraldo, *La tiranía del frac* (Buenos Aires: Biblioteca popular de Martín Fierro, 1905), 39–59.

9 Alejandro Sux, *Bohemia Revolucionaria* (Buenos Aires-Barcelona-Mexico: Biblioteca de la Vida Editorial, 1909), 78.

10 *Luz y Vida*, no. 4, July 20, 1908. This newspaper published a section called "Our Prisoner Support Campaign," in which it publicized the names of detained

anarchists, where they were imprisoned, and the treatment that they received. They also repeatedly denounced the terrible conditions in the prisons generally. Kropotkin's influence is evident in these pieces, particularly in their conviction that prisons are useless because they degrade prisoners and that solidarity—fraternal treatment and moral support—is the only effective response to crime. See, Peter Kropotkin, "Las cárceles y su influencia moral sobre los presos" in *Folletos Revolucionarios,* ed. Roger N. Baldwin (Barcelona: Tusquets, 1977), 51–70. This is the text of a lecture that he gave in 1877, which was turned into an article some years later in France. A version published in Barcelona was circulated in Buenos Aires at the turn of the century.

11   Marotta states that "anarchists organized a demonstration in the Federal Capital against authorities of National Penitentiary, whom they accused of mistreating prisoners. There were 70,000 people in attendance, according to the anarchist newspapers *La Protesta* and *The Battle,* a number never before reached by any fraction of the proletariat," in Sebastián Marotta, *El Movimiento Sindical Argentino,* vol. II (Buenos Aires: Lacio, 1961), 72.

12   We should not forget other, more sporadic forms of solidarity. For example, a cigar cooperative named Germinal formed in 1902 divided half of its profits between the cooperative, the "victims of capital," and the workers' press. See: *La Protesta Humana,* September 21, 1902.

13   *La protesta Humana,* February 4, 1900 and *La Protesta,* August 25, 1904.

14   Sometimes activists raised large sums of money but compromised the value of the effort by dividing the proceeds between too many parties. For example, in late 1901, the Defensores de Nuevas Ideas center organized a party whose profits were split between the organizing center, the Nueva Humanidad school, and the newspapers *La Protesta Humana, The Future, The Rebel,* and *Nuova Civilta.* See *La Protesta Humana,* December 1, 1901.

15   *La Protesta Humana,* February 26, 1899.

16   Of course, anarchists shared this field with socialists, who published around seventy books and pamphlets between 1894 and 1904. Their authors, some of whom anarchists also read, ran from Plekhanov, Turatti, Vandervelde, Laforgue, Jaures, Ferri, and de Amicis to the local writers such as Patroni, Juan B. Justo, Ingenieros, Del Valle Iberlucea, Payró, Palacios, and Ugarte, among others. This information is in *La Vanguardia,* 1894–1904.

17   Paterson, New Jersey, was a focal point for the diffusion of anarchist ideas due to the large number of European immigrant activists, especially Italians, residing there. Writings by the principal libertarian thinkers were printed there and distributed throughout the United States and to cities in the Americas, including Buenos Aires.

18   Gilimón, *Hechos y Comentarios,* 31. This judgment seems correct. Adolfo Prieto, analyzing the emergence of the practice of reading at the end of the nineteenth century, argues: "It is enough to note the formidable amount of printed material that began circulating in the early 1880s to grasp that the public school had already produced a widespread capacity to read," in Adolfo Prieto, *El discurso criollista en la formación de la Argentina moderna* (Buenos Aires: Sudamericana, 1988), 33–34.

19   Gilimón, *Hechos,* 31.

20   It was not only the groups and circles that published by subscription—the printers also utilized the system. For instance, in 1896, the Elzeviriana print shop published *La sociedad futura* by Jean Grave and "to facilitate its diffusion, the editors have

decided to take subscriptions." See *The Woman's Voice*, no. 3, February 20, 1896.

21 *The Rebel*, December 31, 1901. At the end of the nineteenth century, anarchists also began to finance publications with box office receipts from *veladas*. For example, the Modern Youth center used this method. See *La Protesta*, October 15 and 21, 1906.

22 For instance, the Los Ácratas group "has published an interesting pamphlet ... available for a donation," *La Protesta Humana*, February 26, 1899. On the distribution of free material, consider this statement: "The library that founded the *The Rebel* publishing group has initiated a new method for the publication of cheap pamphlets for free distribution among workers who want to learn about our doctrines," in *The Rebel*, July 14, 1901.

23 As an example: Malatesta's pamphlets *En el café* (1904) and *Entre Campesinos* (1901 and 1906) and Etievant's *Declaraciones* had a print run of 10,000 copies. Malatesta was the most popular author after Kropotkin.

24 *La Protesta Humana*, February 26, 1899. There is no doubt that lectures, especially when the orators were talented, prompted audiences to read doctrinal works.

25 With dubious sincerity, the translator of a French-language pamphlet declared: "I did not want to make the mistake of translating letter by letter, truncating not so much the author's style as his ideas, due to discrepancies in the idiom. I attempted instead to make it conform to the Spanish language by changing the place and form of the words—only some of them—but without disturbing the author's intent." "Translator's note" in J. Illenatnom, *Nuestras Convicciones* (Buenos Aires–Montevideo: Biblioteca Acrata, 1900).

26 Although Argentine anarchism was primarily urban, libertarians carried out some propaganda in the countryside, especially during harvest season, when large numbers of militants threw themselves into propagandizing in areas with high concentrations of rural workers.

27 *Cómo nos diezman* (Buenos Aires: Grupo La Expropiación, 1895).

28 The estimate is appropriate if we take into account that print runs for an average of seven or eight publications annually vacillated between 3,000 and 10,000 copies.

29 On this, see Prieto, *El discurso criollista*, 63–82.

30 Public reading—reading aloud—was a form of intellectual sociability that first appeared in England and then in France in the eighteenth century and helped constitute a new public space where, in opposition to the state, members of the bourgeoisie were able to shape a space for critique and debate and constitute themselves as public opinion. See J. Habermas, *Historia y crítica de la opinión pública* (Barcelona: Ediciones G. Gilli , 1986), 63. Also R. Chartier, *El mundo como representación* (Barcelona: Gedisa, 1992), 138. On public reading in Argentina, although dealing with the later period, see Dora Barrancos, "Las lecturas comentadas: un dispositivo para la formación de la conciencia contestaria entre 1914–1930" in *Boletín*, CEIL, no. 16, Buenos Aires, 1987.

31 Tulio Halperín Donghi, "1880: un nuevo clima de ideas" in *El espejo de la historia. Problemas argentinos y perspectivas latinoamericanas* (Buenos Aires: Sudamericana, 1987), 239–252.

32 "Popular reading," said a rationalist publicist, "should not be confused with a lecture, an event in which the public gathers to hear a disquisition, read or spoken, on a specific topic. The goal of popular reading is to engage the masses in the appreciation of works that best reveal the creative faculties of the human spirit ... training the people in the comprehension of the delicacies of thought." Fernando Fusoni, "Las lecturas populares" in *La Escuela popular*, no. 3, December 1, 1912.

33   D. F. Sarmiento, *La educación popular* (Buenos Aires: Librería la Facultad de Juan Roldan, 1915), 402.

34   F. Fusoni, "Las lecturas populares."

35   Alejandro Sux, *Bohemia Revolucionaria,* 78. Enrique Dickmann mentions in his memoirs that he was recruited to the socialist cause after attending a reading of Engels's pamphlet, *Scientific Socialism.* When the talk was over, José Ingenieros and the builder Chacón approached and enlisted him. Enrique Dickmann, *Recuerdos,* 63.

36   Altamirano and Sarlo argue that "lectures institutionalized a new form of cultural communication, in which the features of a meeting are combined with unprecedented modes of relation between the audience and writers." Carlos Altamirano and Beatriz Sarlo, *Ensayos argentinos. De Sarmiento a la vanguardia* (Buenos Aires: CEAL, 1983), 85–86. Of course, the circuit was not only literary: journalists, lawyers, engineers, politicians, and essayists actively cultivated the genre as well.

37   For example, Pascual Guaglianone gave a lecture in April 1900 titled "The Moribund Humanity and the New Humanity," in which he analyzed themes as broad as the role of government, the family, and women. In another, titled "The Religion of Life and the Religion of Death," he attempted a scientific analysis based on the ideas of Darwin, Laplace, and Spencer. A libertarian reporter present at Guaglianone's lectures noted his oratorical talent and expressed surprise at the class background of those in attendance: "An astonishing audience, many of them bourgeois who are happy to listen to such demonstrations and predisposed to study ideas" in *La Protesta Humana,* April 15, 1900.

38   Anarchists and socialists gave 130 and 140 lectures respectively in the city of Buenos Aires and surrounding areas in 1902. This data comes from *La Protesta Humana, La Vanguardia,* and the *La Prensa* newspaper.

39   Dickmann, *Recuerdos,* 37.

40   Nonetheless, a consultation of *La Prensa*'s archives (years 1902, 1904, 1905, and 1908) reveals that anarchist and socialist groups organized 80 percent of the lectures announced. The others of note, alongside the literary ones, were organized by Italian patriotic societies, the Templo Metodista, the Sociedad Sionista Teodoro Herz, the Sociedad Científica Argentina, the Círculo de La Prensa, the Sociedad de Literatura inglesa, the Biblioteca del Municipio, and the Logia Aurora among others.

41   Gilimón, *Hechos,* 32.

42   Santiago Rusiñol, *Un viaje al Plata* (Madrid: 1911), 143.

43   On Anatole France's visit, see Julio and Irene Frydenberg, "Anatole France en Buenos Aires," *Todo es Historia,* no. 291 (1991).

44   Gonzalo Zaragoza Ruvira, *Anarquismo argentino,* 92; M. Reguera, "De *El Perseguido* a *La Protesta,*" in *La Protesta,* January 23, 1909.

45   *La Protesta Humana,* August 1, 1897.

46   Gori went on a propaganda tour for "two years, from 1895 through 1896, covering the entire North American continent, traveling from the Atlantic to the Pacific, from the Gulf of Mexico to Canada, giving close to 280 lectures in cities in the United States." In *La Protesta Humana,* January 1, 1899.

47   Some lectures directed to this end were titled "Association as the Indispensable Foundation of Anarchy" and "Anarchist Free Accord in Organization Does not Weaken but Strengthens Individual Freedom," in *La Protesta Humana,* February 26, 1899.

48   *La Protesta Humana,* January 27, 1899.

49   Ibid.

50   *La Protesta Humana,* August 24, 1899.

51 Patricio Geli, "Los anarquistas en el gabinete antropométrico. Anarquismo y criminología en la sociedad argentina del 1900," *Entrepasados* 2, no. 2 (1992): 13.

52 Reproduced by *La Protesta Humana*, January 27, 1899.

53 Dickmann, *Recuerdos*, 68.

54 Guaglianone joined the anarchist movement after being an active socialist and his conversion was announced at a public event. See *La Protesta Humana*, November 12, 1899. Ghiraldo never hid his admiration for Gori: "He was an accomplished orator … who felt the voluptuousness of the word and lived to be its tribune. He spent hours, whole nights, holding forth on his favorite topics, being a real spectacle to watch and listen to." Alberto Ghiraldo, *Humano Ardor* (Barcelona: Editorial Lux, 1928), 143.

55 About the audience at the lectures, one writer said: "Hearing of libertarian principles perhaps for the first time, they were soon convinced of the goodness of our ideas, which are so slandered and distorted by the bourgeoisie," in *La Protesta Humana*, February 26, 1899.

56 *La Protesta Humana,* February 26, 1899.

57 Dickmann, *Recuerdos*, 89.

58 For example, in 1901, Spartaco Zeo "gave his announced lecture, whose topic was faith in the supernatural, illustrated with scientific data irrefutably proving the absurdity of the belief in God and the falsity of all religions." Later, another lecturer, "speaking on religions, went on at length about spiritualism, this new religion, which is as ridiculous as all the others." *The Rebel*, June 6, 1901.

59 Dickmann, *Recuerdos*, 65.

60 *La Protesta Humana*, November 12, 1899.

61 Dickmann, *Recuerdos*, 76.

62 Often, during crackdowns, disputes were set aside and both tendencies managed to achieve rare moments of accord, which they expressed in joint demands for the restoration of public freedoms. One of the first shared events, which recurred various times throughout the first decade, was a rally in July 1899 against the police ban of a demonstration against executions in Montjuich. It took place in a packed Doria Theater. Gori and Guaglianone spoke for the anarchists and Patroni and Ingenieros for the socialists. See E. Lopez Arango and Diego Abad de Santillán, *El anarquismo en el movimiento obrero* (Barcelona: Cosmos, 1925), 14–15.

63 Abad de Santillán, *El movimiento anarquista en la Argentina*, 85.

64 More than 2,000 people attended the debate on parliamentarianism between Dino Rondani and Félix Basterra that was held in the Doria Theater. See *La Protesta Humana*, September 21, 1902.

65 *La Protesta Humana*, May 13, 1900. While *La Protesta* dismissed some speakers, it praised others. This was the case with Luis Solitro, who "was handy with the word, logical, and conclusive. Solitero is a good lecturer and comrades should exploit his talents, getting him to speak as often as possible." Ibid.

66 Edmundo Calcagno, Manresa Herrero, Francisco Sarache, Roberto D'Angió, Carlos Balsán, Federico Gutiérrez (Fag Libert), Carmelo Freda, Manuel Magdaleno, Esteban Almada, Pedro Planas Carbonell, Francisco Corney, Antonio Loredo, Eduardo Gilimón, Francisco Jaquet, and Lorenzo Mario, among others. With some exceptions, anarchist speakers came and went frequently.

67 Some titles: "Revolutionary Theater," "The People's Theater," "The Theater of Ideas," "The Contribution of Art to Human Perfection," "Life and Art," and "What Is Art?"

68 In addition to Bolten and the aforementioned "*compañera*" Reyes, the following had some standing: Lidia Irigoiti, Elvira Fernández, Ramona Ferreira, Delia Barroso, Julia Rey, Ema Ravizza, Rosa Olivares, Juana Rouco Buela, María Collazo, Belén Sárraga, and Marta Nevelstein. For a discussion of some aspects of female activism, see: Juan Rouco Buela, *Historia de un ideal vivido por una mujer* (Buenos Aires: Julio Kaufman, 1964) and Graciela Sapriza, *Memorias de rebeldía. Siete historias de vida* (Montevideo: Puntosur, 1988).

69 *The Future*, October 22, 1899. Likewise: "an audience composed of some 100 people, of which a small number were of the feminine sex," in *The Rebel*, June 6, 1901.

70 Pietro Gori was undoubtedly a great organizer and played a very important role in the maturation of local anarchism, but he was only active during the formative period (1898–1902) and his influence was confined to the pro-organizational sector. The individualists rejected his views categorically.

71 For the first case, see: Francisco Beazley, Jefe de Policía, Suplemento a la "Orden del Día" de 11 de February de 1903, Buenos Aires, 1903. For the second, see: Informe del jefe de policía Francisco Beazley al ministro del interior J. V. González, Buenos Aires, January 16, 1904, AGN, Sala VII, Archivo Roca, Legajo 157. Although the data is obviously partial, it does suggest tendencies in the social composition of the anarchist movement.

72 Ibid.

73 On the socio-economic profile of the local activists during the early period, see R. Falcón, Darío Macor, and A. Monserrat, "Obreros, artesanos, intelectuales y actividad político sindical. Aproximación biográfica a un perfil de los primeros militantes del movimiento obrero argentino," *Social Studies* 1, no. 1 (1991): 29–73. They argue that Socialists had more support among the classical professions, such as medicine and law, whereas anarchists attracted writers linked to literary bohemia.

74 This is Oreste Ristori's view. His comments appeared in *La Protesta Humana* in 1903 and are reproduced in Abad de Santillán, *El movimiento anarquista en la Argentina*, 141.

75 *La Protesta Humana* published their articles on this topic from November 1900 to February 1901. They articulated their principal ideas in *Conferencias Populares de Sociología*, a pamphlet released in 1905.

76 Here I refer to activists who focused their intellectual efforts on reproducing the anarchist doctrine, but who were not being original thinkers themselves. They functioned as mediators and transmitters, writing articles for anarchist magazines and newspapers, publishing essays in pamphlets, and giving lectures. This is the case for the majority of those mentioned.

77 On Alberto Ghiraldo's trajectory, see: Cordero, *Alberto Ghiraldo* and Hernán Díaz, *Alberto Ghiraldo*.

78 I take this idea from Geli's work. See P. Geli, "Los anarquistas en el gabinete antropométrico." It was very common in other countries with strong anarchist movements for intellectuals to have ties to the movement marked more by a spirit of rebellion than a conscious adhesion to libertarian ideas. Octave Mirbeau, who was one of the most prolific writers in the French libertarian movement and quite familiar to most local activists, explicitly stated his indifference to the doctrine and his attraction to anarchism's violent severity, which even led him to defend Ravachol's terrorism. See André Nataf, *La vie quotidienne des anarchistes en France, 1880–1910* (Paris: Hachette, 1986), 170. The same phenomenon existed in relations between Catalan anarchists and intellectual, artistic vanguards (especially the first literary modernists)

at the end of the nineteenth century. See Rafael Núñez Florencio, *El terrorismo anar-quista, 1888–1909* (Madrid: Siglo XXI, 1983), 111.

79   *The Libertarian*, no. 5, March 2, 1911.

80   Abad de Santillán, *El movimiento anarquista en la Argentina*, 121.

81   When compared to the stability and long-term engagement of socialist intellectuals (for example, consider the case of Juan B. Justo, the Repettos, and Dickmann), the lack of the continuity among Argentine anarchist thinkers is dramatic. But, if youth and impermanence typified anarchist intellectuals, that was not the case among its militant workers. Some police reports indicate that libertarian activists' average age was thirty-one and that they had been active in the movement for approximately one decade when the reports were drafted. See F. Beazley, *Suplemento* and *Informe del jefe de policía*.

82   Abad de Santillán, *El movimiento anarquista en la Argentina*, 113.

83   *La Protesta* published critical pieces on Basterra consecutively for an entire week, indicating that his departure had a powerful impact on the libertarian movement. See *La Protesta,* October 9 through 13, 1906.

84   Geli, "Los anarquistas en el gabinete antropométrico," 16.

85   Julio Ramos, Desencuentros de la modernidad en América Latina. Literatura y política en el siglo XIX (Mexico City: Fondo de Cultura Económica, 1989), 90.

86   *La Protesta,* October 11, 1906.

87   Carlos Altamirano and Beatriz Sarlo, *Ensayos argentinos. De Sarmiento a la vanguar-dia* (Buenos Aires: CEAL, 1983), 71–73.

88   "Like all young people of my generation, I did the socialist thing when I was eighteen years old. This redemptive vocation submerged me in the study of the sociological, historical, and philosophical sciences: I threw myself in the arms of oratory (they say that I'm a good speaker … or a chatterbox). I started anti-clerical magazines in Buenos Aires, a newspaper in Montevideo, I did all the crazy things that one does before loosing a wisdom tooth. After crossing the line, I made a decision"—that is, he left the anarchist movement. In Pascual Guaglianone, *Homenaje de la Facultad de Humanidades y Ciencias de la Educación* (La Plata: Universidad Nacional de La Plata, 1960), 21. Guaglianone became a progressive, liberal academic and Carulla a conservative, nationalist intellectual. Both felt compelled to shrug off their lib-ertarian pasts, characterizing their time in the anarchist movement as a youthful transgression.

89   Santiago Locascio, "Cosas pasadas," *The Martyrs*, May 1, 1917.

CHAPTER IV

1   Gareth Stedman Jones, Lenguajes de clase. Estudios sobre la historia de la clase obrera inglesa (Madrid: Siglo XXI, 1989), 83.

2   Juan Suriano, "Vivir y sobrevivir en la gran ciudad. Hábitat popular en la ciudad de Buenos Aires a comienzos del siglo," *Social Studies* 4, no. 7 (1994): 49–68.

3   Diego Armus, "La idea del verde en la ciudad moderna, Buenos Aires, 1870–1940," *Entrepasados*, no. 10 (1996).

4   Sandra Gayol, "Ambitos de sociabilidad en Buenos Aires: despachos de bebidas y cafés, 1860–1930," *Anuario*, IEHS, no. 8, Facultad de Ciencias Humanas, Tandil, 1993.

5   *Censo General de la ciudad de Buenos Aires de 1910*, vol. II (Buenos Aires: Compañía Sudamericana de Billetes de Banco, 1910), 358–359.

6 A striking quantity of money and people from various social classes participated in gambling. See: "La prensa, August 18, 1901" in Ricardo González, *Los obreros y el trabajo, Buenos Aires, 1901* (CEAL, Buenos Aires, 1984), 82–85. Also: Manuel Bilbao, *Buenos Aires desde su fundación hasta nuestros días* (Buenos Aires: Imprenta de Juan Alsina, 1902), 475–482.

7 *La Protesta*, February 20, 1909.

8 Armus argues that social reformers and Catholics fought alcoholism on behalf of "the virtues of moderation, self-control, productive capacity, family, and race," whereas anarchists and Socialists added "a strong proletarian ethic and the conviction that with greater sobriety, there is greater awareness and dedication to social change." Diego Armus, "Salud y anarquismo. La tuberculosis en el discurso libertario argentino, 1890–1940," in *Política, médicos y enfermedades. Lecturas de historia de la salud en la Argentina*, ed. Mirta Lobato (Buenos Aires: Biblos, 1996).

9 *La Protesta*, August 2, 1908.

10 The percentage of women among attendees at the lectures was small (except when Gori spoke), they made up approximately one-third of the audience at the *veladas*, which were undeniably oriented to families. For example, in the *velada* that took place on April 11, 1909, 759 men and 511 women were present; on May 15, there were 309 and 117 respectively; July 4, 249 and 79; July 31, 85 and 40; September 5, 110 and 44; February 27, 1910, 750 and 272, April 10, 324 and 101; there were 134 men and 47 women on April 24, 1910. See *La Protesta* from the months of May, July, and September of 1909 and February and April of 1910.

11 *Gleam*, No 12, October 13, 1906. Most anarchists supported birth control through contraception and abortion, and promoted it in their newspapers and magazines. However, some disagreed, arguing that large numbers of children were desirable because they would swell the ranks of revolutionaries. For example, Félix Nieves, "Razones para profanar el neomalthusianismo," *La Protesta*, March 3, 1909.

12 Without a doubt, Dr. Arana authored the most complete treatment of the topic in our country. He stressed the need for "woman to receive a rational and scientific education, so that her intellectual level equals that of man's." E. Z. Arana, *La mujer y la familia* (Rosario: Ciencia y Progreso, 1897), 85.

13 *The Rebel*, October 24, 1902.

14 El Caballero del Desierto, *La acción anarquista en la República Argentina* (Buenos Aires: 1906), 31.

15 *The Rebel*, January 19, 1901 (emphasis added).

16 *The Rebel*, October 24, 1902.

17 On the feminism of *The Woman's Voice*, see Maxine Molyneux, "No God, No Boss, No Husband: Anarchist Feminism in Nineteenth-Century Argentina," *Latin American Perspectives* 48 (1986).

18 *The Woman's Voice*, January 8, 1896.

19 *The Woman's Voice*, January 31, 1896.

20 Quiroule discusses some of these topics in his libertarian utopia. See Pierre Quiroule, "La Ciudad Anarquista Americana" in Luis Gómez Tovar, Ramón Gutiérrez, and Silvia Vázquez, *Utopías Libertarias Americanas* (Madrid: Ediciones Tuero, 1991). The issues of marriage, free love, and sexuality are beyond this work, but see Dora Barrancos's previously cited, suggestive work for a valuable discussion.

21 In his autobiographical novel, Alberto Ghiraldo describes the social pressures that he experienced when he decided to live with his girlfriend Angélica as a "test of free love," in Alberto Ghiraldo, *Humano Ardor* (Barcelona: Editorial Lux, 1928), 368.

The same contradiction is evident in the realm of sexuality, where emancipation was pushed off to the future and dominant sexual norms tinted actual practices.

22 *The Rebel*, January 31, 1902 and *Gleam*, March 25, 1906.

23 *La Protesta*, March 22, 1908.

24 *The Rebel*, January 19, 1901. I agree with Pancho Liermur's assertion that in some *La Protesta* articles, "the woman and home evoked do not differ greatly from the self-denying bedrock (the bourgeois mother)." P. Liermur, "El nido de la tempestad," *Entrepasados*, no. 13 (1997): 32.

25 *La Protesta Humana*, May 28, 1899.

26 *La Protesta*, May 14, 1904.

27 *La Prensa*, September 8, 1901.

28 On this topic, see Sergio Pujol, *Historia del baile, de la milonga a la disco* (Buenos Aires: Emece, 1999) [Translator's note: The milonga is a dance form particular to the Río de la Plata region and closely tied to the tango; the haberna is a dance with Cuban roots].

29 *La Protesta*, October 15, 1904.

30 During the tenant strike, the Centro Anarquista Femenino organized a party in a tenement. It began and ended with lectures, but in between "the orchestra broke out with a harmonious waltz, spreading happiness among the audience, which gave itself over to dance completely," *La Protesta*, November 12, 1907, in Juan Suriano, *La huelga de inquilinos de 1907* (Buenos Aires: CEAL, 1983), 60.

31 *La Protesta*, February 20, 1909.

32 Adolfo Prieto argues that creolism was the heart of Carnival celebrations from the 1880s until the period between the 1910 and 1916 centenaries. See Adolfo Prieto, *El discurso criollista en la formación de la Argentina moderna* (Buenos Aires: Sudamericana, 1988), 146–157.

33 *La Protesta Humana*, February 20, 1898.

34 *The Rebel*, February 19, 1899.

35 *La Protesta Humana*, February 20, 1898.

36 *The Rebel,* February 19, 1899.

37 *La Protesta*, February 26, 1906. Ghiraldo's poem expresses similar sentiments: "They tell you: laugh! and there, in the crowd / Always in the crowd, herds of sheep! / You laugh / They tell you: / Kill! And there go your armies! / Always part of the machine, a tool / Either a hangman or bolt: Always an instrument!" A. Ghiraldo, "¡Carnaval," in *Ideas and Figures*, no. 44, February 23, 1911.

38 *La Fusta,* March 22, 1910.

39 *The Rebel,* February 19, 1899.

40 The quote from Darío in "Tribuna," February 26, 1896 and Becher's comments are in "La Nación," February 21, 1906, both in Prieto, *El discurso criollista,* 151.

41 On the Carnival as a rite of inversion or mechanism of reinforcement, see Roberto Da Matta, *Carnavais, malandros e herois. Para uma sociologia do dilema brasileiro* (Río de Janeiro: Zahar Editores, 1979). Also Leander Petzoldt, "Fiestas carnavalescas. Los carnavales de la cultura burguesa a comienzos de la edad moderna" in *La Fiesta. Una historia cultural desde la antigüedad hasta nuestros días*, ed. Uwe Schultz (Madrid: Alianza, 1993); Peter Burke, *La cultura popular en la Europa moderna* (Madrid, Alianza, 1991) and Mijail Bajtin, *La cultura popular en la Edad Media y en el renacimiento. El contexto de F. Rabelais* (Barcelona: Seix Barral, 1974).

42 *The Rebel*, February 19, 1899.

43 *La Protesta Humana*, March 26, 1899. This clash took place in the city of Bolívar

and does not seem to have been repeated on many occasions.

44 Boris Fausto, "Os anarquistas e a minhas lembrancas" in *Libertarios no Brasil. Memorias, lutas, cultura*, ed. Antonio Arnoni Prado (San Pablo: Editora Brasiliense, 1986), 22.

45 I take the idea of the déclassé intellectuals from Claude Grignon and Jean-Claude Passeron, *Lo culto y lo popular: Miserabilismo y populismo en sociología y en literatura* (Buenos Aires: Nueva Visión, 1991), 72. The idea of a field of tension is in Stuart Hall, "Notas sobre la desconstrucción de lo popular," in *Teoría Popular y Teoría Socialista*, ed. Raphael Samuel (Barcelona: Crítica, 1984).

46 On the role of music and song in the workers' movement, see Francisco Foot Hardman, "Lyra de Lpa: acorde imperfeito menor," in Antonio Arnoni Prado, *Libertarios no Brasil*.

47 *1898 Almanac of The Social Question*, Buenos Aires, 1899.

48 Ibid., 57.

49 "Himno Acrático" (with music from the Argentine national anthem), ibid., 60.

50 Ibid.

51 "Himno Anárquico" (with music from the Argentine national anthem), ibid., 57.

52 "A la Revolución Social," ibid., 57.

53 "Milongas Anárquicas," ibid., 58.

54 "Guerra a la burguesía" (tango), ibid., 60.

55 *La Protesta Humana*, September 17, 1899.

56 Interview with Humberto Correale by Daniel James in Buenos Aires.

57 "Declamación. Recitada por la compañerita Fernández en la Verdi el 1º de May de 1906," in *Gleam*, no. 8, July 26, 1906.

58 *La Protesta Humana*, October 14, 1900.

59 Nora Mazzioti, "Bambalinas: el auge de una modalidad teatral periodística" in *Mundo urbano y cultura popular*, ed. Diego Armus (Buenos Aires: Sudamericana, 1990), 72.

60 On Zacconi's visit: *La Nación*, "1816–9 de Julio–1916," 355. On anarchists' admiration for the Italian actor's social commitment, see: *Martín Fierro*, no. 14, June 9, 1904 and *La Protesta*, June 14, 1904.

61 *La Protesta*, December 16, 1906.

62 There was a long debate in 1906 between a drama group and a militant anarcho-syndicalist; the latter thought theatrical performance useless because it consumed energies that he felt should be devoted to other forms of propaganda. In *La Protesta*, November 2 and 4; December 5 and 16, 1906.

63 Alberto Ghiraldo, *Crónicas argentinas* (Buenos Aires, 1912), 85.

64 This view of art was indebted to Grave, Tolstoy, and especially Kropotkin. See André Reszler, *La estética anarquista* (Mexico: Fondo de Cultura Económica, 1974), 56–61. The perspective seems to have origins in Joseph Déjacque's utopia, *Humanisferio* (1858–1859), in which he anticipated the idea of engaged art. He proposed the destruction of bourgeois art, a return to popular roots, and the use of art as a pedagogical tool, in which style and form would be secondary to the ideological message. See Luis Gómez Tovar, Ramón Gutiérrez and Silvia Vázquez, *Utopías Libertarias Americanas* (Madrid: Ediciones Tuero, 1991), 31–33.

65 Alberto Ghiraldo, "El arte para el pueblo," in *Martín Fierro*, no. 7, April 14, 1904. Likewise, see: Alejandro Escobar y Carvallo, "La evolución del Arte en la Anarquía," *The Rebel*, June 4, 1899; Juan Mas y Pi, "El arte social," in *Seed*, December 1, 1906.

66 Sánchez was briefly a figure in the professional circuit, in which he immersed himself completely. Although he frequented anarchist literary circles, unlike Ghiraldo, who directed *La Protesta* and engaged all fronts of the struggle, Sánchez did not have activist commitments. On the contrary, in 1904 he and Belisario Roldán joined the editorial team of the *La Opinión* newspaper, "founded to support the candidacy of Doctor Manuel Quintana." See Enrique García Velloso, *Memorias de un hombre de teatro* (Buenos Aires: EUDEBA, 1960), 84. On *Ladrones* and *Puertas Adentro*, see Luis Ordaz, "Florencio Sánchez," in *Historia de la Literatura Argentina*, vol. 2 (Buenos Aires: CEAL, 1986). Also Eva Golluscio de Montoya, "Sobre Ladrones (1897) and Canillita (1902–1904): Florencio Sánchez y la delegación de poderes," *Gestos*, no. 6 (1988).

67 See Hactor Cordero, *Alberto Ghiraldo, precursor de nuevos tiempos* (Buenos Aires: Claridad, 1962), 136–147. Rodolfo González Pacheco, *Teatro completo* (Buenos Aires: Américalee, 1953).

68 J. Achart, "El estreno de Alas," *La Protesta*, May 13, 1904.

69 Translator's note: The term "Moreirist" here refers to gauchoesque motifs in Argentina culture and literature born of Eduardo Gutiérrez's work *Juan Moreira* (1879).

70 David Viñas, *La crisis de la ciudad liberal* (Buenos Aires: Siglo Veinte, 1973), 79.

71 Ghiraldo, "El regionalismo en el arte," in *Crónicas argentinas*, 93–98.

72 *La Protesta*, July 24, 1908.

73 *The Rebel*, September 23, 1902. Years later another journalist asked: "What can I say about the rendition? As usual, it was terrible. They need to understand that a character has to be played, not imitated," in *La Protesta*, August 11, 1908. However, in some cases reviewers passionately praised the actors-militants: "Mirbeau's *Los Malos Pastores* was so well-performed that it would have been hard for an artist to do a better job," in *The Rebel*, October 26, 1901.

74 *La Protesta*, December 26, 1906.

75 *La Protesta*, July 24, 1908. These critiques were common and had been made for more than a few years. When the works *Dignidad Obrera* and *Venganza Obrera* by "comrade Bergés" were staged in the Lago di Como Theater, a journalist criticized them harshly, recommending "that we deepen our theatrical productions, searching for and getting to the bottom of the present society's ills," in *The Rebel*, September 23, 1902.

76 See *La Protesta*, September 12, 1905.

77 *La Protesta Humana,* August 19, 1900.

78 Scholars have noted similiar characteristics in the Spanish and Brazilian anarchists: Lily Litvak, *Musa Libertaria. Arte, literatura y vida cultural del anarquismo español, 1880–1913* (Barcelona: Antoni Bosch Editor, 1981), 249. Mariangela Alves de Lima and Maria Thareza Vargas, "Teatro operario en Sao Paulo," in *Libertarios no Brasil,* ed. Antonio Arnoni Prado, 173.

79 Serge Salain, "Teoría y práctica del lenguaje anarquista o la imposible redención por el verbo," in *El anarquismo español y sus tradiciones culturales*, ed. Bert Hofmann, Pere Joan i Tous, and Manfred Tietz (Madrid: Vervuert-Iberoamericana, 1995), 330.

80 Ana Ruth Giustachini, "La dimensión verbal en el teatro anarquista: La Columna de Fuego de Alberto Ghiraldo," *Espacio de crítica e investigación teatral* 4, no. 8 (1990): 98.

81 *Seed*, no. 20, May 1908.

82 Litvak, *Musa Libertaria*, 237.

83   *Ideas and Figures,* no. 46, March 20, 1911.

84   Litvak, *Musa Libertaria,* 229–30.

85   This work premiered in a commercial theater in Buenos Aires in 1896 but was canceled almost immediately. A libertarian newspaper exulted: "The work has eminently revolutionary scenes that made the bourgeoisie attending the premiere bristle and shiver." "La Questione Sociale," no. 19, May 15, 1896 in Gonzalo Zaragoza Ruvira, *Anarquismo argentino,* 429.

86   *The Rebel,* March 24, 1901.

87   Reszler, *La estética anarquista,* 62.

88   *La Protesta Humana,* August 17, 1901.

89   *La Protesta Humana,* November 17, 1900.

90   *La Protesta,* June 9, 1907.

91   *The Rebel,* March 8, 1902. There were also complaints about poorly behaved comrades who sang when the orchestra performed, who smoked and "filled the hall with cigarette smoke, despite the ladies," made noise, and did not take off their hats. With this type of conduct, one writer argued, "anarchy will not exist" because "liberty, harmony, fraternity, and love" were transgressed. *La Protesta,* July 24, 1908.

92   There was an appreciable increase in theatrical activity throughout Buenos Aires around the Centenary. "Groups emerged spontaneously," wrote Carulla, "in every workers' society, in every political center, even in the schools, who, as time passed, contributed to the progress of our theater." Juan E. Carulla, *Al filo del medio siglo* (Buenos Aires: Editorial Llanura, 1951), 77–78.

93   *La Protesta,* July 2, 1907.

94   See *Censo,* 358–359.

CHAPTER V

1   Pellicer Paraire, "El diario libertario. Su significación e importancia," *La Protesta Humana,* January 21, 1900.

2   For example, Pedro Gori, "La función histórica del periodismo," *La Protesta Humana,* July 10, 1898; "El diario libertario" *La Protesta Humana,* January 21, 1900; "La función capitalista de la opinión pública," *Vida Nueva,* no. 5 (1904); "La prensa libre," *La Protesta,* June 20, 1906; "Prensa libertaria," *La protesta,* April 10, 1908.

3   J. Habermas, *Historia y Crítica de la Opinión Pública* (Mexico: Edición G. Gilli, 1986), 62–160.

4   Mirta Lobato, "La Patria degli Italiani y el conflicto social en la Argentina de principios del siglo XX," in *Italian Workers of the World: Labor Migration and the Formation of Multiethnic States,* ed. Fraser Ottanelli and Dona Gabaccia (Champaign, IL: University of Illinois Press, 2005).

5   Hilda Sábato, *La política en las calles. Entre el voto y la movilización. Buenos Aires, 1862–1880* (Buenos Aires: Sudamericana, 1998), 62–71. Also, see: Tulio Halperín Donghi, *José Fernández y sus mundos* (Buenos Aires: Sudamericana, 1985).

6   Adolfo Prieto, *El discurso criollista en la formación de la Argentina moderna* (Buenos Aires: Sudamericana, 1988), 35. Also: Tim Duncan, "La prensa política: ⊠Sud-América', 1884–1892" in *La Argentina del ochenta al centenario,* ed. G. Ferrari and E. Gallo (Buenos Aires: Sudamericana, 1980) and Alejandro C. Eujanian, *Historia de revistas argentinas, 1900–1950: la conquista del público* (Buenos Aires: Asociación Argentina de Editores de Revistas, 1999). The transformation of *La República* into an inexpensive paper sold by street venders also contributed to the modernization of

the press. Prior to that, newspapers were costly and sold by subscription. See Manuel Bilbao, *Buenos Aires. Desde su fundación hasta nuestros días* (Buenos Aires: Imprenta de Juan Alsina), 435.

7 The newspapers *La Nación* and *La Prensa* and the magazine *Caras y Caretas* had print runs easily exceeding 100,000 at the turn of the century. The number of people that they employed also indicates the magnitude of the Buenos Aires press as a business: in 1914, *La Nación* employed 100 editors and 400 staff people and *La Prensa* 89 and 532, respectively. Both had luxurious offices. See República Argentina, *Tercer Censo Nacional*, volume IX (Buenos Aires: Talleres Gráficos de L. J. Rosso y Cía, 1917), 282–91. On the modernization of the press, see Aníbal Ford, Jorge B. Rivera, and Eduardo Romano, *Medios de comunicación y cultura popular* (Buenos Aires: Legasa, 1985) and Jorge B. Rivera, *La forja del escritor profesional* (Buenos Aires: CEAL).

8 *Tercer Censo*, 81. On the emergence of popular reading, see Prieto, *El discurso criollista*.

9 Bilbao, *Buenos Aires*, 440. In the late 1880s, the Asociación de Periodistas, the Círculo de Cronistas, and the Círculo de la Prensa were formed expressly to defend the freedom of the press.

10 Joaquín V. González, *Obras Completas*, volume v (Buenos Aires), 155.

11 *Memoria de la Policía de Buenos Aires* (Buenos Aires: Ministerio del Interior, 1909), 261–62.

12 This information is from *La Protesta*, May 19 and 27, 1908; August 26, 1908.

13 *La Razón*, May 17, 1908.

14 See Memoria Policial, 275.

15 Julio Herrera, *Anarquismo y Defensa Social* (Buenos Aires: Librería Europa, 1917), 348.

16 The anarchist press suffered implacable persecution in the months following the approval of the Social Defense Law, its periodicals largely disappeared, and the few that survived went underground. For constant denunciations of these attacks on the freedom of expression and the enormous difficulties that they caused for publishing, see *The Libertarian*, March 2 and 17, 1911 and *Ideas and Figures*, December 1, 1911 and January 4, 1912.

17 See Leonardo Bettini, *Bibliografia dell'anarchismo*, vol. 2 (Florencia: CP Editrice, 1976), 4–5.

18 See Abad de Santillán, *El movimiento anarquista en la Argentina*, 45, 54.

19 Cited by Prieto, *El discurso criollista*, 39.

20 Although one magazine (*Caras y Caretas*, August 11, 1900) counted twenty-four anarchist publications in the 1890s (in the course of this investigation, I have detected thirty-five); Bilbao stated in 1902 "that anarchists have more than ten propaganda papers," in Bilbao, *Buenos Aires*, 454.

21 The print-run figures appear in the ledgers published in the periodicals. The print runs of each vacillated between 2,000 and 3,000 copies. There is not sufficient evidence to determine how many were actually sold and distributed, much less the number of readers.

22 On the history of *La Protesta*, see Abad de Santillán, "*La Protesta*." Also, see Fernando Quesada, "*La Protesta*, una longeva voz libertaria," *Todo es Historia*, no. 82/83 (1974).

23 On the Italian-language libertarian press, see Bettini, *Bibliografia dell'anarchismo*, 3–26.

24 According to the 1914 census, *La Protesta* had its own machines, mechanical type-

setting, and employed eighteen people (four editors and fourteen staff) in that year. This is a very modest number when compared to the nineteen editors and thirty-three staff employed by *La Vanguardia*, its socialist counterpart, but it was enough to keep it publishing. See *Tercer Censo,* 290.

25 Max Nettlau, "Contribución a la Bibliografía anarquista," 12.

26 Abad de Santillán, "*La Protesta,*" 57.

27 *La Protesta Humana,* June 13, 1897.

28 *La Protesta Humana,* November 30, 1901.

29 *La Protesta Humana,* July 22, 1900.

30 Abad de Santillán, "*La Protesta,*" 36.

31 Many articles were signed pseudonymously by authors whose real names will never be known: Sulfuric Acid, Red Soul, Black Soul, Anti-farce, Sonorous Clarion, Attila, Watchtower, Bonaparte, Diogenes, Spartacus, etc.

32 For example, there was a Sociological Studies Competition in 1907 in which the readers submitted works (close to seventy were entered) and voted upon and selected the best, *La Protesta,* May 8, 1907.

33 *La Protesta,* March 4, 1907.

34 Gilimón, *Hechos y Comentarios,* 53. Alberto Ghiraldo was at the head of the paper from September 1, 1904 until August 26, 1906. His egotism and self-important attitude led him to frequently republish articles in *La Protesta* or *Martín Fierro* that he found in other papers that praised him. For example, he reprinted a piece from *La Nación* highlighting his role as the new editor-in-chief of *La Propesta. La Protesta,* September 2, 1904. This tendency became even more pronounced in *Ideas and Figures* (1909–1916).

35 *La Protesta,* January 19, 1908. Rodolfo González Pacheco, Máximo Suárez, and Francisco Sarache made up the editorial group. They were supported by "historicals" like Dr. Juan Creaghe and Eduardo Gilimón. The latter shared the editors' position, but had personal conflicts with González Pacheco, who ended up leaving the paper.

36 Serge Salain, "Teoría y práctica del lenguaje anarquista o la imposible redención por el verbo," in *El Anarquismo y sus tradiciones culturales,* ed. Pere Joan i Tous and Manfred Tietz (Madrid: Vervuert-Iberoamericana, 1995), 328.

37 Ibid., 329.

38 *The Rebel,* December 21, 1899.

39 *The Libertarian,* March 7, 1911 and April 1, 1911.

40 Lily Litvak, *Musa Libertaria. Arte, literatura y vida cultural del anarquismo español* (1880–1913) (Barcelona: Antoni Bosch Editor, 1981), 54–55.

41 *The Rebel,* July 17, 1902.

42 *The Rebel,* December 21, 1899.

43 The Libertarian, March 7, 1911.

44 *The Rebel,* December 21, 1899.

45 *Gleam,* September 28, 1906.

46 Translator's note: Sante Geronimo Caserio (1873–1894) was an Italian anarchist who assassinated French president Marie François Sadi Carnot. Ravachol (1859–1892), whose real name was François Claudius Koenigstein, was a French anarcho-terrorist.

47 Litvak, *Musa Libertaria,* 266.

48 Bettini, Bibliografía dell'anarchismo, 3, 11, 12.

49 *La Protesta Humana,* November 30, 1901.

50   *La Protesta Humana*, June 13, 1897.

51   *La Protesta Humana*, January 21, 1900.

52   I selected these titles randomly among many other, similar ones in issues of *The Rebel, La Protesta, Gleam,* and *The Battle* published between 1900 and 1910.

53   *The Rebel*, January 8, 1899. The Spanish libertarian press used the same propagandistic strategy. See Litvak, *Musa Libertaria*, 194.

54   *La Protesta*, April 1, 1904.

55   *The Rebel*, October 13, 1901.

56   *La Protesta*, April 2, 1904.

57   Juan Suriano, *La huelga de inquilinos de 1907* (Buenos Aires: CEAL, 1984).

58   Alejandro Sux's Sunday columns in *La Protesta* ("My Sundays" or "Sunday Reports") offer a good example of articles resembling folklore loaded with social contrasts (good versus bad, rich versus poor, etc.).

59   Of course, this type of denunciation did not always go smoothly. In 1899, a *La Protesta Humana* writer named Alfonso Pizzi, relying on information from a washerwoman, accused Temperley's Justice of the Peace of mistreating and not paying monies due to an employee. The offical charged Pizzi with slander and injury, compelling him to retract his claims in the absence of proof. See *La Protesta Humana*, November 12 and 26, 1899.

60   See, for example, *The Battle,* March 7 to April 2, 1910.

61   Diego Armus, *"An Autonomous Anarchist Subculture? The Anarchist Press in Argentina"* (paper presented at Eleventh Latin American Labor History Conference, Duke University, April, 1994).

62   The data is from issues of *La Protesta Humana, The Rebel,* and *The Future* published in 1901 and 1902.

63   *La Protesta,* April 7, 1907.

64   *La Protesta*, June 20, 1906.

65   *La Protesta,* August 19, 1908.

66   *New Route*, April 14, 1906.

67   *The Rebel*, June 10, 1900.

68   Abad de Santillán, *"La Protesta,"* 51.

69   *The Rebel,* March 3, 1901.

70   *La Protesta*, November 10, 1908.

71   Abad de Santillán, *"La Protesta,"* 49.

72   *La Protesta*, October 5 and 21, 1904.

73   *The Battle*, March 16, 1910. On the newspaper sellers' union, see Bilbao, *Buenos Aires*, 456–57.

74   I have uncovered ninety specifically anarchist publications in the city of Buenos Aires between 1879 and 1912, although the real sum was probably greater given that not all were preserved.

75   *The Rebel*, October 26, 1899. The newspaper made it clear that it relied on voluntary subscriptions. It ran the motto: "Appears when possible."

76   *La Protesta Humana*, October 10, 1900.

77   Manuel Tuñón de Lara, "Prensa e historia," in *Prensa obrera en Madrid,* ed. various authors (Madrid: ALFO 2-Cidur), 27.

78   *La Protesta*, December 7, 1904.

79   *La Protesta Humana*, February 9, 1901.

80   *La Protesta Humana*, February 9, 1901.

81   The balance sheet for March 1908 indicates that *La Protesta* paid: $887 for

typography; $540 to editing and proofing personnel; $180 for administrative personnel; $180 to dispatch personnel; $150 to a machinist; and $100 to a collector. This figure represented 65 percent of the publication's expenses and demonstrates the importance of salaries in the overall cost of the publication. See *La Protesta*, April 7, 1907.

82   *Gleam,* October 13, 1906.

83   *La Protesta Humana*, January 21, 1900.

84   *La Protesta*, December 26, 1904.

85   *La Protesta*, July 2, 1908.

86   *La Protesta*, February 13, 1904.

87   *La Protesta*, July 6, 1904.

88   Subscribers expressed their convictions and beliefs with their pseudonyms, sometimes humorously: "Broke foundry worker," "One who eats the higher-ups," "A chill," "A nephew of the Pope," etc. Others pointed to a predilection for violence: "One who sharpens the dagger and waits," "Long live the avenger's hand," and "One who donates to the vigilante," etc. Some referred to hatred for religion: "Death to priests," "Burn down the convents," "Let the Pope go to hell," "Destroyer of religion," etc. The most common bespoke shared certainties: "Viva anarchy," "Neither God nor country," and "Viva the social revolution," etc. Pseudonyms were furnished when subscriptions came from anonymous sympathizers in the public sphere: "An honest bourgeoisie," "A lady who likes the idea," "A storekeeper," etc. This information is from *The Rebel, The Future, La Protesta Humana,* and *La Protesta.*

89   *La Protesta*, February 20, 1904.

90   *La Protesta,* July 6, 1904.

91   *La Protesta*, December 6, 1904. Most libertarian publications published their balances regularly, but in global figures of income and expenditures.

92   In March 1907, the income for advertising reached 11 percent of the costs of publication. *La Protesta*, April 7, 1907.

93   *La Protesta,* April 1 and 8, 1904. Considering that the libertarian press as a whole was relatively late in incorporating advertising, it is surprising that the *Caserio* newspaper (1896), which was pro-individualist and supported terrorism, carried ads for Quilmes beer.

94   For example, *The Battle* was firmly committed to avoiding the habitual penuary of the libertarian press. Three of its eight pages were dedicated to advertising: the workers' clothing shops Casa Roveda, Cabezas, and Defensa Obrera took up an entire page; ads for Avanti cigars, Alpini cigarettes, Quilmes beer, and La Nacional vegetable oils were intermixed with the customary announcements from activists and sympathizers (for Bautista Fueyo's bookstore, The Modern School, etc.).

CHAPTER VI

1   Taken from Lilia Ana Bertoni, "Nacionalidad o cosmopolitismo. La cuestión de las escuelas de las colectividades extranjeras a fines del siglo XIX," *Anuario*, no. 11 (1996): 181.

2   On the many dimensions of libertarian education, see Félix García Moriyón, ed., *Escritos anarquistas sobre educación* (Madrid: Editorial Zero, 1986); Mikhail Bakunin, *La Instrucción Integral* (Barcelona: Pequeña Biblioteca Calamus Scriptorius, 1979); Maurice Dommanget, *Los grandes socialistas y la educación* (Madrid: Editorial Fragua, 1978); Gabriel Giroud, *Paul Robin: sa vie, ses idées, son action* (Paris: Mignolet

y Stoy, 1937); Tina Tomassi, *Breviario del pensamiento educativo libertario* (Cali, Colombia: Ediciones Madre Tierra, 1988); George Woodcock, *El anarquismo* (Barcelona: Ariel, 1979).

3   Andrés Girard, *Educación y autoridad paternal* (Buenos Aires, 1898). The Los Acratas group translated and published this pamphlet by the French educator. It also sponsored the first (and failed) attempt to start a libertarian school.

4   *The Battle*, March 29, 1910.

5   *La Protesta*, November 5, 1904.

6   Bertoni argues correctly that the constitution of the national educational system began in the 1880s, although it deepened in the following decade due to the polemic with foreign schools and truly ended up taking shape during the first years of the century. What was novel during the latter stage was the patriotic fervor linked to border disputes, which had not existed previously, and that climaxed during the Centenary festivities. See Bertoni, "Nacionalidad o cosmopolitismo."

7   Juan Suriano, ed., *La cuestión social en Argentina, 1870–1943* (Buenos Aires: La Colmena, 2000).

8   Translator's note: Buenos Aires declared its independence from Spain on May 25, 1810; the country as a whole declared indepence on July 9, 1816.

9   Proyecto Sobre Saludo a la Bandera, en La Escuela y el Patriotismo: Documentos de las iniciativas por las cuales se estableció que la enseñanza en las escuelas públicas se impartiera al amparo de la bandera nacional y saludo a la bandera, Buenos Aires, 1930, Expediente no. 4.588, Consejo Escolar 4to, año 1908, 18.

10   See Carlos Escudé, *El fracaso del proyecto argentino. Educación e ideología* (Buenos Aires: Editorial Tesis, 1990), 1–61; also, Juan Carlos Tedesco, *Educación y Sociedad en la Argentina (1880–1900)* (Buenos Aires: Ediciones Pannedille, 1970). On the origins of this process, see Lilia Ana Bertoni, "Construir la nacionalidad: héroes, estatuas y fiestas patrias, 1887–1891," *Boletín del Instituto de Historia Argentina y Americana Dr. Emilio Ravigna*ni, no. 5 (1992).

11   Tulio Halperín Donghi, *El espejo de la historia* (Buenos Aires: Sudamericana, 1987), 112. On Ramos Mejía's ideology: Oscar Terán, *Positivismo y Nación en la Argentina* (Buenos Aires: Puntosur, 1987).

12   On social control and reproduction, see Pierre Bourdieu, *La Reproducción. Elementos para una teoría de la enseñanza* (Barcelona: Laia, 1977) and Pierre Vilar, "Enseñanza primaria y cultura de los sectores populares en Francia durante la III República," in *Niveles de cultura y grupos sociales*, ed. J. Bergeron (Madrid: Siglo XXI, 1977).

13   *La Protesta*, July 6, 1906.

14   *La Protesta*, March 1, 1910.

15   On this topic, one can consult: *Cincuentenario de la ley 1420*, volume II, "Memoria sobre el desarrollo de las escuelas primarias desde 1884 a 1934" (Buenos Aires: Consejo Nacional de Educación, 1938).

16   *La Protesta,* July 6, 1906.

17   Bakunin, La Instrucción Integral, 57.

18   For the ideas of the Catalan educator, see Francisco Ferrer y Guardia, *La Escuela Moderna* (Madrid: Ediciones Júcar, 1976). On Ferrer's work, see Buenaventura Delgado, *La Escuela Moderna de Ferrer i Guardia* (Barcelona: CEAC, 1979); M. Dommanget, *Los grandes socialistas y la educación*; Pere Sola, *Las escuelas racionalistas en Cataluña, 1909–1939* (Barcelona: Tusquets, 1979); Tina Tomassi, *Breviario del pensamiento educativo libertario*. On rationalism in Argentina, see Barrancos, *Anarquismo, educación y costumbres*.

19 *La Protesta Humana*, July 27, 1901.
20 Esteban Almada, "Pan y Letras," *Luz y Vida*, no. 4, July 20, 1908, 25–26.
21 Eduardo Gilimón, "La Escuela Moderna," *La Protesta*, October 1, 1908.
22 Ibid.
23 Ricardo Mella, "El problema de la enseñanza" in Various Authors, *Escritos sobre educación* (Madrid: Zero, 1986), 85–103. Mella's work contains articles that he wrote for Gijón's *La Acción Libertaria* between 1910 and 1912 summarizing ideas on rational education that he had developed in lectures he gave during the first decade of the century.
24 *La Protesta Humana* said that the congress "also voted to start free schools," whereas the *La Organización* and *El Obrero* newspapers said "it was resolved to create practical-theoretical schools." This discrepancy was noted by Oved, *El anarquismo*, 169.
25 Edgardo Bilsky, *La FORA y el movimiento obrero (1900–1910)* vol. 2 (Buenos Aires: CEAL, 1985), 203.
26 The congress resolutions have been taken from Bilsky, *La FORA*, 208, 212, 218.
27 *La Protesta Humana*, February 13, 1898.
28 On Molina y Vedia's educational effort, see *La Protesta Humana*, February 13 and 20, 1898 and March 6, 1898.
29 *The Rebel*, May 19, 1901.
30 Ibid.
31 It then reported the balance of the last *velada* held to benefit the institution, indicating the meager results obtained:

Table 3: Balance of the party held on March 16, 1901 by the Los Corrales group to benefit the libertarian school:

INCOME		EXPENDITURES		BALANCE
113 Entrance tickets	$113	Room	$80.00	
Flowers	$11.65	Music	$43.00	
Raffle	$20.90	Flowers	$8.30	
Donation	$0.63	Tranway	$7.85	
Surplus	$18.05			
TOTAL	**$147.03**		**$139.35**	**$7.68**

Source: *The Rebel*, March 24, 1901.

32 *La Protesta Humana*, November 9, 1901.
33 *La Protesta Humana*, July 27, 1901.
34 Elam Ravel, "Pro Causa," *The Rebel*, July 27, 1901. The article continues in the same paper on August 17, 1901.
35 Ibid. Coinciding with *The Rebel*'s defense of alternative education, *La Protesta Humana* published several articles in the same vein. See for example Halma Dejah, "Por la instrucción," *La Protesta Humana*, August 10, 1901.
36 Antonio Pellicer Paraire, "Los Círculos de Estudios Sociales y las escuelas libertarias," *La Protesta Humana*, January 7, 1900.
37 The preceding information was taken from *La Prensa*, June 23, 1902, June 27, 1902, March 26, 1904 and November 5, 1904; *La Protesta Humana,* June 14, 1902, June 28, 1902, August 9, 1902, July 25, 1903, and August 22, 1903; *La Protesta*, December 31, 1904.
38 For the list of deportees, see Oved, *El anarquismo*, 272–277.

39　*La Protesta Humana*, July 25, 1903 and August 22, 1903.

40　*La Protesta*, June 27, 1905.

41　*La Protesta*, May 8, 1906.

42　*La Protesta*, October 4, 1905.

43　*La Protesta*, October 7, 1905.

44　His encounter with Latin American educational issues led Julio Barcos to participate in the revolutionary movement against Tinoco in Costa Rica and the drafting of public education legislation in El Salvador. Close to the group of heterodox intellectuals linked to Ghiraldo (he, Barcos, and Maturana created the publishing business, Luz del Día) and put off by doctrinal generalizations, he always operated with a degree of independence from anarchism, which generated more than a few problems with the doctrinal purists and anarcho-syndicalists. In any case, due to his own ideological evolution and knowledge of the official educational system, he came to conclude that he should do battle from within the state educational apparatus, which is why he left the anarchist movement around 1920 and joined the Yrigoyenist Radicals, even becoming a functionary of the National Education Council. From then on, he played a distinguished role in the educational arena within the "framework of the system," as his ex-comrades put it critically. He authored numerous works, among which the following stand out: *Cómo educa el Estado a su hijo*, *La felicidad del pueblo es la suprema ley*, and *La libertad sexual de las mujeres*. He also co-edited the pan-American magazine *Quasimodo* in Buenos Aires and edited the *El auto argentino* magazine for twenty-five years. He died in Buenos Aires in 1960.

45　*La Protesta*, May 19, 1906.

46　See *La Protesta*, June 17, 1906, August 2 and 31, 1906.

47　*La Protesta*, October 4, 1906.

48　Ibid.

49　See *La Protesta*, April 5, 1908.

50　*La Protesta*, April 5, 1908.

51　*La Protesta*, March 1, 1907.

52　See *La Protesta*, February 27, 1907.

53　*La Protesta*, July 16, 1907.

54　Ibid.

55　*La Protesta*, July 14, 1908.

56　*La Protesta*, March 29, 1908.

57　*La Protesta*, November 17, 1908 and July 12, 1909.

58　*La Protesta*, October 1, 1908.

59　*La Protesta*, March 1, 1910. There are many examples of ad hoc, volunteer teachers. For instance, in 1907, one Octavio Tonietti gave a night course in the Cart Drivers building to thirty-four enrollees. Three months later the class had to be suspended because all of the students had fled. He complained of a lack of support, but a writer from *La Protesta* (Lorenzo Mario) categorically dismissed his claims, citing his limited intellectual capacities and total inability to speak Spanish.

60　Félix Nieves, "A propósito de las Escuelas Modernas de Buenos Aires," *La Protesta*, January 23, 1910.

61　Comunicado de la Comisión Administrativa de la Escuela Moderna: "Una cuestión de conciencia. Lo que no se puede callar," *La Protesta*, May 18, 1909.

62　*Ideas and Figures*, no. 23, January 11, 1910.

63　*The Battle*, March 24, 1910.

64　See Barrancos, *Anarquismo, educación y costumbres*, 134–148.

65 "Bases y Fines de la Liga de Educación Racionalista," *The Modern School,* no. 3, December 1, 1912, 1.

66 The League's trajectory is beyond the scope of this work, but the breadth of its activity was remarkable (lectures, talks, classes, participation in educational conferences, etc.), even if it did not manage to open a school until 1916. I have taken information about the League's activity from *The Modern School,* no. 1–16, and the *Boletín de la Liga de Educación Racionalista,* no. 1–6, corresponding to the 1912–1915 period. For a meticulous account of rationalist activity, see Barrancos, *Anarquismo, educación y costumbres,* 134–148; 217–236.

67 Mercedes Gauna, an active and effective contributor and member of the Advisory Council of *The Modern School,* published a passionate critique of coeducation in the magazine, after which its editors felt compelled to register their disagreement with her. Mercedes Gauna, "Moral y educación sexual," *The Modern School,* no. 13, November 15, 1913. Months later, there was a report stating that a "notable contributor" had departed due to differences over coeducation. Ibid, no. 16, March 15, 1914, 23.

68 *The Modern School,* no. 12, October 15, 1913.

69 J. Erlijman, "La educación racionalista y la lucha por la libertad," *Boletín de la Liga de Educación Racionalista,* no. 6, May 1915.

70 Ibid.

71 Heriberto Staffa, "La Vanguardia y la Liga," *The Modern School,* no. 13, March 15, 1913.

72 *La Protesta,* January 14, 1915 and Boletín de la Liga de Educación Racionalista, No 3, January 25, 1915.

73 *The Modern School,* no. 16, March 15, 1914.

74 This contains seven notes published by *La Protesta* on the days of December 16, 17, 18, 19, 20, 21, and 23, 1913.

75 Julio Barcos, "Plan de una Escuela Integral," *La Protesta,* August 21, 1913.

76 It is interesting to note that the National Educational Council's publication (*El Monitor de la Educación Común*) did not discuss libertarian schools. It was preoccupied by the presence of anarchism in society as a whole, but not anarchist pedagogy. When closures occurred, it was due to schools' failure to satisfy structural norms, not ideological issues. Closures during periods of martial law were justified by the global political context, not educational activities per se.

77 This affirmation contradicts Dora Barrancos's essentially unsupported claim that anarchist labor and educational fronts worked together closely. See Barrancos, *Anarquismo, educación y costumbres,* 87.

CHAPTER VII

1 Political representation is "an institutionalized system of political responsibility, realized through the free electoral designation of fundamental political organisms (generally parliaments)," in Norberto Bobbio, Nicola Matteucci, and Gianfranco Pasquino, *Diccionario de política* (Mexico: Siglo XXI, 1983), 1389. See also Hanna Pitkin, *The Concept of Representation* (Berkeley: University of California, 1967).

2 Juan Suriano, "La oposición anarquista a la intervención estatal en las relaciones laborales," in *La cuestión social en Argentina, 1870–1943,* ed. Juan Suriano (Buenos Aires: La Colmena, 2000).

3 Leopoldo Bonafulla, "Anatema," *La Protesta Humana,* February 9, 1901.

4   Eduardo Gilimón, *Para los que no son anarquistas* (Buenos Aires: Ediciones Libre Iniciativa, 1920), 5.

5   *The Rebel*, August 14, 1899.

6   Ibid.

7   *The Rebel*, July 14, 1901.

8   "Los anarquistas y el Estado," *La Protesta*, June 30, 1906.

9   *La Protesta*, September 5, 1909.

10 *The Rebel*, October 8, 1899.

11 Rafael Barrett, *Escritos de Barrett* (Buenos Aires: Proyección, 1971), 65.

12 *The Rebel*, June 22, 1901.

13 Félix Basterra, *Sobre Ciencia Social*, 10.

14 Alberto Castro and C. García Balsas, *Crítica al proyecto González* (Montevideo and Buenos Aires: Ediciones del Grupo Aurora, 1904), 31.

15 "Fundamentos del ideal anarquista," *La Protesta*, December 31, 1913.

16 *Gleam*, no. 14, December 12, 1906.

17 Castro and García Balsas, *Crítica al proyecto González*, 13.

18 Ibid., 33.

19 Ibid., 7.

20 See *La Protesta*, October 2 and 4, 1904.

21 *La Protesta*, February 16, 1906.

22 Juan Suriano, Trabajadores, anarquismo y Estado represor: de la Ley de Residencia a la de Defensa Social (1902–1910) (Buenos Aires: CEAL, 1988).

23 "Resoluciones del Primer Congreso de la Federación Obrera Argentina," in Edgardo Bilsky, *La FORA y el movimiento obrero (1900–1910)* vol. 2 (Buenos Aires: CEAL, 1985), 192.

24 *La Protesta*, May 15, 1904. The author refers to the defeated National Labor Law.

25 *La Protesta*, June 21, 1906.

26 Francisco Jaquet, "El proyecto de ley de trabajo," *La Protesta*, May 31, 1904.

27 Rafael Barrett, *Escritos de Barrett*, 74.

28 See Eric Hobsbawm, *Naciones y nacionalismo desde 1780* (Barcelona: Crítica, 1991), 111–140 [*Nations and nationalism since 1780: programme, myth, reality* (Cambridge: Cambridge University Press, 1992).

29 *La Protesta Humana*, January 7, 1900.

30 *La Protesta*, May 24, 1906 and Augustin Hamon, *De la patria* (Buenos Aires: Biblioteca Germen, 1907).

31 *La Protesta Humana*, January 7, 1900.

32 Hamon, *De la patria*, 14.

33 Pedro Gori, "Sin Patria," in *Ideas and Figures*, no. 46, March 20, 1911. This antipatriotic work premiered in Buenos Aires in 1899 and was featured regularly at anarchist *veladas*. It was performed in Italian for years; *Ideas and Figures* only printed a Spanish version in 1911.

34 *El Cuartel*, no. 3, May, 1909.

35 Ibid.

36 *El Cuartel*, no. 1, March, 1909.

37 *La Protesta*, May 24, 1906.

38 *La Protesta Humana* discussed local militarism, in the context of Argentina's conflict with Chile, on March 18, April 1, May 1, and October 9, 1898; also on October 1 and December 24, 1899.

39 See Darío Cantón, "Notas sobre las Fuerzas Armadas argentinas," in *Los fragmentos*

del poder, ed. Torcuato S. Di Tella, and Tulio Halperín Donghi (Buenos Aires: Editorial Jorge Alvarez, 1969); Alain Rouquié, *Poder militar y sociedad política en la Argentina* (Buenos Aires: Emecé, 1981). On the early years of patriotic education in public schools and its links to militarism, see Lilia Ana Bertoni, "Construir la nacionalidad: héroes, estatuas y fiestas patrias, 1887–1991" in *Boletín*, No. 5, Instituto de Historia Argentina y Americana, Dr. Emilio Ravignani (1992).

40   *La Protesta Humana*, October 25, 1902.

41   *Gleam*, no. 2, March 25, 1906.

42   *Gleam*, no. 6, June 12, 1906.

43   Edgardo Bilsky, *La FORA*, volume 2, 219.

44   *Soldier's Enlightenment*, no. 5, February 1, 1908.

45   For example, in 1908, it helped form an anti-militarist center in La Plata. See *Soldier's Enlightenment*, no. 5, February 1908.

46   It is not clear exactly when it ceased publication. The last issue held by Amsterdam's Institute for Social History bears the date September 1913.

47   See *Gleam*, no. 2, March 25, 1906; no. 6, June 12, 1906; no. 8, July 26, 1906; no. 12, October 13, 1906; no. 13, November 11, 1906 and no. 14, November 12, 1906.

48   *Soldier's Enlightenment*, no. 5, February 1, 1908.

49   The print run data comes from the "Balance" section. For instance, see *Soldier's Enlightenment*, no. 48, February 1910, which records a print run of 4,000. The newspaper published 2,000 copies when it reappeared a year after the Centenary repression. See ibid., February 15, 1911.

50   *El Cuartel*, no. 3, May, 1909.

51   G. Inglán, "La mentira de la democracia," *La Protesta Humana*, May 25, 1901.

52   Ibid.

53   *The Rebel*, October 24, 1902

54   *The Rebel*, July 27, 1901.

55   The anarchist vision of life without government rested on the idea of natural order, "because everything is anarchic in nature" and human beings are born equal: "We are all born anarchists. We have the same origins." Individuals have equal rights and duties, but, as life unfolds in bourgeois society, inequalities are imposed that disrupt and deform the natural order." See José Mas Gomeri, "La Anarquía," *The Rebel*, May 31, 1902.

56   I rely on Agnes Heller's definition: "Political activity *sensu stricto* is always directed to power," that is, to preserving or obtaining power. Agnes Heller, *Sociología de la vida cotidiana* (Barcelona: Península, 1977), 172.

57   *The Future*, October 25, 1896.

58   Rodolfo González Pacheco, *Carteles* (Buenos Aires: Américalee, 1956), 72.

59   *La Protesta*, March 10, 1906.

60   Errico Malatesta, "Candidaturas anarquistas," London, March 30, 1900. Published in *La Protesta Humana,* July 8, 1900.

61   The debate took place throughout 1897 in the *Il Messagero*, *Avanti*, and *L'Agitazione* newspapers. See Malatesta-Merlino-Bonano, *Anarquismo y elecciones* (Barcelona: Colección A, undated).

62   *The Rebel*, April 22, 1900.

63   Osvaldo Saavedra, "Caricaturas políticas," *Martín Fierro*, no. 7, April 14, 1904.

64   Bakunin argued that "universal suffrage … is the surest way to get the masses to build their own prison," in Mikhail Bakunin, *La Libertad* (Buenos Aires: Ediciones

del Mediodía, 1968), 165. In an opposing perspective, Engels asserted that "preaching apoliticism to the workers is to toss them into the arms of bourgeois politics," in Carlos Marx and Friedrich Engels, *Obras Fundamentales* (Mexico: Fondo de Cultura Económica, 1989), 125.

65 Eduardo Gilimón, "La acción política y la emancipación del proletariado," *La Protesta Humana*, January 23, 1898.

66 *The Future*, April 24, 1898.

67 *La Protesta*, September 3, 1905. This conclusion, though exaggerated, made sense. Interior Minister Joaquín V. González himself had enthusiastically welcomed Palacios's arrival to the parliament: "How lucky we are," he said, "to see his first steps on the terrain of legality and constitutional order." Minister González's speech in the Chamber of Deputies, May 11, 1904, in Juan Suriano, "El Estado argentino frente a los trabajadores urbanos: política social y represión, 1880–1916," *Anuario*, (1989–1990): 119. [Translator's note: Alfredo Lorenzo Palacios (1880–1965) was the first Socialist to be elected as a deputy in the Argentine Congress.]

68 For the Spanish case, see Paul Heywood, "El movimiento obrero en España antes de 1914," in *Movimientos obreros y socialistas en Europa antes de 1914*, ed. Dick Geary (Madrid: Ministerio de Trabajo y Seguridad Social, 1992), 327–372. On Italy, see "Socialismo y clases trabajadoras en Italia antes de 1914" in Ibid, 259–326.

69 *La Protesta*, March 3, 1906.

70 Enrique Dickmann, *Recuerdos*, 102.

71 Natalio Botana, El orden conservador. La política argentina entre 1880 y 1916 (Buenos Aires: Sudamericana, 1985), 191.

72 Although the proportion of voters was negligible, the majority were workers, as has been demonstrated recently for the 1850–1880 period. See Hilda Sábato, "Ciudadanía, participación política y la formación de una esfera pública en Buenos Aires, 1850–1880," *Entrepasados*, no. 6 (1994): 68–69.

73 *La Protesta,* March 10, 1906.

74 E. Almda, "A los trabajadores," *La Protesta*, March 9, 1906.

75 *The Rebel*, April 1, 1900.

76 In 1906, the quantity of votes cast in the Federal Capital was 31,957. The number fell to 24,732 in 1910. See Natalio Botana, *El orden conservador*, 191.

77 *La Protesta*, March 8, 1908.

78 *La Protesta*, March 15, 1910.

79 For an analysis of the role of violence in anarchism, see Rafael Nuñez Florencio, *El terrorismo anarquista, 1888–1909* (Madrid: Siglo XXI, 1983).

80 In the 1890s, anarcho-terrorist bombings and assassinations in Europe and the United States cost the life of Italy's King Humberto; Austria's Empress Isabel; French President Sadi Carnot; United States William President McKinley, and Spain's Minister Cánovas. Assessing the impact of these acts, Hobsbawm convincingly argues that they did not alter the course of political democratization timidly initiated during the period, because the European bourgeoisie was more concerned with mass movements than acts of terror. Eric Hobsbawm, *La Era del Imperio (1875–1915)* (Barcelona: Crítica, 1992), 101. On the repercussions of the bombings and assassinations in Argentina, see Oved, *El anarquismo*, 110–116 and 192–196.

81 Lombroso saw the anarchist as a born delinquent whose principal characteristic was fanaticism and violent, anti-social behavior. See Cesare Lombroso, "Los anarquistas," in *Los Anarquistas*, ed. C. Lombroso and R. Mella (Barcelona: Jucar, 1977). On the link between positivism, criminology, and anarchism, see Patricio Geli, "Los

anarquistas en el gabinete antropométrico. Anarquismo y criminología en la sociedad argentina del 900," *Entrepasados*, year II, no. 2 (1992): 7–24. The influence of positivist criminology on ruling groups is analyzed in chapter six and seven of Eduardo Zimmermann, *Los liberales reformistas. La cuestión social en la Argentina, 1890–1916* (Buenos Aires: Sudamericana-Universidad de San Andrés, 1995).

82 *La Autonomía Individual*, no. 2, August 1, 1897.

83 Ibid.

84 *La Autonomía Individual*, no. 2, August 1, 1897.

85 *Gleam*, no. 6, June 12, 1906.

86 *Gleam*, no. 8, July 26, 1906.

87 Alejandro Escobar y Carballo, "Elocuencia del atentado," *The Rebel*, January 8, 1899.

88 Félix Basterra, "Gaetano Bresci," in *1900 Illustrated Almanac of The Social Question* (Buenos Aires: Librería Sociológica, 1900), 30.

89 *The Rebel*, August 26, 1900.

90 *La Protesta*, January 20, 1910. Firing Colonel Falcón from the police was one of anarchists' unsatisfied demands for ending the long strike in May 1909.

91 *La Protesta Humana*, October 31, 1903 and *La Protesta*, January 10, 1908. They also commonly defended tyrannicide from a point of view that celebrated heroic, individual action, "noting in such acts the heroism of the deed with which the fanatics of freedom—a glorious fanaticism—know how to respond in liberty's name to those who barbarously mock the people." This is how Julio Barcos spoke of the attack that took the life of Czar Alexander II. In his view, such acts enlightened the soul of the oppressed. And individual action was an effective stand-in for collective struggle, whose erruption was delayed due to the people's ignorance. Though "small is the army of terrorism … it takes only one of those fascinating Lucifers of rebellion to make the heart of the omnipotent monarchy shudder with fright." See Julio Barcos, "La cabeza del terrorista," *La Protesta*, June 1, 1909 and June 13, 1909.

92 See *La Protesta*, June 28, 1904 and August 6, 1904.

93 Errico Malatesta, *Anarquismo y anarquía* (Buenos Aires: Tupac Ediciones, 1988), 35–51.

94 *La Protesta Humana*, September 14, 1901.

95 *The Rebel*, May 31, 1902.

96 Pascual Guaglianone, "La huelga general" in *Vida Nueva*, no. 2, November 22, 1903.

97 At the begining of the industrial revolution, William Bembow and, later, Robert Owen promoted the general strike, which Chartists called "the holy month." At the end of the nineteenth century, North American syndicalists used the general strike to win the eight-hour working day. In France, anarchists as well as revolutionary syndicalists turned to the tactic in 1885. On the general strike and the disputes provoked by its adoption, see Hubert Lagardelle (editor), *Huelga general y socialismo* (Buenos Aires: Cuadernos de Pasado y Presente, 1975). Also Edward Shorter and Charles Tilly, *Las huelgas en Francia, 1830–1968* (Madrid: Ministerio de Trabajo y Seguridad Social, 1985) and Colin Crouch and Alessandro Pizzorno, *Conflitti in Europa* (Milan: Etas Libri, 1977).

98 *La Protesta Humana*, September 14, 1901.

99 *La Protesta Humana*, November 9, 1901.

100 Taking issue with the "right to work" slogan used in France during the revolution of 1848, Kropotkin emphasized workers' right to well-being: "They claim the right to

possess the wealth of the community—to take the houses to dwell in, according to the needs of each family; to seize the stores of food and learn the meaning of plenty, after having known famine too well. They proclaim their right to all wealth—fruit of the labour of past and present generations—and learn by its means to enjoy those higher pleasures of art and science too long monopolized by the middle classes." Peter Kropotkin, "Lo que entendemos por revolución," *The Rebel*, November 11, 1898 and November 27, 1898.

101 *La Protesta Humana*, October 19, 1901.

102 El Caballero del desierto, Declaración de guerra al orden o la acción anarquista en la República argentina (Buenos Aires, 1906), 7.

103 Heller, *Sociología de la vida cotidiana*, 173.

104 *La Protesta*, October 1, 1907.

105 *La Protesta*, October 16, 1907.

106 *La Protesta*, October 20, 1907.

107 *The Libertarian*, no. 7, April 1, 1911.

108 See Aníbal Vighera, "Participación electoral y prácticas políticas de los sectores populares en Buenos Aires, 1912–1922," *Entrepasados*, no. 1 (1991).

109 Teodoro Antilli, "Hacia una acción práctica," *La Protesta*, August 7, 1913.

110 *La Protesta*, August 14, 1913.

111 Ibid.

112 Translator's note: "Kraussism" refers to the ideas of German philosopher Karl Christian Friedrich Krause, whose supporters were politically and intellectually influential in Argentina for a time. See, O. Carlos Stoetzer, "Krausean Philosophy as a Major Political and Social Force in the Modern Argentina and Guatemala" in *Bridging the Atlantic: toward a reassessment of Iberian and Latin American Cultural Ties*, ed. Marina Pérez de Mendiola (Albany, NY: State University of New York Press, 1996), 99.

113 Alberto Ghiraldo, *Crónicas Argentinas. Balance social de un pueblo* (Buenos Aires: Malena, 1912), 170–171.

114 Batlle y Ordóñez governed Uruguay between 1903 and 1907 and again between 1911 and 1915; in the interim, Claudio Williman, his first minister of government, served as president. Williman was much more conservative and distanced himself from the labor movement, although he continued state reforms, creating the Labor Office in 1908. On *batllismo*, see Benjamín Nahdn, *La época batllista, 1905–1929* (Montevideo: Edición de la Banda Oriental, 1993).

115 For many libertarian militants, the Río de la Plata area was a region of its own and their activity alternated between one country and the other.

116 *The Libertarian*, no. 9, March 17, 1911.

117 The case of Francisco Corney was different. Once a distinguished FORA leader, he emigrated to Montevideo toward the end of the first Batlle government, where he would play an important role in Uruguay's Regional Workers' Federation. He ultimately left the anarchist movement and joined the Colorado Party, serving as an "informant" for Montevideo's Chief of Police between 1915 and 1919, to whom he provided information on the workers' movement on both shores. See Universindo Rodríguez Díaz, *Los sectores populares en el Uruguay del novecientos* (Montevideo: Editorial Compañero, 1989), 17.

118 The anarchist press was still under the censorship imposed during the Centenary in early 1912 and, as a result, there is little information on this interesting process. Mention of it can be found in Abad de Santillán, "*La Protesta*," 60.

119 Santiago Locascio, "La tradición revolucionaria," *Seed*, Revista Quincenal Ilustrada, Buenos Aires, year VI, no. 10, November 30, 1911.

120 Santiago Locascio, *Maximalismo y Anarquismo* (Buenos Aires: Vicente Bellusci Editor, 1919), 3.

121 Abad de Santillán, "*La Protesta*," 59.

CHAPTER VIII

1 Bronislaw Baczko, *Los imaginarios sociales. Memorias y esperanzas colectivas* (Buenos Aires: Nueva Visión, 1991), 44.

2 Eric Hobsbawm, "Come si inventa una tradizione," in *L'invenzione della tradizione*, ed. Eric Hobsbawm and T. Ranger (Torino: Giulio Einaudi editore, 1984), 3–4. See also chapter seven by Hobsbawm in the same work: "Tradizioni e genesi dell'identitá di massa in Europa, 1870–1914."

3 See Oscar Cornblit, "Inmigrantes y empresarios en la política argentina," in *Los fragmentos del poder*, ed. T. S. Di Tella and T. Halperín Donghi (Buenos Aires: Jorge Alvarez, 1969), 402–405.

4 Joaquín V. González, *El juicio del siglo* (Buenos Aires: CEAL, 1979), 150.

5 *Martín Fierro*, no. 1, March 13, 1904.

6 Journalists' accounts of anarchists' May Day rallies in Buenos Aires and Rosario and their mobilizations during general strikes offer excellent insights into their use of rites and symbols. See, for example, *La Nación*, May 2 & 3, 1904; May 22 & 23, 1905; May 2 to 9, 1909.

7 Comments on the orderliness of Socialist rallies and demonstrations are abundant. For example, see *La Nación*, May 3, 1909 and *La Prensa,* May 2, 1909.

8 Enrique Dickmann, *Recuerdos*, 93.

9 *La Prensa*, May 2, 1909.

10 Another even more aggressive image circulated in Argentina in the 1890s. In the context of the anarchist bombings and assassinations in Europe, it influenced dominant groups and encouraged their highly negative view of anarchism. In its introductory editorial, a libertarian newspaper not coincidentally named *Caserio*— in homage to the man who assassinated the French president Carnot—argued: "We break the law; we are delinquents, criminals; we have no God, fatherland, or flag; for us, the family doesn't exist; we are eternal outlaws, the exiled of the Earth" in *Caserio*, February 14, 1896.

11 See Miguel Cané, *Proyecto de ley de residencia* (manuscrito), AGN, Sala VII, Archivo Cané, Legajo NO. 6, 1899; Joaquín V. González, "Proyecto de Ley Nacional de Trabajo," *Diario de Sesiones,* Cámara de Diputados, Buenos Aires, 1904, volume I, 76; Ernesto Quesada, "La cuestión obrera y su estudio universitario," *Boletín,* Departamento Nacional del Trabajo, No 1, 1907.

12 *Suplemento de La Protesta Humana,* March 18, 1899. The drawing by Marius, who was a frequent contributor to the paper, largely reproduced an image distributed since the times of the First International.

13 See Jan Bialostocki, *Estilo e iconografía. Contribución a una ciencia de las artes* (Barcelona: Barral Editores, 1973), 114. These images also refer directly to Delacoix's painting, "La libertad guiando al pueblo en las barricadas." See Donald Drew Egbert, *El Arte y la Izquierda en Europa. De la Revolución Francesa a May de 1968* (Barcelona: Editorial Gustavo Gili, 1981), 174.

14 See José E. Burucúa, Andrea Jáuregui, Laura Malosetti, and María Lía Munilla,

"Influencia de los tipos iconográficos de la Revolución Francesa en los países del Plata" in AA.VV., *Imagen y recepción de la revolución francesa en la Argentina* (Buenos Aires: Grupo Editor Latinoamericano, 1990). [Translator's note: "The May Revolution" refers to a series of events that occurred in Buenos Aires in 1810 that marked the beginning of the Argentine War of Independence.]

15   Adrián Patroni, *Los trabajadores en la Argentina* (Buenos Aires, 1907), 30. For creollism's influence on the workers, see Adolfo Prieto, *El discurso criollista en la formación de la Argentina moderna* (Buenos Aires: Sudamericana, 1988).

16   Cornelius Castoriadis, "La Institución imaginaria de la sociedad," in *El Imaginario Social*, ed. Eduardo Colombo (Montevideo-Buenos Aires: Tupac Ediciones, 1989), 39.

17   See Bialostocki, *Estilo e iconografía*, 160–161.

18   *La Protesta Humana*, May 1, 1898.

19   *Gleam*, no. 12, October 13, 1906.

20   See Juan-Eduardo Cirlot, *Diccionario de símbolos* (Colombia: Editorial Labor, 1994).

21   *La Nación,* May 2, 1904.

22   The emergence of the red flag as a symbol of social revolution "and later, of the working class was, it seems, absolutely spontaneous: from February 1848, when barricades appeared across the world, until the French strikes of 1871–1890, red, when it appeared, almost always did so spontaneously." Eric Hobsbawm, *El mundo del trabajo. Estudios históricos sobre la formación y evolución de la clase obrera* (Barcelona: Crítica, 1987), 107.

23   "A un símbolo," *Gleam,* no. 11, September 28, 1906.

24   This is a fragment of the poem "Mi Bandera" written by Juan B. Medina in Montevideo in 1907 and published by the "Almanaque de la revista Germen para 1908," Buenos Aires, 1908, in Jean Andreu, Maurice Fraysse, and Eva Golluscio de Montoya, *Anarkos. Literaturas Libertarias de América del Sur, 1900* (Buenos Aires: Corregidor, 1990), 188–189.

25   *La Nación,* May 2, 1904.

26   *La Protesta Humana,* May 13, 1900. 3. This was a common pattern during the first decade of the century. The description from *La Prensa* is to the point and surprisingly similar to that of *La Protesta*: "The red banners fluttered over the demonstrators' heads," in *La Prensa*, May 2, 1909.

27   *La Nación*, May 2, 1904.

28   See *La Protesta Humana*, May 5, 1901.

29   *La Nación*, May 22, 1905.

30   Cámara de Diputados, "Interpelación del diputado A. Palacios al Ministro del Interior Rafael Castillo," *Diario de Sesiones*, Buenos Aires, 1905, volume I, 358.

31   Police killed Cosme Budeslavich when they attacked striking workers at the Rosario Refinery. After a struggle with authorities, workers and their representatives managed to carry out his funeral. More than one thousand people marched in the entourage, which a group of seventy women led, including one who carried a red flag with a black band. Despite being encircled by an imposing array of security forces, the burial of the first casualty in the Argentine workers' movement occurred without incident.

32   *El Tiempo*, October 24, 1907.

33   The twenty-five-year-old worker, José Ocampo, had been born in Chaco and worked as a longshoreman at the Drysdale y Cía. yard located on Palos and Mendoza Streets

in the La Boca neighborhood.

34 As an example: "The Graphic Arts Federation invites workers to gather at 8:00 this morning in the eastern cemetery to pay homage to the late Ferruccio Zapallotti, who died, you will recall, on the port during the longshoremen's strike," in *La Nación*, May 1, 1904.

35 See Bialostocki, *Estilo e iconografía*, 115, 161.

36 *La Protesta*, May 3, 1904.

37 The desacralization of the figure of the king and the destruction of idols gave way to the cult of heroes and revolutionary martyrs. See Michel Vovelle, *La mentalidad revolucionaria* (Barcelona: Crítica, 1989) 132–140. Also: Maurice Agulhon, *Marianne au combat. L'imagerie et la simbolique republicaines de 1789* (Paris: Flammarion, 1979).

38 *La Protesta Humana*, November 2, 1901.

39 Utopian socialists also depicted labor in heroic terms, a motif embraced by realists and naturalists, whose art anarchists frequently turned to. On this topic, see Lily Litvak, *Musa Libertaria. Arte, literatura y vida cultural del anarquismo español (1880–1913)* (Barcelona: Antoni Bosch editor, 1981), 121.

40 *The Rebel*, March 18, 1899. The publishers dedicated this entire issue to commemorating the Paris Commune.

41 *The Rebel*, November 11, 1900.

42 *Gleam*, no. 5, May 24, 1906. A number of libertarian circles and centers organized events and rallies demanding that Planas be freed. An account of one such event that occurred in the Plaza Constitución in September 1907 is in *La Protesta*, September 10, 1907.

43 Litvak, *Musa Libertaria*, 174.

44 *La Protesta Humana*, February 4, 1900.

45 Pierre Ansart, "La ideología política," *El Imaginario Social*, ed. Colombo, 107.

46 *The Rebel*, November 11, 1901. Felipe Layda authored a similar piece called "Idols out" that appeared in *The Rebel*, July 14, 1901: "We just gave up a paganism that kept humanity in misery and barbarism for centuries when, by way of emancipation, we ourselves the emancipated, or, better, those who wish to be emancipated, created another paganism that, while not consisting precisely in putting a few mortals in a shrine, is close enough to that." This article was a response to (false) reports of the construction of a monument in homage to Bakunin in Switzerland.

47 *Popular Almanac* by *The Social Question* from 1895 (Buenos Aires: Imprenta Elzeviriana, 1894), 3.

48 *La Vanguardia's Almanaque Socialista* circulated at the same time as the *Popular Almanac*, but celebrated Socialist instead of anarchist actions. See the *Almanaque Socialista* from *La Vanguardia* for 1900 (Buenos Aires: 1899).

49 For a history of May Day and its origins as a commemoration, see Maurice Dommanget, *Histoire du Premier Mai* (Paris: Société Universitaire d'Éditions, 1953); Andre Rossel, *Premier Mai. Quatre-vingt-dix ans de luttes populaires dans le monde* (Paris, 1977).

50 Hobsbawm, *El mundo del trabajo*, 109.

51 This also occurred among Spanish anarchists. See José Alvarez Junco, *La ideología política del anarquismo español (1868–1910)* (Madrid: Siglo XXI, 1976), 208–209.

52 *The Rebel*, February 25, 1900.

53 *La Protesta Humana*, May 1, 1899.

54 *La Protesta Humana*, November 10, 1900.

55 See *La Protesta Humana*, May 1, 1902 and May 1, 1903. Also, *L Avvenire*, November 10, 1900. [Translator's note: In fact, Louis Lingg committed suicide in his cell.]

56 *La Protesta Humana*, November 12, 1899.

57 Viguera made this point in his interesting work on the evolution of the meaning of May Day during the first half of the twentieth century. See Aníbal Viguera, "El 1º de Mayo en Buenos Aires, 1890–1950: evolución y usos de una tradición" in *Boletín*, Instituto de Historia Argentina y Americana Dr. Emilio Ravignani, no. 3, first half of 1991.

58 This memory is "essentially construed, [and] does not stop being an object of struggle and power." Michelle Perrot, "O primeiro Primeiro de Maio na Franca (1890): nascimento de un rito operaio," in *Os excluidos da historia*, ed. Michelle Perrot (Rio de Janeiro: Paz e Terra, 1988).

59 See Viguera, "El 1º de May en Buenos Aires." For the specific case of Peronism: Mariano Plotkin, *Mañana es San Perón* (Buenos Aires: Ariel, 1994), 75–140.

60 *Polémicas,* Buenos Aires, no. 6, May, 1928.

61 *New Route,* May 1, 1906.

62 *The Rebel,* May 10, 1902.

63 *La Protesta Humana,* May 1, 1903.

64 *La Protesta,* April 17, 1904.

65 *La Protesta Humana,* May 1, 1902.

66 Viguera, "El 1º de Mayo en Buenos Aires," 61.

67 *La Protesta Humana,* May 1, 1902.

68 *La Nación,* May 3, 1904.

69 *Memoria de la policía de Buenos Aires,* 1900–1909 (Buenos Aires, 1909), 258, 259, and 267.

70 In his memoirs, Dickmann repeatedly mentions libertarian's predisposition for irrational violence and the irritation that this caused Socialists. See Dickmann, *Recuerdos,* 65–69, 76–80, and 91–94.

71 Before the 1903 May Day mobilization, an anarchist newspaper warned: "We suggest that comrades conduct themselves in a serious, dignified way throughout the march and do not compromise the true meaning of the May Day demonstration, which is a robust protest against the present social regime." *L Avvenire,* May 1, 1903.

72 For example, during the 1904 May Day rally "workers with firearms repelled the attack and their bullets also found their way to some of the security troops," in Diego Abad de Santillán, *La FORA. Ideología y trayectoria* (Buenos Aires: Proyección, 1976) 43. On the same incident, a witness comments: "The workers guarded the body, revolver in hand," in Gilimón, *Hechos y Comentarios*, 43. The Police Chief affirmed these assessments. While speaking of the events during May Day, 1909, he argued that, from a column of demonstrators, "revolver shots came from different areas, while the bulk of the column imitated the example," in *Memoria*, 259. It was fairly common to possess firearms at that time and it seems to have been an accepted practice among anarchist militants. An ad for a libertarian cultural event announced that at the end of the evening there would be a raffle of Michelet's history of French Revolution and "a revolver with a load of bullets," in *La Protesta*, August 25, 1904.

73 The anarchist press urged militants to ignore the socialist event held in the Prado Español on May 1, 1891. With a certain unjustified haughtiness, a paper said. "We are preparing for the general strike, and we've promised the scoundrels [the socialists]

that we'll treat them as they deserve," *La Miseria*, No. 4, May 1, 1891.

74 *La Protesta Humana*, May 5, 1901.

75 Ibid.

76 Ibid.

77 Though most likely an exaggerated figure, due to the partiality of the person who calculated it, an anarchist leader of the period claimed that between 40,000 and 50,000 people attended the 1904 May Day rally. See Gilimón, *Hechos y Comentarios*, 43.

78 *La Protesta Humana*, May 10, 1902 and *The Future*, May 3, 1902. These newspapers said that 20,000 people were in attendance.

79 *La Nación*, May 2, 1904.

80 *La Prensa*, May 2, 1909.

81 Writers from newspapers like *La Prensa, La Nación*, and *La Argentina*, who would not be partial to anarchists, accused police of indiscriminately and disproportionately suppressing demonstrators during the events of 1904, 1905, and 1909, among others.

82 *La Nación*, May 1, 1904.

83 Gilimón, *Hechos y Comentarios*, 43

CONCLUSION

1 *Ideas and Figures*, no. 34, October 1, 1910.

2 Note from the Italian consul to the Italian Minister of the Interior. ACC, MI-PS, AAGG- RR- 1911, b.57.f.

3 Policía de Buenos Aires, *Memoria*, 1900–1901 (Buenos Aires: 1909), 273. On Lombroso's influence, see Oscar Terán, *Positivismo y nación en la Argentina* (Buenos Aires: Puntosur, 1987), 52–53.

4 Eduardo Gilimón, *Hechos y Comentarios* (Buenos Aires-Montevideo: Imprenta B. Puey, 1911), 86.

5 Cámara de Diputados, "Intervención del Ministro del Interior José Gálvez," Buenos Aires, *Diario de Sesiones*, 1910, volume I, 55.

6 Libertarian publications released in 1911 contain numerous complaints about the difficulty of carrying out propaganda. See *The Libertarian*, no. 5, March 2, 1911; No. 6, March 17, 1911, and No. 7, April 1, 1911.

7 *The Libertarian*, No. 7, April 1, 1911.

8 Ibid

9 Ghiraldo's last organizational act within the anarchist movement was to assume the leadership of *La Protesta* on November 25, 1913. He quit fourteen days later due to opposition from the doctrinal anarchists and left the country shortly thereafter. Gilimón remained an anarchist, but gave up active militancy and wrote only sporadically for anarchist publications.

10 See Diego Abad de Santillán, "*La Protesta*," *Certamen Internacional*, 59–63.

11 Ofelia Pianetto argues that the decline of labor conflicts between 1910 and 1916 was a result of unemployment: "Workers faced unfavorable occupational circumstances and this weakened the cohesion achieved during the first decade; disintegration and competition put a parenthesis around the development of the class." Ofelia Pianetto, "Mercado de trabajo y acción sindical, 1890–1922," *Desarrollo Económico* 94 (1984): 305.

12 Hugo del Campo, *El "sindicalismo revolucionario" (1905–1945)* (Buenos Aires: CEAL, 1986), 19.

13 Syndicalism's stronger influence among native workers has been emphasized in David Rock, *El radicalismo argentino*, 1890–1930 (Buenos Aires: Amorrortu, 1977), 102.

14 On syndicalism, see July Arraga, *Reflexiones y observaciones sobre la cuestión social*, (Buenos Aires, 1910); del Campo, *El "sindicalismo revolucionario"*; Maricel Bertolo, "El sindicalismo revolucionario en una etapa de transición," *Social Studies* vol. 3, no. 4 (1993).

15 Abad de Santillán, *La Protesta*, 61. On the strikes between 1917 and 1919, see Rock, *El radicalismo argentino*, 138–166.

16 The experience of the anarchist-led renters' strike in 1907 shows how easily they exploited sentiments of discontent and hopeless among workers. See Juan Suriano, "La huelga de inquilinos de 1907 en Buenos Aires," in *Sectores populares y vida urbana*, ed. José Pedro Barrán (Buenos Aires: Clacso, 1984).

17 Leandro Gutierrez and Luis Alberto Romero, *Sectores Populares, Cultura y Política. Buenos Aires en la entreguerra* (Buenos Aires: Sudamericana, 1995).

18 Translator's note: the *sociedades de fomento* emerged in the context of Buenos Aires's rapid growth and the sudden appearance of new, poverty-stricken neighborhoods in outlying areas. As neighborhood organizations, they served as intermediaries between the state and residents, and came to represent an ideology based on neighborhood values and interests. See, *Urban Social Movements in the Third World*, ed. Frans Johan Schuurman and A. L. van Naerssen (New York: Routledge Kegan & Paul, 1989), 48.

19 Humberto Correale, interview by Daniel James in Buenos Aires.

20 I take the expression "strategy of exile" from Francisco Foot Hardman, *Nem Patria, Nem Patrao* (San Pablo: Brasiliense, 1984), 59.

21 Xavier Paniagua, "Una gran pregunta y varias respuestas. El anarquismo español: desde la política a la historiografía," *Historia Social* 12 (1992).

INDEX

"Passim" (literally "scattered") indicates intermittent discussion of a topic over a cluster of pages.

Support AK Press!

AK Press is one of the world's largest and most productive

anarchist publishing houses. We're entirely worker-run and democratically managed. We operate without a corporate structure—no boss, no managers, no bullshit. We publish close to twenty books every year, and distribute thousands of other titles published by other likeminded independent presses from around the globe.

The Friends of AK program is a way that you can directly contribute to the continued existence of AK Press, and ensure that we're able to keep publishing great books just like this one! Friends pay a minimum of $25 per month, for a minimum three month period, into our publishing account. In return, Friends automatically receive (for the duration of their membership), as they appear, one free copy of every new AK Press title. They're also entitled to a 20% discount on everything featured in the AK Press Distribution catalog and on the website, on any and every order. You or your organization can even sponsor an entire book if you should so choose!

There's great stuff in the works—so sign up now to become a Friend of AK Press, and let the presses roll!

Won't you be our friend? Email friendsofak@akpress.org for more info, or visit the Friends of AK Press website: http://www.akpress.org/programs/friendsofak